Small Town
Economic Development

Small Town Economic Development

Reports on Growth Strategies in Practice

Edited by
JOAQUIN JAY GONZALEZ III,
ROGER L. KEMP *and*
JONATHAN ROSENTHAL

McFarland & Company, Inc., Publishers
Jefferson, North Carolina

RECENT WORKS OF INTEREST AND FROM MCFARLAND: *Privatization in Practice: Reports on Trends, Cases and Debates in Public Service by Business and Nonprofits*, edited by Joaquin Jay Gonzalez III and Roger L. Kemp (2016); *Immigration and America's Cities: A Handbook on Evolving Services*, edited by Joaquin Jay Gonzalez III and Roger L. Kemp (2016); *Corruption and American Cities: Essays and Case Studies in Ethical Accountability*, edited by Joaquin Jay Gonzalez III and Roger L. Kemp (2016); *Urban Transportation Innovations Worldwide: A Handbook of Best Practices Outside the United States*, edited by Roger L. Kemp and Carl J. Stephani (2015); *Global Models of Urban Planning: Best Practices Outside the United States*, edited by Roger L. Kemp and Carl J. Stephani (2014); *Town and Gown Relations: A Handbook of Best Practices*, Roger L. Kemp (2013); *The Municipal Budget Crunch: A Handbook for Professionals*, edited by Roger L. Kemp (2012); *Cities Going Green: A Handbook of Best Practices*, edited by Roger L. Kemp and Carl J. Stephani (2011)

LIBRARY OF CONGRESS CATALOGUING-IN-PUBLICATION DATA

Names: Gonzalez, Joaquin Jay, editor. | Kemp, Roger L., editor. | Rosenthal, Jonathan, 1955– editor.
Title: Small town economic development : reports on growth strategies in practice / edited by Joaquin Jay Gonzalez III, Roger L. Kemp and Jonathan Rosenthal.
Description: Jefferson, North Carolina : McFarland & Company, Inc., Publishers, 2017 | Includes bibliographical references and index.
Identifiers: LCCN 2017014040 | ISBN 9780786476787 (softcover : acid free paper) ∞
Subjects: LCSH: Small cities—United States. | Urban renewal—United States. | Community development—United States. | Economic development—United States.
Classification: LCC HT384.U5 S63 2017 | DDC 307.3/4160973—dc23
LC record available at https://lccn.loc.gov/2017014040

BRITISH LIBRARY CATALOGUING DATA ARE AVAILABLE

ISBN (print) 978-0-7864-7678-7
ISBN (ebook) 978-1-4766-2852-3

Front cover photograph of downtown West Jefferson, NC © 2017 Kim Hadley

Printed in the United States of America

McFarland & Company, Inc., Publishers
Box 611, Jefferson, North Carolina 28640
www.mcfarlandpub.com

Jay:
To the magnificent Gonzalez, Lucero, and Hong families

———⊶⊷———

Roger:
To my granddaughter, Anika, the best and the brightest

———⊶⊷———

Jonathan:
To my wonderful, brilliant sons Geoffrey Harrison
(Gershon Herschel) and Alexander Marshall
(Hanim Mordecai) Levitt Rosenthal

Acknowledgments

We are grateful for the support of the Mayor George Christopher Professorship, the Russell T. Sharpe Professorship at Golden Gate University, the Bibbero Trust, and GGU's Pi Alpha Alpha Chapter. We appreciate the encouragement from Dean Gordon Swartz and our wonderful colleagues and students at the GGU Edward S. Ageno School of Business, the Department of Public Administration, and the Executive MPA Program.

Our heartfelt "Thanks!" goes to the contributors listed in the back of the book and the individuals, organizations, and publishers below for granting permission to reprint the material in this volume and the research assistance. Most waived or reduced fees as an expression of their support for practical research and information sharing that benefits our community.

American Planning Association

American Society for Public Administration

Auburn University

Mark Brodeur

California Planner

eRepublic

Dr. Mickey McGee

Elise Gonzalez

Governing

Government Finance Officers Association

Government Finance Review

Paul Harney

Michelle Hong

International City/County Management Association

Iowa State University

Livability (www.livability.com)

MarketingModo

Becky McCray

Erin Mullenix

National League of Cities

PA Times

Beth Payne

Pew Charitable Trusts

Planning

PlannersWeb

PM Magazine

Purdue News

The Rural Center, North Carolina

smallbizsurvival.com

Smart Growth America

Stateline

University of North Carolina

Table of Contents

Appendices

Preface

Most of the time America's small towns and cities (those with populations under 50,000) live in the shadow of large metropolises—San Francisco, New York, New Orleans, and Chicago, among others. Few people outside their metro areas even know their names. So when small town residents are asked where they come from they usually mention the city which is the economic hub of the region. Some would provide more detail and say that they live in a "suburb of" and name the big city close by.

Not surprisingly, many small towns never get the visibility (and revenue) associated with hosting national sporting events and commemorations. Thus they are seldom in the news. And when they go viral it's because something really bad happened. Take, for instance, Ferguson. We are sure that when you are asked if you've heard of this small Missouri suburb that you are going to say "yes." Why? It's because of a sad and tragic event that happened there in 2014.

Most urban dwellers associate the economic development of small towns with the rural United States. Some may even picture many small towns as ghost town America. Not only are residential homes empty, factories are also closed and rusting. They imagine main streets and downtowns sprinkled with shuttered shops. Many speculate that it's because small towns lack the sophistication and lifestyle amenities that attract innovative businesses and creative hipsters. Consequently, in the era of mass urban renewal and megacities

this makes the small town's outlook rather bleak.

But our experiences living and serving in small town America say otherwise. We have seen their progress and especially their potential. There is a lot to share between and among small towns. Big cities need small towns in a symbiotic relationship. We believe that many have quietly kept big lessons that even large cities should consider emulating. We think they possess hidden gems.

In our travels, we've met millennials born and bred in small towns who leave for college and work in exciting big cities. But when it came down to raising a family some went back to their small town and started-up "big city"–inspired businesses, like the owners of Café Duet, a Brooklyn-inspired coffee experience, in downtown Stroudsburg, Pennsylvania. Returnees feel that the ingredients for livability, creativity, and inclusive growth are present in their small towns. And if they are not, then they will make them happen.

Thus, in *Small Town Economic Development*, we compiled case studies which not only looked into small town America's trials and struggles but also their successful rise and revival practices. Some involved old school approaches while some used contemporary and hip strategies. Many even enhanced local government revenues without having to increase taxes. Demographically, aging hippies and young hipsters, rustics and gentrifiers, artists and techies found common ground to co-exist.

Part I: The State of Small Towns

We begin our story with a selection of nine essays on the state of small towns and cities in the United States. Where are they headed? What are their challenges?

Straight away, in Chapter 1, veteran small cities manager Tommy Engram predicts that the winds of growth or decline will be dictated largely by demographic shifts—particularly the coming and going of the young and the creative. Reinforcing this demographic forecast are two Smart Growth America (SGA) research findings, Chapters 2 and 3, which reveal that cities in metro areas are gaining population—and most are growing faster than their suburbs.

How then will the suburbs—which in some metro areas are comprised of villages, towns, cities, and similar sized jurisdictions—survive? At a gathering organized by the National League of Cities (NLC) and documented in Chapters 4 and 5, Emily Robbins reports that America's mayors promised economic development that will place equal attention to equity and inclusion concerns while Trevor Langan elaborates on the "how" based on the mayors' speeches.

But most of the NLC mayors who gave speeches were from urban cities. What about the small rural towns and cities? In response to this question are Chapters 6 and 7, wherein the Council of Economic Advisers details the federal government's view of the situation and the corresponding policies, programs, and incentives they seek to implement for rural communities so they are not left behind by urban metropolises. They should not only rely on the generosity of big cities. They could take matters into their own hands if they wish.

In Chapter 8, writing from her home base at Iowa State University, Erin Mullenix, a community development specialist, shares her thoughts on the economic, infrastructure, and fiscal challenges of small towns.

However, the context may be different during hard times—much more challenging. Thus, in Chapter 9, the highly respected International City/County Management Association (ICMA) suggests actions that cities, big and small, could and should be taking when pursuing economic growth initiatives during a recession.

Part II: Bright Ideas, Good Practices

Given the state of small towns outlined in Part I, we sought out bright ideas and good practices for effective small town economic development. Our search of case studies did not disappoint. We uncovered a gold mine which we divided into 15 sections. Lessons came from tiny Judith Gap, Montana (pop. 216), to not-so-tiny Olympia, Washington (pop. 48,000).

The first cluster of sections describes the must-have hardware to be effective and efficient. The next two clusters provide the classic and contemporary bright ideas and best practices (or the software options) for citizens and leaders to consider and replicate. We think it's possible to mix and match old school approaches with trendy tactics depending on a town's growth needs and aspirations.

From Sections A through C, 18 chapters identify and elaborate on what our contributors have found as essential organizational practices for implementing successful small town economic development: leadership and strategy, marketing and branding, and capital and financing.

A leader who understands the politics and not just the economics of small town America is essential. This is what Christiana McFarland and Katie Seeger, in Chapter 10, outline as the role of local elected officials in economic development. The succeeding chapters in this section, 11 through 18, reinforce this theme and provide a range of strategies, ideas, and measures not just for leaders, but also for citizens. They are based on practices and ideas from Bedford, Pennsylvania; Brookings, South Dakota; Lauderdale Lakes, Florida; Mooresville, North Carolina; Union City, Georgia; Marlborough, Massachusetts; Mission, Kansas; Littleton, Colorado; Tuscumbia, Alabama, to Centralia, Illinois.

To attract visitors, businesses, and residents, many small towns are being advised by planners and consultants to aggressively brand and market. Our contributors in Chapters 19 through 23 share useful tips and how-to guides on how to effectively achieve this. Ideas and practices were derived from Pretty Prairie, Kansas; Poquoson, Virginia; Corning, New York; Galesburg, Illinois; Petersburg, Alabama; Brookings, South Dakota, to Goshen, Indiana.

Good leadership and strategies and branding and marketing plans must be backed by sufficient funding and sustained investments. Chapters 24 through 27 in this section elaborate on some creative approaches for small towns in these two critical areas, from the use of tax increment financing, to capital improvement districts, and nudging state governments to act like "venture capitalists."

Classics. Sections D through I are about classic ideas and old school practices for small town economic development. These basic approaches are tried and tested, prescribed by economists during recessions and depressions for big and small cities. Nineteen chapters describe the use of infrastructure, brownfield, downtown, main street, retail, and tourism programs for renewal and revitalization.

Chapters 28 through 32 are case experiences about constructing public infrastructure or rehabilitating old ones to create better access and enhance the attractiveness of small towns to residents and entrepreneurs. Chapters 33, 34, and 35 discuss the vast potential for brownfields—empty or abandoned sites previously used for industrial or commercial purposes. Another classic economic development practice is to encourage business or public-private partnership investments downtown as discussed in Chapters 36 through 39. Connected to downtown development is main street development according to our case studies on Sandy, Oregon, and Marion and Morganton, North Carolina (Chapters 40 and 41).

The other classic economic development practices discussed are attracting retailers (Chapters 42 and 43) and tourists (Chapters 44 through 46). The assumption is that downtowns and main streets need to be connected to major highways by wider roads and bridges so that tourists and local consumers can reach retail shops. These are discussed in our retail cases from Bartlett, Tennessee, and Marion, Indiana, as well as tourism cases from Park City, Utah; Pigeon Forge, Tennessee, and New Mexico's old West Country.

Contemporary. The 15 chapters in Sections J through O discuss the contemporary ideas and trendy practices that resonate with hip millennials but are also amenable to retiring baby boomers. They involve a mix of public, private, and nonprofit investments in the arts, technology, food, creative space, transportation, and multigenerational programs.

Our arts section is based on two quaint Kentucky towns. Chapter 47 is on Paducah's Artist Relocation Program while Chapter 48 is about creating a community of artisans in Berea, a town of 14,000 residents. Our technology section is on tiny Judith Gap, Montana's Green Technology program (Chapter 49), Chaska and Moorhead, Minnesota, and St. Cloud, Florida, experiences with providing municipal WiFi (Chapter 50), and Pelahatchie, Mississippi's hotspot project (Chapter 51).

In our food section, we have not just economic development but community development examples, including using the supermarket as a neighborhood building block (Chapter 52) and sustainable food sources (Chapter 53). Creative space is an increasing demand from millennials. Hence, we selected two chapters on how creative spaces were conceptualized and constructed in Greensburg, Kansas (Chapter 54), as well as Biddeford and Saco, Maine (Chapter 55). After all, community building is economic development!

Another big trend popularized by the millennial generation is environmentally friendly transportation, covered in Chapter 56 on bike sharing as a critical livability issue as demonstrated in the case of College Park, Maryland. But it seems that rural legislators in Washington, D.C., disagree and are not in favor of federal government livability initiatives (Chapter 57).

Finally, our concluding section covers multigenerational economic development that not only attracts the hipsters but also the hippies, including brilliant ideas and good practices to: get millennials to revive small cities (Chapter 58), attract young professionals to return home and stay (Chapter 59), build intergenerational communities (Chapter 60), and utilize retirees for growth and prosperity (Chapter 61). Our small town case studies in this multigenerational section came from Auburn, New York (pop. 27,000); Shorewood, Michigan (pop. 13,100); Coeur d'Alene, Idaho (pop. 46,000), and Olympia, Washington (pop. 48,000).

Part III: Caveats and the Future

Because Part II already focuses on a plethora of bright ideas and best practices, we felt we should balance them with essays providing important caveats on moving forward in Part III. After all, based on our experiences, leaders and citizens should always be ready for the unexpected dips and bumps.

Manhattan Institute Senior Fellow Aaron M. Renn posits in Chapter 62 that before starting, small town leaders should ask residents if they really want economic devel-

opment, especially the trendy kind. *Governing*'s William Fulton adds in Chapter 63 that the latest economic development fad grounded in Richard Florida's "Creative Class" prescription might not be the silver bullet for all or any of small town America's ills. This is exactly the problem with the hip but underutilized new community center in blue-collar Johnsburg, New York (pop. 2,395), as reported by Rob Gurwitt in Chapter 64.

Instead of multigenerational harmony, what if intergenerational conflict erupted like in the case of Newtown, Connecticut (pop. 27,000), where schools and senior services were the two tax funding choices, according to *Stateline*'s Jenni Bergal in Chapter 65? Another worst-case scenario, shared by Joseph McElroy in Chapter 66, is when a redevelopment project stalls and a pretty town like Petoskey Pointe, Michigan (pop. 6,000), is left with an ugly "dirt hole."

In Chapter 67, *Governing*'s data editor Mike Maciag suggests localities should evaluate just how effective tax breaks and other incentives are at boosting economic development when they look to expand or renew programs. Moreover, cities that are being enticed to merge with larger ones to maximize economies of scale should read Aaron M. Renn's cautionary piece in Chapter 68. As businesses and jobs become more fluid, i.e., project to project, economic development planners have to prepare for an emerging 1099 labor force, according to William Fulton in Chapter 69.

Appendices

Our four appendices yield useful economic development prescriptions and guides for leaders, followers, businesses, residents, advocates, voters, constituents, and taxpayers.

First, we would like to inspire you with a ranking of the best of the best. There are a lot of "best small town" rankings out there but we chose Livability's because of its rigorous methodology. Second, we encourage you to consider the International City/County Management Association's nationally and internationally tried and tested blueprint for community-based economic development. Third, for those interested in the how-to-do economic development, we have the Government Finance Officers Association's how-to guide for communicating capital improvement strategies. Fourth and finally, we developed a handy glossary of essential economic development practices to help you wade through the technical language and acronyms thrown back and forth by both scholars and practitioners.

Small Town Economic Development is the result of a national literature search in the fields of economic development and renewal in small urban and rural cities and towns in the United States. It is the only book of its kind in America wherein public officials and citizens throughout our nation could read about bright ideas and best practices and how to adapt them in their own communities.

This book is easy to read and incisive. We cover small towns from the East Coast to the West Coast, from Crescent City, California, to Corning, New York, as well as small cities from the North to the South, from Chelsea, Michigan, to Tuscumbia, Alabama. The reputable publications and contributors offer a spectrum of ideas and opinions representing America's diversity and democracy.

Read on!

1. Towns in the Age of Megacities[*]

TOMMY ENGRAM

Management guru Peter Drucker describes demographics as the most powerful force impacting society. Fortunately, it is also the easiest to quantify and the most predictable in time perspective.

Demographics shape our destiny and there can be little doubt that we are living in the age of the megacity. Aldous Huxley forecast this in 1932 in his futuristic novel *Brave New World*. Edward Glaeser proclaimed it in his *Triumph of the City*. Richard Florida provided abundant statistical confirmation that the shift to large scale megacities is happening in *Cities and the Creative Class*.

For those who have any doubt, get off the interstate highway and drive across the nation on a two-lane blacktop. The hollowing out of rural America is obvious and unrelenting.

Big metropolitan areas are growing in population and that trend has continued since the Renaissance. They grow because the aggregation of people and the comingling of their ideas enhance productivity and improve the standard of living. As technology and circumstances have changed, this wellspring of creativity has allowed cities to reinvent themselves.

With our economy generating so much wealth, why—unlike megacities—have many small cities and towns in the hinterland failed to grow and prosper? Why are they left dependent on one or a handful of local industries to fuel their ailing economies? More importantly, what can be done to reverse this trend?

Florida and others claim the reason for the decline of smaller communities is that their human capital is being drained by megacities that offer young creative people more opportunities for work, entertainment and finding a mate. Companies at the cutting edge of technology need smart young minds so they gravitate to areas with a density of talent. This frequently translates into megacities.

Companies that have stayed in the hinterland tend to be low tech or old tech manufacturing and service industries. They need steady, dependable employees who will do repetitive tasks for relatively low wages.

Florida claims that, over time, the accumulation of task workers in small communities shapes the public psyche and results in sets of amenities attuned to the preferences of low-wage workers. In turn, these communities become less attractive to their own young residents and likewise unacceptable to outsiders who may be seeking a site for a new business.

---

[*]Originally published as Tommy Engram, "Towns in the Age of Megacities," *PA TIMES*, July 19, 2016. Reprinted with permission of the publisher.

I had the opportunity to observe the commencement exercise of a youth leadership program for the top 50 high school seniors from a rural county. When the moderator asked how many students planned to go to college, all 50 planned to go. When he asked how many planned to return to that community after college, only one answered yes.

But what Florida and others describe is a trend, not a law of nature. Chattanooga, Tennessee, is not a megacity. But it has transformed itself from a declining southern industrial town into a mecca for talented and creative young people.

On a visit to a high-tech incubator on Market Street, I asked the proprietor how much of Chattanooga's success in attracting smart young people was due to its "Gig City" technology. "Not much," he answered. He explained that young creative people come to Chattanooga for the quality of life. High technology employers follow.

Given the unsustainable loss of their highest-potential young people, how can small towns and rural areas get more of the best and brightest to return and repay the investment made in their education?

First, small communities must want to become attractive to younger people.

Unfortunately, many of these communities are locked in the past with leaders who have been unable to cope with a vision of a future that might be attractive to younger people. To paraphrase a biblical admonishment, when the leaders lack vision, the community dries up and blows away.

But for those more fortunate communities that have overcome that obstacle, relatively small investments in restaurants, attractive downtowns, Wi-Fi, canoeing, biking, hiking and (especially) places to meet and mingle with potential mates may yield excellent returns.

Young adults returning from college or technical school may get very excited about an affordable loft apartment on the town square or studio in an old factory. They may care more about a Main Street pub with a good local band than proximity to a professional baseball venue. They may be willing to trade the convenience of public transportation in a distant megacity for bike lanes, good sidewalks and greenways closer to home.

Also, small towns and rural communities may yet benefit from the rush to the megacity. As the quantity of desirable and available living space in large metropolitan areas becomes scarcer, housing costs tend to rise. Urban residents find themselves priced out of the megacity market.

When that economic pressure is combined with the increasing bandwidth available in even remote areas, a new option may emerge. Attractive smaller communities, with reasonably priced and varied housing options, may actually enjoy significant advantages in attracting young creative people, especially those under the heavy burden of student loans.

2. Where Is America Growing?*

Smart Growth America

Cities are growing faster than their suburbs for the first time in recent history, and this trend applies to the country's biggest as well as some of its smallest.

New analysis of U.S. Census data from Smart Growth America reveals that cities in small metro areas are gaining population—and most are growing faster than their suburbs. This finding reflects population trends revealed in 2012 in research from the Brookings Institution, which examined growth rates the country's 51 largest metropolitan areas. But whereas that report looked only at large metro areas like New York, San Francisco and Chicago, Smart Growth America's research examines what's happening in the nation's slightly smaller—but no less important—metro areas.

The results are surprising.

"Small metro areas' cities are doing just as well, if not better than, big cities," says Smart Growth America President and CEO Geoffrey Anderson. "The trend in terms of population growth is toward city living, and that's happening at a greater rate in our smaller metro areas and the middle of the country."

"Many of these small cities are investing in new smart growth ideas. Clarksville, Tennessee is creating a historic downtown shopping district. Lincoln, Nebraska has a citywide Complete Streets policy. These kinds of investments are starting to pay off, and it's only going to continue in coming years."

Smart Growth America calculated population change between 2010 and 2011 in 171 of the nation's smaller metropolitan areas based on 2010 Census figures and 2011 Census estimates. Overall, 22 percent of the U.S. population lives in these small metro areas—more than 69 million people. Of these, 39.3 percent, or 27 million people, lived in the Census-defined cities of the small metro areas in 2011.

Between 2010 and 2011, 86.5 percent of small metro areas saw an increase in the number of people living in the city. El Paso, Texas, saw the largest growth in the city population, gaining a total of 13,687 residents. Overall, cities in the smallest metro areas (150,000–250,000 people) saw the largest increase in people within their boundaries.

Perhaps more noteworthy is the fact that small metro city population growth is now outpacing growth in the suburbs. In one year, cities in the small metro areas grew in population by 0.89 percent. In comparison, their suburban counterparts grew by 0.67 percent. Though these growth rates may

---

*Originally published as Smart Growth America, "Where Is America Growing? The Answer May Surprise You," December 2012, www.smartgrowthamerica.org. Reprinted with permission of the publisher.

seem small, they can have a big impact on a small city or town.

In addition, small metro area cities are seeing more growth than big cities. 55.0 percent of cities in small metro areas grew at a faster rate than their suburban counterparts between 2010 and 2011. Comparatively, 51.0 percent of cities in large metros added population at a greater rate than their suburbs.

The top ten small metros where cities added population at a greater rate than their suburbs were:

1. Clarksville, TN–KY
2. Lexington-Fayette, KY
3. Fort Smith, AR–OK
4. Lynchburg, VA
5. Athens–Clarke County, GA
6. Lincoln, NE
7. Davenport, IA–Moline, IL–Rock Island, IL
8. Greensboro–High Point, NC
9. Bloomington, IN
10. Durham–Chapel Hill, NC

All of the cities in this top ten list grew at least 60 percent faster than their suburbs. In the case of Clarksville and Lexington, the city population grew at more than double the rate of the suburban population.

"When people talk about how cities are making a comeback, they often have this image of the big metropolises," Anderson says. "They might think it's only happening in places like Washington D.C. But that's just not true. It's happening everywhere."

3. City Versus Suburban Growth in Small Metro Areas[*]

Smart Growth America

The Brookings Institution released new research which revealed cities in the country's 51 largest metropolitan areas were, on average, growing faster than their suburbs for the first time in decades (Frey 2012).

Smart Growth America wondered if this was true in smaller metro areas as well. Following a methodology similar to that used by Brookings, we calculated population growth between 2010 and 2011 in 171 of the nation's smaller metropolitan areas.

This analysis looked at U.S. Census–designated Metropolitan Statistical Areas (MSAs) with populations between 150,000 and 1 million that also have at least one primary city of at least 50,000 people, based on 2010 Census figures and 2011 Census estimates. These "small metro areas" are the focus of our examination. Some of the biggest gains were made in the smallest metro areas.

Overall, 22 percent of the U.S. population lives in small metro areas—more than 69 million people. Of these, 39.7 percent, or 27 million people, lived in cities in 2011. Between 2010 and 2011 small metro area cities grew in population by 0.89 percent, whereas their suburban counterparts grew by 0.67

percent. These growth rates may seem trivial, but in small towns and cities they can make a big difference.

Our findings reveal that some of the biggest population gains were made in the smallest metro areas. Our analysis examined absolute increase in population, the rate of growth, and how small metro areas compared to large ones. We found that not only are small metro areas part of the larger national trend, many are leading the way.

At the end of this report we discuss why this might be happening. We take a brief look at 5 of the 171 cities included in this study, and examine the new projects, policies and initiatives that could be contributing to these new population gains.

"City" and its boundaries are defined by the U.S. Census Bureau. One primary city and up to two additional cities were used to calculate the "city" population of each MSA; the suburban population was found by subtracting the city population from the total population of the MSA. Population data for cities smaller than 50,000 was not available from the Census for 2011. The Census Bureau's methodology for allocating the population change between cities

---

*Originally published as Smart Growth America, "City Versus Suburban Growth in Small Metro Areas: Analysis of U.S. Census Data in Metropolitan Statistical Areas Under One Million People," www.smartgrowthamerica.org. Reprinted with permission of the publisher.

and suburbs from 2010 to 2011 within metropolitan areas is based on past trends.

Findings

The research revealed four clear trends about small metro areas: (1) city populations grew from 2010 to 2011; (2) city populations grew at a faster rate than their suburbs; (3) the smaller the metro area, the greater the city population growth; and (4) small metro areas in the Heartland grew fastest.

1. In small metro areas, city populations grew from 2010 to 2011.

Between 2010 and 2011, population increased in 86.5 percent of cities in small metro areas. El Paso, Texas saw the largest growth in city population, gaining a total of 13,687 residents.

SMALL METRO AREAS WITH LARGEST CITY POPULATION GAINS, 2010–2011

1. El Paso, TX: +13,687
2. Colorado Springs, CO: +6,643
3. McAllen–Edinburg–Mission, TX: +6,452
4. Albuquerque, NM: +5,412
5. Fresno, CA: +5,181
6. Omaha, NE–Council Bluffs, IA: +4,987
7. Boise City–Nampa, ID: +4,874
8. Durham–Chapel Hill, NC: +4,847
9. Lexington–Fayette, KY: +4,777
10. Laredo, TX: +4,683

These numbers are good news for these cities. In at least some cases, population gains may be a result of new economic opportunities and civic efforts to attract and retain new residents.

The metro areas with the highest city population gains were also among the biggest (with populations between 750,000 and 1 million people). Overall, however, the smallest metro areas (150,000–250,000 people) had the largest number of cities gain population.

2. In small metros areas, city populations grew at a faster rate than their suburbs.

Between 2010 and 2011 small metro area cities grew, in total by 0.89 percent, whereas their suburban counterparts grew in total by only 0.67 percent. Below are the top ten small metros where cities added population at a greater rate than their suburbs.

FASTEST-GROWING SMALL METRO AREA CITIES COMPARED WITH THEIR SUBURBS, 2010–2011

1. Clarksville, TN
2. Lexington-Fayette, KY
3. Fort Smith, AR
4. Lynchburg, VA
5. Athens–Clarke County, GA
6. Lincoln, NE
7. Davenport, IA–Moline, IL–Rock Island, IL
8. Greensboro–High Point, NC
9. Bloomington, IN
10. Durham–Chapel Hill, NC

All of these cities grew at least 60 percent faster than their suburbs. In the cases of Clarksville and Lexington, the city population grew by more than double the rate of the suburban population.

This data indicate that people are increasingly choosing to live in cities in small metro areas. Notably, this trend is even stronger in small metro areas than large ones: 55.0 percent of cities in small metro areas added population between 2010 and 2011; 52.9 percent of cities in large metro areas did so in the same period.

Overall, the smallest metro areas had the highest share of cities growing faster than their suburbs, at 63.0 percent.

These figures suggest that cities are gaining popularity in small metro areas. In fact, cities in small metro areas may be gaining popularity faster than large metro area cities. In small metro areas, 45.6 percent of cities added more residents (in absolute numbers) than did their suburban counterparts. This is more than double the number of large metro areas, where only 21.6 percent of cities gained more residents than the suburbs.

3. The smaller the metro area, the greater the city population growth.

Not only did the smallest metro areas— ranging from 150,000 to 250,000 people— have the most cities where population increased and the most cities growing at a faster rate than suburbs, they also had the most cities that added more population (in absolute numbers) than their suburbs.

4. Small metro areas in the Heartland grew fastest.

Census Division 4—consisting of Iowa, Kansas, Minnesota, Missouri, Nebraska, North Dakota, and South Dakota—showed the strongest growth of small metro areas across the country. All small metro cities in this division saw population increases between 2010 and 2011.

In addition, 66.7 percent of cities in the division added more people than in their suburbs—the highest percentage nationally. This division also had the second highest percentage of small metro area cities growing at a faster rate than suburbs (77.8 percent). Finally, population rose in a greater number of small metro area cities than large metro area cities in this division.

A Closer Look at City Growth

Why are so many cities in small metro areas growing? Every place has different reasons, but many share common traits. We looked at five examples from across the country.

Abilene, Texas, *Population: 166,416*

Abilene, Texas, was the first city in the state to create a downtown reinvestment zone through tax increment financing. The goal of this innovative strategy was to create the kind of downtown that would attract people and businesses alike. The city is also committed to preserving historic buildings that contribute to the character of Abilene. There are over 700 businesses and 6,000 employees downtown and the city boasts more arts and cultural institutions per capita than any city in Texas besides Houston—and 95 percent of these attractions are located downtown.

Tuscaloosa, Alabama, *Population: 221,553*

Tuscaloosa, Alabama, has won awards for the quality of life it affords residents and businesses alike. Tuscaloosa has been listed among the top 100 best cities for young people by America's Promise Alliance, named the most livable city in America by the U.S. Conference of Mayors, and one of the best places to launch a small business by CNN's *Money*. Tuscaloosa is deeply engaged in making the city a cultural and artistic destination, and its Culture Builds initiative supports downtown development projects like a new amphitheater on the Black Warrior River and an outdoor market.

Clarksville, Tennessee, *Population: 277,701*

Clarksville, Tennessee, is deeply proud of its historic downtown, which is home to locally owned shops, restaurants, the Downtown Clarksville Association and an artist co-operative founded in 2001 to bring creative vibrancy to the area. In 2010, the City of Clarksville adopted a city plan entitled Smart Growth 2030, dedicated to making Clarksville a "model for economic growth, alternative energy strategies, recreational facilities, aesthetic appeal, cultural experiences and environmental stewardship" as the city grows to exceed a projected 250,000 people within the next two decades.

Lincoln, Nebraska, *Population: 306,503*

Lincoln, Nebraska, is working hard to make its downtown a destination for visitors and new residents. The area is home to several universities and an extensive park system. Lincoln has a robust primary transit authority, StarTran, and together with its city-wide Complete Streets policy, it's no surprise that Lincoln households have a 30 percent shorter commute time than the national average. Lincoln is also home to an extensive park system throughout the city, demonstrating its commitment to creating a great place for its residents.

Grand Rapids, Michigan, *Population: 779,604*

Grand Rapids, Michigan, is known for its thriving arts culture, including numerous festivals anchored around downtown's Calder and Vandenberg plazas and the Grand Rapids Art Museum. The Downtown Development Authority has partnered with local businesses in the Downtown Alliance to host events in downtown Grand Rapids and provides financial assistance in small grants through an initiative called "Let's Go. Out." In 2002, the city adopted a master plan focusing on creating a broader range of housing types, more balanced transportation choices and concentrated business activity.

Conclusion

Similar to their large urban counterparts, many small cities across the country are seeing populations increase—and increase faster than their suburban counterparts.

Nowhere is the trend more clear than in the country's smallest metro areas of 150,000–250,000 people. These areas have the most cities with population increases, the most cities growing at a faster rate than their suburbs, and the most cities that added more population than their suburbs.

Cities in metro areas between 250,000 and 1 million residents saw similar gains. This trend mirrors what's happening in large metropolitan areas, where cities are gaining population faster than the suburbs for the first time in recent history.

Small metro area cities, like their larger counterparts, are working hard to attract new residents and new businesses. And many are using smart growth strategies to achieve these goals. Great neighborhoods attract new residents, who in turn help to make those places even better. These city population increases stand to benefit municipal budgets and local economies—great news as our country's metro areas continue to rebound from the recession.

REFERENCES

Frey, W. (2012). "Demographic Reversal: Cities Thrive, Suburbs Sputter." Brookings Institution. *State of Metropolitan America.* December 7, 2012. http://www.brookings.edu/research/opinions/2012/06/29-cities-suburbs-frey.

4. Pushing for Inclusive Economic Development*

Emily Robbins

The 2016 National League of Cities analysis of State of the City speeches reaffirms that mayors are optimistic about the growth of their local economies, and also that cities are developing economic development agendas to ensure this prosperity is widespread.

Mayor Emily Larson of Duluth, Minnesota, said in her speech, "We intend to expand the number of local businesses in our purchasing pool, and make renewed efforts to ensure that local area businesses know about bid opportunities. We'll lead an effort to identify local vendors (particularly minority and women-owned businesses) who want to be notified by the city about purchasing opportunities. And then we'll mentor those businesses on how to navigate the city's contracting process."

It makes sense that mayors are feeling positive about the state of their cities. Municipal budgets in many regions are returning to pre–Recession levels. Jobs gains and business growth are on the rise. Overall, crime is down, and local housing markets are improving. However, recent studies about the income inequality and socioeconomic disparity in cities are worrisome, and likely the driving force behind the mayoral push we're seeing for more equity and inclusion, particularly in economic development.

More than half (55 percent) of the mayors referenced recent job gains as an economic win for their cities. Baton Rouge, Louisiana, Mayor Kip Holden said, "Today, we're at a record level of jobs in our parish. I could tell you about the more than 7,000 jobs created, or the $327 million in new payroll." Muriel Bowser, Mayor of Washington, D.C., acknowledged local employment growth reached 1,000 new jobs in her city. Mayor Joseph Curtatone of Somerville, Massachusetts, touted that the workforce in his city grew by 15 percent in the previous year.

At the same time, mayors of nearly one third (30 percent) of cities described workforce development efforts to help fill these new employment opportunities, often with the goal of inclusive job readiness. As San Diego Mayor Kevin Faulconer explained in his speech, "The impact of this skills gaps is particularly harsh on low income communities—especially for our young adults." Apprenticeships and on-the-job training, vocational programs, and alternative education were put forth by mayors as policy

*Originally published as Emily Robbins, "State of the City Speeches Reveal Push for Inclusive Economic Development," July 22, 2016, https://citiesspeak.org/. Reprinted with permission of the publisher.

15

solutions that will help level the playing field in terms of accessing well-paying jobs in their communities. Columbus, Ohio, Mayor Andrew Ginther summarized this approach well by saying, "[A] college degree is not the only road to the middle class. There are many different paths to success."

A large number of state of the city speeches also highlight the strength of local business environments, and feature city programs proactively ensuring minority and female small business owners are thriving in this period of growth. Overall, business growth was mentioned by a third (33 percent) of mayors, and 22 percent of speeches highlighted local small businesses. In particular, mayors shared how their cities are becoming more business-friendly by streamlining processes and providing more business services online, such as business license applications. In Columbia, South Carolina, Mayor Stephen Benjamin shared in his speech, "We will be expanding our online offerings for business—where now, for the first time ever, business licenses can be acquired through our city's website, and soon, the entire building permit process will be available in a single, seamless online system."

In this current climate where businesses are opening and expanding, mayors are cognizant that all businesses should have an equal chance at success. That's why several cities are implementing procurement programs that encourage local businesses to apply for city contracts.

In Jersey City, New Jersey, Mayor Steven Fulop noted the city's new Office of Diversity and Inclusion would spearhead similar efforts to assist minority and women-owned businesses with accessing city contacts. Mayor Fulop said in his speech, "It is our hope that this initiative will encourage the growth of our minority and women-owned businesses, while also working to foster inclusive neighborhoods and increase the diversity of the city's small businesses."

As the 2016 State of the Cities report describes, these mayoral speeches help forecast the future priorities of cities. It's welcomed news that so many local economic development agendas are giving attention to equity and inclusion. It is our hope that even more cities join this movement and strive to do what Syracuse, New York, Mayor Stephanie Minor calls "creat[ing] a concentration of opportunity to combat our concentration of poverty."

5. The State of America's Cities*

TREVOR LANGAN

The nation's mayors are leading our country with a critical focus on the issues that matter to citizens. From sustainability and entrepreneurship to public health, mayors described their policy goals in their State of the City speeches. In our recent analysis of these speeches, we found the following trends.

Mayors continue to be focused on improving their local economies and encouraging entrepreneurship.

"Our unemployment rate is down by more than a third, and we have created more than 20,000 new jobs," said Mayor Stephanie Rawlings-Blake, touting her record leading the city of Baltimore. "We focused on the small entrepreneurs in our neighborhoods who are at the heart of job creation, as well as the larger development projects and established businesses that support hundreds, if not thousands, of jobs." More and more cities are making it easier for entrepreneurs to apply for the permits and licenses needed to start or grow a business. "We will be expanding our online offerings for business—where now, for the first time ever, business licenses can be acquired through our city's website, and soon, the entire building permit process will be available in a single, seamless online

system," said Mayor John Tecklenburg of Charleston, South Carolina.

Mayors are seeing improved revenue and are being judicious about how to spend it.

Many cities are returning to pre–Recession levels of fiscal health. Detailing the economic success his city has felt these last few years, Kansas City, Missouri, Mayor Sly James said that the 2016 budget continues that momentum and "supports our neighborhoods and our young people. We'll be able to demolish dangerous buildings and invest more in summer youth employment." In Covina, California, Mayor Peggy Delach talked about the need for fiscal restraint. "We are continuing to identify ways to reduce our costs and make our organization more efficient and more responsive and ensuring that more of our tax dollars are available to be used for community improvements," she said.

Mayors are cautiously optimistic about the future and are leading in the development of sustainable communities where people want to live.

The year 2015 was a monumental one for green mayors, like Boston's Marty Walsh and Atlanta's Kasim Reed, both of whom traveled to Paris to sign the Compact of Mayors on climate change. In their speeches,

*Originally published as Trevor Langan, "The State of America's Cities," 2016, https://citiesspeak.org/cities/. Reprinted with permission of the publisher.

mayors made the case for sustainable development. "Being green makes great social sense," said Mayor Rusty Bailey of Riverside, California. "Greener living means more local parkland for running, walking, biking, and playing outside. It means better access to healthy food."

Mayors are concerned about the uptick in the murder rate even though overall crime rates are historically low.

Many mayors reported an uptick in crime within their cities, and this trend, noticeable across the country, was particularly alarming for homicide. "Many of our homicides are the result of domestic violence. In the past two years, we have made significant changes in the way we deal with these situations. We are handling the calls differently. We are handling the investigations differently. We are learning more and more about which cases are likely to escalate," said Mayor Mick Cornett of Oklahoma City. Research has shown, however, that even though the short-term homicide trend is pointed in the wrong direction, crime overall is still at the lowest point in decades nationally.

Mayors are concerned about the increasing opioid epidemic.

Seventy-eight Americans die every day from an opioid overdose. The fact that this epidemic has grown at such an expansive rate in recent years has led NLC to join with the National Association of Counties (NACo) to form the National City-County Task Force on the Opioid Epidemic. Policies addressing substance abuse, fueled by an increase in opioid addiction, consumed much of the coverage of health-related topics in State of the City speeches. "It's a living and breathing epidemic—like a virus—infecting residents of all walks of life. It's dashed young people's dreams of going to college or landing a job. It's torn families apart. Parents have had to bury their children," said Binghamton, New York, Mayor Richard David.

Mayors are helping their cities see the value of using technology and data to drive decisions and make their city governments more efficient and effective.

In the speeches, multiple cities committed to becoming smart cities, where classrooms, neighborhoods and businesses leverage data and technology to become better connected and more productive. "We need to focus on new technologies, because the solutions we envision today may be obsolete 10 years from now," said Mayor Megan Barry of Nashville, Tennessee. Cities are also moving their operations online and into the cloud to increase transparency and efficiency. "Greenwood is the first city in Indiana to use OpenGov, a software platform that is transforming how governments analyze, share and compare financial data," said Mayor Mark Myers. "It's a remarkable tool, and I urge all citizens to visit the City's website and take a look." In Syracuse, New York, residents can submit and track requests for things like sewer backups, trash removal and pothole filling anytime online using "City Line."

6. Strengthening the Rural Economy[*]

COUNCIL OF ECONOMIC ADVISERS

While rural America offers many opportunities, it also faces unique challenges in growing its economy and maintaining an educated and healthy labor force. In this section, we begin by describing how the U.S. population is distributed geographically and the sectors in which the rural population is employed. We then examine how rural communities have fared compared with their urban counterparts in labor force participation, educational attainment, poverty rates, and access to health care.

The Diverse Rural Economy

About 17 percent of the U.S. population lives in rural counties. Virtually every state contains rural areas, reflecting the country's diversity of communities. That said, rural counties are not uniformly distributed. With the exception of the coast, the Western United States is dominated by low-density rural land where the distance between metropolitan areas is larger and population density is lower, while the Eastern United States is mainly a mixture of high-density rural and urban areas.

Today's rural economy has diversified substantially since 1970. Manufacturing, government, services, and wholesale and retail trade are important sources of employment for rural America. In total, they represented 68 and 76 percent of total employment for the low and high-density rural population in 2007, respectively, up from 61 and 73 percent in 1970. Growth in services was particularly large over this time period in both rural and urban areas. Earnings show a similar pattern by industry over time.

The agricultural sector is also an important but declining source of employment and earnings for rural America. In 2007, the agriculture, forestry, and fishing sector constituted about 6 percent of employment in high-density rural areas and about 12 percent of employment in low-density rural areas, down from 13 percent and 23 percent in 1970, respectively. Note that these shares somewhat understate the importance of agriculture in rural America, since ancillary businesses are counted in other sector categories. For example, workers who truck or wholesale crops or livestock are generally not included in the agriculture sector classification, though livestock breeders and cotton ginners are.

Among individuals who identify them-

[*]Originally published as Council of Economic Advisers, "Strengthening the Rural Economy," www.white house.gov.

selves as farmers, agriculture has become a less important source of income. Half of farm household income came from the farm in 1960. Today, the vast majority (89 percent in 2008) comes from off the farm. Because agriculture is one of the key industries that distinguishes rural America from urban areas and because of its continued contribution to productivity and trade, we discuss it in greater detail below.

The U.S. Agricultural Sector. Perhaps the defining feature in the history of U.S. agriculture is its persistent gains in efficiency. Even relative to America's surge in productivity over the past half century, American agricultural productivity has grown rapidly. Farm productivity nearly tripled in the second half of the twentieth century, while nonfarm productivity increased by about 75 percent. Almost all of this divergence in productivity growth occurred after 1980. A consequence of this tremendous increase in productivity is that, despite increases in total agricultural output, employment has declined. In 1900, about 41 percent of the total U.S. workforce farmed. This share dropped to 16 percent in 1945, 4 percent in 1970, and only 2 percent in 2000.

The productivity of the agricultural sector in the United States compares with that of other high-income countries. As measured by agriculture value added per worker, the United States has remained substantially more productive than other Organisation of Economic Co-operation and Development (OECD) high-income countries. Specifically, value added per worker grew from $16,000 in 1970 to $59,300 in 2005 in the United States, compared with an increase from $8,000 in 1970 to $35,700 in 2005 in high-income OECD countries.

International Trade Plays an Important Role in Rural America. It should not be surprising that the U.S. agricultural sector is very competitive in the international market. Indeed, in 2008, U.S. agricultural exports were worth $70 billion according to Census definitions, and $115 billion using the Department of Agriculture's broader definition. The share of American agricultural output exported in 2007 (using the Census definitions) was 15 percent, having increased from 11 percent in 1999. Thus, access to foreign markets is very important for American agriculture. Likewise, although gross agricultural output only constituted about 2.5 percent of total GDP over this period, agriculture made up 2.8 percent of total exports in 1999, rising to 3.4 percent in 2007, according to Census definitions. Notably, this competitiveness is not primarily driven by farm support programs. Since 1991, high-value commodities (for instance, fruit and meat) have made up a larger fraction of exports than bulk commodities (for instance, wheat and rice), though they receive far less Federal support.

In addition to productivity growth, removing trade barriers has played an important role in agriculture's success. Analysis by the CEA of major free trade agreements (FTAs) between 1985 and 2005 confirms that U.S. agricultural exports increased while import growth remained largely unchanged following these FTAs. The weighted-average growth rate in exports and imports before and after the implementation of these FTAs. On average, in the five years following an FTA, agricultural exports to the FTA partner grew at a very rapid pace (14 percent), up from a rate of 6 percent beforehand.

Exports to the rest of the world also grew, but only at a rate of 3 percent, up from 1 percent growth beforehand. Prior to the FTAs' implementation, exports to the partner country were growing 5 percentage points faster than exports to the rest of the world, but after, they were growing 11 percentage points faster. There is no evidence that import growth from FTA countries accelerated after the implementation of an FTA. Thus, on net, American agriculture appears to have benefited from recent trade liberalization agreements, and increased access to foreign markets has translated into increased opportunity for American agriculture.

The Labor Force in Rural America

While the rural economy has become increasingly diverse, it faces a number of unique challenges regarding its labor force. First, incomes are lower and poverty rates are higher in rural areas than they are in urban areas. Second, a lower proportion of the rural population is of working age (20–64), which presents challenges for future job creation, and the share of the U.S. population living in rural counties has steadily declined over time. Third, a higher portion of rural residents are on disability and therefore unable to participate in the rural workforce. Fourth, educational attainment lags behind that of urban areas for the working-age population. Recognizing these challenges, the Administration has made education a major pillar in its policies for rural America. Its focus on expanding opportunities for small businesses, tourism and recreation, and clean energy will also help to make rural households better off while attracting a new generation of young workers.

Income and Poverty Rates. On average, rural residents have notably lower incomes than urban residents. Between 1979 and 1999, the average urban resident experienced greater increases in income, in both level changes and percent growth, compared with his or her rural counterpart. The poverty rate paints a similar picture. While the rural poverty rate decreased sizably between 1979 and 1999, the average rural county posts poverty rates at least several percentage points above those observed in urban counties. Note that the cost of living is higher in urban areas and ideal measures of income and poverty would adjust for these differences. We have not done so here.

Labor Force Participation. The extent to which a population is comprised of able, working-age people is an important indicator of potential employment. The trajectory of the labor force, measured by the age and training composition of the rural population, helps predict its future economic health. To examine the current and future economic health of rural America, we compare the average age composition in urban, high-density rural, and low-density rural counties in 1970 and 2000. The share of the population under age 20 has declined since 1970 but remains similar across urban and rural classifications. While the share of the population in the prime working ages (20–49) has increased in both urban and rural counties since the 1970s, it continues to be substantially lower in rural counties. Rural counties also tend to be relatively older, which holds among the elderly (65+) and near-retirement (50–64) age groups.

The overall share of the U.S. population living in rural counties also has been steadily declining over time, with high-density rural counties experiencing particularly sharp declines. From 1900 to 1970, rural counties lost nearly 0.3 percentage point of the U.S. population per year. From 1970 to 2008, this trend has continued, albeit at a slower rate, costing rural counties almost 0.1 percent of the U.S. population annually. The net effect of these declines is a broad-scale population shift from rural to urban America. In 1900, about 40 percent of the population lived in a county that ultimately would be classified as rural in present-day America, whereas today that share has dwindled to half this amount.

An additional measure of labor force depth is the share of the working-age population (25–64 years old) healthy enough to be counted as an active member of the labor force. The Federal Social Security

Disability Insurance (SSDI) program provides monthly cash benefits to people who are unable to work due to a disability. In 2008, disability insurance enrollment as a share of the working-age population was 6.5 percent in high-density rural areas and 5.7 percent in low-density rural areas, compared with 3.9 percent in urban areas. Thus, the average rural resident was much more likely to be enrolled in SSDI than his or her urban counterpart. Because individuals enrolled in SSDI are unlikely to exit from the program, these disparities are also likely to impact future labor force capacity.

Educational Attainment. Over time, the share of the population of ages 25–64 with more than a high school education in an average urban county has been persistently above the share in an average rural county. While rural counties have made great strides in ensuring that larger proportions of their populations pursue schooling beyond high school, they have been unable to close this gap. Additionally, the rate of progress in educational attainment has been slightly slower in rural areas, causing education levels in rural areas to slip further behind those in urban areas. In 2000, an urban resident was between 10 and 15 percentage points more likely to have attended college than a rural resident. Two decades earlier, this difference was between 9 and 13 percentage points.

This growth differential is driven by the share of the working-age population that has completed only high school. In the average urban county, this share fell 11 percentage points over the two decades, compared with just 3 to 6 percentage points in the average rural county. Put another way, in 1980 rural residents were 1.1 times more likely to stop attending school after high school than urban residents. By 2000, this ratio was up to 1.3–1.4.

The Status of Health Care in Rural America

Health care costs have continued to rise for individuals and families throughout the United States, while health insurance coverage has eroded for hundreds of thousands of Americans. Because health care costs account for a much larger share of rural residents' average income, the relentless rise in health care costs in recent years has disproportionately impacted them. In this section we lay out the health care challenges faced by rural residents. In Section VI, we discuss how these challenges are being addressed through the Recovery Act and health care reform.

While residents of non-metropolitan areas have comparable rates of health insurance coverage to metropolitan areas and the nation overall, they are more likely to be enrolled in public programs such as Medicaid for low-income families, the Children's Health Insurance Program, and especially Medicare for the elderly (due to the relatively older rural population) rather than holding private insurance. Residents of rural areas have less access to doctors and other health care providers than their counterparts in urban areas. As a result, they are more likely to forego needed care. Finally, improvements in health status in rural areas have not kept pace with those in urban areas.

The Burden of High Costs. Families in non-metropolitan areas are more likely than families in metropolitan areas to have a high burden in affording health insurance coverage, defined as health expenses exceeding 10 percent of after-tax family income. While total out-of-pocket health expenses are comparable in metropolitan and non-metropolitan areas ($3,265 versus $3,216 in 2005, the year with the most recent available data, in 2007 dollars), incomes in non-metropolitan areas tend to be lower. As a result, 24.2 percent of families in non-metropolitan areas spend more than 10 percent of their income on health insurance coverage, compared with 18.1 percent of families in metropolitan areas (Jones et al. 2009).

Lack of Access to Doctors and Health Services. In addition to the higher burdens from the cost of health insurance coverage, rural families have less access to health care services. For instance, rural areas tend to have fewer active doctors and specialists per person than metropolitan areas. As a result, rural residents face greater difficulties in accessing care. This complicates early detection and regular treatment of diseases such as cancer.

Non-metropolitan counties had on average 1.2 active doctors for every 1,000 residents in 2007, compared with 3.0 active doctors for the same number of residents in metropolitan areas. Metropolitan counties also had more than 3 times as many specialists, 1.1 for every 1,000 residents compared with only 0.3 for every 1,000 residents in non-metropolitan counties.

Finally, in addition to disparities in health care infrastructure and workforce capacity, rural residents face specific geographic challenges in accessing medical care. One report found longer travel times for emergency services in small and geographically isolated rural communities (Chan, Hart, and Goodman 2006). This can be especially problematic for acute events such as heart attacks and strokes, where the time that elapses until the patient reaches the hospital can mean the difference between life and death.

Diverging Mortality Rates. While mortality rates in the United States overall have declined over the past few decades, mortality rates in metropolitan and non-metropolitan areas have diverged since the early 1990s. Since 1990, non-metropolitan mortality has declined at an average annual rate of only 0.73 percent, significantly slower than the metropolitan rate of 1.27 percent.

While the source of this divergence is unclear, it is likely that improvements in access to health care and in the affordability of that care in rural areas could help to narrow this gap in mortality rates.

Traditional Federal Support for Rural America

A key aim of Federal policy is to increase economic opportunities and overall standards of living in rural areas. While the Department of Agriculture has a significant focus on rural development, other Federal agencies also play a role, including the Small Business Administration, the Department of Health and Human Services, the Department of the Interior, and the Environmental Protection Agency, among others. Long before the Administration's recent efforts to strengthen rural America, Federal support for rural areas through these many agencies was extensive.

To illustrate this traditional support, consider expenditures in 2007. About $390 billion in Federal funding was directed to rural areas through non-loan, non-insurance programs in that year. Approximately 84 percent of this funding went to health care, Social Security, military wages and procurement, and non-military wages and procurement (including the Postal Service). The remaining 16 percent—denoted as "other spending"—is further broken out in the right-hand pie chart. This "other" component of rural spending constituted about $62 billion in 2007. About one-quarter of this spending was directed toward transportation infrastructure. Spending on social services and food assistance (17 percent), income security (16 percent), the agricultural sector (15 percent), and education (13 percent) represent the next largest areas of spending. Spending on housing and other infrastructure, while smaller, was still a substantial portion of Federal funding.

REFERENCES

Chan, Leighton, L. Gary Hart, and David C. Goodman. (2006). "Geographical Access to Health Care for Rural Medicare Beneficiaries." *Journal of Rural Health* 22, no. 2: 140–146.

Jones, Carol, et al. (2009). "Health Status and Health Care Access of Farm and Rural Populations." *Economic Information Bulletin* 57. Department of Agriculture, Economic Research Service. August.

7. Growing New Businesses in Rural America*

Council of Economic Advisers

The previous essay highlighted both the strengths of rural America and the challenges it faces. The Obama Administration is committed to building on those strengths and addressing the challenges. One key set of the Administration's policies for rural America are programs to help businesses grow and flourish in rural areas. These policies include supporting small businesses, jump-starting the transition to clean energy, and new opportunities for rural tourism and recreation.

Strengthening Small Business

Background. In the second half of the twentieth century, a diversifying rural economy gave the Federal government reason to expand its rural business programs beyond the agricultural sector. The three main organizations that house these programs are the Small Business Administration (SBA), the Department of Commerce's Economic Development Administration, and the Department of Agriculture's Office of Rural Development.

The Small Business Administration has supported loans to small businesses for over fifty years through numerous loan and financing programs, the biggest of which are the 7(a) and 504 loan guarantee programs. The 7(a) program has historically offered guarantees of up to 85 percent on loans to small businesses that would not otherwise be able to get funding. The 504 program is designed to help businesses get long-term financing to acquire fixed assets for expansion or modernization. Both programs work through qualified lenders and generally require fees for participation. Over 2007 and 2008, an annual average of more than $2 billion in loan guarantees by the 7(a) and the 504 programs went to rural counties, representing 12 percent of their total loan volume.

The Economic Development Administration provides a variety of services to stimulate economic development and to protect underserved businesses, including a revolving loan fund program to small business owners and entrepreneurs, a trade adjustment assistance program, and an economic adjustment assistance program for businesses affected by sudden economic changes. In fiscal year 2008, it reported investing almost 69 percent of its funds for infrastructure and revolving loan funds in rural areas.

Programs in the Department of Agricul-

---

*Originally published as Council of Economic Advisers, "Growing New Businesses in Rural America," www.whitehouse.gov.

ture's Office of Rural Development are explicitly geared towards encouraging economic development in rural communities. In 2008, these programs supported more than $1.5 billion in loans and grants, $1.4 billion of which was in the Business and Industry (B&I) Guaranteed Loan program. The B&I Guaranteed Loan program provides loan guarantees on up to 80 percent of the loan amount for loans to rural businesses.

New Policies. The Administration is committed to supporting rural businesses both by providing short-term relief and by promoting long-term economic growth. Small businesses were hit particularly hard in the recession. With limited access to capital markets, small businesses rely more heavily on bank lending than large businesses do, making them vulnerable to difficulties in the banking sector. Small businesses in rural areas are no exception, and the struggles that they have faced during this recession have required timely action. The Administration and Congress reacted swiftly to the needs of small businesses by passing the Recovery Act in February 2009.

The Recovery Act included legislation that increased the resources of many of the programs that generally support small business and economic development in rural areas. The Small Business Administration's 7(a) and 504 programs were expanded by temporarily eliminating or reducing fees and raising the guarantee rates. The Rural Development Administration's B&I Guaranteed Loan Program was granted budget authority to support nearly $1.7 billion of new loans to rural businesses. The Economic Development Administration received $150 million to create jobs and boost development in parts of the country hit hard by the recession, and particularly those that would qualify for help under their economic adjustment assistance program. The Community Development Financial Institutions Fund also received funds to be used

for technical and financial assistance for American Indian and Alaska Native communities.

The Recovery Act provided support at a critical time for many rural small businesses. New monthly lending in the SBA's 7(a) and 504 programs in rural counties from January 2007 through December 2009. There are two principal findings. First, small business SBA-backed lending in the rural sector dropped substantially during the course of the financial crisis of 2008, as banks reined in their lending (an equivalent drop occurred in the urban sector). Second, the success of the Recovery Act program to expand credit to small business is evident. The fee elimination or reduction and the higher guarantee rates coincided with a substantially increased loan volume. By December 2009, the dollar amount of loans issued in rural counties was more than 2.5 times larger than the amount issued at the low point in January 2009.

This substantial increase after the Recovery Act occurred in both rural and urban communities. However, recent SBA policies and general improvements in the lending environment appear to have especially benefited rural communities. The percentage of SBA-backed loan dollars issued to rural counties jumped in 2009 after the Recovery Act was put into effect. The percentage of loans issued to rural counties increased to an average of 15 percent after the Recovery Act was enacted through the end of 2009, up from an average of 12 percent in 2008 and 11 percent in 2007.

The Administration's policies are not limited to the short-term response that was essential during the recession. Long-term investment in innovation and entrepreneurship is critical for the economic health of rural communities. In addition to continuing strong support of existing programs, the Administration has introduced new policies that will foster rural revitalization. In particular, the Department of

Agriculture will lead a strategy to promote economic opportunities through regional planning among Federal agencies and state and local governments through its Rural Innovation Initiative. Recognizing that rural areas often suffer from higher poverty and unemployment rates, the Department of Agriculture and the Small Business Administration recently announced their intent to work together to better coordinate development programs and increase the number of guaranteed small business loans (Small Business Administration and Department of Agriculture 2010).

The fiscal year 2011 budget also includes almost $100 million for the promotion of regional innovation clusters through the Small Business Administration and the Economic Development Administration. The Economic Development Administration will use its budget allocation to distribute regional planning and matching grants to support the creation of regional innovation hubs. The Small Business Administration will promote small business participation in regional economic clusters by awarding grants on a competitive basis to facilitate the coordination of resources through business counseling, training, and mentorships. The proposed fiscal year 2011 budget also expands the Emerging Leaders Initiative and the Minority Business Development Agency, both of which will play critical roles in supporting American Indian and Alaska Native businesses by providing technical assistance and connecting business leaders to regional networks.

Jump-Starting the Clean Energy Transformation

The rural economy will also benefit from policies aimed at moving the American economy toward cleaner domestic sources of energy. Existing Administration policies—the Renewable Fuel Standard recently enacted under the Energy Independence and Security Act of 2007 (EISA) and Recovery Act incentives for the development of bio-energy—will increase the amount of bio-based transportation fuels and renewable energy produced in rural areas. Further energy and climate legislation could greatly expand the use of energy sources located in rural areas such as bio-energy, solar, wind, biomass, and geothermal to produce electricity and transportation fuels.

Increased Demand for Bio-Based Feedstocks. The EISA requires that a minimum volume of renewable fuel be added to any gasoline sold in the United States. Renewable fuels are defined by statute as fuels derived from bio-based feedstocks such as corn, soy, sugar cane, or cellulose that have fewer lifecycle greenhouse gas emissions than the gasoline or diesel they replace. This provision will increase the volume of renewable fuel blended into gasoline from 9 billion gallons in 2008 to 36 billion gallons by 2022. While petroleum refiners will initially rely on conventional biofuels to meet the requirement, the EISA mandates that 58 percent of the total requirement be met by advanced biofuels in 2022. Fuel sources that could be used to meet this mandate in future years include sugar cane, switchgrass, agricultural residues, algae, and waste.

Greater use of biofuels is already leading to the location of bio-refineries in rural America, and this trend is expected to grow over time. The number of operating ethanol refineries in the United States more than doubled between 2005 and 2009, with capacity concentrated in the Midwest. The number of ethanol plants built each year and their average capacity also have increased over the past several years. In 2002, about six ethanol plants were built annually, each with an average capacity of 50 million gallons. In 2008, the number of ethanol plants built annually had increased to 26, each with an average capacity of 100 million gallons. Over the next decade, the

Environmental Protection Agency (EPA) projects that between 10 and 15 ethanol plants will be built annually (Environmental Protection Agency 2010).

The increased demand for bio-based feedstocks is expected to increase net incomes in rural America. The EPA estimates that the increase in renewable fuel production due to the renewable fuel standard will result in a $13 billion increase in net U.S. farm income in 2022 (Environmental Protection Agency 2010). This represents a 36 percent increase in net income relative to what is projected to be without the renewable fuel standard. Biofuel production tends to occur relatively close to where the feedstock is grown. Thus, the employment associated with greater biofuel production from the feedstock will further increase earnings in rural areas.

The Recovery Act Will Spur Investment in Renewable Energy. The Recovery Act's substantial investments in America's renewable energy future. In the short term, they will help achieve the President's goal of doubling renewable energy production by 2012. Over the longer term, they will help ensure that renewable energy sources become a major part of our supply of energy. This increased production of renewable energy from geothermal, wind, solar, and biomass will generate increased income, particularly for residents of rural communities.

The Energy Information Administration's (EIA) revised Annual Energy Outlook for 2009 projects that the fraction of electricity generated from renewable energy will grow due to the renewal of Federal tax credits and the funding of new loan guarantees through the Recovery Act (Department of Energy 2009b). Wind generation is expected to be more than double what it would have been without the Recovery Act by 2012. Geothermal and biomass capacity are also projected to grow significantly more due to the Recovery Act.

States with largely rural populations have some of the highest technical potential for renewable development and therefore will likely be the principal recipients of renewable energy projects spurred by these Federal incentives. Low-density rural counties have the highest technical potential for solar and wind-based energy, while high-density rural counties have the highest technical potential for crop and forestry biomass and for renewable energy from animal waste residues. In particular, North Dakota, Montana, and other portions of the Great Plains rank highest in terms of wind intensity, while the most certain wind resources are located in the southeastern plains. States in the West—Utah, Arizona, California, New Mexico, Colorado, and Nevada—have the highest solar energy potential. Western states also tend to have the highest proportion of geothermal potential (where magma has penetrated the Earth's upper crust).

There is also some evidence that certain types of renewable generation may be more labor-intensive than traditional power generation. For instance, CEA analysis suggests that a 100-megawatt concentrated solar plant may require up to seven times the number of workers necessary to operate a 100-megawatt combined cycle natural gas plant. While the operation and maintenance of the power plant is similar to a conventional combined cycle plant, concentrated solar requires additional workers to maintain large solar fields. For instance, the mirrors must be washed frequently during summer months. Since these facilities will be disproportionately located in rural areas, this is expected to expand rural employment opportunities.

In addition to incentives to spur investment, both the Recovery Act and the President's proposed fiscal year 2011 budget increase funding for research and development for renewable energy, biofuels, and energy efficiency to help ensure that investments in these areas continue to contribute to future economic growth. For instance, of about $2.5 billion to support energy research and development in the Recovery Act, $400 million is allocated to the Advanced Research Projects Agency-Energy (ARPA-E). The President's fiscal year 2011 budget proposes adding another $300 million in funding to this program. ARPA-E uses a highly entrepreneurial approach by funding potentially transformative technologies that "industry by itself is not likely to undertake because of technical and financial uncertainty" (U.S. Congress 2007). The proposed 2011 budget also includes $220 million for biofuels and biomass research and development.

A Market-Based Approach to Controlling Greenhouse Gas Emissions Will Spur Generation of Renewable Energy in Rural America. The President has included an economy-wide cap-and-trade program in his fiscal year 2011 proposed budget that reduces greenhouse gas emissions by more than 80 percent by 2050. The American Clean Energy and Security Act (ACES) that was passed by the House of Representatives last summer includes a cap on greenhouse gas emissions that is consistent with this goal, and the Senate is currently engaged in an effort to develop a bill.

A cap-and-trade system limits total annual aggregate greenhouse gas emissions and requires that a firm hold an allowance for each ton it emits. Trading allows firms the flexibility to meet the cap at least cost. Based on two analyses, the CEA estimates that U.S. actions consistent with the President's emission reduction goals would reduce greenhouse gas emissions by approximately 110–150 billion metric tons (in CO_2 equivalents) cumulatively by 2050 (Environmental Protection Agency 2009; Paltsev et al. 2009).

A number of analyses find that renewables such as wind, solar, geothermal, and biomass will play an important role in meeting these long-term emission goals. For instance, in its analysis of the ACES legislation, the EIA projects that renewables will make up a substantial proportion of the new generation capacity added between 2012 and 2030, representing an almost 50 percent increase over what occurs without the legislation (Department of Energy 2009a). Further, the EPA estimates that generation from biomass and municipal solid waste will increase by 44 percent and generation from wind and solar will increase by almost 70 percent in 2030 relative to what occurs without the legislation (Environmental Protection Agency 2010).

As previously discussed, technical capacity for wind and solar is highest in less-densely populated areas. Further, land is less expensive in rural areas. Consequently, increased reliance on these technologies will likely translate into a greater number of large-scale wind farms and concentrated solar plants in these communities. Furthermore, rural communities in particular will likely benefit from revenues from increased biomass production, since large quantities of fuel will require some conversion of existing land to growing feedstocks and the use of currently fallow lands for this purpose.

A common feature of a cap on greenhouse gas emissions is the flexibility to purchase offsets. Offsets allow emissions sources in covered sectors of the economy to purchase a reduction in emissions from a source that is not covered. Since greenhouse gases cause the same damage no matter where they are emitted, offsets offer the appealing prospect of achieving emissions reductions specified by the cap at lower cost. For a variety of reasons, the agriculture and forestry sectors are unlikely to be covered by a cap on greenhouse gas emissions, making them eligible for offsets. Offsets represent a potential new source of income for these sectors. A recent study by Baker et al. (2010) finds that the overall impact on U.S.

farmers' net welfare of a market-based cap on greenhouse gas emissions consistent with the Administration's emission reduction goals is positive. The gains in farm income from higher output prices, increased bio-energy use, and demand for domestic offsets outweigh any increases in input costs.

New Opportunities in Recreation and Tourism

Background. America's Federal lands are precious national assets that are an important source of employment in rural areas through their support of the tourism industry. These lands—wildlife refuges, national parks, national forests, and Bureau of Land Management lands—are located disproportionately in rural areas. Recently, there have been more than 620 million annual visits to these lands, including over 310 million to national parks and wildlife refuges. The Department of the Interior estimates that its lands support over 320,000 jobs in tourism and recreation (Department of the Interior 2009). Recent studies estimate that the National Park Service alone annually contributes $6.3 billion in labor income and $9 billion in value added (Stynes 2009), the wildlife refuges provide an estimated $1.7 billion in sales and $542.8 million in employment income (Carver and Caudill 2007), and recreational visits to the National Forests contribute $11.2 billion to GDP (Department of Agriculture 2010a).

America's Federal lands support a wide variety of activities. Every year, about 7 million anglers visit national wildlife refuges, as do 2 million hunters and many millions of birders (Carver and Caudill 2007). Of those surveyed on their national forest recreation visits, the primary activities were hiking or walking, downhill skiing, viewing natural features, hunting, and fishing. Additionally, about 40 percent listed viewing wildlife as an activity in which they partic-

ipated. Recreation and tourism on Federal lands is a growth industry, with the potential to increasingly benefit rural America. For example, the Department of Agriculture estimates that the number of visitors has increased at national forests from 134 million in 1964 to 206 million in 2007 (Department of Agriculture 2008, 2010b). Likewise, the number of recreation visits to the national parks has increased from 205 million in 1979 to 275 million in 2008.

Unfortunately, two problems—deferred maintenance and damaged ecosystems—prevent America's Federal lands from reaching their full economic potential. In 2009, the Fish and Wildlife Service, Bureau of Land Management, National Parks Service, and Forest Service had a combined deferred maintenance project backlog of between $16 and $22 billion. The Forest Service estimates that 37 percent of its administrative facilities need major repairs or renovations (Department of Agriculture 2009). The failure to do needed maintenance leads to eroded roads, closed-off trails, and hazardous dilapidated buildings, and reduces the safety and accessibility of America's Federal lands. In turn, this makes them less attractive tourist destinations.

Similarly, a legacy of damaged ecosystems has decreased the attractiveness of many Federal lands. Aside from the reduction in ecosystem services that these lands provide to the whole country, the harms to recreation and tourism take many forms. Whether through decreasing bird biodiversity that attracts birders, fish abundance that attracts recreational fishermen, the population of native species prized by amateur naturalists, or the quality and quantity of water available for water recreation, ecosystem degradation is harmful to tourism on Federal lands. For example, the Forest Service estimates that 25 million acres of its lands are at future risk from insects and diseases (Department of Agriculture 2009). Furthermore, a legacy of counterproductive fire suppression has led to an excessive build-up of combustible material on Federal lands, leading to more extreme wildfires which—aside from endangering surrounding communities—harm ecosystems and site facilities, keeping away visitors.

New Policies. Through the Recovery Act, the Administration has increased investment on Federal lands, reducing the problems of deferred maintenance and ecosystem degradation and creating a stronger foundation for the future of rural tourism. The Recovery Act invests over $2.3 billion to preserve and improve the accessibility and experience of America's extraordinary Federal lands. Much of this spending goes disproportionately to rural areas; for example, the CEA estimates that 65 percent of Forest Service spending has been allocated to rural counties. The funding is roughly evenly split between the Department of the Interior (National Park Service, Fish and Wildlife Service, and the Bureau of Land Management) and the Department of Agriculture's Forest Service.

To make parks and forests safer and more accessible, these funds will repair eroded trails and roads, close hazardous abandoned mines near tourist sites, build visitor facilities, and invest in many other assets. For example, the Forest Service is replacing unsafe and unhealthful bathrooms in Pike-San Isabel National Forest, in rural Chaffee County, Colorado, responding to the number-one complaint received from forest visitors. To improve the natural capital that draws people to Federal lands, these funds will reforest, reduce hazardous fuel build-up, remove structures preventing fish from accessing spawning and feeding areas, and remove damaging invasive species. The Department of the Interior is funding the construction of water control infrastructure that will increase the wetlands available to migratory birds at Tule Lake, in rural Siskiyou County, California, which attracts one of the largest concentrations of migratory waterfowl in the world.

The President's proposed fiscal year 2011 budget continues to support these types of investments through a variety of targeted programs. For instance, it proposes the establishment of a Forest Service pilot program for long-term, landscape-scale forest restoration activities that emphasize resiliency, health, and sustainable economic development. Likewise, the 2011 budget proposes to fully fund the ten-year average cost of fire suppression and additional discretionary funding if the ten-year average funding is exhausted due to excess wildfire activity.

Finally, the 2011 budget includes funding for conservation on private and public lands. For instance, it proposes to fund the Wetlands Reserve Program at a level that will support the conservation of almost 200,000 additional acres of wetlands; a 67 percent increase in funding over 2010 to decrease nutrient loading in the Chesapeake Bay; funding for the installation of conservation practices on 1.5 million acres of priority landscapes, including the Bay-Delta region in California and the upper Mississippi River; and a 31 percent increase in funding for the Land and Water Conservation Fund to acquire and conserve landscapes and ecosystems that lack adequate protection and improve wildlife and public enjoyment on Federal lands.

In the short run, these investments provide jobs in rural communities that will help them weather the recession. In the long run, they will expand the opportunities for tourism-related businesses in rural America.

REFERENCES

Baker, Justin S., et al. (2010). "The Effects of Low-Carbon Policies on Net Farm Income." Working Paper. Duke University, Nicholas Institute for Environmental Policy Solutions (February).

Carver, Erin, and James Caudill (2007). "Banking on Nature 2006: The Economic Benefits to Local Communities of National Wildlife Refuge Visitation." Division of Economics, Fish and Wildlife Service. September.

Department of Energy (Energy Information Administration) (2009a). Energy Market and Economic Impacts of H.R. 2454, the American Clean Energy and Security Act of 2009. SR-OIAF/2009-05.

Department of Energy (Energy Information Administration) (2009b). An Updated Annual Energy Outlook 2009 Reference Case Reflecting Provisions of the American Recovery and Reinvestment Act and Recent Changes in the Economic Outlook. SR-OIAF/2009-03.

Environmental Protection Agency (2009). "EPA Analysis of the American Clean Energy and Security Act of 2009 H.R. 2454 in the 111th Congress." June.

Environmental Protection Agency (2010). "Renewable Fuel Standard Program (RFS2) Regulatory Impact Analysis." EPA-420-R-10-006.

Paltsev, Sergey, et al. (2009). "The Cost of Climate Policy in the United States." Report 173. Massachusetts Institute of Technology, Joint Program on the Science and Policy of Global Change (April).

Small Business Administration and Department of Agriculture (2010). "Memorandum of Understanding." April.

U.S. Congress (2007). "America Competes Act." Public Law 110–69.

8. The Challenges of a Small Town

Erin Mullenix

Living in a small town has its advantages and disadvantages, both administratively and financially. As statistics point to an increasing trend of migration to urban centers, smaller communities face ever-present challenges. Identifying and addressing the needs of small communities is not a particularly simple task.

Administrative Challenge

The definition for the population threshold of a "small city" may vary greatly; smaller communities may face relatable challenges. Small communities struggle to keep up with local administration and requirements. Some have mainly a one-person clerk's office, part-time administrative staff, or elected officials who work full-time beyond their commitment to the city. Many have a tough time filling elected official seats.

When jurisdictions are very small, services are often also very limited. Transparency is key to both the community understanding its own limitations and where spending is prioritized. Often, the small community may have a hard time marketing itself due to the limited services it can afford. However, local grassroots efforts to share new advancements, projects or concepts the city is committed to can be helpful. Social media may also provide an additional avenue to help bolster local communication efforts, though communities should take care in how it is used.

Economic and Financial Factors

Economic development. Economic development strategies can be critical for cities' well-being when planning for the future. The further the distance from regional centers and economic drivers, the more difficult it may be to boost economic activity. Careful planning to build a stronger economy, support the history and character of the community and make it a place where people can thrive are critical.

Planning for future local needs can be one of the most important, and potentially equally challenging parts of economic development related to a small community. All cities should plan regularly, refresh plans frequently and plan out several years in strategic planning and capital planning to address the future. While undoubtedly, new challenges will arise that change initial planning, keeping future needs in mind now will help ensure city preparedness down the road.

Local infrastructure. Some small communities have difficulty meeting the infrastructure needs of potential new development. Clearly, aging infrastructure is a common problem that has surfaced as the useful lifespan of older infrastructure systems approaches its end. Careful proactive

33

planning can be instrumental to a city anticipating maintenance and replacement costs projected over the lifetime of local infrastructure. Additionally, regulatory requirements, and new changes as new technology and information becomes available, can be a particularly tough barrier in small communities.

In terms of economic development; transportation, logistics, water and wastewater facilities, etc., may need to be expanded to help grow the community. There is typically an element of financial uncertainty related to infrastructure needs for smaller communities very actively engaged in economic development activities.

Fiscal stress. With the cost of government rising alongside other economic drivers, small communities may have difficulties keeping up. Trends in many states indicate that small towns are generally feeling at least some financial strain. Some very small communities are pushed near the brink of dissolving as they are unable to continue basic local operations.

Local political factors can play a significant role in influencing local governmental decisions; many such decisions can impact local finance. New local laws can impact local decisions in a multitude of ways, but budget planning must continue on. It is especially critical for small cities to accurately assess the local financial picture, plan, and make decisions accordingly. Communication amongst local officials, appointed and elected, is crucial, particularly related to finance.

Solutions for Small Communities

Plan for the future. City officials can prioritize and plan now. By exploring options, risks and requirements, and discussing the current status, the city can plan for its continued growth. A basic strategic plan in even the smallest of cities is helpful.

Make use of its geographic/regional advantages. If the town has advantages, such as a nearby freight line, transportation hub, major city, etc., these may be marketable for growth. Finding what is marketable can make smaller communities destinations for recreation, tourism or other activities.

Seek grants. Small cities may be able to obtain grants. Though writing and managing grants does take some time and effort, grants can help the efforts of small cities. There are often more opportunities than small communities are aware of. Connecting with other local or regional public resources may help small communities understand where to find strong possibilities and how to submit grant requests.

Share. There may be great opportunities to enter into mutual aid agreements and shared services with neighboring communities. Additionally, there has been an increasing trend in communities collaborating amongst the public, nonprofit and private sectors. Always consult legal assistance when needed. Use state or regional resources for information and advice, when needed. Explore partnerships with local colleges or universities as well.

Advocate. Join the state's municipal league, council of government, foundations or other organized local efforts to advocate for the small city interests in the state. Reaching out to other local partners can help magnify the "voice" of smaller communities. Also, make use of advancements in technology to communicate the positive steps forward the city is making or considering.

9. Economic Development in Hard Times[*]

INTERNATIONAL CITY/COUNTY MANAGEMENT ASSOCIATION

One of the greatest challenges to state and local economic developers is to be tasked with developing their communities in times of economic recession. As large companies lay off workers, small businesses close, and money for investment becomes tight, tax receipts dwindle as well. This causes government to tend to use its remaining resources to ensure the continuation of basic services rather than expending them on development efforts.

However, there are actions that can and should be taken:

Engage in Economic Development Strategic Planning. One of the main functions of strategic planning is to help organizations achieve their goals within the limitations of the resources available to them. Thus, an economic recession is a prime time for engaging in economic development planning. It not only can help the community weather the storm but also takes advantage of the slack time created by a slowdown to prepare for times of economic boom ahead.

Find Partners and Build Networks. Each community is part of a regional economy. Each regional economy is a component of the national economy, which in turn is a player in the global economy. This suggests that communities that share boundaries and economic realities and build social capital among themselves can benefit from what Brandenburger and Nalebuff call "co-opetition," or collaborating to compete.

Mutual benefit can be reached only when each party knows what it wants and why and can express that clearly to the other parties in the partnership. This becomes the basis for negotiating an agreement that is effective and will last the lifetime of the partnership.

Invest in Entrepreneurship. Entrepreneurship can be a low-cost, bottom-up strategy for fostering economic development. It is economically sustainable because it is small scale, draws largely on local resources, and produces home-grown businesses that tend to be loyal to the community in which they were spawned. These qualities help make entrepreneurship assistance, or enterprise development, an attractive economic development strategy for hard times.

---

[*]Originally published as International City/County Management Association, "Economic Development in Hard Times," July 5, 2012. http://icma.org, and from *Economic Development: Strategies for State and Local Practice*, 2d ed. (Washington, D.C.: International City/County Management Association, 2010), Chapter 3, "Planning for Economic Development." Reprinted with permission of the publisher.

35

Engage in Bootstrapping. Entrepreneurs not only can help build economies but also can be role models for how to do more with less. In the world of entrepreneurship, this is called *bootstrapping....* Bootstrapping involves a variety of techniques for attracting and utilizing other people's resources to help entrepreneurs accomplish their goals.

For example, a small rural community in the Midwest wanted to start a kitchen business incubator, but the community could not afford to buy a building and outfit it with the kitchen equipment.... Community planners negotiated with the local high school to give their clients access to the school's home economics lab when school was not in session.

Make Investments in Economic Good Times with Foresight. Rather than waiting until the economy takes a turn for the worse and reacting to that, it is far better to look forward in good times and make the kinds of investments that will cushion the blow of a recession.... Of course, this requires the kind of long-range anticipation that only planning can provide, which brings us full circle. Planning ahead is absolutely the best way to manage hard economic times.

• A. Leadership and Strategy •

10. The Role of Local Elected Officials in Economic Development[*]

CHRISTIANA McFARLAND *and* KATIE SEEGER

Economic development is the process of building strong, adaptive economies. Strategies driven by local assets and realities, a diverse industry base and a commitment to equality of opportunity and sustainable practices have emerged as those that will ensure a strong foundation for long-term stability and growth. Even within the parameters of these principles, what constitutes success in economic development and the specific strategies to accomplish it will look different from place to place. Despite these differences, leadership is consistently identified as a critical factor in effective economic development.

Dedicated leadership is needed to raise awareness, help develop and communicate a common vision, and motivate stakeholders into action. Although leadership can come from many places within the community, local elected officials are particularly well-positioned to take on this role. The political influence of elected leadership is critical to helping communities stay the course toward a vibrant economic future. From the bully pulpit to the design and coordination of public policies, mayors and councilmembers have opportunities every day to effect change and promote a strategic vision of economic growth for their community.

The goal of this guide is not to provide a one-size-fits-all solution to economic development or even to offer an Economic Development 101. Nor does this guide contend that elected officials should be economic development experts. The goal is instead to identify fundamental ways elected officials can become informed and strategic decision-makers who can connect the policy "dots," be effective communicators and take a leadership role in economic development. The guide is based on the premise that elected officials can and should actively participate in and lead long-term development strategies that make sense for their community.

The format of the guide is a "top 10 list" of things elected officials should know about economic development in order to be effective leaders. These include:

Your Local Economic Strengths and Weaknesses

Your community's strengths and weaknesses, such as quality-of-life amenities, infrastructure and workforce skills, deter-

---

[*]Originally published as Christiana McFarland and Katie Seeger, *The Role of Local Elected Officials in Economic Development* (Washington, D.C.: National League of Cities, 2010). Reprinted with permission of the publisher.

mine the potential of your local economy to support economic growth. This economic profile lays the foundation for creating a realistic vision and strategic direction for economic success that is unique to your community. Information about your local economy can also help engage and educate constituents and build community support for economic development decisions.

Your community's strengths and weaknesses, such as quality-of-life amenities, infrastructure and work-force skills, determine the potential of your local economy to support economic growth. This economic profile lays the foundation for creating a realistic vision and strategic direction for economic success that is unique to your community. Information about your local economy can also help engage and educate constituents and build community support for economic development decisions.

With the assistance of your economic development staff and input from stakeholders, you can identify factors within and outside of the control of local government that impact and shape your local economy. Identifying strengths and opportunities is crucial, but local officials also should pay attention to weaknesses and potential threats.

For example, what industries in your community and region are growing or struggling? What are the skills of your workforce, and are they sufficient to meet the needs of business? What barriers and support services exist for local entrepreneurs and small businesses? Is the local and regional housing stock diverse enough to provide for a wide range of housing needs?

All of these factors should be understood in comparison to other communities and in the context of broader economic trends. As a result of this process, you will have a stronger sense of your unique local assets, as well as what you can and should be doing to build on strengths and mitigate weaknesses.

Constituents have expressed concern that the city has too great a risk exposure in these investments. "There are requests that we redirect the money from the fund back to general government operations each time we face additional budget cuts, but due to political will and improved communications with our constituents, so far we have been able to maintain funding," said Councilmember Neal Andrews. City leaders have made a special effort to bring community opinion leaders into a position where they understand what a Jobs Investment Fund (JIF) is about and why it's important.

Your Community's Place in the Broader Regional Economy

Understanding your local economy also means knowing how your community fits into the broader region. Although increased competition for jobs, tax base and private investment can put political pressure on elected officials to go toe-to-toe with neighboring jurisdictions, the reality is that local economic success depends on regional economic success.

This is particularly true in the context of the global economy, where economic competition may not be with your neighbor, but with a city in China, India or Ireland. Firms engaged in global economic activity rely on a breadth of resources available in a region, including workers, transportation, housing, and amenities. In nearly all cases, one community does not have full capacity needed to support these activities. Cities that focus on competition within the region, instead of collaborating for economic development, are placing their economic future at risk.

With a firmer grasp of your community's place in the region, you're better prepared to work with other jurisdictions to share responsibility for promoting regional economic success. Cities in the Denver region, for example, work together to draw businesses and other economic activity to the region while agreeing not to compete or offer incentives to firms to locate in their specific communities. Similarly, many cities work together on regional marketing efforts, typically via participation in a regional council. These collaborative efforts attract firms, investment, and employment that benefit the entire region.

Participating in regional activities may present some political difficulties if the local economic benefits are not well understood by your constituents. Local elected officials should be prepared with the facts about how regional economic success translates into improved employment opportunities, tax base, or amenities for your city and the people who live there. Local officials can work with their staff to craft a clear, accurate message about their involvement in regional activities, and communicate this message to community through the media, neighborhood meetings or other public venues. It can serve as a starting point for a community dialogue about the importance of regional collaboration to local success.

Your Community's Economic Development Vision and Goals

A primary challenge in the practice of economic development is choosing among many competing priorities and various activities. A clear economic vision and goals are needed to provide a framework for strategically assessing and coordinating these efforts. The vision stems from the community's values, its collective sense of local economic strengths and weaknesses, and consensus on a desired future. Goals are more tangible expressions of the vision and provide specific direction for actions.

For example, the City of Albuquerque, New Mexico's economic development initiative "thrive!ABQ" identifies the city's economic vision as a city with a vibrant business climate that's accessible, user-friendly and welcoming to all. The three primary goals of "thrive!ABQ" are:

- Albuquerque First: Retain existing businesses and industries by fostering partnerships with local businesses and increasing spending in the community.
- Albuquerque Easy: Remove barriers to conducting business within the city.
- Albuquerque Recruits: Make the city an attractive place for businesses to locate.

According to the American Planning Association's *Economic Development Toolbox* (2006), a sound economic vision and goals should:

- Balance what the jurisdiction would like to achieve with what resources and public support the jurisdiction can realistically expect to muster in support of that vision.
- Be consistent with the role of the jurisdiction's economy in the larger regional and state economies.
- Be understandable to citizens without technical training or experience in economic development.
- Be produced in a way that makes it possible to incorporate it in the jurisdiction's comprehensive plan.

If your city already has an economic development vision, make sure your policy decisions reflect the principles in the vision. In cities that do not have an economic vision, local elected officials can help initiate a community visioning effort. A well-designed visioning process will surface an array of ideas, opinions and objectives from a diverse group of stakeholders. An important role for elected officials is to help bring people to consensus and agreement on a common purpose.

Case Study: Mission, Kansas (pop.

9,727). Mission, a community less than three square miles in area, was at a crossroads when many large parcels of land became available for redevelopment. In response, the city began a planning process that involved all facets of the community, including residents, businesses and shoppers, to create a vision that would serve as the framework for future development. The vision, which ultimately called for more compact, walkable, and sustainable development, was challenged when Mission was offered a lucrative deal by a big-box developer.

With a strong commitment to the vision, Mission denied the big-box store and has accepted an offer for a new mall from a developer who has embraced the city's vision for a vibrant, pedestrian-friendly, mixed-use destination. Although the developer typically works on retail projects only, his collaboration with the city and understanding of the community vision has led him to include residential, hotel, office and entertainment as potential project components.

The city's resolve to stick with its vision also resulted in overwhelming community support for the project. Instead of Not in My Back Yard (NIMBY) opposition, city officials received acclamation from those attending its Planning and Zoning hearings. Among the most common questions the city received from residents: "When will the project be complete?"

Your Community's Strategy to Attain Its Goals

Once the economic development vision and goals are defined, it is important that they not be shelved, but that they guide and determine you community's economic development strategy. If the community has been involved in the process and believes in the vision and goals, residents will hold political leadership accountable for putting them into practice. Strategic implementa-

tion of the economic development vision involves linking economic development goals to specific activities, allocating a budget and staff to these activities, and evaluating performance based on specific, measurable, agreed-upon outcomes.

There are many local activities that can be used to accomplish your city's long-term economic vision. The types of economic development policies and tools pursued by your community will depend on those permitted by your state, as well as how your local government perceives its role in stimulating private sector economic activity.

The traditional local government role in economic development is to facilitate economic activity by offsetting the cost of doing business in your community (in terms of time, opportunity and money). Strategies include land assembly, modifying the permitting process and providing job training. More entrepreneurial roles, as well as strategies that more directly address the demand for local products, may include seeding and investing in local small businesses, matching gaps in supplier/buyer linkages and international trade promotion. Local elected officials can work with city staff, businesses and other stakeholders in the community to educate themselves about the types of programs and tools that are available to them and to decide which economic development role is best for their city.

You can also look to "best practices" in other communities; however, it is important to remember that economic development activities that work in one place will not necessarily work in another. Following economic development fads or strictly replicating another city's approach without putting it in the context of your community is a recipe for failure. Instead, elected officials can learn how and why another city was successful and adapt those practices to local realities.

Elected officials should also work with their staff to determine a set of expected outcomes, the necessary level of resources (staff and budget) needed to achieve these outcomes and performance metrics to evaluate and measure them. In the context of short-term political cycles, it may be tempting to stray from the strategy and only consider economic development in terms of traditional, more tangible successes, such as attracting a new, large employer. For this reason, it is important that elected officials and staff agree upon, are committed to and accurately measure even incremental economic achievements. This will allow political leaders to demonstrate success and champion all various ways the community is supporting economic activity.

Strategic implementation of economic development, from selecting activities that support the vision to accurately measuring progress, enables local governments to be more responsive in an increasingly complex and uncertain economic environment. It allows the community, staff and elected officials to be part of a "continuum" of leadership and to make more deliberate progress toward long-term economic success.

Case Study: Littleton, Colorado (pop. 43,055). In 1987, the City of Littleton pioneered an entrepreneurial alternative to the traditional economic development practice of recruiting industries. The "economic gardening" program, developed in conjunction with the Center for the New West, is as an effort to grow local jobs through entrepreneurial activity.

The approach is based on research that indicates the great majority of all new jobs in any local economy are produced by small, local businesses already in the community. According to Chris Gibbons, Littleton's director of business/industry, an entrepreneurial approach to economic development has several advantages over attraction strategies. First, the cost per job is much less than the $250,000 to $300,000 incentives typical in major relocations. Second, the investment is in the community and its infrastructure; should a business choose to leave, it does not take that investment with it. Third, it is a healthier approach in that a community's future is no longer tied to the whims of an out of state company. Its future is entirely a function of its own efforts and investments.

Littleton's economic strategy focuses on creating a nurturing environment for entrepreneurs and "second-stage" companies, those with 10–99 employees and/or $750,000–$50 million in receipts. In a typical engagement, the city's Economic Gardening team will assist a company with core strategy, market analysis, competitor intelligence, and other priority tasks. Since the start of the program, Littleton's job base has grown from 15,000 to 30,000, the retail sales tax has tripled from $6 million to $21 million, and the population has grown by 23 percent.

Connections Between Economic Development and Other City Policies

It would be nearly impossible to list all of the various ways in which local government policies interact and overlap. When crafting economic development policies, it is essential to consider how other city policies support or discourage your economic development goals. For example, are your transportation initiatives supporting local retail? Are your local workforce training programs aligned with your sustainability plans? Is the regional housing stock adequate to meet the needs of workers in your community? By thinking about policies holistically, you can avoid detrimental policy interactions and create an environment for different policies to support and enhance each other.

Policy integration has become even more important over the past 30 years as the drivers of economic growth have broadened significantly. Today, the scope of economic development and the interests and needs of the business community extend well beyond market access and transportation networks. Social and professional networks, educational institutions, quality-of-life amenities, talent and workforce skills and housing are important assets that contribute to your community's economic profile. Additionally, there is increased recognition that improvements in economic equity and the natural environment are critically important to a strong local economy.

For example, the City of Portland, Oregon, has created a Sustainable City Partnership to foster a collaborative, citywide effort to integrate sustainable practices and resource efficiency into municipal operations and to strengthen existing policies and efforts. A primary partnership role for city officials and staff is to develop connections between environmental quality and economic vitality. The city has encouraged sustainable business practices and has leveraged sustainability as a key economic sector.

One strategy to ensure that all of the various sources of economic growth and the key elements impacting economic development are coordinated is to develop your economic development activities in conjunction with your community's comprehensive planning process. Some communities have formalized this process through implementation of an Economic Prosperity Element.

Your Regulatory Environment

Your regulatory environment directly impacts the ease of doing business in your city. For business leaders, time is money; they want to know that the regulatory process provides for timely, reliable and transparent resolution of key issues. If your city's regulatory policies are riddled with delays, confusing and redundant steps and multiple approval processes, a prospective

business may very well choose to locate or expand in another community.

Local officials can improve the regulatory environment for businesses by ensuring that the development review process and other policies are streamlined and transparent. The key to success is ensuring consistency and clarity about expectations, timelines, regulations, and costs. This will alleviate much of the uncertainty involved in economic development projects by allowing businesses to accurately anticipate the timing of the process and to build their plans accordingly. In addition, a better regulatory environment can promote information-sharing and better communication with local businesses so you can work together to identify potential challenges or problems.

As a local elected official, your first step is to ensure that you have an understanding of the current regulatory system and where there may be problems. This will require you to gather input from the business community about their frustrations and experiences. Working with your local chamber of commerce or other local business organizations may be helpful in this process. To gain additional perspective, you may want to consider going through the process yourself, as if you were a developer or a new business. This will allow you to have firsthand knowledge of the time, costs, hassles and clarity of the process.

When examining your regulatory process, be mindful not to throw the good out with the bad. Not all development is good development, and it is important that your regulatory processes reflect your long-term economic development vision so you can safeguard against detrimental projects. The key for your city is to find a balance and remove unnecessary delays and hurdles, while still preserving the integrity of the community's economic development vision and goals.

Your Local Economic Development Stakeholders and Partners

A group of diverse stakeholders within and outside local government contribute to economic development. These include both large and small businesses, nonprofit organizations, workforce and training organizations, universities, department staff and many others. Economic development partnerships will likely change depending on the activity, so it is important to think strategically on a project-by-project basis about who needs to be involved and the resources they bring to the table.

Collaborative partnerships are especially important given the increased complexity and diversity of interests in economic development. Harnessing the breadth of resources, knowledge, leadership, and skills of stakeholders that may not typically interact is essential for effective implementation of your city's economic development strategies. By facilitating broader and deeper interaction among local government, business, the community, and economic development activities, local elected officials can ensure that policy decisions will be in tune with all of the other work that is happening in the community to advance the city's economic development goals.

Your local government may not always be the lead organization for an economic development project. Sometimes, the chamber of commerce might lead the way. In other instances, it might be a different community organization or business leader. But even if the city is just one stakeholder among many, local elected officials can make themselves available to help bring the right people and organizations to the table. Important roles for municipal leaders include: reaching out to the various parties; working to break down communication barriers; helping to facilitate consensus; and ultimately, coordinating and leveraging action.

The Needs of Your Local Business Community

Local businesses are essential to a stable and diverse local economy. In recent years, many cities have shifted their primary economic development focus away from attracting large firms from outside the community to growing new businesses from within and helping existing businesses survive and thrive. Local officials can help create an environment that supports the growth and expansion of local businesses.

In the case of entrepreneurs and small businesses, many fail not for lack of ideas, but on planning and management. By allocating resources for entrepreneurial and new business support services, local governments can help these businesses overcome critical barriers to success. Such services include small business development centers, entrepreneurship training, market information, networking opportunities, marketing assistance, business incubators and even financing opportunities.

Running a business is a full-time job, and even if local services are available, business leaders may be unaware of the assistance available to them. Even more likely, they may not automatically view the city as a resource or an ally. By making the effort to reach out and communicate with your local business community, whether through your local chamber of commerce, organized events or visiting businesses individually, local officials can gather input to help improve local business policies and demonstrate that the community cares about the success of their business.

It is important for local elected officials to bring the same commitment and enthusiasm to existing business as they do to new business prospects. The city often creates incentives or other policy packages to attract new employers, and celebrates a new, large company with ribbon cuttings and stories in the local media. By similarly celebrating local business accomplishments, you can show the city's support, increase the business's profile and draw attention to economic development success stories that often go unnoticed.

Additionally, by publicly highlighting the achievements of your local companies, you will build your city's reputation as a business friendly community. This, in turn, may encourage outside businesses to take a second look at your community as a desirable location, while providing existing businesses with even more reasons to stay in your jurisdiction.

When making policy decisions focused on business retention and expansion, including small business and entrepreneurial development, it is important to remember that many local businesses need time to mature and grow. Although this form of business support may not deliver an overwhelming, immediate economic impact, the benefits of staying the course with your local businesses can provide greater long-term pay-offs. These include a more diversified, stable economy, a business community with stronger local ties and maybe even the next, great Fortune 500 company.

Your Community's Economic Development Message

Strong communications and a compelling message are vital to successful economic development and a primary responsibility for local elected officials. An economic development message that is based on your community's collective vision and is conveyed by all key stakeholders will establish a consistent community "brand" and competitive identity to the outside world.

Local elected officials can use public speeches, interviews and other communications to rally the community around their economic development message. In addition to publicly promoting the message,

local elected officials can work with their staff to ensure that all economic development partners have the information that they need to support the message or to accurately convey the message to others. This may be data about the economic role they play in the community, or marketing materials that they can use to engage others outside the community. These small steps go a long way in generating a positive reputation of your community.

Sometimes, cities let politics and minor disagreements about the direction of economic development affect their city's public image. This can detrimentally impact the confidence investors have in your community as a place to do business. Developers, business owners and others want to be assured that their investment in your community will have broad support among local leaders, residents and key partners. If those who impact the success of a business or economic development project are not unified, the confidence of the investor will falter. Local elected officials can help manage internal disputes and ensure that all stakeholders remain committed to the message and the vision it conveys.

Your Economic Development Staff

As discussed throughout the guide, local elected officials have clear and specific roles to play in their cities' efforts to build a strong local economy. However, success in filling these roles often depends on the relationship between elected officials and staff members who work on economic development issues on a daily basis.

As a local elected official, you are often the public face and the cheerleader for your city on economic development. When you are giving a speech, talking to a local business or discussing a new project with constituents, you must be prepared with the facts or run the risk of seeming uninformed and out of touch.

Staying up to date requires open and regular communications with and trust in your city's economic development staff. Your relationship with staff will enable you to gain a better understanding of the economic position of your city, changing local and regional conditions and your city's economic development plans and priorities. You will be better able to articulate economic goals to constituents and the media and make more informed policy decisions based on the most current information. This is especially important in the current economy, as city resources are scarcer and businesses and citizens alike are looking for informed leadership.

Local officials should begin building a strong relationship with economic development staff at the beginning of a political term or new project. Economic development is a complex topic; most newly elected officials may not have an in-depth understanding of the current economic policies or the city's long-term vision and strategy. By forging a relationship early on, local officials can come up to speed more quickly and be able to make better policy decisions in the long run.

It's also important to consider what expertise and knowledge you bring to the relationship that city staff may not have. Most elected officials come to office with a professional background in an area other than local government, such as banking, small business or healthcare. This can make you uniquely qualified to represent the city to important economic interests. With open communication, your city's economic development staff can become more aware of your skills and seek opportunities to use them.

Conclusion

As an elected official, you make decisions every day that impact the future of your community. It is of critical importance that your decisions and actions support your community's vision and do not work at cross purposes with existing efforts. This is particularly true in today's rapidly changing economic environment.

You can use this guide to initiate conversations—or ask questions—with key players within your community. The first step will most likely be to initiate conversations with your economic development staff about how to best use your skills and political capital to support a strategic economic direction. Even if you are already engaged in economic development, this guide can serve as a reminder of all the leadership roles needed for economic success. It can also help you identify how your economic development role should vary over time to support the changing needs of your community and economic development stakeholders.

Your city may have all the right assets, partners and tools, but may never realize its full potential without a leader to bring all the pieces together. You have the power and the ability to do what's needed to advance the cause of successful economic development for your city.

11. All Economies Are Local*

Christopher Robbins

Local governments can no longer rely on state or federal aid to fill their budget gaps. If local governments want to enjoy the benefits of a robust economy, each community must become a high-performing, self-reliant economic engine operating on four cylinders: residential, business, public sector, and nonprofit.

Each cylinder represents an indispensable component of the local and regional economy, employing thousands and fueling millions of dollars of activity through wages, the purchase of goods and services, and the payment of taxes.

In Massachusetts, Governor Deval Patrick's Economic Development Policy and Strategic Plan, Choosing to Compete in the 21st Century, recommends that each local government have a "CEO" and a team to create and implement an economic development plan for job growth. Communities must learn to take advantage of economic development opportunities and tax revenues.

They must understand how to create the optimum number of local jobs and how their local metrics determine their economic well-being. They must know their industry sectors, especially which ones are thriving or struggling, and the decision makers at those enterprises who pay taxes and create jobs. In short, each local government must take responsibility for its own economic fate.

Massachusetts localities are forming economic development corporations or committees to encourage new business establishments, developing supportive customer service policies, and providing predictable regulatory processes that are committed to respecting developers and residents. An incubation center for technology and science start-ups, TechSandbox moved to Hopkinton after selectmen voted to waive building permit fees and explore a special tax arrangement.

Marlborough (pop. 38,000), Massachusetts, formed an economic development corporation that works with local and private investors to create jobs and revitalize the community. The cities of Cambridge (pop. 100,000) and Somerville (pop. 78,000) implemented Buy Local First programs to support sustainable local economies and vibrant communities.

Three Steps

To understand how various components influence local and regional economies, local governments can design and implement this type of three-step process:

---

*Originally published as Christopher Robbins, "All Economies Are Local," *PM Magazine*, November 2014. Reprinted with permission of the publisher.

Develop an economic profile of your city or county. Include an appropriate set of metrics, and then examine historical performance. Examples of these metrics include payroll data from local employers; the tax base and rates; commercial land available; office and retail vacancies; school budgets and per-pupil expenditures; housing starts and trends; local revenues; cost-of-living measures; number of employers by sector; job statistics; and population trends and demographics. With this information, a city or county can better understand how the local economy works, including its strengths, weaknesses, and hidden potential.

Develop an economic portrait of your community's primary industry and small business sectors. This portrait should include nonprofits. In Worcester, Southborough, and Cambridge, for example, nonprofits are major employers, and they have a significant influence on the performance of a community's economy.

Do not forget to track and support the DBA (doing business as) companies, too. They are potential incubators for larger enterprises, new jobs, and growing your municipality's economy. Additional industry possibilities may include manufacturing, software, medical devices, finance, education, health care, information technology, tourism (leisure/hospitality), public sector, construction, legal, retail, and professional and business services.

The economic portrait will provide a wealth of information and assist local leaders to answer three questions:

1. How do we support local businesses and nonprofits?
2. What industries should we strive to retain or attract?
3. Are we too dependent on any particular industry? If so, how might that dependence be a problem or strength for encouraging job growth?

Only a diverse business base can help local governments survive economic storms and capitalize on opportunities during prosperous times. Certain metrics can be highlighted within industry sectors that include number of local employees, top employers, income data, products and services made or provided locally, economic outlook for each sector, and contact information for business and nonprofit leaders.

Outreach then becomes possible. Southborough's Economic Development Committee schedules meetings monthly with business and nonprofit leaders to learn how the town can help them prosper.

The Massachusetts Institute of Technology (MIT) developed a community economic development toolbox, where profiles can be viewed of economic indicators by county and profiles compared to state and national data. At the website mass.gov/lwd/economic-data, click on Municipal Data under Other Resources. State offices of economic development and local tax rolls are also good sources for identifying local businesses.

Create and communicate an action plan to interested parties. Assemble and interpret your local government's financial data and trends. Assess the strengths and weaknesses for retaining and attracting business; integrate economic profile, portrait information, and economic development action plan into the annual municipal budget process.

A review of this information can be useful in determining the best opportunities and planning next steps for job creation and growth. Armed with data, cities and counties can also explore opportunities to create public-private partnerships to reduce the cost of government and improve the delivery of core services.

Officials committed to job growth and economic well-being must come forward in each community and lead in a way that will help ensure fiscal sustainability and quality of life.

12. Defining Small Towns for Economic Development

Jonathan Rosenthal

Cities, towns, villages, boroughs, and hamlets are large and permanent human settlements. The significance of cities and towns is that they generally have complex systems for sanitation, utilities, land usage, housing, education and transportation. The concentration of development greatly facilitates interaction between people and businesses, benefiting both parties in the process. Their existence may also present physical, ecological and social challenges. (US Census Bureau, October 1995.)

- A center of population, commerce, and culture; a town of significant size and importance.
- An incorporated municipality in the United States with definite boundaries and legal powers set forth in a charter granted by the state.

Interestingly, there is no agreement on how a city is distinguished from a town or other jurisdictions including by population size. Many cities have a particular administrative, legal, or historical status based upon state laws. In fact, these municipalities are creatures of larger governments, state governments, who allow them to incorporate under certain rules and determine their boundaries. The federal government and its agencies has no standard definition for types of municipalities. There is no agree-ment as to what constitutes a small city or town but we have identified a few program elements that can be used for some guidance.

The Census Bureau defined "urban" for the 1990 census as comprising all territory, population, and housing units in urbanized areas and in places of 2,500 or more persons outside urbanized areas. More specifically, "urban" consists of territory, persons, and housing units in:

1. Places of 2,500 or more persons incorporated as cities, towns, villages, hamlets, boroughs and places.
2. Census designated places of 2,500 or more persons.
3. Other territory, incorporated or unincorporated, included in urbanized areas.

So one might utilize a population of 2,500 persons as a semi-sanctioned minimum size for a small town.

So What Are the Limits of a Small Town?

Researchers and policy officials employ many definitions to distinguish rural from urban areas, which often leads to unnecessary confusion and unwanted mismatches in program eligibility for communities. However, the existence of multiple rural

48

definitions reflects the reality that rural and urban are multi-dimensional concepts. Sometimes population density is the defining concern, in other cases it is geographic isolation. Small population size typically characterizes a rural place, but *how small is a small city or town? Population thresholds used to differentiate rural and urban communities range from 2,500, a number deemed to be sufficiently large, up to 50,000 persons.*

Because the U.S. is a nation in which so many people live in areas that frequently are not clearly rural or urban, seemingly small changes in the way rural areas are defined can have large impacts on who and what is considered rural. Researchers and policymakers share the task of choosing appropriately from among alternate rural definitions currently available or creating their own unique definitions.

Nonmetro Counties Are Commonly Used to Depict Rural and Small-Town Trends

Researchers who analyze conditions in "rural" America most often use data on nonmetropolitan (nonmetro) areas, defined by the Office of Management and Budget (OMB) on the basis of counties or county-equivalent units (such as parishes or boroughs). Counties are the standard building block for publishing government economic data, for conducting research and for tracking and explaining regional population and economic trends.

In 2013, OMB defined metropolitan (metro) areas as broad labor-market areas that include:

- Central counties with one or more urbanized areas; urbanized areas are densely settled urban entities with 50,000 or more people.
- Outlying counties that are economically tied to the core counties as measured by labor-force commuting.

Outlying counties are included in metropolitan areas, that is to say cities, if 25 percent of workers living in the county commute to the central counties, or if 25 percent of the employment in the county consists of workers coming out from the central counties—the so-called "reverse" commuting pattern.

Nonmetro counties are outside the boundaries of metro areas and are further subdivided into two types:

- Micropolitan (micro) areas, which are nonmetro labor-market areas centered on urban clusters of 10,000–49,999 persons and defined with the same criteria used to define metro areas.
- All remaining counties, often labeled "noncore" counties because they are not part of "core-based" metro or micro areas

What may be most telling in considering the importance of a community is examining how a small city or town is connected with and impacts its region and nearby communities and populations. It is important not only to ask what services are provided but also to look at the impact if those services were to disappear or move further away.

Economic and community development practitioners as well as planners and researchers cannot simply scale up small towns or shrink down large cities. Their characteristics remain unique in many ways … but not all. Lessons can be drawn but must account for specific conditions.

SWOT Analysis

If community leaders decide that some economic development action plan is desirable they may begin by assessing community's assets. A SWOT Analysis (Strengths, Weaknesses, Opportunities and Threats) can be a useful exercise for determining how to effectively commit limited resources. Some communities will undertake *Place-making—that is* planning, design and management of public spaces. Some will pursue *Branding* that markets the positive differentiator(s) of a community, which can help it stand out relative to the competition.

Community leaders might start by asking themselves a few questions.

- Is your community the biggest population or center in the county or other area?
- Even if the community is smaller than a relatively close urban area, can it provide an intervening opportunity by transportation path for shopping or recreation and so on?
- Can the community provide a qualitatively different opportunity?

Where is your Small Town/City? Location matters. Does the community contain the largest center in the area; let's say an hour and a half from any significantly sized municipality? One can determine if the community is an isolated, stand-alone municipality or if it's located within the circle of influence of another municipality. Is the other municipality smaller, larger or of similar size? If the town is close to a large city, like it or not, the community may be part of another metropolitan area or market area. It may be an inner ring or outer ring suburb, regardless of a jurisdiction's population and its land uses.

Assessing Your Small Town/City. Some large cities are truly able to be almost all things to all people. Most communities probably won't have a large array of resources, so they will need to inventory their strengths and those that might be improved upon.

An assessment of a community's *Strengths, Weaknesses, Opportunities and Threats* is commonly called a *SWOT Analysis*. With a facilitator, many communities can successfully complete these analyses on their own.

Local colleges and community colleges may be able to provide someone to help your group with a facilitator or in tabulating results. Recruit local stakeholders (businesses, educational institutions, colleges, recreational groups, government leaders and so on) to offer their views. Do not forget to have strong representation of ethnic groups and gender participation.

Another mechanism for looking for economic opportunities is *Cluster Analysis*. Clusters examine employment clusters. Theses clusters can provide insight into industry skill sets that may be possible to build upon in similar or transferable industries.

After assessing the overall strengths, opportunities and correctable deficits of a community its leaders will want to determine what economic development opportunities can be promoted. These efforts can be part of a *Community Branding* effort, that is marketing and business strategy activities. Out of your analysis(es) a vision and aspirations for the community can be formulated.

Can the community be the regional or destination center? Does the community have a unique resource(s) such as natural features (lake, mountains, gorges, waterfall, river, fishing, skiing, etc.) or historic sites and buildings, or cultural resources including special events or can the community offer a concentration of resources.

- For infrastructure (sewer, water, utilities, telecomm)
- Civic Center (government offices, libraries, and post offices)
- Medical Center
- Cultural Center (theatres, museums, sites)
- Recreational Center (movies, water features)
- Dining Center (restaurants and inns)
- Office Center
- Shipping or Transportation Center (highways, rail, buses, ports)

- Housing Center (density of population)
- Motel and Hotel Center (infrastructure, transportation access)
- Manufacturing Center—including agricultural processing (infrastructure, labor force)

The more centers a community has the more strengths are established through interrelations.

Spatial Behavior/Gravity Analysis. If retail uses are considered as a component of an economic development strategy determining market feasibility might include calling in a consultant to look at gravity analysis.

The Retail Gravity Model is a modified version of Sir Isaac Newton's Law of Gravitation applied to retail behaviors and demographics. Gravity modeling studies retail choice and the probability of a customer visiting a particular center. As with planetary bodies, the larger the object, the greater the pull of gravity.

The idea behind gravity modeling is that the probability of a given customer visiting and purchasing at a given outlet is a function of the distance to that outlet from a customer's home or work, and its "Attractiveness" for the customer to want to use that outlet rather than other retail opportunities. Retail gravity is based on the simple theory that any consumer's choice of where to shop will be based on two fundamental considerations: Proximity (travel time); and, the attractiveness of the choice (venue), often linked to size. Attractiveness of the retail outlet can be defined in a number of ways including the size, store density, internal or external characteristics, choice of products/services, and appeal to a certain lifestyle and brand. The probability of a consumer patronizing a shopping center can be predicted especially where there are differentiations of size and quality. Remember that larger venues generally exert more gravity.

Right Sizing for the Community. As with most market decisions, community demographics will determine economic viability, especially costs and the number of realistically available customers and their available or disposable income. Small communities need services but may need to look for their delivery at a scale appropriate for their community.

Certainly a number of smaller communities may be able to aggregate demand into one or more convenient, local and central locations. A full service hospital may not be viable for a community but a medical clinic may provide adequate emergency service for all but the most severe medical issues. Where a clinic isn't viable a medical office might be an alternative.

Retail and other services can be a very important part of the small city's economic base from such stores as groceries, fuel, hardware and clothing. Clustering these retail services can increase the convenience of shopping as well as increase their economic viability. Competition from some big box stores can actually undermine better inventory and selection of local stores by creaming the market for the majority of goods and leaving only a fraction of sales for the local stores. It's worth remembering that the profits of local stores are kept in the local community, notably in a living wage for the storeowners. Storeowners vary in their commitment to staying current in their selections and providing quality goods. It can be helpful for them to receive a critical evaluation of how to best serve their customer base.

Restaurants can be an important feature for people to gather and for utilizing retail space. The conundrum of paying for improvements by either property owner or the restaurant tenant is common. Restaurant uses often require substantial power, cooling, fire suppression, sanitary and plumbing leasehold improvements. Property owners don't want to pay for renters who are not strong credit risks (so-called credit tenants). Tenants don't want to pay for improvements on buildings they don't own. Communities that want to attract restaurants my wish to consider incentives for building improvements or rent guarantees.

Resurrecting an old movie house can create a special attraction. A community in northern Michigan is now supporting two successful "art houses" showing foreign, independent and other limited release films. Their success defies the conventional wisdom that only college towns and big cities support such efforts. And before we cede all on-screen entertainment to streaming services such as Netflix, pay per view or HBO and other cable subscriptions, we should remember that people like getting out and watching movies on a big screen, in-the-dark, with an audience. And maybe throw in dinner out as well.

Community leaders can look at what a community is doing well and consider if those efforts could be expanded. They can also look at what the community might be missing—and is exporting its dollars to—and consider if that use might be supported with a new, local location. This so-called "leakage" outflow of sales can be supported by proper zoning and working with property owners. Rent support can encourage an end-user and recruitment efforts may include speaking with successful current operators who might wish to open a second or third location.

There are options for communities trying to expand their economic base. It takes some vision and cooperation and commitment from property owners but there are a number of silk purses that can be found in small communities who commit themselves to economic diversity and improvement.

13. The Secrets of Successful Communities*

EDWARD T. MCMAHON

There are over 25,000 incorporated communities in America. How many of these are truly successful? How is it that some small towns and rust belt cities are prospering, while many others are suffering disinvestment, loss of identity, and even abandonment? Why are some communities able to maintain their historic character and quality of life in the face of a rapidly changing world, while others have lost the very features that once gave them distinction and appeal? How can communities, both big and small, grow without losing their heart and soul?

From coast to coast, communities are struggling to answer these questions. After working in hundreds of communities in all regions of the country, I have come to some conclusions about why some communities succeed and others fail. There are many communities that have found ways to retain their small town values, historic character, scenic beauty and sense of community, yet sustain a prosperous economy. And they've done it without accepting the kind of cookie-cutter development that has turned many communities into faceless places that young people flee, tourists avoid and which no longer instill a sense of pride in residents.

Every "successful" community has its own strengths and weaknesses, but they all share some common characteristics. It's clear for instance that successful communities involve a broad cross-section of residents in determining and planning the future. They also capitalize on their distinctive assets—their architecture, history, natural surroundings, and home grown businesses—rather than trying to adopt a new and different identity.

Sometimes a community's assets are obvious, like in Annapolis (pop. 38,000), Maryland. Sometimes they are not obvious. In the 1970s Lowell (pop. 108,000), Massachusetts, was dying industrial city. It had an unemployment rate of 25 percent. It thought it had no assets. But it had abandoned textile mills. Today almost all of these mills have been restored and repurposed.

Most successful communities also utilize a variety of private-sector and market incentives to influence to influence their development, instead of relying solely on government regulations. Not every, successful community displays all of the following characteristics, but most have made use of at least three or four:

---

*Originally published as Edward T. McMahon, "The Secrets of Successful Communities," PlannersWeb.com, July 29, 2013. Reprinted with permission of the publisher.

- Have a vision for the future
- Inventory community assets
- Use education and incentives, not just regulation
- Pick and choose among development projects
- Cooperate with neighbors for mutual benefit
- Pay attention to community aesthetics
- Have strong leaders and committed citizens

1. Have a Vision for the Future

Successful communities always have a plan for the future. Unfortunately, "planning" is a dirty word in some communities, especially in small towns and rural areas. In some places, this is the result of today's highly polarized political culture. In other places, it results from a misunderstanding of planning and its value.

The truth is, failing to plan, simply means planning to fail. It is difficult to name any successful individual, organization, corporation or community that doesn't plan for the future.

Try to imagine a company that didn't have a business plan. It would have a very hard time attracting investors or staying competitive in the marketplace. The same is true of communities.

A community plan is simply a blueprint for the future. People may differ on how to achieve the community's vision, but without a blueprint, a community will flounder. Understandably, people in small towns don't like change. But change is inevitable. Technology, the economy, demographics, population growth, market trends and consumer attitudes are always changing and they will affect a community whether people like it or not. There are really only two kinds of change in the world today: planned change and unplanned change. Communities can grow by choice or chance. Abraham Lincoln used to say that "the best way to predict the future is to create it yourself." Communities with a vision for the future will always be more successful than communities that just accept whatever comes along.

2. Inventory Community Assets Creating

A vision for the future begins by inventorying a community's assets: natural, architectural, human, educational, economic, and so on. Twenty-first century economic development focuses on what a community has, rather than what it doesn't have. Too many cities and towns spend all their time and money on business recruitment. They build an industrial park out by the airport and then they try like crazy to attract a plant, factory or distribution center to move there. The few communities that are "successful" at this strategy usually accomplish it by giving away the store.

The old economic development paradigm was about cheap land, cheap gas and cheap labor. It was about shotgun recruitment and low cost positioning. In the old economy, the most important infrastructure investment was roads. Today, successful economic development is about laser recruitment and high value positioning. Today highly trained talent is more important than cheap labor and investing in education is far more valuable than widening the highway.

American communities are littered with projects that were sold as a "silver bullet" solution to a city's economic woes: the New Jersey State Aquarium in Camden, New Jersey; Vision Land Amusement Park in Birmingham, Alabama; the Galleria Mall in Worcester, Massachusetts; the Winter Garden in Niagara Falls, New York—to name just a few. Too many communities think that economic revival is about the one big thing. Whether it is a convention center, a casino, a festival marketplace, a sports arena, or an aquarium, city after city has followed the copycat logic of competition.

If your city has a big convention center, my city needs an even bigger one. Festival marketplaces worked fine in cities like Boston and Baltimore, but similar projects went bankrupt in Toledo, Richmond, and a dozen other communities.

Successful economic development is rarely about the one big thing. More likely, it is about lots of little things working synergistically together in a plan that makes sense. In her award winning book—The Living City—author, Roberta Brandes Gratz says that "successful cities think small in a big way." Two examples of this are Silver Spring, Maryland and Cleveland, Ohio. Cleveland had an aging, undersized convention center. Civic boosters argued for a huge new convention center that could compete with much bigger cities like Chicago, Atlanta, or Minneapolis.

But small cities like Cleveland will never win in an arms race to build the biggest convention center. Instead Cleveland took a look at its assets, one of which is the Cleveland Clinic—a world renowned medical center located a short distance from downtown. Instead of trying to compete with every other convention city, Cleveland decided to build a smaller, less expensive meeting facility—the Cleveland Medical Mart and Global Center for Health Innovation—focused on medical conventions and which would have an attached medical mart, affiliated with the Cleveland Clinic.

Another example of asset based economic development is Silver Spring, Maryland. For many years, Silver Spring was among the largest suburban commercial centers in the Mid-Atlantic region. But, by the early 1990s Silver Spring had fallen on hard times. In 1996, a story in the *Economist* said "You can see America wilting in downtown Silver Spring. Old office blocks stand empty. A grand art deco theater is frequented only by ghosts. Glitzy department stores have decamped to out-of-town shopping malls. Tattoo parlors, pawnbrokers and discounters remain."

To combat this decline, local officials and an out of town developer proposed to build a second Mall of America (like the one in Bloomington, Minnesota). The proposed mega-mall would have 800 stores and it would cover 27 acres. The projected cost was $800 million and it would require a $200 million public subsidy. It would also mean the demolition of most of downtown Silver Spring's existing buildings. So what happened? The county rejected the massive American Dream Mall and set their sights on a succession of more modest developments.

First, they realized that despite its decline, Silver Spring had some important assets that were probably more valuable than a giant mega-mall. First, Silver Spring was adjacent to Washington, D.C., the nation's capital. Second it was served by transit (i.e., the Washington Metro system), and third it was surrounded by stable middle-class neighborhoods. Rather than spending $200 million subsidizing a giant mall, county and state officials collaborated to find a site for the new headquarters for the Discovery Communications Corp, which was then housed in several different locations around the Washington area.

The site where Discovery Communications decided to build their new headquarters was adjacent to the Silver Spring Metro Station. Bringing 1500 employees to downtown Silver Spring was a huge boost to the community, but what really synergized the renewal was Discovery Corp's agreement not to build a cafeteria in their new headquarters building. This meant employees would have to patronize local restaurants.

3. Use Education and Incentives, Not Just Regulation

Successful communities use education, incentives, partnerships, and voluntary initiatives not just regulation. To be sure, land use regulations and ordinances are essential to protecting public health and to setting minimum standards of conduct in a community.

Regulations prevent the worst in development, but they rarely bring out the best. Regulations are also subject to shifting political winds. Often one county commission or town council will enact tough regulations only to see them repealed or weakened by a future town council or commission with a different ideology or viewpoint.

If regulations aren't the entire answer, how can a community encourage new development that is in harmony with local aspirations and values? Communities need to use carrots, not just sticks. They also need to use education, partnerships, and voluntary initiatives. Successful communities have identified a variety of creative ways to influence the development process outside of the regulatory process. Some of the incentives they use include: conservation easements; purchase of development rights; expedited permit review; tax abatements that promote the rehabilitation of historic buildings; award and recognition programs; density bonuses for saving open space; and other techniques.

In Staunton, Virginia the Historic Staunton Foundation offered free design assistance to any downtown business owner who would restore the façade of their building. They did this after the city council had rejected a measure to create an historic district in downtown Staunton. At first, only one business owner took advantage of the incentive, but then a second business owner restored his building facade, and then a third, and then many more. Today, there are five historic districts in Staunton including the entire downtown, but it all began with an incentive.

Successful communities also use education to encourage voluntary action by citizens. Why do cities and towns need to use education? Because, education reduces the need for regulation. Also, because people and businesses will not embrace what they don't understand. Finally, community education is important because, citizens have a right to choose the future, but they need to know what the choices are.

4. Pick and Choose Among Development Projects

All development is not created equal. Some development projects will make a community a better place to live, work, and visit. Other development projects will not.

The biggest impediment to better development in many communities is a fear of saying "no" to anything. In my experience, communities that will not say no to anything will get the worst of everything.

The proof is everywhere, communities that set low standards or no standards will compete to the bottom. On the other hand, communities that set high standards will compete to the top. This is because they know that if they say no to bad development they will always get better development in its place. Too many elected officials have an "it'll do" attitude toward new development. Worse yet, they'll accept anything that comes down the pike, even if the proposed project is completely at odds with the community's well thought out vision for the future. They are simply afraid to place any demands on a developer for fear that the developer will walk away if the community asks for too much.

This is especially true when dealing with out of town developers or with national chain stores and franchises. The bottom line for most developers, especially chain stores and franchises, is securing access to profitable trade areas. They evaluate locations based on their economic potential. If they are asked to address local design, historic preservation, site planning or architectural concerns they will usually do so. Bob Gibbs, one of America's leading development consultants says that "when a chain store developer comes to town they generally have three designs (A, B, or C) ranging from Anywhere USA to Unique (sensitive to local character). Which one gets built depends heavily upon how much push back the company gets from local residents and officials about design and its importance." One community that has asked chain stores and franchises to fit-in is Davidson, North Carolina. Chain drugstores, like CVS, Rite Aid, and Walgreens are proliferating across the country. They like to build featureless, single-story buildings on downtown corners, usually surrounded by parking—often after one or more historic buildings have been demolished.

This is what CVS proposed in Davidson. The town could have easily accepted the cookie cutter design (Plan A), but instead it insisted on a two story brick building, pulled to the corner with parking in the rear. CVS protested, but at the end of the day they built what the town wanted because they recognized the economic value of being in a profitable location. The lesson learned is that successful communities have high expectations. They know that community identity is more important than corporate design policy.

5. Cooperate with Neighbors for Mutual Benefit Historically

Elected officials have tended to view neighboring communities, the county government, and even the managers of adjacent national parks or other public lands as adversaries rather than allies. Some community leaders see economic development as a "zero-sum" game: if you win, I lose. Successful communities know that today's world requires cooperation for mutual benefit. They know that the real competition today is between regions. They also understand that very few small towns have the resources, by themselves, to attract tourists or to compete with larger communities.

Regional cooperation does not mean giving up your autonomy. It simply recognizes that problems like air pollution, water pollution, traffic congestion and loss of green space do not respect jurisdictional boundaries. Regional problems require regional solutions. There are numerous examples of communities working together for mutual benefit. In the Denver region, 41 communities cooperated to support funding for a regional transit system (i.e. FasTracks). Cleveland area communities cooperated to build a Metro parks system. Metro Minneapolis and St. Paul collaborate on tax base sharing.

Even small rural communities can cooperate for mutual benefit. Small towns in Mississippi have worked together to organize and promote U.S. Route 61 as "the Blues Highway." Similarly, five rural counties on Maryland's Eastern Shore collaborated with the Eastern Shore Land Conservancy to create a regional agreement to preserve farmland and open space.

6. Pay Attention to Community Aesthetics

During the development boom of the 1980s, *Time Magazine* had a cover story article about what they called "America's growing slow-growth movement." The article began with a quote from a civic activist in Southern California, who said "we were in favor of progress, until we saw what it looked like." Looks count! Aesethics matter!

Mark Twain put it this way, "We take stock of a city like we take stock of a man. The clothes or appearance are the externals by which we judge."

Over 80 percent of everything ever built in America has been built since about 1950 and a lot of what we have built is just plain ugly. There are still many beautiful places in America, but to get to these places we must often drive through mile after mile of billboards, strip malls, junk yards, used car lots, fry pits, and endless clutter that has been termed "the geography of nowhere."

The problem is not development, per se; rather the problem is the patterns of development. Successful communities pay attention to where they put development, how it is arranged, and what it looks like. The image of a community is fundamentally important to its economic well-being. Every single day in America people make decisions about where to live, where to invest, where to vacation and where to retire based on what communities look like. Consider tourism, for example. The more any community in America comes to look just like every other community the less reason there is to visit.

On the other hand, the more a community does to protect and enhance its uniqueness whether natural or architectural, the more people will want to visit. Tourism is about visiting places that are different, unusual, and unique. If everyplace was just like everyplace else, there would be no reason to go anyplace. Successful communities pay attention to aesthetics. Typically they control signs, they plant street trees, they protect scenic views and historic buildings, and they encourage new construction that fits in with the existing community.

7. Have Strong Leaders and Committed Citizens

Successful communities have strong leaders and committed citizens. A small number of committed people can make a big difference in a community. Sometime these people are longtime residents upset with how unmanaged growth has changed what they love about their hometown. Others times, the leaders might be newcomers who want to make sure that their adopted hometown doesn't develop the same ugliness or congestion as the one they left. More often than not, they're simply citizens who care a great deal about their community.

An example of a citizen who made a big difference is Jerry Adelman. Jerry grew up in the small town of Lockport, Illinois. Almost single-handily Jerry created the Illinois and Michigan Canal National Heritage Corridor which helped restore an abandoned canal linking Lockport with Chicago. Adelman's success at building local support for the canal convinced Congress to add the canal corridor to the national park system. What about the Naysayers?

Every community has naysayers. Whatever the civic or community leaders propose to do, some people will always say things like: "you can't do it," "it won't work," "it costs too much," "we tried that already." And, "no," is a very powerful word in a small community, but leaders of successful communities know that "yes" is a more powerful word. Yes, we can make this town a better place to live in, to look at, to work in, to visit. A pessimist sees difficulty in every opportunity. An optimist sees opportunity in every difficulty.

Summing Up

We live in a rapidly changing world. In his new book, *The Great Reset*, author Richard Florida says that "the post-recession economy is reshaping the way we live, work, shop and move around." He goes on to predict that "communities that embrace the future will prosper. Those that do not will decline." One big change is that people and businesses can now choose where to live or operate a business. In today's world, communities that cannot differentiate themselves will have no competitive advantage. This means that quality of life is more important than ever. Successful communities know that sameness is not a plus. It is minus. Successful communities set themselves apart. They know that communities that choose their future are always more successful than those that leave their future to chance.

14. Big Ideas for Small Cities*

NATIONAL LEAGUE OF CITIES

The Big Ideas for Small Cities series serves as a platform for small city officials to share compelling and creative ideas that they have used to drive change in their communities. These TEDx-style talks are meant to inspire local leaders to think "big" for their small cities.

The Big Ideas for Small Cities series serves as a platform for small city officials to share compelling and creative ideas that they have used to drive change in their communities. These TEDx-style talks are meant to inspire local leaders to think "big" for their small cities.

What Is a Small City? Traditionally, a "small city" is a city with a population of under 50,000. As an organization that represents over 19,000 municipalities, the National League of Cities recognizes that these communities comprise the backbone of our country.

What Makes a Big Idea, Big? With smaller budgets, part-time city staff, and a state and national focus on larger cities, America's small cities often face challenges that require unique and innovative solutions. From converting vacant and abandoned buildings into industrial complexes and movie sets to partnering with private sector consultants to nurture small business development, city officials are thinking out-side of the box to make real change happen.

In March of 2015, NLC University launched the Big Ideas for Small Cities series, drawing nearly 300 attendees. Six small city mayors from all over the nation shared how they implemented creative programs to solve challenging problems.

In an effort to further our commitment to small cities, the National League of Cities decided to continue the series and hosted a second Big Ideas for Small Cities at the 2015 Congress of Cities in Nashville. The next event will take place at the 2016 City Summit (formerly called the Congress of Cities) in Pittsburgh.

Auburn Growth Strategy

What are the target goals? In the absence of any tax increment financing options (TIF) available under Washington State law, the City of Auburn (pop. 74,000), Washington, sought to stimulate development in its city center with infrastructure projects financed through alternative means. Revitalization started with the construction of a new regional transportation center in 2000 to link the city with Sounder Transit trains that run between Seattle and Tacoma. BNSF (Burlington Northern Santa Fe) rail and

*Originally published as National League of Cities, "Big Ideas for Small Cities," www.nlc.org. Reprinted with permission of the publisher.

Sounder Transit joined forces with the city to complete the project. City officials then drafted a comprehensive redevelopment plan, the result of which lead to the clearing of three blocks of downtown land in 2010 (formerly a shopping mall) and an overhaul of the city's zoning plan.

The city also used federal grants through the Economic Development Administration (EDA) to replace its aging clay water pipe system and install a fiber optic telecommunications network. On its own, the city established small business assistance centers, invested approximately $100,000 in storefront façade improvement projects for existing businesses, and implemented certain tax and fee waivers for construction and new development to further promote growth. The program ultimately resulted in its crowning achievement—a large mixed-use development that includes a combination of market rate and subsidized housing units.

Who are the partners? The City of Auburn largely relied on partnerships with local small businesses and federal agencies to implement this program. Business partnerships were formed through fiscal incentives offered by the city. The Economic Development Administration also worked with the city to complete infrastructure updates. The city offered tax cuts and construction fee waivers and EDA provided infrastructure grants.

Bedford Historic Downtown Revitalization

What are the target goals? In the wake of a declining auto manufacturing industry, city leaders in Bedford (pop. 2,700), Pennsylvania, sought to target business growth and development in the historic downtown. For this community, the downtown remained an important community venue and one that offered some distinctive retail diversity.

Through a partnership with a private merchandising firm, the city offered marketing expertise and training to local business owners to improve economic growth opportunities and rejuvenate shopping downtown. The city used its business incubator, known as the Bedford Catalyst, as a key tool to fill vacant store fronts with a diverse retail industry (including pop-up stores) and preserve Bedford's historic downtown image.

Who are the partners? The city retained the firm of Paradise + PEOPLE as the merchandising advisor. The Downtown Historic Business Owners Association has been revived through this effort and the local Chamber of Commerce is adapting its mission and focus to support this revitalization agenda.

How is the effort financed? The city offers the Bedford Catalyst's classes free of charge to local businesses, and finances the program completely through its own budget.

Brookings Crowdsourcing Creativity

Community leaders in Brookings (pop. 23,000), South Dakota sought ways to jump-start economic development, boost public spiritedness, and unleash the creative ideas of residents in the city and the region. The resulting Creativity Week festival, begun in 2014 and continued in 2015, gives credence to the city's claim as "Creative Capital of the North."

What are the goals? With a goal of "crowdsourcing creativity," Brookings adopted a model familiar to anyone who has ever watched a TED talk. In the case of Brookings, the Creativity Week festival was not just one event in one venue. Rather, the festival, showcasing the creativity and innovation of the local community and region, encouraged individuals to hold their own events ranging from TED-style talks to music and arts performance.

At the heart of the effort was a recognition that a community vision and the energy to achieve that vision starts at the grassroots. Whatever big challenge may confront residents of Brookings, whatever outcomes they wanted to achieve, the solutions can be found through the innovative ideas of residents, business owners, neighborhood leaders, high school students, and grandparents. Participation in the Creativity Week events has proven to be a catalyst for idea sharing that engaged a significant portion of the community.

How is the project being executed? With just $20,000 in financing, the city launched its first "Creativity Week" in 2014. Although the city manages the event, citizens host the local sessions which helps keep costs down. The city has committed funding to the 2016 event and accepted donations and sponsorships for the 2015 event. In fact, the 2015 event is financed almost entirely with donations from the Bush Foundation, local businesses, and the Chamber of Commerce and the Convention and Visitor's Bureau.

What are some of the results? Combined unique attendance in 2014 topped 4,500 attendees. YouTube videos of the event gained more than 75,000 views.

Major lessons from the experience thus far include:

1. Be radically inclusive in all events and activities, show off a welcoming community;

2. Take risks and think big, possibilities are unlimited;

3. Energize the arts—music, dance, painting, performance—are the inspiration for creativity; and

4. Capture what is learned, share it widely and build on the bright spots that capture people's imagination.

Gaithersburg Book Festival

City leaders sought to raise the prominence and economic prowess of Gaithersburg (pop. 65,000), Maryland, through creation of a world class book festival. Five years after its creation in 2010, the event has solidified the city's position as one of the most literate communities in the U.S. as well as a literary destination for bibliophiles throughout the country. This is especially significant in light of the fact that nearby Washington, D.C., hosts the annual National Book Festival (sponsored by the Library of Congress and established in 2001). In addition to adding a desired sense of culture to the city, the festival has also fostered economic development by attracting thousands of visitors each year.

The event itself is run by the city and the Gaithersburg Cultural Arts Advisory Committee. Gaithersburg partners with other municipal and county level organizations as well as literary organizations and local education institutions such as the University of Maryland.

The effort is largely funded by generous sponsors and donors, with some assistance provided by the City of Gaithersburg. Sponsors are offered varying levels of monetary donations in exchange for corresponding opportunities for marketing and publicity. Individual patrons may also make personal donations and be recognized as sponsors. Admission is free during the event.

Much of the festivals success can be attributed to Gaithersburg's unique location within the Baltimore Washington area, one of the most educated regions of the country. During 2014, the festival attracted over 20,000 visitors.

Lauderdale Lakes Economic Revival

What goals were the initiatives designed to address? Even before the Great Recession, the city of Lauderdale Lakes (pop. 34,000), Florida, was experiencing a weakening economy due to a loss of middle income residents and the departure of major national retail shopping stores. Toward the goal of establishing a process and a set of tools to lead a redevelopment effort, a Community Redevelopment Agency was created in 1999.

What steps were taken as part of the program? The first step for the Redevelopment Agency was to define and study the area targeted for investment and improvement. The charge included an inventory of vacant land, evaluation of road traffic flows and bottlenecks, and a review of the general characteristics of existing and proposed development in terms of its aesthetics and its commercial viability. The agency had the power to acquire land, execute contracts, and borrow money.

Fundamentally any revitalization needed to be a community process; one with buy-in from residents. In order to achieve a set of concrete goals and policies, a vigorous community engagement process was undertaken. Using community charrettes and other techniques, residents helped to envision what they wanted their city to look like over the long-term.

What was achieved? As part of a community master plan (adopted in 2003), city leaders and residents focused on vital outcomes. These outcomes included improved walkability and pedestrian safety, more dedicated park and open space, affordable housing, targeting priority development areas, allowing mixed-use development along certain roadways, making better use of the waterfront, and building both a new town center and a new library.

Implementation of the master plan required development of a comprehensive plan and amendments to existing land use and zoning codes. A commercial façade renovation grant program was launched to assist existing businesses upgrade to the new plans. Also, citizens approved a $15 million bond for public improvements within the plan area.

To date, the CRA plan has brought new life to the heart of the city and precipitated numerous building renovations and infill development throughout the district. Streetscape improvements at city gateways along State Road 7 have been completed, maintaining the road width, incorporating signature bus shelters and landscaping. New roads have been constructed and others linked, increasing connectivity throughout the CRA. Traffic calming features have been introduced in strategic locations. All of these efforts have resulted in revived investment, a return of national retailers, newly revitalized commercial activity and greater pedestrian activity overall.

Mooresville Technology Infrastructure

The City of Mooresville (pop. 34,000), North Carolina, made the decision to establish high speed Internet as a basic utility to which all citizens have access. Through a robust technology infrastructure, the city will better equip its students, citizens, and businesses with the tools necessary compete in a global market. Schools will have access to the fastest Internet speeds available and each student in the district will receive a school issued laptop or tablet. Additionally, the strong data network provides low-cost Internet to citizens and businesses, fostering economic development, supporting municipal planning, and even enhancing disaster relief.

How was the project executed? In 2007, the City of Mooresville bought a local cable company after it went up for sale. Mooresville and its neighboring communities filed to jointly buy the company for $64 million. After a lengthy process, the coalition of cities gained control of the company and its fiber optic network. That same year, the Mooresville School District began its "21st Century Digital Conversion."

Having secured access to a high speed telecommunications network, Mooresville sought advice and help from industry experts like Apple and Discovery education. In keeping with the education goals outlined above, Mac Book computers and iPads have been leased annually from Apple on three or four year contracts. The funding for this equipment and software updates comes through city and school district budgets and is partially offset by reductions in costs for textbooks. Additionally, the district has received grants to support equipment costs or for various upgrades from sources including Lowe's Home Improvement.

Despite state education funding cuts, the Mooresville School District is able to maintain over 5,000 laptops and tablets and support a large IT staff. Although the school district has grown in the population served, the use of one-to-one technology has been an essential factor in managing increasing class sizes—in some cases increases of 50 percent. The city also has partnered with local Internet service provider My Connection to offer broadband service at home for as little as $9.99 a month and to offer the service free to families with children eligible for free or reduced cost meals.

What are the results from this initiative? Since beginning this venture, the city has received acclaim for its actions, including from President Obama who visited the local middle school in 2013. Students from kindergarten to grade 12 each have their own computer and every classroom has wireless Internet access. Graduation rates have risen and the city has seen a dramatic reduction in the performance gap between black and white students and between wealthy and poor students.

In other areas, Mooresville also used its enhanced GIS technology to help Niagara Bottling Company find a new home in existing facilities just outside of Mooresville. All city parks and municipal buildings offer public access Wi-Fi to 100mbps while sports venues webhost live footage of youth sports so that out of town parents can watch their children play.

Union City Film Industry Attraction

Following the closing of a large anchor-employer (Union Station Shannon Mall), Union City (pop. 20,000), Georgia sought to create a vision for the 90-acre lot site and has been working with the film industry to bring a $100 million project to fill the vacancy. After four years of searching for a partner to redevelop this vacant land the city welcomed 404 Studio Partners, a newly formed media production company, to this Metro Atlanta community close to Hartsfield International Airport. Officials expect the project to create up to 1,200 new jobs in the first year alone, with the potential of indirectly spurring an additional 800 related support jobs.

Who are the partners? 404 Studio Partners was recently formed by executives from Turner Entertainment, and Universal and plans to build both Georgia's largest movie studio, and a warehouse on an additional parcel of land left by the mall's exodus. City officials have also worked with the Atlanta Regional Commission to develop the TIF plan to finance the project. Local high schools also have worked with the city on implementing video production training programs to their students as part of a job training pipeline.

How is the effort financed? The effort has largely been funded by Georgia's "Opportunity Zone" tax write-offs, which offer incentives of $3,500 for each new job created, and tax increment financing to launch the project. Donations from local philanthropies and start-up expenditures from the film companies also will help finance educational programs.

Other Details Beyond simply the establishment of a new business venture, the city expects this facility to be a catalyst for job training and educational opportunities for high school students aspiring to go on to work in the film production industry.

Smart Growth in Artesia

With California's expected population increase of 8 million people by 2040, the city of Artesia is in a unique position to utilize growth. Of the 88 cities in Los Angeles County, Artesia has a population of 17,000 and is 1.6 square miles. The median age is above the state average and so are the housing prices, yet there are no malls, movie theatres, or large businesses. To improve quality of life and increase revenue from sales tax, Mayor Canales plans to use a strategy of Smart Growth.

What are the goals? The goal for Artesia is to anticipate the state's growth and respond with Smart Growth. The community will need to manage growth so that it drives economic development while improving quality of life. Economic development will be improved by making the community more competitive for businesses and expanding tax bases. Quality of life will be improved by making the community more walkable and livable, and by improving public safety. Mayor Canales' ultimate goal is to change the commute through Artesia to the commute to Artesia.

How is the project being executed? Space is being better utilized; there are motivations for lot consolidation and buildings will be built higher, as most buildings in Artesia are only two stories. Development is becoming more mixed use, with business on the bottom and living area on top. Government officials are incentivizing underutilized commercial properties to be developed.

A specific example of Artesia's Smart Growth execution is Pioneer Boulevard. The city's main street has been consolidated from four lanes to two lanes, and the sidewalks have been expanded. The next major step in the city's plan is to build a promenade in the center of the city with free Wi-Fi, allowing people to relax in the center of their downtown space.

What are some of the results? For the past two years, Artesia has been nominated as Most Business Friendly City in Los Angeles County. Mayor Canales encourages the audience to rethink how they want to market their cities, and to not be afraid to rebrand themselves.

15. Small Towns, Big Ideas*

WILL LAMBE

From June 2006 to June 2007, researchers from the UNC–Chapel Hill School of Government screened, researched and documented 45 case studies of small towns across the United States that are using a wide range of community and economic development strategies to advance their communities' vision for prosperity. The case studies are a response to the demand for examples of real communities facing challenges related to globalization, geographic isolation, urban sprawl, aging populations and natural disasters.

This project was designed to be a broad qualitative research assessment. It is not a study of best practices, which, as the term implies, ought to be subject to rigorous evaluation and replication. Rather, small towns were selected to provide the reader with exposure to a wide variety of strategies and tools at work across a range of local conditions. An arbitrary decision was made to produce 10 analytic cases and 35 descriptive cases. The analytic cases describe the communities in depth, identify and discuss the varied development strategies at work in each community, and venture to answer questions about how and why a particular combination of strategies produced positive outcomes within the local context. Descrip-tive cases are shorter and describe strategies that small towns are using to advance their vision incrementally.

The selection of cases began with a list of more than 150 small towns that were known, either by word of mouth or in print, for success or innovation in community economic development. Each features a small town with fewer than 10,000 people in which a development strategy (or strategies) is currently being implemented and where the development activities are controlled locally. In other words, we did not want to re-tell old stories and we did not want stories in which local civic leaders were not playing a major role in strategic decision-making.

The cases were then screened by various criteria. First, we sought to ensure geographic and strategic diversity. Analytic cases were further screened for evidence that the community's strategy was successful, in economic, social, civic and/or environmental terms. Analytic cases also were screened for evidence that the strategy was financially sustainable and that it demonstrated some measure of adaptability to changing circumstances. For example, we sought evidence that a particular approach continued across more than one term of

---

*Excerpt from Will Lambe, *Small Towns, Big Ideas* (Chapel Hill: UNC School of Government, N.C. Rural Economic Development Center, December 2008). Reprinted with permission of the publisher.

local political leadership. Descriptive cases were screened for evidence that the town's strategy was innovative or that the strategy was distinctive within the local context.

For the 10 analytic cases, interviews were conducted in-person, over a one- to four-day visit to the community. For the descriptive case studies, interviews were conducted over the telephone or by e-mail. Data collected during interviews were supplemented by newspaper articles, scholarly articles and other written content.

After final selection, case studies were categorized by the predominant characteristic of each community with bearing on its development opportunities and challenges.

These categories became the sections in *Small Towns, Big Ideas*. Towns were characterized as:

1. recreation or retirement destinations or adjacent to an abundance of natural assets
2. having historic downtowns or prominent cultural or heritage assets
3. home to or adjacent to a college campus adjacent to a metropolitan area or an interstate highway

These categories are not, nor were they intended to be, mutually exclusive. For example, a community categorized as being a recreation or retirement destination (Brevard, N.C., for example) might also have a historic downtown. Communities were categorized based on the relationship between the local asset being categorized and the community's approach to development. Categories were intended only to ensure that the full sample of case studies covered a diverse range of community contexts and to provide the reader with a relevant starting point for identifying similarly situated communities in *Small Towns, Big Ideas*.

Lessons Learned

Seven themes emerged from stories in *Small Towns, Big Ideas*. These themes are offered as take-away lessons for other communities hoping to learn from small towns with big ideas.

1. In small towns, community development is economic development. If community development—compared with economic development—is generally considered to include a broader set of activities aimed at building the capacity of a community, then these case studies demonstrate that capacity-building and other strategies typically associated with community development are analogous with actions designed to produce economic outcomes. This is especially true, it seems, when these efforts are included as parts of a comprehensive package of strategies designed to address a community's core challenges and opportunities.

For example, in Ord, Neb., a broad-based and inclusive approach that included leadership development, youth entrepreneurship and philanthropy enhanced the community's capacity to take on more traditional economic development projects, such as recruiting an ethanol facility (with dozens of new jobs) into the jurisdiction.

Further, communities that incorporate economic and broader, longer-term, community development goals stand to gain more than small towns that take a piecemeal approach. Selma, N.C., for example, had made significant investments in revitalizing both its downtown area and the train depot. Lack of consideration of a four-block area between these two investment zones, however, limited the positive impacts of the community's work. By viewing redevelopment in a more comprehensive way, and by including community development considerations such as revitalization of blighted downtown properties in its strategy, the town was able to identify a barrier to continued revitalization and a potential means of overcoming this barrier that may pay off in the years ahead.

Finally, because community development

includes short-range and long-range strategies, it is by definition a long-term and transformative process (a fact that is recognized more in community development circles than in economic development). Successful small towns tend to balance short-term economic gains with longer-term community development goals. In Davidson, N.C., Mayor Randall Kincaid said that every decision about development is weighed against the question of whether "this project is something that our grandchildren will be proud of." Civic leaders in Ord, Neb., invest time and resources into entrepreneurship training in the local school system, with the hope that these activities will transform the local economy for the next generation.

Similarly, Big Stone Gap, Va., having developed a strategy based on entrepreneurship, had to "help people think about economic development differently." Over a period of six years, entrepreneurs harvested local opportunities, and slowly but surely, new small businesses started appearing in town—new businesses with local ownership and local roots. These outcomes, however, were not realized during the typical political cycle.

2. Small towns with the most dramatic outcomes tend to be proactive and future-oriented; they embrace change and assume risk. These general characteristics of small towns (specifically, of leadership in small towns) perhaps relate to the fact that most communities featured here "hit bottom" and their stories evolved from circumstances in which local folks were willing to try new things and take new risks. For example, in Helena, Ark., the town's collective sense of hitting bottom presented local leaders with an opportunity to step up, to initiate a new way of planning and implementing development efforts and to convince locals to participate in the process. Similarly, in Scotland Neck, N.C., difficult economic and civic circumstances in the

late 1990s presented an opportunity for Mayor Robert Partin and other civic leaders to look inward for new ideas and angles on old problems.

Being proactive (as opposed to reactive) can be measured by a small town's willingness and ability to act on a particular challenge before it becomes a problem. In Tennessee, for example, Etowah's proactive approach to building and occupying its industrial park, as opposed to reacting to trolling industries, has paid major dividends in terms of maintaining a diverse array of living wage jobs in town. In Ord, Neb., proactive meant preparing the community for opportunity. Having tackled a number of small-scale challenges in the community and seeded the roots of teamwork around development activities, Ord was prepared to act when the ethanol production facility project arrived.

Cases from Chillicothe, Mo.; Douglas, Ga.; and Farmville, N.C., demonstrate that taking a proactive approach to development also includes reaching out to existing industries.

In Chillicothe, Mayor Rodenberg called his core team together on the day the prison announced it was closing. Rather than wasting valuable time, the town initiated an aggressive lobbying campaign and offered an alternative to closure that helped the prison system financially.

Finally, most of the communities profiled in this collection demonstrate a willingness to embrace change and assume risk. For example, Etowah had a history of adapting to shifts in social and economic conditions. Local leaders, therefore, tended to be less steeped in a mindset of "well, this is just the way it's always been done." In the face of a growing tourism economy, downtown merchants embraced change and adapted their business models to the shifting circumstances. Similarly, Fairfield, Iowa, is a small town where the entire strategy of building an entrepreneurial culture is based on the natural business cycle of success and failure. According to a local leader, "there was a lot of trial and error—and failures—to get to where we are today, but the failures of some companies have provided cheap space, office furniture and equipment for another round of start-ups. Failure has freed up talented people who again ask what new concepts and companies can we start here in Fairfield."

3. Successful community economic development strategies are guided by a broadly held local vision. Most communities in *Small Towns, Big Ideas* demonstrate the importance of establishing and maintaining a broadly held vision, including goals for all manner of development activities. This idea is perhaps illustrated most dramatically by Helena, Ark., where the inclusiveness of the planning and visioning process was crucially important. In this case, it included representatives from government, community organizations, for-profit and nonprofit interests, resource providers and average citizens of the community. In fact, anybody could join the effort, and this perception of an inclusive and open-door process was widespread across Helena. Similarly in Ord, Neb., where so much of the momentum comes from one-on-one conversations, local leaders take the time to meet individually with members of the community to ensure that opposition to development efforts does not take root for lack of understanding the larger vision. In terms of maintaining momentum, Douglas, Ga., demonstrates how a local organization (the Chamber of Commerce in this case) can take responsibility for calling stakeholders together on a regular basis to recommit themselves to the community's vision.

A separate but related point is that in small towns, people are always the most important resource and communities with limited resources cannot afford to exclude anyone from planning or development efforts. Pelican Rapids, Minn., appears to be on the front end of an economic reawakening based on the entrepreneurial tendencies of new immigrant residents who were settled in the area by various refugee organizations. Case after case has demonstrated that people (as opposed to money or other resources) are the one absolutely necessary ingredient to successful development. A committed group of local residents who are willing to work hard for their community's interests can change the fate of an otherwise hopeless community. In Nelsonville, Ohio, an informal group of civic entrepreneurs and artists came together to revitalize the historic downtown square and in the process injected a new dose of energy into the community.

Importantly, it seems, special attention needs to be paid toward integrating newcomers into the community. Newcomers, including young leaders, bring a fresh perspective and new energy to local challenges. In Douglas, Ga., local leaders recognized that newcomers are valuable assets and the town has worked hard to integrate new residents into the community. In Farmville, N.C., new residents are welcomed every spring, when the mayor and town manager invite all newcomers to a "New Residents Picnic." In Nelsonville, Ohio, several young professionals, including an attorney and real estate developer, are forcing the community to think creatively about new economic opportunities.

4. Defining assets and opportunities broadly can yield innovative strategies that capitalize on a community's competitive advantage. In almost any setting—urban or rural, small or large—shell buildings, low tax rates, limited regulation and access to trained workers, highways, railroads or professional services might all be considered economic development assets and justifiably so. Small towns, however, cannot afford to stop there. Given limited sources of competitive advantage, they must redefine economic development assets in a much broader framework.

For example, Allendale, S.C., capitalized on a regional university to create a local leadership development program that, in turn, trained new economic development leaders for the entire region. Brevard, N.C., demonstrates that retirees within a community can be economic development assets. The Retiree Resource Network is a group of retirees with private sector experience who mentor local entrepreneurs. In Columbia, N.C., local leaders recognized that their region's natural beauty was an asset that could drive an ecotourism strategy. In an ironic twist on small town development, the arrival of Wal-Mart became an asset for the small community of Oakland, Md., when local leaders took the opportunity to help Main Street retailers diversify their product lines. Assets for small town development might include individual people, nonprofit organizations, businesses, open space, farms, parks, landfills (biomass), museums, schools, historic architecture, local attitudes or any number of other things.

Further, the mere fact that a particular town is small can become an asset. In some cases, locating a business in a small town can provide a competitive advantage for the business. In Fairfield, Iowa, local leaders are taking advantage of the perception that businesses located in small-town, rural locations carry a moral and ethical standard above their urban competitors. Civic and business leaders in Fairfield have exploited this perception to their competitive advantage. In Oxford, N.C., the Kerr-Tar Mini Hub concept is based on the idea that rural communities within driving distance of the Research Triangle Park can capture a market of technology companies that need to be near the park, but can thrive outside it, where business costs are lower.

A final emerging trend in this category is the increasing use of small town assets as either fuel or triggers for innovation in the area of environment-friendly development or clean energy.

In Dillsboro, N.C., the town turned an environmental challenge, in this case methane gas migrating from the community landfill, into an opportunity to create jobs and provide space for entrepreneurs. The Jackson County Clean Energy Park (in Dillsboro) is using methane gas from a nearby landfill to power the studios of local artisans. In Cape Charles, Va., the town's investment in an eco-friendly industrial park was an innovative strategy to bridge the dual challenges of environmental degradation and job creation. And, in the most extreme case, Reynolds, Ind., is capitalizing on latent energy contained agricultural waste from 150,000 hogs to become Bio-Town, USA, the nation's first energy-independent community.

5. Innovative local governance, partnerships and organizations significantly enhance the capacity for community economic development. Most towns featured in *Small Towns, Big Ideas* include an innovative element of either organization or governance. It is clear that innovative local governance, in a variety of forms, can strengthen a community's development strategy. In Columbia, N.C., the town's ability to design an alternative arrangement for generating tax revenues on protected lands helped turn a potential obstacle into a local innovation. In Selma, N.C., the town used an innovative property tax incentive tool to focus redevelopment on a blighted area of town. In New York Mills, Minn., the town structured a public investment in the Regional Cultural Center so the town assumed ownership of the building, thereby reducing long-term risk and creating a win-win situation for artists, public officials and local residents. The key is to think creatively about organizational structure, but always to keep the community's overall net benefit in mind.

Regionalism, or identifying opportunities and partnerships beyond municipal boundaries, is another emerging theme in successful cases. Cross-jurisdictional partnerships can help small towns to pool resources toward shared objectives. Strategies in Ord, Neb., and in Davidson, Oxford and Hillsborough, N.C., involve commitments to interlocal revenue- and responsibility-sharing among varying jurisdictions. Davidson and Oxford are partnering with neighboring communities in industrial development while Hillsborough is partnering with the county to manage growth beyond the town's municipal boundaries. Ord joined with the county and the Chamber of Commerce to share costs and revenues from a wide range of development activities. In Washington, N.C., local officials recognized the growing marine trades cluster in eastern North Carolina and created a workforce and entrepreneurship development strategy to harness the regional economic opportunity.

In addition to regional partnerships and opportunities, successful small towns tend to have local leaders who connect with higher level policy makers and business leaders. Mayor Partin in Scotland Neck, N.C., and several key leaders in Helena, Ark., make explicit efforts to link the interests of their individual communities to policy makers in their respective state capitals. Further, as demonstrated by Douglas, Ga., leaders in small towns must forge partnerships with state-level developers, bankers and power companies, each a critical player in state economic development.

Finally, public-private (including nonprofit) partnerships are emerging as the prominent organizational model for small town development. In Siler City, N.C., for example, the successful establishment of an incubator was the product of a partnership of the community college, local government and a state-level nonprofit organization. In Spruce Pine, N.C., the town's approach to supporting local entrepreneurs requires that the Chamber of Commerce and the craft community work closely together for the first time, to ensure successful marketing and branding. After the plant closures in Morrilton, Ark., Mayor Stewart Nelson brought area churches together to discuss how the faith community could contribute toward economic recovery efforts. In Chillicothe, Mo., an ad-hoc partnership between the town administration and a local business (a prison) demonstrates the influence that towns can have on strategic management decisions within a business, which in turn can have a tremendous impact on the local economy.

6. Effective communities identify, measure and celebrate short-term successes to sustain support for long-term community economic development. Given the long-term nature of community development, and the fact that measurable results from a particular project may be decades in the making, leaders in small towns must repeatedly make the case for the importance of their efforts. Making the case is important to maintain momentum, invigorate volunteers and donors, convince skeptics and, most importantly, keep the focus on the vision or the goals established in a community's strategic plan. Many of the communities profiled in this study recognize that making the case is an ongoing and continuous effort and that there are a number of strategies for doing it.

First, short-term success can build long-term momentum. Obviously, the best way to make the case for any intervention is to demonstrate success. Along these lines, Scotland Neck, N.C., began with actions that would demonstrate success quickly. Town leaders decided to support local hunting and fishing guides, to start bringing more tourists into town and to show local residents that there was reason to be optimistic. This initial success helped them build momentum before beginning to tackle more intractable challenges. Similarly, to maintain buy-in from the Arkansas community, the initial action steps in Helena's strategic plan were those that could be accomplished in short order and for which there was already some momentum. By starting with "low-hanging fruit," town leaders demonstrated that change was possible. Once people started seeing change happen, there was more of an incentive to join in the process. Short-term success is a means for making the case that particular CED activities are worth the investment.

Second, many communities profiled here make an explicit effort to measure and monitor the impacts of their efforts. It seems obvious, but measuring progress and evaluating programs tend to get pushed to the end of priority lists. Not so in successful small towns. In Ord, Neb., impacts of the community's development programs are monitored and have become useful for both external and internal audiences. Data are used to attract additional investment from outside sources. Moreover, by demonstrating a reasonable return on investment, these data may be used to convince a community's naysayers to join the efforts. In Hollandale, Miss., an analysis of local data helped the community to convince outside grant-makers that a rural transportation network was a smart investment. In addition, it helped to convince policy makers that rural transportation was a viable (if incremental) strategy for alleviating a range of economic challenges.

Finally, small towns profiled here tend to communicate and celebrate success. For example, in Douglas, Ga., community leaders work hard to keep local papers informed about various economic development projects and publicize even the most modest success, including stories of local entrepreneurial successes. Leaders in Ord spend an ever-increasing amount of time publishing newsletters and writing articles for the local newspaper. They send e-mails to as many residents as possible and appear on radio broadcasts regularly. The idea is to replace rumors and coffee shop chatter with accurate information about what the community is trying to accomplish.

7. Viable community economic development involves the use of a comprehensive package of strategies and tools, rather than a piecemeal approach. The capstone lesson is, perhaps, a reaffirmation of a point that we have heard over and over again: there is no silver bullet. No single strategy saved any community in this study. Successful development in small towns is always multifaceted. Small towns should take nothing off the table in selecting strategies to pursue. Successful communities tend to have evolved to the point where they have a comprehensive package of strategies and tools that are aligned with the core assets, challenges and opportunities within their regional context.

Furthermore, given the basic strengths, weaknesses, opportunities and threats affecting each community and the virtually limitless menu of possible strategies, no single package of strategies necessarily fits with a particular type of community. That is, there is no universally applicable formula for community development. Decisions about what to do and why to do it have to be based on local conditions, context and capacity. The lessons from these small towns, however, provide insights and inspiration for other community leaders as they begin the important process of building locally driven strategies that create economic opportunities and improve the social, civic and environmental conditions that face their hometowns.

16. Strategies for Small Town Success*

Joe A. Sumners

Leaders in struggling rural communities and small towns often pin their hopes for economic prosperity on the recruitment of a large manufacturing plant to "save" their town. In Alabama, our success in attracting large automotive plants like Mercedes-Benz, Honda, and Hyundai has fueled such a lust for industrial recruitment. Many small towns are sure that their big break is just around the corner, if only they can come up with the right financial incentives and recruitment strategy.

An unfortunate consequence of relying on strategies that focus exclusively on industrial recruitment is that many communities undervalue, or don't understand, the importance of other determinants of a strong local economy. Business retention and expansion, small business and entrepreneurial development, tourism and retiree attraction, for example, receive short shrift compared to industrial recruitment. More significantly, local leaders pay too little attention to building community and civic infrastructure. Put another way, many small towns overemphasize marketing and sales (industrial recruiting) without adequate attention to product development (improving the quality of life in the com-munity). But prosperous small town economies are built upon the foundation of strong communities.

Strategies for Small Towns and Rural Communities

Successful development strategies in small towns will typically include the following elements:

1. Community Leadership: Create leadership that is inclusive, collaborative, and connected. "Leaderful" Communities. Successful communities all over the United States understand the importance of an expansive view of community leadership. The traditional notion of the community leader—often a mayor or other powerful "position-holder"—as chief community problem-solver has given way to a new, more dynamic model of the community leader as catalyst, connector, and consensus-builder.

Dr. David Mathews, President of the Kettering Foundation, in summarizing the findings of the Foundation's research on community politics, writes:

> What stands out in the high-achieving community is not so much the characteristics of the leaders as their number.... The high-achieving

---

*Originally published as Joe A. Sumners, "Strategies for Small Town Success," https://ecdi.wordpress.com, November 29, 2009. Reprinted with permission of the publisher.

community had ten times more people providing leadership than communities of comparable size. This [high-achieving] community is "leaderful"; that is, nearly everyone provides some measure of initiative. And its leaders function not as gatekeepers but as door openers, bent on widening participation.

This new leadership model recognizes that leadership is not confined to a few elected officials and business leaders. Rather, successful leadership requires mobilizing the knowledge, talents, and perspectives of every segment of the community. Successful communities tend to be full of leaders.

2. Community Assessment and Planning: Identify all community assets and create a plan to take strategic advantage. Strategic Planning. There is an old saying that goes, "If you don't know where you're going, any road will take you there." Citizen leaders and stakeholders in high-achieving communities know where they are going. They understand that an era of rapid social, cultural, and technological change requires a proactive approach to addressing current and future problems. They engage in a strategic planning process to identify what makes their place special and to decide how to cultivate and promote their unique assets—e.g., a river, a lake, a mountain, or a unique history. The result of this process is a strategic plan that identifies community priorities and outlines specific strategies to make best use of available assets and to address local challenges. It becomes a road map for the future and a benchmark for community progress.

The benefits of strategic planning are not limited to the final product. In fact, one of the most beneficial aspects of strategic planning is the process itself. A successful strategic planning process brings together a diverse group of stakeholders, who address basic questions for the community: "Where are we now?" "Where do we want to go?" and "How do we get there?" There

are few other occasions when representatives from throughout the community come together for an extended period of time to discuss shared hopes, dreams, knowledge, perspectives, ideas, and concerns. Broad-based strategic planning is a "mega-crossroad" and one of the best tools available for building and strengthening community connections.

3. Local and Regional Partnerships: Connect local stakeholders and join forces with neighbors. From Planning to Action: Connecting Community Stakeholders. The process must not end with the creation of a strategic plan. If so, it would resemble most other community planning efforts. The result would be a plan that looks good on paper, but ends up collecting dust on a shelf. To prevent this, the community should create an entity responsible for seeing that the major objectives in the plan are actually implemented. This group, which should include representatives from government, business, education, and faith-based institutions, should meet regularly to monitor the community's progress on the plan and make needed modifications to ensure that the plan remains relevant to community priorities and needs.

The value of the group is not just that it checks items off of the list of community objectives. It can serve as an important community "crossroad" where key community stakeholders have the opportunity to think, work, and act together. Most communities have many excellent people, programs, and projects. All communities have at least some institutional assets—city government, churches, schools, civic clubs, and Chambers of Commerce. But far too often, individuals and organizations work independently, rather than in concert with one another. The truly high-achieving communities are those that create crossroads where leaders from all of these community organizations and institutions can come together to accomplish shared community objectives.

Joining with other jurisdictions to maximize limited resources. Because small towns and rural areas are sparsely populated, they lack a critical mass—of taxpayers, leadership, financial capacity, infrastructure, and skilled labor. So if small towns are to survive, they must join forces and work together. Small towns must learn to see their neighboring community as a competitor only for the Friday night football game.

While a holistic strategy for economic development is needed, attracting new businesses clearly should be one part of the overall approach. However, small towns rarely possess adequate resources to be effective in the increasingly competitive arena of economic development. Hiring a professional economic developer is an impossible dream for most small communities. That is, unless they decide to partner with their neighbors.

Conclusion

Small towns, and larger jurisdictions for that matter, are best served by a holistic approach to economic development. Industrial development may be an appropriate strategy, especially if done in partnership with regional neighbors. However, it should not be the only strategy. To be successful, small towns need to cultivate strong and diverse community leadership that is inclusive, collaborative, and connected. They need to identify their unique assets, create and implement a strategic plan, and establish strategic partnerships among community stakeholders and with other jurisdictions. And they need to be proactive in creating community and regional crossroads—organizations, or structures, where leaders can connect on a regular basis to assess, plan, and work together.

If small towns aggressively pursue these strategies, they have excellent potential for success. Many city-dwellers long for what people in small towns already have, and often take for granted: a slower pace of life, friendly people who know their neighbors, attractive open spaces and beautiful scenery, quaint shops, historic homes and buildings, parades, festivals, and streets that are safe and free of traffic congestion. Many of our small towns still possess a sense of authenticity and charm that cannot be replicated in bigger cities.

These inherent quality-of-life advantages, enhanced by community leadership, planning, and partnerships, ultimately make the community more attractive to both existing and potential residents and employers. In other words, investments in product development make the community much easier to market and sell. The irony is that strategies emphasizing community development ultimately make small towns much more attractive in the competition for those large manufacturing plants they covet.

17. Using Networks for Economic Development*

CAMILLE CATES BARNETT *and* OSCAR RODRÍGUEZ

Only hours before Hurricane Katrina hit, Lieutenant Governor Mitchell J. Landrieu of Louisiana connected the dots at a conference in New Orleans. He emphasized the connections between creative individuals and the potential for wealth and job creation in various cultural industries. Later, making the connections clear, he said, "In Louisiana, we don't refer to 'your home as where you live.' In Louisiana, 'your home is where y'at.'"

Now Wynton Marsalis and other cultural icons are raising money to help hurricane victims and to guide the long rebuilding of Louisiana's cultural economy. Thousands of families and friends have hosted evacuees, who are relying on their connections with individuals.

A few years ago, Tuscumbia (pop. 8,500), Alabama, birthplace of Helen Keller, was so broke it could not afford the match for federal development grants. The downtown was dying; tax revenue was paltry. Then a millionaire businessman named Harvey Robbins returned to Tuscumbia, his hometown, to retire. Once resettled, he led a successful movement to turn things around. He invested in economic development and spurred others to do the same. The town's finances are now back in shape and so is a sense of community.

In El Salvador, Jamaica, and Nicaragua, remittances sent by expatriates working abroad account for more than 15 percent of gross national income, an amount larger than total exports and larger than foreign investment and foreign aid combined. The extended communities of many of these countries have even come to represent significant export markets.

Pollo Campero, a popular fried-chicken restaurant chain once found only in Central America, now has outlets in Los Angeles and Washington, D.C., serving primarily a Central American clientele. Likewise, the Dominican Republic and Central America, served by airlines with a majority of passengers traveling to and from the United States, are members of a large, extended community (Orozco 2005)

The city of Philadelphia is serious about the advice offered by *New York Times* columnist Thomas Friedman on August 3, 2005: "The world is moving to an Internet-based platform for commerce, education, innovation, and entertainment. Wealth and

*Originally published as Camille Cates Barnett and Oscar Rodríguez, "Connections Matter: Using Networks for Economic Development," *PM Magazine* 88, no. 2 (March 2006). Reprinted with permission of the publisher.

productivity will go to those countries or companies that get more of their innovators, educators, students, workers, and suppliers connected to this platform via computers, phones, and PDA's." Philadelphia is making the entire city a "hot zone," where any resident can have cheap, high-speed access to the Internet.

A Common Theme

What do these stories have in common? Connections. Using connections that people have to their communities is a key to economic development. Developing and using the ties that bind will help to build the economy.

It works. Your community's connections can be a major asset for promoting economic development, just as a university's alumni are a main support for its endowment and just as some developing countries' expatriates are their vital source of foreign income.

Economic development today takes understanding your community's networks. It takes seeing the connections and making them.

To take full advantage of such an asset, however, you have to see the world of public management as a world of networks. To do a good job, public managers have to design and facilitate those networks. In the past, economic development meant marketing a community's competitive advantages in natural resources, labor, or existing industry. The goal was to attract new industry and win new business for existing industry that would employ local residents and buy locally produced goods and services. Of course, this needed to be done while keeping other communities from stealing your existing employers.

Today, economic growth and wealth accumulation depend increasingly on information technology and intellectual capital, and the critical factor is the talented work-force that runs these new economic engines. Now, regions of multiple communities compete globally. The economic development game has changed. Success means attracting your fair share of this new workforce and working with your network of residents and former residents to do it.

In his book, *Cities and the Creative Class*, Richard Florida (2005) explains how the economic development game has changed for cities. The case he makes is that highly skilled workers have become the critical factor of economic growth and that industry now follows them-instead of the other way around. Florida argues that the presence of workers engaged in creative industries is the best predictor of future growth and wealth accumulation today. It is a greater predictor than housing prices and the quality of public schools.

In this new environment, the key for communities wanting to promote economic development is being able to attract highly skilled workers so industry will follow them. This is the reverse of the adage from the 1990s movie Field of Dreams: build it and they will come.

According to Florida, these workers' preferences are known well enough that local governments can assess-even improve-how they stand with regard to the critical markers that creative workers seem to look for when they decide where to live. Using a series of indexes that correlate strongly with each other and with recent growth and prosperity trends, Florida points out the salient characteristics of the most competitive localities:

- Tolerant local society
- Proximity to a quality natural environment
- Abundance of entertainment and cultural opportunities
- Existing critical mass of creative workers.

Washington, D.C., New York, Boston, Austin, and Seattle are among the cities that have fared well by this rising class of workers. Richard Florida shows that creative workers are attracted to places with the three Ts: technology, talent, and tolerance.

So how does a city play the new game? Here are some strategies to help you develop a game plan.

1. Know where you are; assess your locality and region. Use Florida's research to see how your community and region look to the creative class. His books have ranked the large and small regions in the country by the percentage of creative workers and by a "creativity index" that combines data on the creative class, high technology, innovation, and diversity.

Louisiana commissioned a groundbreaking report on the economic impact of the cultural economy. It's called Louisiana: Where Culture Means Business (Mt. Auburn Associates 2005). This study also helped Louisiana learn something about how to use connections to residents to shape strategies to improve tourism. Here is what Louisiana learned:

- One-quarter of Louisiana tourists are residents of the state who are exploring other areas.
- One-third of all nonresident visitors to Louisiana stay with friends and family while visiting Louisiana.
- Two-thirds of all Louisiana visitors use information from friends and family as their primary source for planning a leisure trip.

Therefore, the image of Louisiana offered by Louisiana residents themselves can be extremely important to potential visitors who have ties to families and friends to Louisiana.

For more information, visit the Web site at http://www.crt.state.la.us/CulturalEcon omy/MtAuburn/culturaleconomyreport.htm.

2. Know who your community is; in-clude everybody with connections to your area. If you count only the people who live within your jurisdiction today, you have fewer options than if you recognize everybody who considers your city their hometown. Your population of creative workers is likely to be higher if you use the more inclusive definition, allowing you greater leeway to market your community to creative workers.

The same goes for the effectiveness of your marketing effort because it is driven for the most part by your ability to reach a receptive audience. If your target is the creative class at large, you will end up spending more time and resources on people who will never consider moving into or investing in your community than if you focus on creative workers whose heartstrings are already pulling them there.

Today, economic growth and wealth accumulation depend increasingly on information technology and intellectual capital, and the critical factor is the talented workforce that runs these new economic engines.

Many communities in the developing world have been on this road for decades. Along the way, they have learned a lot about why and how to keep in touch with their expatriates. Their experience demonstrates that working with extended communities improves the prospects for local economic development. To cope with so many of its people living abroad, the community as a whole began to see itself less as a place fixed in time and space and more as the center of a network of its members' life paths. This new way of seeing themselves allowed both the expatriates and the hometown to stay engaged no matter how far or for how long they were apart.

To be sure, mass emigration is not restricted to the developing world. Of the top countries with sizable national populations living abroad today, one-third come from the ranks of industrialized countries.

What is true for these countries may very well be true for your community. Most communities in the United States have significant expatriate populations. Residential mobility has always been an important characteristic of American life. Americans are more stationary today than in the past, but still one out of every six Americans has moved during the past five years (Francese 2002). Chances are that a lot more people contribute to your community's sense of itself than just those who live there now. Getting to know who they are will pay off.

The purpose of knowing your broader community is not to simply identify the people who share a particular tie to your community, but to understand the networks that connect them and the strings that pull at them, and what can be done to strengthen the other strings.

Check the box ahead to find the basic questions you should ask about your extended community.

3. Pull on the heartstrings. Once you have a clear picture of who makes up your extended community, identify the strongest ties that bind your expatriates and the ones that tug at the largest numbers of them. Then pull on those ties. In the new economic development game where the aim is to attract creative workers, this means making your extended community the target of promotional and marketing efforts.

Targeting your extended community sharpens the focus of your marketing efforts. Your focus is creative workers who still harbor ties to their hometown. You tap into an audience that is already receptive to your community. It will make you a more viable tourist destination and a more attractive investment site. It may also help your local businesses gain access to external markets that would otherwise not exist or be accessible without the presence and assistance of your expatriates.

The goal is to maximize the contribution of the extended community to the economic development of your community. Not everybody will contribute in the same way or for the same reason. Some expatriates may move themselves and their companies or capital back home. This happened in Tuscumbia, Alabama, when Harvey Robbins moved back home and saw he needed to help his hometown recapitalize its downtown (Warren 2005).

New Zealand saw this too when Peter Jackson filmed his award-winning film trilogy Lord of the Rings in his home country and jump-started a national film industry that has become a magnet for creative talent from around the world. Now the government's national economic development agency, New Zealand Trade and Enterprise, is targeting music, design, digital innovation, fashion, and gaming for strategic development (Mt. Auburn Associates 2005).

To attract expatriates to enhance your local economy, you will have to show them that you are not seeking a one-way relationship, that you are not calling on them only when you are raising funds or marketing locally produced or locally owned products. A network functions because it serves everybody who supports it. If you can demonstrate to expatriates that their support of your community is also in their best interests, their commitment will be greater and more sustainable.

Your promotion and marketing strategies should include activities for helping your expatriates help each other. You may decide to promote economic development in your community by strengthening the network itself through information and contact sharing among your expatriates, so they too can prosper and become even stronger and more able supporters of your community.

4. Facilitate your community's networks; develop networks where there are none. Economic development today takes understanding your community's networks. It takes seeing the connections and making them. It also takes developing them when there are none, strengthening them when they are weak, and maintaining them so they remain effective. College alumni associations and international emigre communities offer a lot of experience from which public managers can draw lessons learned and pick up best practices. These range from simple newsletters to high-stakes public-private investment matching programs. Connections matter.

What to Know About Your Extended Community

Basic Questions to Ask	Sample Answers
1. Who are they?	Alumni from the local high school, summer camp, or college; retirees who moved away; second-home owners; snowbirds
2. What ties do they have to the community?	Family, schools, churches, nostalgia, property
3. What image do they have of the community?	Perfect place to raise a family, vacationland, refuge from the city, ideal spot to retire, the "only place I call home"
4. Where are they?	In the same region, in the nearest metropolitan center, in a vacation or retirement center
5. Who among them are creative workers?	40-year-olds living in large cities, second-home owners, wealthy alumni from the local summer camp, alumni from the local college who majored in film
6. Among the creative workers, which ones want to return?	50-year-olds who own their own companies, new families whose children are still in elementary school, women who are heads of households, middle-aged couples with elderly parents still living in the community
7. When do they visit?	Holidays, long weekends, funerals, weddings, class reunions, special ceremonies at the local summer camp or college
8. Why do they return; why would they return?	Raise a family, vacation, retire, take care of elderly relatives, get away from city life, start a business
9. How do they stay in touch?	E-mail, column in the local newspaper, alumni newsletter, blogs, informal calling tree, reunions and special events in their current location
10. What networks do they use?	Local-newspaper readers, local summer camp association or college alumni association, family connections, key individuals, Internet

The most successful communities and the most successful managers are those that master the art of networks.

REFERENCES

Florida, Richard. *Cities and the Creative Class.* New York: Routledge, 2005.

Francese, Peter. "A Nation of Homebodies: People Moving Less Often." *American Demographics*, January 1, 2002.

Mt. Auburn Associates. *Louisiana: Where Culture Means Business.* Baton Rouge: State of Louisiana, 2005. http://www.crt.state.la.us/CulturalEconomy/MtAuburn/culturaleconomyreport.htm.

Orozco, Manuel. "Transnacionalismo y desarrollo: Tendencias y oportunidades en AmŽrica Latina." *Foreign Affairs en Espanol* 5, no. 3 (July-September 2005): 19. http://www.iadia log.org/publications/oped/july05/orozco_fa.pdf; http://www.iadialog.org/programs/policy/trade/remittances.

Warren, Chris. "Re-Creation Instead." *American Way*, July 15, 2005. http://americanwaymag.com/aw/business/feature.asp?archive_date=7/15/2005.

18. State-of-the-Art Measures in Economic Development*

DAVID AMMONS *and* JONATHAN MORGAN

For years local governments have invested resources into efforts to spur economic growth. And for years the officials heading most of these economic development initiatives tracked their efforts with little more than output measures—for instance, the number of industrial contacts made or assisted, the number of meetings held or presentations made, the number of information packets or brochures distributed, the number of trade shows attended, and similar measures of activities. They focused on showing that they were trying hard.

More recently, as local governments have gained greater experience with economic development and as more attention has been directed to outcomes and accountability across the range of local government programs and services, the state of the art has begun to change. Now, economic development officials—and those who monitor their performance—are increasingly tuned in to a broader and more meaningful array of measures to document their performance.

Limited Control of Outcomes

Simple outputs, such as raw counts of meetings and contacts, were appealingly easy to compile and report, but another factor also led to the tendency to report activities rather than results. By reporting numbers of contacts made, meetings held, and brochures distributed, economic development officials reported on things they controlled. Many were reluctant to claim outcomes that were dependent on more—sometimes much more—than their own efforts.

Taxpayers and public officials, however, want results from their investments. They want to see outcomes. The state of the art for measures of economic development has evolved accordingly.

More and more economic development officials are showing a willingness to move beyond the customary raw counts of outputs and have begun to report on outcomes—even outcomes over which they have limited control. Having only limited control might not be as desirable as having complete control, but the absence of full control over an important goal is not a characteristic unique to economic development among local government programs.

Many factors beyond police performance influence crime rates, yet the police are expected to hold the rate down; many outside

*Originally published as David Ammons and Jonathan Morgan, "State-of-the-Art Measures in Economic Development." *PM Magazine* 93, no. 5 (June 2011). Reprinted with permission of the publisher.

factors influence the rising incidence of teen pregnancy in a given community—many beyond the full control of a local program established to battle the problem—but the program is expected to make a dent. Other local government programs also tackle problems that lie beyond the government's full control, often by leveraging the assistance of others.

Limited control is neither unique to economic development among local government programs nor is it likely to be considered an adequate alibi for unsatisfactory results. Although far short of *absolute control*, limited control is by no means the same as *no control*.

Economic development efforts can influence outcomes; otherwise, local governments would have little reason to fund them. Economic development outcomes—at least in the form of intermediate outcomes—are now being reported by local governments.

Results in Raw Terms

Some localities have supplemented their workload measures with measures that demonstrate results. Nearly two-thirds of the respondents to a 2009 survey conducted by ICMA and the National League of Cities reported that they used performance measures to track outcomes specified in the economic development plans of their cities and counties.

Increasingly, local governments are reporting on new capital invested, jobs created, and businesses attracted or retained. Measures from Austin, Texas; Olathe, Kansas; and Scottsdale, Arizona, for example, show important characteristics of economic development: investment, new jobs, downtown construction, and new business licenses.

Economic development officials in these cities are not claiming sole responsibility for any advances from one year's number to the next, but they are suggesting that they have had a role in influencing the results.

Results in Terms That Could Serve as Benchmarks for Others

Among the new generation of economic development measures are some that report performance in a manner that could serve as useful benchmarks for others. These are outcome measures that convert raw improvement into percentage improvement or, better yet, into measures that reflect conditions of economic development vitality that can serve as inspiration to other communities.

Communities often establish economic development programs with a principal hope of boosting the local tax base. Increasingly, these programs are reporting data relating to that goal.

A sure sign of economic vitality is a high occupancy or low vacancy rate for existing office, retail, and industrial buildings. Of course, this can be a moving target. Achieving a low vacancy rate is likely to spur new construction with new vacancies, perhaps causing the vacancy rate to edge upward—but the tax base will get a boost.

The occupancy or vacancy rates reported by economic development programs in several local governments.

Other measures focusing on different aspects of economic development success are also being reported by various programs. Each of these measures goes well beyond simple counts of activities and provides an indicator of quality or results.

Different clusters of measures have been selected by different communities. A set of complementary measures for the city and county of Denver, Colorado.

Yet another approach to measuring outcomes has been adopted by a few communities that track their standing or progress on national indices of economic vitality. Centralia (pop. 13,000), Illinois, for example, tracks its economic strength ranking through a feature of the POLICOM Corporation national rankings; and Mesa, Arizona, reports new jobs created on the basis of metrics compiled for metropolitan regions by the Milken Institute and Greenstreet Real Estate Partners.

Although these national ratings typically pertain to entire metro areas rather than to individual communities, the economic development programs that choose to include metro area rankings among their measures implicitly acknowledge the link between the success of the region and their own.

Value of Advances in Results-Focused Measures

Leading economic development programs are increasingly focused on results. Several have also demonstrated a willingness to declare their results in a format that permits others to compare their own results with the results of these leaders. Some have even tied their claims of success to advancement in national rankings.

These advances in performance reporting provide other program models of better measurement. Perhaps more important, this approach to performance measurement can increase other programs' aspirations to achieve similar results.

Looking Ahead: New Strategies, New Measures

A changing economy, major shifts in industrial structure, and increased global competition for jobs and private investment have challenged traditional approaches to economic development and led local governments to pursue new job creation strategies. What had been an almost exclusive focus on marketing and industrial recruitment is being augmented by approaches that emphasize homegrown sources of economic activity—efforts that develop entrepreneurial skills, creativity and talent, and promote innovation.

The cutting edge of economic develop-

ment performance measurement reflects the reality that economic development has expanded to become so much more than activities aimed at recruiting large manufacturing facilities or filling commercial office buildings. Some analysts call for new metrics that are better aligned with the dynamics of a knowledge-based, global economy and that use regional economies, not political jurisdictions, as the units of analysis (Klein, 2007).

This approach to measuring performance in economic development emphasizes outcome metrics focusing on the number of high-tech jobs, levels of personal income, and number of new businesses as well as indicators that gauge the local assets that can be thought of as the "inputs" to regional competitiveness. These assets include a skilled workforce, ample financial capital, and a community's innovative capacity.

The new set of performance measures will reflect the fact that so much of what communities do now to promote economic development involves enhancing local and regional competitiveness and boosting the local capacity to support private investment and economic growth from both within and without. This new approach to measuring success will assume that economic growth, as measured by a quantitative increase in certain indicators—jobs, capital investment, and tax base, for example—is an intermediate outcome that should lead to qualitative improvements in a local and regional economy over the longer term.

Communities, therefore, will be following Denver's lead and will be emphasizing such indicators as job quality, wealth creation, economic diversification, and sustainability.

REFERENCE

Klein, Eva. (2007). "Your Regional Knowledge Economy Strategy: Is It Succeeding?" *Economic Development America* (Spring): 26–29.

19. Jump-Starting a Small-Community Economy[*]

R ANDALL W HEELER

As almost every new local government manager can tell you—and every aspiring manager will one day find out—one of the most important expectations of a new manager is to "do something about economic development." Exactly what that is and how to do it are unique to each community.

The one thing that has been consistent with every community I have worked with is a desire for "more" and "better." Seems simple enough, right? I sure wish it was. This one area of Poquoson's governmental mission is unlike most traditional government services and in almost every instance, smaller localities are woefully under-resourced.

Poquoson (pop. 12,000) is a small coastal city located on a peninsula in Virginia literally at the end of the road. When I accepted the position of city manager six years ago in the midst of the Great Recession, one of my main responsibilities was to jump-start its economic development program.

Like any good applicant would, I had studied the comprehensive plan, read the pertinent economic development plans, and was eager to hit the ground running. What I discovered, however, was that the city had no dedicated staff, no resources to speak of, and economic development efforts were almost completely reactive.

For the past several years, city staff and I, working closely with the city council and the economic development authority, have made great strides in the areas of economic development and marketing. Poquoson recently received the Virginia Municipal League's Communications Award for community rebranding efforts.

If you, like me, are called upon to essentially create a high-quality economic development program in an extremely constrained resources environment, it is my hope that our experience, which I have broken into six overlapping stages here, offers helpful insights.

Stage One: Strategic/Resource Alignment. The birth of the city's current program began at a council retreat. With the support of the mayor, I asked for the opportunity to engage the councilmembers in a discussion of their priorities, specifically economic development.

In my discussions with them, it was clear that economic development was in the top three priorities for each member. But unlike the other two, education and public safety,

---

[*]Originally published as Randall Wheeler, "Jump-Starting a Small-Community Economy," *PM Magazine*, October 2015. Reprinted with permission of the publisher.

which were the city's two largest budgetary priorities, economic development had essentially no dedicated resources.

If we were going to be successful in meeting the council's expectations, we needed at least a small bundle of dedicated resources. The importance of this step cannot be overvalued. It required the staff and me to do something that can be unusual in the local government management profession. That is, admit that we would not succeed without help. To their credit, councilmembers responded affirmatively.

Stage Two: Assessment. We took a critical look at our efforts up to that time, changed unproductive strategies, and clarified goals and objectives. The main marketing strategy, for example, had been placing signs on properties and hoping someone would drive by and call with an economic development initiative. While this might be an effective strategy if Poquoson was located on a major highway, it is not particularly powerful when the property is in a remote location.

In another instance, we were meeting with an important prospect and much to my chagrin, our marketing materials consisted solely of a photocopied magazine article someone else wrote about Poquoson a few years prior. Clearly, marketing efforts had room for improvement and so did planning documents.

The economic development authority had a strategic plan located "somewhere," and a marketing study and plan conducted a few years before for a main development area was on a shelf gathering dust. It was critical that before we moved forward, we carefully studied these previous efforts.

At the conclusion of this assessment, we brought forward a plan for economic development, which the council endorsed. This plan included implementation strategies for marketing, outreach, land development, and performance measurement.

Stage Three: Branding. One key aspect of any successful economic development marketing campaign is branding. What about your smaller-sized community is special, unique, or highly competitive? Whose attention are you trying to attract? What is attractive to this constituency? These are important questions to ask when establishing a community brand.

Ask yourself, or better yet, ask your residents and business owners: What is great about your community? Do this enough times and your brand will emerge. In this case, we learned that Poquoson itself was the brand.

Just as we had "developed" this brand ourselves, we also realized that given our limited resources we would need to develop all the supporting marketing materials in-house. Though you may not have a team of marketing professionals on staff, chances are staff members have experience marketing your community.

They could be employed anywhere in your organization, but I suggest you start looking first in the parks and recreation department, local library, and school system. I am proud to say that Poquoson's award-winning marketing program was developed on several large pieces of butcher paper by the assistant director of parks and recreation.

Stage Four: Outreach. As noted previously, Poquoson is an end-of-the-road location on a peninsula. During my settling-in period as the new manager, I was often struck by the number of people I met who said they had never been to Poquoson even though, in many cases, they lived within a 15-minute drive.

Clearly, we were located close to a large, untapped market area. We began by reaching out to two groups—the commercial development community and residential realtors. In separate events, we invited them to the community to unveil our marketing program and to discuss the unique and special aspects of the community.

One of the highlights of the realtor event was a bus tour of the city when I told them about the community's history, which in turn helped them to relay it to their customers who would be our future residents. Both events now occur on an annual basis.

We also hosted an extended visit and tour with the editorial staff of the local newspaper, sharing with them the many positive and unique aspects of Poquoson, including our economic development and marketing plans. As a result, we received some outstanding regional press coverage.

Another important element of our outreach plan was to engage with business leaders, asking them to help us "champion" the community. We also asked for their candid feedback and suggestions on how best to achieve the city's objectives. The first big economic development project was a direct result of a referral from one of these business leaders.

A final component was to reach out to landowners in the city's planned development area and facilitate a nearly year-long dialogue intended to give them the information and tools necessary to develop their properties and just as importantly, create an opportunity for owner-to-owner dialogue. As I prepared this article, the council was in the midst of considering the city's largest ever mixed-use development project in the primary development area that is a direct result of this dialogue.

It is important to note that one of the first things we had to do was make it clear that the city had no interest in or ability to buy landowners' properties; meaning if their property was going to be developed, they would need to seek a private sector alternative. This understanding helped set the stage for all that has since occurred.

Stage Five: Marketing. As we began outreach efforts, we marketed our community as never before. We successfully built upon initial branding and marketing efforts by again looking for help internally to make things happen.

We were fortunate that one of the Economic Development Authority members happened to be an award-winning maker of short films. We used her expertise and contacts to produce high-quality aerial footage of Poquoson for which we have found many uses.

These include placement of short, quality-of-life spots in movie theatres across Virginia, promotional videos, and still images that capture our unique coastal community. We also expanded the city's website and added the app EnjoyVA.com, which I encourage readers to try.

A little more information about the app: It was developed for about the same cost that was used in the past to print and mail a yearly business guide. My thinking was that most people would rather have something they can readily access from their cellphones rather than a guide left forgotten in a drawer.

Among other things, the app includes marketing videos, links to area businesses, an e-coupon section, a direct link to the city website, community recreation information, and residential and commercial property listings.

Since we had limited money to spend, we have had to be extremely careful in targeting marketing dollars. We have, for example, focused a good portion of our efforts on recreational boaters.

The thinking here is that water access is one of the community's strengths, and we firmly believe that if recreational boaters visit us once, they'll be hooked on our community. We are also keenly aware that in order for visitors to get to the waterfront, they must drive through the central business district.

One last word about marketing: The council and I recognize and appreciate the important role that every city employee contributed in making Poquoson a great place to visit and to live. The same can be said for residents and business owners. Everyone recognizes that collectively we are all ambassadors and cheerleaders for the city.

Stage Six: Organizational Alignment. During meetings with residents and business owners, we have actively sought feedback and suggestions on how we can better promote economic development. As a result we have changed ordinances, removed unnecessary barriers, and streamlined the development-review process.

The resultant changes have added speed and certainty to city processes. Another area of strategic alignment was in the tax code. A few years ago, the council eliminated the tax on boats. As a waterfront community that is heavily reliant on commercial and recreational boating, this was seen as an investment in Poquoson's way of life rather than solely a tax issue.

Again, if your community is struggling with economic development, I hope this information will be helpful. My advice includes these priorities: Always look forward, use hidden talent within your organization, and change strategies that have not borne fruit.

Start first by clearly understanding the goal, be honest about the tools you need to achieve that goal, and build a coalition of the willing.

20. Ten Tips for Branding Your Small Town*

Thomas Ford

Most know that I come from a small town, a very small town. Pittston (pop. 7,600), Pennsylvania is located in the heart of the Pennsylvania coal fields on the banks of the Susquehanna River smack dab between Wilkes-Barre and more well-known Scranton. Pittston, just like many small towns across the country are seeing a new renaissance but many face the same problems namely many businesses that make up these small towns are outdated in their marketing and the town itself does not follow standard marketing practices.

In this article we will look at how small towns can revitalize their marketing efforts and take their place on the digital roadmap. The first thing to keep in mind is about how people search when we're looking for somewhere to go. We search on *activity* first, then *location* second. For example, we'll search "river kayaking eastern Pennsylvania" or "sailing Outer Banks."

Unfortunately, most towns don't care advantage of this and as a result, 97 percent of community-based marketing is ineffective. Something else to keep in mind when marketing a town, community or city is that we filter out everything that isn't directly relevant to us. The main concept to focus on is the following:

Locations/Destinations must act like businesses and narrow their focus:

- What do you have that the people you are hoping to attract can't get or do closer to home?
- What makes you worth a special trip?
- What sets you apart from everyone else?

Whatever it is that makes you different or clearly better, you must take it and capitalize on it. But it isn't enough for you claim that you're different or clearly better. Every small town can do that. That difference has to come not from the town but by third party endorsement. In other words, other people have to say it, too. Most communities and small towns are stuck in what one might consider "group hug mentality." They try to make everyone happy with their tourism marketing.

The "membership mentality" of "we don't want to leave out any of our members" leads to generic, "something for everyone" market that is ineffective. Essentially, you try to be a jack of all trades while being a master of none and this dilutes your small town marketing. So, how does one go about marketing small town America? Check out these 10 tips on how you can take your town's branding efforts to the next level.

1. Don't get hung up on logos and slogans. Logo and slogans are not brands. They are merely marketing messages that support your brand. Logos and slogans are 2 percent of marketing, but 98 percent of local attention goes to them. Think of it from a consumer marketing standpoint. You don't choose Ford over Chevy because of their logo or slogan.

2. A brand is a perception. A brand is what people think of you, not what you say you are. What we see if often the polar opposite. Towns create a brand based on how they perceive themselves and only how they perceive themselves and this results in a disconnect with the people they are trying to connect with. We create brand experiences through visual cues, people and attitudes, word of mouth, publicity, and social media. Negative perceptions can require a repositioning or rebranding effort. Good brands evoke emotion. They make a statement. They sell a feeling, not a place or a product. Brands are all WHY, not WHAT or WHERE.

3. Successful brands have a narrow or niche focus. If I can take out your town's name, and plug in any other town, it fails. You're not doing anything wrong, you're just saying the same thing everyone else is saying. You must drop the generic. You cannot be all things to all people. Promote your primary lure. Here are some of those "generic" words and phrases to delete from your marketing immediately:

- explore
- discover
- outdoor recreation
- so much to do
- four season destination
- historic downtown
- center of it all
- best kept secret
- close to it all
- playground

I am sure you can think of many more. Drop these words like bad habits.

4. Narrow focus so much that your name becomes synonymous with your brand. In the end, you want your name and your brand to become one. One wouldn't think of Napa Valley without its wine nor would you think of Las Vegas without associating it with casinos and gambling. How do you accomplish this? It is actually quite simple. Find your brand and make it everything you are about. Live, eat and breath your brand. Looking back at my hometown of Pittston, Pittston has branded itself as "Tomato Capital of the World." Even though it may not be true, though I can testify that many of the local are extremely competitive in growing their tomato plants during the summer, you would never be able to tell. Pittston has embraced this image thoroughly. Every summer, the city holds a "Tomato Festival" which includes a large scale tomato fight. Streets have taken on the name of the rotund vegetable and even the artwork dotting the city pays tribute to the almighty tomato.

5. Brands are built on product, not just marketing. A key concept of tourism marketing is that people are looking for things to do, not just things to look at. That's why it's difficult to market your history in tourism just based on the history itself. You have to find ways to make people involved in the experience of that history. Brands are also always experiential. Tourism organizations sell cities, towns and counties before experiences. Economic Development groups sell infrastructure and land before opportunities. These are mistakes. Avoid hiring any branding company that does not talk about product—what it is that sets your community apart from the rest.

6. Never, ever use focus groups. They are never the way to build a brand. In fact, in over seven years I have never seen one work and in all actuality they lead to more of that generic speak we discussed earlier more often than not. Cute and clever very seldom work in tourism marketing. Never do branding by public consent. Period. When lots of people get involved, that carefully crafted narrow niche gets spread out into making everyone happy. Build your brand by feasibility, not local sentiment. Top-down branding efforts fail 98 percent of the time.

7. You never "roll out" your brand until you can "deliver on the promise." If you market your community for a niche you really don't deliver on, you are setting up for upset visitors. Brands are earned, good or bad but they are earned. Communities have used transitional brands to talk about what they are becoming. If you are a small town that is struggling to reinvent itself do not go about creating a brand reflecting the end goal of what you want to be. First create brand that focuses on the effort to become that end goal. Too many towns try to pass themselves off as the end goal when in reality they cannot deliver on more than half of their promises.

A good example is of a small town on the Chesapeake in Maryland. The town was planning on building a beautiful waterfront that would tie the community with the Chesapeake Bay and during the planning stages they developed a brand for their community based on this upcoming feature even though it was entirely in concept drawings. Five years later and still no work has been done and the project had entered "development hell" and is unlikely ever to become a reality. This doesn't prevent the town from using it as a selling point for tourists. Once they arrive hoping to make use of the park, they find it not even built and they leave, in some cases very angry. These angry tourists have taken to the Web to blast the community for its "lies and falsehoods." This user generated content now outranks the town's own webpages and is the first thing anyone researching the town will see. The damage it has done is incalculable. Remember this lesson and only promise what you can deliver.

8. Great brands always start with a plan. You would be surprised to see how often town's create their brands without a plan of action at all. Unfortunately, this lack of organization is clearly see in the brand itself: The ideal plan for creating a brand for your community follows the four basic questions below:

- What do you want to be known for?
- What do you need to own the brand?
- How will you tell the world?
- What goes on the "to do" list?

9. Build your brand by feasibility, not local sentiment. Start your brand building with an assessment. Where you are today? Then, ask the locals, where do you want to go as a community? When someone mentions your community in 10 years, what do you want them to mention? Next, do the research. Which of all the ideas make the most sense? Answer these key questions about feasibility:

- Is this something the markets we are hoping to attract can't get or do closer to home?
- Can the community buy into it over time?
- Can the private sector invest in it?
- How much will it cost and when will we see return?
- Does it have legs? Can we start with a niche, then add extensions to the brand?
- Can we make it obvious and pervasive throughout the city?
- Will it extend our seasons?
- Do we have tireless champions for this cause?

- Is it experiential? Things to do, not things to look at.

Only once the concept is proved feasible do you begin developing an action plan. The strategies, goals and objectives should fill no more than 10 pages. An action plan is a "to do" list. Each item on the plan should include:

- the recommendation—what is to be done
- who's in charge
- what it will cost
- the source of funds
- when it must be completed
- the rationale—give the reason

10. Don't let local politics kill your branding efforts. There are actually three areas that can rapidly kill any branding efforts:

1. local politics, especially "membership" politics that try to please everyone
2. lack of champions
3. lack of money

The most dangerous of all of them is politics. Many a good branding effort has been destroyed by petty politics. Someone with political clout has one vision while someone else has another vision and the result is an all-out political war with the town becoming a desolate no man's land. This is a very sad situation as the actions of selfish men and women can derail and postpone a community's renaissance. Push politics aside and make sure you take a good deal of the branding out of the hands of politicians. Entrust it to third parties such as MarketingModo and those without political interference or form a committee that includes all major factions plus members of the community. Far too often, the branding efforts of a town are solely in the hands of political figures or the top citizens in the community who have political clout of their own. Try to make sure that your efforts include everyone. Some towns break it down into neighborhood committees and they are responsible for their own area of the town. That is one way but there are many others.

21. Are Municipal Branding Campaigns Worth the Price?*

RYAN HOLEYWELL

For the last 12 years, Don McEachern has been traveling the United States and making a relatively simple pitch to city leaders coast to coast. For a modest sum—typically somewhere between $80,000 and $200,000 for a medium-sized city—he can help improve a city's image, contributing to gains in tourism, economic development and citizen pride.

Many of his clients are places you've probably never heard of and will probably never visit, like Brookings (pop. 22,000), S.D.; Walton County, Ga.; and Goshen (pop. 32,000), Ind. But if McEachern has his way, once acquainted with them, you'll never forget them. McEachern's Nashville-based North Star Destination Strategies is one of the leading firms in the field of place branding, a specialized type of marketing that promises to help tell a community's story by drawing on lessons learned from market research, focus groups and surveys. In short, McEachern helps cities develop their brand. Call it their essence, their character, their spirit—whatever it is, a brand, McEachern explains, "is what they say about you when you're not around."

The field has its skeptics. Critics of place branding say McEachern and his ilk are selling a false promise. A city's brand is developed over years by its policies and its amenities, and a glorified marketing effort can't change that, they argue. But advocates for place branding say services provided by firms like North Star are so integral to the success of a city that it's nearly impossible to compete without them.

Ultimately, does place branding really work? That depends on whether you trust McEachern. He insists it does. But he's also the first to acknowledge that he has almost no proof.

Every city is trying to capture a little bit of the branding magic that has helped put some of America's best known cities on the map. Many are associated with catchy slogans—not necessarily developed by city governments themselves—like "Keep Austin Weird" or "What Happens in Vegas Stays in Vegas." Other places have an instantly recognizable nickname, like the Windy City, the Motor City or the Big Easy. Those in the branding community say that while a slogan or motto is part of a brand, they're more concerned with projecting a broader image of a community, like the reputation Portland, Ore., has as a haven for independent-minded hipsters, Santa Fe's

*Originally published as Ryan Holeywell, "Are Municipal Branding Campaigns Worth the Price?," *Governing*, December 2012. Reprinted with permission of the publisher.

position as a destination for those embracing Southwest arts and culture, or Miami's role as a place for sun, surf and nightlife.

But most cities aren't Portland, Santa Fe or Miami. The vast majority of America's small and midsize cities don't have much of a reputation very far beyond their borders. That's where branding consultants like North Star and its competitors come in, pledging to help communities distinguish themselves.

North Star officials speak at events run by groups like the National League of Cities and the International City/County Management Association. The firm distributes information about successful campaigns to potential clients, and its efforts have been well documented in local newspapers across the country. So when city leaders decide to pursue branding, McEachern says, "people think of us."

The typical product provided by North Star and other companies includes a logo, a slogan and a broader message or narrative about a community, as well as a list of steps that should be taken to help spread that story. "I wish I had a dollar for every time I heard 'small-town charm with big-city amenities,'" McEachern says. "That might be extremely relevant about a place, but it's not the least bit distinct."

If a community has done a particularly good job at identifying and understanding its brand, it won't just serve as a marketing tool. Rather, it will actually be used to guide decision-making, almost like a citywide mission statement. Advocates for the process don't shy away from emphasizing how important they believe developing a brand to be. A report by the group CEOs for Cities says branding can help repair a city's image problem and raise awareness of what makes a city a good place to live. It goes so far as to call branding the foundation of what makes a place desirable. "A city is not Coca-Cola," says Alison Maxwell, deputy director of economic development for Glendale,

Calif. "It's a living, breathing, amorphous entity. Good branding can bring the sum of the parts together and give you a hook to hang your identity on."

You've likely never heard of Petersburg, Alaska, pop. 3,000. The tiny town about 110 miles southeast of Juneau sits on a coastal island that's only accessible by boat or plane. With snowcapped peaks towering over a quaint harbor, it's a picturesque Alaska fishing town—which doesn't make it all that different from many of its neighbors.

So, in an effort to distinguish itself, Petersburg hired North Star for the full branding treatment. (Since landing Sumner County, Tenn., as its first client in 2000, North Star has provided services to about 180 communities.) The firm conducted a series of focus groups, interviews and surveys of stakeholders, residents and Alaskans from other parts of the state. The data revealed some interesting aspects of the city. Its best assets, research found, include its reputation as an authentic town not inundated with tourists like other Alaskan coastal communities, and the fishing industry in Petersburg is well known and respected. Petersburg is also unique in having a deep-rooted Norwegian culture. While residents overwhelmingly said they'd recommend it as a place to visit, they weren't as enthusiastic about recommending it as a place to live. Ultimately, the city's historic lack of messaging meant many Alaskans—even those living near Petersburg—weren't that familiar with the city. While obstacles like high transportation costs weren't helping Petersburg get visitors, neither was its hesitancy to be its own advocate.

The key to a good brand, McEachern says, is linking up research with an authentic message that resonates. North Star concluded that while Petersburg can't claim the distinction of being Alaska's best fishing village, it could own the title as Alaska's best Norwegian fishing village. That, North Star says, works to the city's advantage because it plays into the town's reputation as industrious and hardworking. North Star—as it does with all clients—boiled it all down into one sentence known as a "brand platform" that's meant to be the driving force behind all the city's messaging efforts: "For those seeking adventure and independence, Petersburg is at the heart of Southeast Alaska on Frederick Sound, where the fishing culture is distinguished by a strong Norwegian heritage, so your hard work and pursuit of authenticity are rewarded."

In addition to developing a logo for the city (featuring six fishing ships) and a new slogan ("Little Norway. Big Adventure."), North Star suggested some other ways the city could spread the brand. McEachern typically proposes strategies beyond traditional advertising, largely because he works with cities that don't have big budgets for major ad campaigns. For starters, North Star told Petersburg to inventory all things "Norwegian" about the city—festivals, foods, traditions—and highlight them. It also recommended developing an online community calendar, a citywide Flickr account (followed by a photo contest), an endurance race through area trails and online job listings—all to generate buzz about the town.

The firm designed signage for the airport and harbor, and directional markers around town that feature Petersburg's new logo and color scheme. It offered suggestions for content and design of a new website, print advertisements and trade show booths. It gave ideas for merchandise to be branded with the new city logo, like workboots and fleece jackets. It provided city leaders with words they should use in written materials and even in conversation to spread the brand, like "authentic Alaska," "small-town feel" and "adventure." It even suggested a new way for city staffers to answer their phones that plays up the Norwegian angle: "Velkommen to Petersburg."

The city and affiliated entities are using the new logo and slogan on business cards, stationery and websites. A new public library will include a totem pole that incorporates Norwegian designs, per North Star's recommendation. A recent promotion with Dodge Ram at the Alaska State Fair offered fairgoers the chance to win a free trip to Petersburg. The chamber of commerce is scheduled to have a booth at the upcoming Seattle boat show in January. The community is even planning on advertising in Alaska Airlines' in-flight magazine. "I couldn't believe the number of people who came up to me and told me 'I'm so excited about this project,'" says Liz Cabrera, coordinator of the Petersburg Economic Development Council. "It was almost like the horses got let out of the corral."

Skeptics may wonder why Petersburg needed to spend $75,000 to get consultants to travel 2,500 miles and confirm that the Norwegian fishing town is, in fact, exactly that. But McEachern says that in the case of Petersburg, his company's value is in providing insight on how the city should convey its message, as opposed to the message itself.

Still, skeptics contend that at a time when cities are struggling financially, it's irresponsible to spend money on amorphous branding campaigns that don't provide a concrete return on investment. Many have also questioned whether a process originally designed for corporations can work for a community. A 2006 paper on city branding by a pair of Danish professors noted that city branding campaigns tend to be bland—and thus fail to stand out—thanks to the manner in which they're developed. Cities are diverse places: In order for a brand to see the light of day, it needs buy-in from a broad group of stakeholders. So while the intent of place branding is to emphasize what makes a city unique, the messages that come from branding efforts can sometimes be anything but that. "The result may appear well meant," the researchers concluded, "but the remarkable and catchy will elude the branding effort."

Indeed, while Petersburg gave North Star a lot to work with, other communities offer greater challenges. Some slogans developed by North Star—like "Bring Your Dreams" for Brookings, S.D., or "Yours Truly" for Lee's Summit, Mo.—could probably be used in any city in America. Steve Arbo, the city manager of Lee's Summit, a Kansas City suburb of 91,000, says that there was some skepticism when that slogan was first revealed. "There are those that said, 'This is a waste of money and you could have paid me $75,000 to come up with "Yours Truly,"'" Arbo says. But he dismisses those critics as people who "don't have a full understanding of what we're trying to do." The slogan is part of a broader message that emphasizes Lee's Summit as a place that values community.

Critics also wonder why an outside consultant is even necessary. Glendale, Calif., for example, finalized a branding campaign led by North Star. The city didn't have a bad image, says Maxwell, the deputy director for economic development. It just didn't have much of a reputation at all. Ultimately, the city and North Star selected "Your Life. Animated." The intent is to highlight Glendale's position as home to DreamWorks Animation, the studio behind animated movies like "Shrek" and "Kung Fu Panda," and Walt Disney's Imagineering, which develops components for Disney's theme parks. The phrase has a double meaning meant to convey positive feelings about the city beyond the industry. "It gives you something we can talk about," Maxwell says. "It helps everyone coalesce around an image and sense of self."

Dave Weaver, a retired engineer who serves on the Glendale City Council, says he's not convinced the city needed to hire an outside consultant. "I said, 'You've come from the East Coast, and you want me to tell you about the town I was born and raised in so you can tell me how to brand

ourselves?'" He says the effort could have been done internally, or the city could have used creative types from the area. "Let the entertainment people come with their ideas," Weaver says. "It's in their own backyard."

City officials would be better off focusing on concrete improvements they can make to their communities, some have argued. "I said from the beginning: If you want to change the image of the city, change the city," says Steven Holzman, a city commissioner in Boynton Beach, Fla., which spent about $15,000 on a branding campaign. "We have areas that are blighted. There's trash strewn. The landscaping needs to be replaced. We don't have sidewalks and curbs on major streets. You can tell people all you want about how beautiful it is, but when they drive and see it with their own eyes, it's not as beautiful."

That kind of criticism isn't unique. North Star's own Petersburg report, for example, notes that the city faces serious hurdles: a declining population, a lack of higher education opportunities and few entertainment venues to attract new, young residents. It's hard to imagine a branding campaign reversing all of that. Scott Doyon, a principal with PlaceMakers, a firm that specializes in urban planning and marketing, says cities undergoing branding campaigns risk advancing a message that's too aspirational and not rooted in reality. The best plan, he says, is to try to leverage positive qualities—not dupe people. "Cities already have a brand whether they've done anything to cultivate one," Doyon says. "They tend to get the most respect if they can find a way to leverage that reputation."

Still, Holzman wonders if the relatively small amount of money that his city and other midsize communities spend on branding will have much impact, considering that they don't have the resources to spend millions of dollars on advertising campaigns that will get lots of eyeballs. If they can't go all out, he reasons, then what's the point? But McEachern counters that his efforts give cities the power to get the smartest use out of the limited dollars they've already budgeted for marketing.

Sometimes—for reasons that can't always be anticipated—branding efforts flop when they're first rolled out. When Oak Park, Ill., revealed its new logo, bloggers suggested it resembled a stylized phallus. Critics of Dunwoody, Ga.'s new logo, which featured sky-blue text and a large neon asterisk, said it was remarkably similar to Walmart's. And Colorado Springs faced a double dose of criticism. After committing $111,000 on a branding project, city officials didn't get the reception they had hoped for. Its slogan, "Live It Up," was panned as generic and unoriginal (it turns out Battle Creek, Mich., had used the same one), and some said the logo looked like clip art.

"You spend months working on a strategy, and people say 'Show me the logo, show me the tagline,'" recalls Doug Price, president and CEO of Colorado Springs' Convention and Visitors Bureau. "We got to the end, and when we announced it was going to be 'Live It Up' … everybody's a critic. People say, 'How did you come up with something that stupid?'"

Colorado Springs ultimately kept the slogan. Price is a fan, noting its double meaning ("It's an attitude and it's an altitude"). But it still responded to the criticism of the logo with a redesign contest and wound up with a new logo that was vastly more popular. "My advice is to pull the tent flaps back as far as you can and get as many people involved," says Price.

In the end, the most critical question is whether branding matters. Experts in the field say that, to an extent, its return on investment can be measured by social and economic indicators, job creation numbers, tourist trips and opinion surveys of the brand itself. Indeed, the New Mexico Tourism Department, which recently launched a multimillion dollar "New Mexico True" campaign, says it's so critical to measure the ROI that it's budgeted for a consultant to study the ads' impact.

Still, it can be difficult to measure the true return, since indicators like jobs don't change in a vacuum. Ask a new resident whether the "Yours Truly" campaign helped convince her to move to Lee's Summit, and she'll probably say no—even if the campaign really did play a role—since marketing done well is subtle. "I've been asking people all over the country if anyone's ever moved anywhere or even spent a vacation somewhere because they had a great logo and a line," McEachern says. "Nobody's raised their hands."

Cities may not be able to point to specific effects of a branding campaign, but in many cases, McEachern says, a new brand will infuse existing city efforts with new energy. "There are so many variables at play, there's no clean return on investment on this, and if anyone tells you there is, they're selling you something. There simply isn't."

Arbo, of Lee's Summit, says he knows the campaign on its own won't prompt people to move to his city or open businesses there. But he hopes—and expects—that it might be enough to get people to give Lee's Summit a second look. "The rest," Arbo says, "is up to us."

22. How to Market a Small Town*

Becky McCray

Recently, I listened to a session on "How to Market a Community" with Roger Brooks of Destination Development International. I wanted to share my notes with you.

The first fact he mentioned is about how we search when we're looking for somewhere to go. We search on *activity* first, then *location* second. So we'll search "mountain biking western Oklahoma" or "sailing southern Ontario." Brooks' examples showed people searching on an activity and then a town name.

"Have you ever gone anywhere because they 'have something for everyone' or they are the 'gateway to' someplace else?" Brooks asked.

He says 97 percent of community-based marketing is ineffective. The reason is that we filter out everything that isn't directly relevant to us.

Pretty Prairie (pop. 688), Kansas, promotes only one thing on their highway sign: the largest night rodeo in Kansas.

Destinations must act like businesses: narrow your focus.

- What do you have that the people you are hoping to attract can't get or do closer to home?
- What makes you worth a special trip?

- What sets you apart from everyone else?

(If you read my weekly emails, you know I hammer on this one, as well.)

Whatever it is that makes you different or clearly better, you must hang your hat on that, Brooks said. But it isn't enough for you claim that you're different or clearly better. That difference has to come by third party endorsement. Other people have to say it, too.

Most communities are stuck in the "group hug mentality." They try to make everyone happy with their tourism marketing. The "membership mentality" of "we don't want to leave out any of our members" leads to generic, "something for everyone" market that is ineffective.

Ten Things You Need to Know and Do to Win

To drive home the message about narrowing your tourism marketing to a niche, Brooks presented 10 things to know.

1. Don't get hung up on logos and slogans. They are not brands. They are just marketing messages that support your brand. Logos and slogans are 2 percent of marketing, but 98 percent of local attention

*Originally published as Becky McCray, "How to Market a Small Town," http://smallbizsurvival.com. Reprinted with permission of the publisher.

goes to them, Brooks said. You don't choose Ford over Chevy because of their logo or slogan.

2. A brand is a perception. A brand is what people think of you, not what you say you are, Brooks said. We create them through visual cues, people and attitudes, word of mouth, publicity, and social media. Negative perceptions can require a repositioning or rebranding effort. Good brands evoke emotion. They make a statement. They sell a feeling, not a place or a product. Brands are all WHY, not WHAT or WHERE.

3. Successful brands have a narrow focus. If I can take out your town's name, and plug in any other town, it fails, Brooks said. You're not doing anything wrong, you're just saying the same thing everyone else is saying. You must jettison the generic. You cannot be all things to all people. Promote your primary lure. Memberships kill attempts to specialize tourism marketing.

Here are some of those "everyone uses them" words and phrases to delete from your marketing:

- explore
- discover
- outdoor recreation
- so much to do
- four season destination
- historic downtown
- center of it all
- best kept secret
- close to it all
- playground

I'm sure you can think of many more. Don't just market what you have, market what will close the sale, Brooks said.

4. Narrow focus so much that your name becomes synonymous with your brand. Brooks listed off destinations that have succeeded at this: Napa Valley for wine, Las Vegas for adult fun.

5. Brands are built on product, not just marketing. People are looking for things to do, not just things to look at, Brooks said.

That's why it's so hard to market your history in tourism. You have to find ways to make people involved in the experience of that history. Brands are always experiential. Tourism organizations sell cities, towns and counties before experiences. Economic Development groups sell infrastructure and land before opportunities. These are mistakes according to Brooks. Avoid hiring any branding company that does not talk about product, he said.

6. Never, ever use focus groups. They are never the way to build a brand, Brooks said. Cute and/or clever seldom work in tourism marketing. Never do branding by public consent. Period. When lots of people get involved, that carefully crafted narrow niche gets spread out into making everyone happy. Build your brand by feasibility, not local sentiment. Top-down branding efforts fail 98 percent of the time, Brooks said.

7. You never "roll out" your brand until you can "deliver on the promise." If you market your community for a niche you really don't deliver on, you are setting up for upset visitors, Brooks said. Brands are earned, good or bad. Communities have used transitional brands to talk about what they are becoming.

8. Great brands always start with a plan. Brooks outlined a simple plan:

- What do you want to be known for?
- What do you need to own the brand?
- How will you tell the world?
- What goes on the to do list?

9. Build your brand by feasibility, not local sentiment. Brooks said to start with an assessment. Where you are today? Then, ask the locals, where do you want to go as a community? When someone mentions your community in 10 years, what do you want them to mention? Next, do the research. Which of all the ideas make the most sense? Answer these key questions about feasibility:

- Is this something the markets we are hoping to attract can't get or do closer to home?
- Can the community buy into it over time?
- Can the private sector invest in it?
- How much will it cost and when will we see return?
- Does it have legs? Can we start with a niche, then add extensions to the brand?
- Can we make it obvious and pervasive throughout the city?
- Will it extend our seasons?
- Do we have tireless champions for this cause?
- Is it experiential? Things to do, not things to look at.

Only once the concept is proved feasible does Brooks recommend developing an action plan. The strategies, goals and objectives should fill no more than 10 pages. An action plan is a to do list. Each item on the plan should include:

- the recommendation—what is to be done
- who's in charge
- what it will cost
- the source of funds
- when it must be completed
- the rationale—give the reason

10. Don't let local politics kill your branding efforts. Brooks listed three killers of branding efforts:

1. local politics, especially "membership" politics that try to please everyone
2. lack of champions
3. lack of money

What lessons have you learned in marketing your community?

23. Seven Elements of Effective Community Marketing[*]

John Gann, Jr.

What happens to your property tax revenues when existing home values head south as they've lately been doing with a vengeance? Or when home building shuts down and other development projects are cancelled because of turmoil in the credit markets?

What happens to sales tax revenues when families hit by high gasoline and food prices stop spending? How do real estate transfer tax receipts fare when homes aren't selling? What does a soft job market do to income tax revenues? And what does budget distress in the state capitol mean for funds that pass through to localities?

And what happens when all of these things come at the same time, as is happening to some of us right now?

What happens is that smart communities start thinking more seriously about how to expand their tax bases by marketing to bring in economically valuable businesses and populations. Consistent with constrained budgets, they also look for ways to market their communities much more cost-effectively.

Brochures, Billboards, Branding

Just about every place today has a Web site and a marketing brochure, and communities do other things, too.

They run ads in business and travel publications, rent billboard space, send officials to trade shows, produce videos, develop branding logos and slogans, and do other things to make themselves—or their downtowns, industrial parks, tourist spots, neighborhoods, or highway corridors—more visible and attractive to industry, retailers, tourists, shoppers, young people, retirees, convention and special-event planners, and college graduates.

Such undertakings cost money, of course, and it's not always clear that they produce results that can be counted in tax receipts. One reason is that so many competing cities and counties are doing exactly the same things, and because they entail major outlays and can sometimes—as in the case of logos on the letterhead or cute slogans—seem a bit frivolous to people, these efforts can be politically controversial as well.

To avoid problems and get the most out of what is invested in marketing, local

---

[*]Originally published as John Gann, Jr., "Grow Your Tax Base: Seven Elements of Effective Community Marketing," *PM Magazine*, December 2008. Reprinted with permission of the publisher.

officials would do well to look at seven things that greatly affect marketing success.

The Seven Elements

The marketing effectiveness of everything from Web sites, to trade show displays, to special events downtown largely hangs on how well communities handle four elements of marketing planning and three elements of execution:

Planning:

1. The product
2. The market
3. The strategy
4. The appeal

Execution:

1. The message
2. The graphics
3. The media

In a number of their activities, local governments tend to copy what they see other local governments doing. In marketing, however, it can be better to draw not upon what your peers have done but on what has been learned in the world of business.

Businesses have to know how to market because a business that does not market probably won't be around long. For businesses, expert marketing is what they need to survive. For communities, it can be what they need to thrive.

Marketers in the business world have developed measures in each of these seven areas that make their work more successful. Local officials can adapt them to more successfully grow their tax bases.

Planning/The Product. The "product" in this case is, of course, your community. Although marketing is often thought of as just selling the locality, it's vitally important to make sure you have a product you can sell.

If your community doesn't have what people or businesses want, what you spend on Web sites, videos, or printed literature won't matter very much. So one of the best things you can do in marketing is simply to make improvements to your community in ways that are important to the people you want to sell it to.

The Market. Your community's market is the entity you're selling to. It can be the corporate real estate executive, the conference planner, the home buyer, the tourist, or the real estate investor. Because of the competition for growth today, it's important to select the right market(s) for your particular community and not try to be all things to all people.

The currently hot markets that all those other places are going after aren't always the best choices, especially if they aren't a good fit with what your community offers. Two of the biggest business successes of our time—Wal-Mart and Starbucks—happened when small companies took markets with seemingly little growth potential—small, rural towns and coffee drinkers—and found value that larger competitors couldn't see.

The Strategy. Here is the strategy portion of marketing planning. The most valuable thing that marketing professionals can do for you is not write clever copy, not shoot appealing photographs, not put animation and dazzle into your Web pages, and not slap a colorful logo on the sides of your police cars. The biggest value-added component of any marketing effort is thought.

Good thinking can do more than anything else to make any ad, brochure, or Web site effective. But strategic marketing thought is also the most likely element to be missing from a community's marketing, especially when marketing is piecemeal (a video here, a trade show there) rather than part of an overall program.

The best marketing strategies are consistent, focused on results, and directed to the prospective customer on the outside. Normally, special efforts must be made to achieve all three because these qualities don't always come naturally in local government.

The Appeal. Finally, there is the appeal. The heart of anything you do to market your locality is what specifically you offer prospects who are seeking that specific thing from a location. Places sometimes try to avoid defining their appeal by claiming—ineffectively—that they've "got it all." Or they boast about something their market doesn't care about (like how great their Web site is). And some places run ads that give prospects information on how to contact them but give no good reason why they should do so.

Communities will do better if they define their appeal in terms of benefits to prospects rather than just point-with-pride facts about the locality. You have to show the business decision maker, tourist, shopper, or prospective resident how your community's advantages will make him or her better off.

Execution/The Message. The message is at the top of this list. To most local officials, "marketing" means media: brochure, video, trade show, or advertisement. So they spend big on media while they make little or no investment in developing a compelling message to convey in the media.

Top marketing pros emphasize that the nature of the message is much more important for getting results than the vehicle you use to get that message out. Three critical parts of marketing messages have to be done right:

- The opener is what you do to get attention and motivate someone to take in the rest of your message. It's the most important part of any message because if it fails the rest of what you have to say goes to waste. An ad to get Manhattan companies to move their offices across the river to New Jersey got a powerful message across in a six-word opener headline: "Move 6 Miles. Save $60 Million." What cost-conscious company wouldn't read further?
- The argument is the case you make for how being in your community will benefit your prospect. One of the benefits of living in a good, older, city neighborhood rather than a suburban subdivision is the money you can save on housing, transportation, and other things. An ad I wrote a few years ago detailed those savings for home buyers under the headline, "What will you do with an extra $30 a week?" (At today's prices it would be more like $60.)
- The close is what you do to get your prospect to take some action. If you don't get any action on your message, you've just wasted your money.

If the marketing points you make about your community in a brochure, print ad, or Web site could validly also be made by dozens of other places, you need a better message. If you look like everyplace else, you're likely to remain invisible.

The Graphics. Making a place look good with graphics, whether it be video, graphic elements, color, fancy typography, and the like can do a lot to enhance a marketing message. But these same actions also too often serve to sabotage that message.

Poorly thought-out graphics an compete with or obscure your message, miss opportunities to make it more powerful, and even turn off prospects by looking too much like advertising.

Communities tend, for example, to overuse logos (one of the least effective elements in marketing communities) and underuse things like photo captions (one of the most effective). Contrary to common assumptions, it can hurt your marketing to display too many pictures of your locality in a booklet or Web site.

And photos of people enjoying your community have much greater marketing power than the much more common shots of buildings. Corning, New York, and Galesburg, Illinois, have used to good effect pictures in their brochures of people enjoying their downtown areas.

The Media. You can spend a lot of money on the ways—what's called the medium—used to get your message out, whether through advertising, Web sites, trade missions, or a dozen other media. That makes it important to choose carefully to get the most bang for your buck.

Saving money on media doesn't always mean compromising effectiveness. A half-page print ad, for example, is paradoxically more likely to be successful than a more costly full-pager.

A Time of Opportunity

The term "marketing smarter" means using limited resources more thoughtfully to produce better results. Smart marketing calls for greater attention to substance and less to form. It's easy to be dazzled by the glitz often associated with marketing. But it's useful to remember that every dollar you spend on fancy icing is a dollar not available to make a more appealing cake.

Times like the present—of change and economic difficulty—have always offered opportunity for enterprising businesses and communities because the business-as-usual that favored competitors has been disrupted. Places that act now to sell themselves more effectively instead of just cutting budgets or raising taxes can find themselves ahead of the game once the economy turns around.

24. Creation, Implementation and Evaluation of Tax Increment Financing[*]

GOVERNMENT FINANCE OFFICERS ASSOCIATION

Tax incremental financing (TIF) can be an important tool for local governments to attract economic development projects, create jobs, foster infrastructure investment, and/or redevelop blighted areas. TIF is a technique for funding a qualifying capital project, its related infrastructure, or maintenance of the project from a stream of revenue generated within the geographic area defined as a TIF district. Depending on state and provincial regulations, primary governments with taxing powers can often use TIF, but redevelopment agencies may also be party to a TIF project.

When a redevelopment agency uses TIF, the agency may share or redirect property or other taxes imposed by other taxing entities. TIF generally relies on incremental property taxes generated in a specific area, but it can also apply to other taxes, including sales taxes. Any organization considering the use of TIF should be aware of the risks involved. As demonstrated in previous economic downturns, TIF can significantly constrain an organization's ability to generate tax revenues, once a TIF is crafted, it

can be very difficult to change the terms or cancel the agreement, especially if bonds have already been issued and the various interests in the flow of funds have been established. As a result, there is a need to focus on the long-term nature of TIF, and the long-term forecasts of the tax revenues that support it. The basic principles outlined herein are applicable to any type of TIF.

While TIF laws differ among states or provinces, most states have established laws and eligibility requirements to create or designate an area as a TIF district (e.g., blight, dilapidation or deterioration, age of structures). Once an area is legally designated as a TIF district, the base valuation amount of the property values is "frozen." Improvements to properties within the boundaries of the TIF district will then result in increases to this base of "the increment" which is captured through additional taxes and expended solely within the TIF district. This increment can serve as a source of revenue to pay debt service, upfront development costs for additional

---

[*]Originally published as Government Finance Officers Association. "Creation, Implementation and Evaluation of Tax Increment Financing," February 2014, http://www.gfoa.org. Reprinted with permission of the publisher.

improvements, or for individual projects on a "pay-as-you-go" basis. The maximum period of time a TIF may exist is determined by state law; legislation generally allows time for development efforts and a traditional 20- to 30-year financing period.

All TIF and TIF districts should be developed in a manner consistent with a government's TIF or economic development policies. Specific components that organizations should include in a TIF policy include:

1. Objectives or strategic goals that the organization can satisfy by using TIF (e.g.: job creation, removal of blight, meeting infrastructure needs).

2. Eligible projects where TIF can be used.

3. Non-eligible projects or users where TIF may not be used.

4. Standards for creating a TIF district and/or evaluation criteria.

5. Processes for considering, reviewing, and implementing a potential TIF agreement.

Recommendation: The Government Finance Officers Association (GFOA) recommends that local governments carefully evaluate whether TIF and TIF districts are the most appropriate and effective tool to assist the local government in its economic development plans. TIF can be a powerful economic development tool, but when tax revenues from the TIF increment is diverted to a TIF district, local governments will be affected by not receiving these revenues, which can constrain a government over the duration of the TIF. Additionally, the development project itself may contain risk, if the project fails to realize the projected results, it could subject the TIF (and the government) to significant financial pressures, particularly with respect to TIF debt service.

When adopting a TIF policy, the governing body needs to identify when TIF dis-

tricts are appropriate, taking into account risk, financial conditions, and the relationship of a project to the organization's overall plans, including maintenance and sustainability. The policy may be based solely on enabling statutes but should provide flexibility for the local governing body and be consistent with local preferences. The policy also should address the following steps to evaluate whether a TIF district should be created. These steps assume that the government has already compared TIF with other options, including other financing sources, and that the TIF aligns with community development goals and complies with the jurisdiction's development policies and objectives. Recommended evaluation steps include the following:

- Identify the area for the TIF district designation to determine whether a proposed district meets the criteria under applicable state law and the priorities established by the governing body. TIF districts may vary in size, depending on the applicable state laws and local government objectives.
- Conduct feasibility studies, including an evaluation to determine whether development or redevelopment could take place within an acceptable timeframe, without economic assistance from the local government (e.g., but for the TIF assistance, the development would not be possible).
- Include an evaluation of debt limitations.
- Identify any taxpayer concentration, tax appeal history, and overlapping taxing jurisdictions contribution and commitment to pledged revenues.
- Identify any laws that might cap assessed value growth or the effect of tax rates on the taxing entity's credit ratings.
- Evaluate the jurisdiction's ability to

meet the proposed TIF plan objectives and its ability to mitigate potential risks to local agencies, including the inability to repay debt in the event of revenue declines.

- For property tax increments assessed value (AV) annual growth limits, for example, look at past and future AV growth trends and collection performance and delinquency rates.
- For sales tax increments, look at historical sales tax collections, change in sales tax rates, pending re-authorizations of the sales tax, tax exemption status and any potential changes to it, and overall economic forecasts.
- Subject assumptions and methods for all feasibility studies to sensitivity analysis and other modeling techniques (see the GFOA best practice, *Evaluating Data and Assumptions in Economic Development Proposals*).
- If the government does not have the technical skills available on staff to conduct a feasibility study, then the use of a qualified consultant is appropriate and recommended. Additionally, an alternative analysis should be prepared to evaluate pay-as-you-go financing and/or debt financing options that the TIF could support.
- Prepare a forecast of the costs and revenues applicable to the project.
- Analyze the long-term economic benefit to the local economy for the term of the TIF, the fiscal impacts to the affected jurisdictions and over-lapping tax entities (e.g., school districts), and the economic cost of TIF incentives. Use various forms of analysis, including sensitivity analysis.
- Evaluate the risk to general government operations when the TIF-related revenue is no longer available, including an evaluation of the total impact of all TIF districts on the tax base.
- Prepare a maintenance plan for the TIF district's projects, incorporating ongoing costs and future capital costs, and considering the revenue sources available to help cover those costs. If a third party or private-sector partner such as a developer is to maintain the TIF district, provide a maintenance plan that incorporates those components. Document any risk sharing between local government and the third party or private sector partner in a development agreement that clearly states each party's responsibilities. For example, the agreement should identify who is responsible for the following:
- Project upkeep.
- Who backs up project revenue if increments are not sufficient. (There are inherent risks any time the government's credit is used as a backup pledge.)
- Ongoing maintenance responsibilities.
- Maintaining designated reserves, if required.
- Project reporting and monitoring.
- Adherence with state and local laws.

If a government believes a TIF is warranted, based on a comprehensive evaluation, the following implementation steps are recommended, in addition to verifying compliance with state and local laws:

- Prepare a thorough development or redevelopment plan that includes the projects identified and an estimate of the incremental increase in real estate valuation the proposed projects will create. Governments may also consider hiring outside professionals to assist with this process. The development plan and agreement are critical, and should include the following:

o Detailed performance measures.
o Milestones for identified performance measures.
o Steps for monitoring and evaluating the plan, enforcing the agreement (e.g., are target job creation numbers met?).
o Steps to be taken if performance goals are not met, including descriptions of the consequences for either better or worse performance. (One option is to outline future benefits and burdens under all possible economic scenarios.)
o Monitor bond covenants.
o Determine which party is responsible for making any post-agreement filings.
o Thoroughly investigate any third-party or private-sector partners, and their ability to meet the obligations outlined in the development agreement. This includes due diligence in examining the developer's financial and other resources, and its track record with similar projects.
o Obtain input from all parties involved in the project. In the case of multi-jurisdictional TIF districts, consider establishing an oversight board. Also obtain public input on the TIF and make adjustments accordingly, including public hearings if required or desired.
o Periodically review of TIF and TIF district to determine if the TIF is functioning as intended. This periodic review should include measures of actual performance, as compared to projected performance. Measurements could include items such as actual versus projected tax base, jobs created, and the potential impact of shifting economic development from non–TIF district to TIF district.
o Ensure that there is adequate understanding of governmental monitoring and reporting requirements. Also, identify who will be accountable for monitoring the TIF and preparing any necessary reports.

25. Community Improvement District to the Rescue[*]

TY LASHER, MICHELLE MEYER
and ALISON MCKENNEY BROWN

A struggling housing development project in Bel Aire (pop. 6,900), Kansas, provides a prime example of how a rapidly changing economic environment requires local governments to find flexible financing solutions. Bel Aire used the Community Improvement Districts Act (CID Act) as an innovative financing tool in order to resolve a housing development issue. Although the CID Act is intended more for economic development that is related to retail and commercial uses, the city used it to successfully revitalize a failed residential subdivision.

The dilemma began in 2007 when an experienced developer planned a 60-acre upscale housing community in Bel Aire, for homes ranging in price from $450,000 to $800,000. The city accepted the petitions for installation of infrastructure and issued a temporary note to cover the cost of installing streets, water lines, sewer lines, and storm drainage.

The developer built 10 upscale model homes on the site and was able to sell several of them relatively quickly. In 2008, the "housing bubble" burst and residential development slowed to a halt as the recession hit Kansas. The developer struggled to keep the project moving, but was eventually forced to claim bankruptcy and walk away.

The few remaining unsold homes and the remaining residential lots reverted to the ownership of an out-of-state bank.

Special Assessments

In 2011, Bel Aire issued a general obligation bond to refund the temporary note that was issued in 2008. In Kansas, special assessments are used where the cost of infrastructure is spread to a benefit district in accordance with state law and paid by the homeowner over a period of 20 years. The bank, however, owned 57 lots and chose not to pay the special assessments or property taxes on any of them. (Note: The authors recognize that special assessments and related legislation are handled differently in various states and that this example may not be relevant to all states and readers.)

The bank understood that Kansas law allows a property to accrue three years of back taxes and special assessments before such property is eligible to be sold at a sheriff's sale. So, while the bank held the lots in limbo for three years incurring no cost, Bel

[*]Originally published as Ty Lasher, Michelle Meyer and Alison McKenney Brown, "CID to the Rescue," *PM Magazine*, November 2014. Reprinted with permission of the publisher.

Aire was responsible for repaying the debt service payments on the bond, yet receiving no revenue from the special assessments. The total special assessments on the bank-owned lots amounted to $150,000 per year.

The city was in a no-win situation. Not only were taxpayers having to cover the special assessment payments for at least three years, the city was also losing out on the revenue from the general property taxes for that same time period. In all likelihood, at the end of the three-year period, Bel Aire would end up purchasing the lots at the sheriff's sale and taking possession of the property in order to protect its investment.

Stakeholder Meetings

In 2012, a successful developer contacted the manager's office seeking assistance in acquiring the lots and dealing with the special assessments. Staff held meetings with the bank and the developer, both jointly and separately, to determine what each party needed from the other to allow this developer to move forward with construction.

The bank agreed to sell the lots to the developer for the value of the outstanding real property taxes and special assessments in order to validly transfer the lots.

The developer could not turn the project into a successful development if such a significant portion of cash was tied up in paying the annual special assessments. With the existing special assessment law, there was no flexibility to delay or reduce the payments.

Manager Lasher began with the premise that Bel Aire might be open to covering costs of the special assessments.

Councilmembers were open to the idea, but needed to know how these costs would be recovered. The developer agreed that the pace of development would be increased without the burden of the special assessment payments for the initial two years of the development.

Working with the idea that the special assessments would need to be initially absorbed by Bel Aire as a cost of development, Attorney Brown began to look for a secondary means of spreading these costs to the benefitting lots. It was determined the best tool to make this happen was to overlay a secondary special assessment on the benefitting lots through a community improvement district (CID).

Such an assessment would extend the period of time for paying the original special assessments. They would eventually be paid for by the owner(s) of these lots so that Bel Aire would receive reimbursement for initially covering some of the special assessment payments.

The Kansas Legislature approved the Community Improvement District Act in 2009 under K.S.A 12-6a26 et seq. The CID Act is generally recognized as authorizing local governments to create CIDs for the purpose of imposing and collecting a community improvement district sales tax on retail sales. Other states have enacted similar legislation to help spur economic growth coming out of the Great Recession. As the Bel Aire case study illustrates, local governments may have additional options to use CIDs as an innovative financial tool.

Prior to the property being sold to the developers, the bank petitioned for creation of the CID, and Bel Aire accepted the petition. The CID process was streamlined since it was created at the beginning of the process and the land was still held by a single owner.

The Solution

Clearly, the sale of the lots to the new developers would directly benefit Bel Aire, as the sale would result in the unpaid special assessments being brought up-to-date, as well as the payment of the outstanding back taxes. Bel Aire, however, also needed some reassurance that its two-year investment in this development would eventually be repaid.

As the special assessments had initially been spread in 2011, by state law the actual owners of the lots would automatically be responsible for the payment of those assessments. Bel Aire and the developers decided that the best approach for paying the special assessments for the 2014 and 2015 tax years was for the developer to pay both these assessments and real estate taxes when billed by the county.

The developer would then provide Bel Aire with a receipt showing the special assessments had been paid, verifiable through the county's online tax information system. In turn, Bel Aire would reimburse the amount of the special assessments that had been paid.

Based on the possibility that a subsequent purchaser of a lot would choose not to seek the initial two-year reimbursement or would pre-pay its special assessments, it was important not to assess the CID special assessment upon all lots equally. Assistant Manager Meyer will be responsible for tracking the amount of reimbursement provided to each lot over the two-year period.

This approach meant that only those special assessments actually advanced by the city would be spread through the CID assessment process to the benefiting lots. The innovative use of the CID Act allowed every participant in the process to achieve some level of success.

The bank was able to sell all of the lots that it had been holding without putting further investment into the properties, thereby avoiding the negative ramification of having the county foreclose on the property.

The developers who purchased the lots were able to invest more cash into constructing model homes as they were able to avoid incurring the carrying cost of special assessments, which meant that construction began immediately and added a vibrant and exciting new development to the community.

Bel Aire was paid for delinquent special assessments associated with the lots that had been unpaid prior to 2013, as well as the delinquent real estate taxes. Both the city and the community benefitted because a previously failed development was rejuvenated.

The homes currently being constructed will add to the city's tax base, as well as residential valuation in the future. Finally, the burden of the city paying special assessments for the failed development has been eliminated.

While it will take two years longer than what was anticipated in 2008 to receive total payment for the infrastructure improvements provided for the home lots, for Bel Aire it is encouraging to know that eventually the special assessments will be paid by the lot owners. We consider these successful results.

26. State Governments
*The Latest Venture Capitalists**

RUSSELL NICHOLS

Driving around Youngstown (pop. 65,000), Ohio, can feel eerily like exploring a decimated city in a war-torn nation. Brick buildings downtown look like hollow, bombed-out shells. Houses abandoned by blue-collar workers sit empty. Bruce Springsteen's ode to the Rust Belt city sang of the steel mills that "built the tanks and bombs that won this country's wars." But those factories were shuttered long ago, their idle smokestacks looming over a crime-ridden town that for decades was better known as "Bomb City" and "Murdertown, USA."

But there's life emerging beneath these hardened scars. In the shadow of the iconic 1919 Home Savings and Loan Company building downtown, a managed cluster of high-tech startups is injecting new energy into the city. It's the Youngstown Business Incubator (YBI), a nonprofit corporation, and it's not only redefining the industry of this hardscrabble valley on the eastern edge of Ohio; it's changing the notion of what cities and states can do to spur innovation and investment. In the past decade, CEO Jim Cossler, who also refers to himself as "chief evangelist," has revamped the model of an incubator from a klatch of unrelated businesses to a targeted group of niche entrepreneurs—in this case, business-to-business software firms. Unlike traditional business incubators, Cossler doesn't "graduate" successful companies and send them packing. Instead, he keeps the portfolio companies on a single, mixed-use campus that promotes open source collaboration. He provides them with cheap or free rent, utilities and Wi-Fi to help them convert IT ideas into dollars and, in turn, jobs.

Bringing Silicon Valley into the Mahoning Valley was a hard sell at first, Cossler says. "When we announced to the world in 2001 that we were going to launch world-class software companies in the global market, the kindest thing that was said to us was, 'You're kidding, right?'" But in 2002, the Ohio Department of Development backed him up, pumping $375,000 per year into the incubator from the Ohio Third Frontier, a 10-year, $1.6 billion project designed to support innovation ecosystems around the state with early stage equity investment capital. The gamble has been paying off. The YBI now boasts eight onsite companies with a total of 320 employees, many in highly skilled technical jobs. In 2010, Cossler says, the entire portfolio made about $65 million in global sales. One of the

---

*Originally published as Russell Nichols, "State Governments: The Latest Venture Capitalists," *Governing*, March 2011. Reprinted with permission of the publisher.

businesses, Turning Technologies, which makes audience response systems, was ranked by *Inc.* magazine in 2007 as the nation's fastest growing software company.

The YBI is definitely a crown jewel in Ohio's push to cultivate small businesses, but it's only one piece of the state's venture capital efforts. Since 2002, the Third Frontier has created more than 60,000 jobs in Ohio. It has helped create, attract and capitalize more than 600 businesses and leveraged more than $5 billion in private investment. Last May, voters overwhelmingly approved a $700 million bond issue to extend the program for another four years. "It's helped create companies and careers that didn't exist in Ohio, or anywhere, just a few years ago," then–Gov. Ted Strickland said following the renewal. "They are inventing the cure for the Rust Belt."

Now more than ever, states are playing the part of venture capitalist—and despite the recession, it turns out they're uniquely suited for the role. As the recession froze private-sector investment, venture capital firms began avoiding early stage deals, saving their money for less risky, later stages of development. That created a void. Governments began to realize they could fill the gap by providing seed money to new startups in all sorts of emerging industries, from biotech and health care to nanotechnology and solar power.

The idea isn't to supplant private-sector firms, but to plug a hole in the marketplace by funding new companies during the high-risk early stage frequently referred to as the "valley of death." It makes for riskier deals, but it also means that relatively small amounts of cash could bring a big payoff to governments that invest. "Many states are saying 'We see that valley of death, and we think we can fill it and create jobs for our residents,'" says Robert Atkinson, founder and president of the Information Technology and Innovation Foundation, a Washington, D.C.-based technology policy think tank. "It's something government knows how to do: They just write a check or give a tax break."

The idea of government as venture capitalist isn't exactly a new one. Around the globe, governments have been experimenting with that role for decades. Some efforts have produced positive results, while others serve as cautionary tales on how to blow billions of taxpayer dollars on a bad idea. Decades ago, Norway squandered some of its oil wealth on sketchy business ventures, and recently the Dubai government's investment in real estate projects led to massive deficits as the financial crisis hit. According to *The Economist*, Canada's venture capital experiment flopped because the Canadian Labor Fund Program had so much money that it scared off private venture capitalists. And in 2005, the Malaysian government opened its huge $150 million complex, called BioValley, prematurely, and it became mocked as the "Valley of the BioGhosts."

The United States, especially in recent years, is no stranger to tech incubation and venture capital efforts. As part of his State of the Union pledge to "win the future" by boosting innovation, President Obama in February launched a national campaign to provide mentorship and funding to help cultivate new businesses. Dubbed "Startup America," the program will eliminate the capital gains tax on some small business investments and speed up the patent process. The U.S. Small Business Administration will direct $2 billion over the next five years to match private-sector investment capital for under-the-radar startups and firms with high-growth potential.

The modern venture capital industry goes back to the 1970s. Private-sector capital firms set their sights on electronic, medical or data-processing technology, and began investing in the startups that soon would populate Silicon Valley. As the number of firms grew, leading venture capitalists formed the National Venture Capital Association and by 1978, the industry experienced its first major fundraising year, with venture capitalists raising about $750 million. At the same time, states were getting into the venture capital game. In the earliest approaches, state governments set up quasi-public corporations and made direct investments in companies, according to Dan Berglund, president and CEO of the State Science and Technology Institute (SSTI), a nonprofit organization that helps states build tech-based economies. "For more than 30 years, states have put money into programs to encourage access to capital," he says. "Over time, it's shifted. Now, more investment decisions are being made by private investors and states play a more passive role as a limited partner."

During the 1980s and '90s, the venture capital wave rose and fell and rose again, leading up to the boom in 2000, followed by the dot-com bust and a decade in recovery mode. Today, in the face of an unstable market, state governments, desperate for jobs, are aiming to capitalize on untapped potential with seed money, investment programs, partnerships and economic development funds to nurture new businesses and create innovation clusters. California and Massachusetts dominate the country in earlier-stage per capita growth and deals. But several states, including Colorado, Connecticut, Maryland, Ohio, New York and Washington, are boosting capital opportunities for early stage entrepreneurs, according to the SSTI.

In New York State, for instance, Empire State Development joined forces with the University of Rochester Medical Center to help high-tech startups commercialize their ideas through a $2 million pilot seed fund project. In February, Maryland Gov. Martin O'Malley announced plans to spur job creation in cutting-edge industries by unlocking $100 million in venture capital through InvestMaryland. Various other states, from Oregon to Georgia to Connecticut, have been setting up similar programs to advance innovation in emerging fields. "We know these kinds of programs do work and make a difference," Berglund says. "In a down economy, now is the time when you really have to invest in the future. It's even more critical at this point."

While state-funded venture capital efforts promise payoffs around the country, they're particularly valued in the Rust Belt and Midwest, where the recession has exacerbated the existing hardships of the shift to a post-industrial economy. In addition to Youngstown, cities such as Ann Arbor, Mich.; Madison, Wis.; and Pittsburgh have powered forward with business acceleration strategies that have attracted up-and-coming entrepreneurs and generated millions from venture capital firms, not to mention the cash coming in from individuals who invest in startup businesses, known as angel investors. For example, Ann Arbor Spark, a nonprofit and business acceleration organization, serves as the administrator over the Michigan Pre-Seed Capital Fund. As of January, 52 startups had received investments from the fund, which have totaled more than $11.6 million.

"The West Coast and Boston and Texas, they don't need money the same way that the Midwest states do," says Jim Jaffe, president and CEO of the National Association of Seed and Venture Funds. "There is an emphasis in some of these areas and some money is starting to flow."

But the key for a successful state venture capital program, Jaffe says, comes down to how much money governments can afford to put on the table. Not all states can invest on the level of Ohio Third Frontier. And places that can't put up enough capital run the risk of handicapping all their venture capital efforts. "The states have to be willing to invest enough money in this process to make it worthwhile," Jaffe says. "If you're investing $500,000 or you've got $20 million over a few years, you can't make enough of a difference at that rate to create a lot of jobs."

That lack of sufficient investment is what usually undermines government efforts to spur innovation, says Harvard Business School professor Josh Lerner. In his book, Boulevard of Broken Dreams, Lerner examines the history of government venture capital activity. True, he says, government investments helped create success stories like Silicon Valley. "But for each effective government intervention," he writes, "there have been dozens, even hundreds, of failures, where substantial public expenditure bore no fruit."

In addition to underinvesting, Lerner says states that set up capital programs tend to rush to give away cash. "In their eagerness to jump-start entrepreneurial activity, governments frequently race to hand out capital," he writes. "This is equivalent to serving the main course before setting the table and unlikely to lead to a successful dinner party." Expecting quick results can torpedo a state's venture capital program.

That was part of the problem with a program in Florida designed to attract biotech firms to the state. In January 2010, news media made hay of a state report showing that Florida's hefty investment in biotech firms hadn't had much of an impact. According to the report from the Florida Legislature's Office of Program Policy Analysis and Government Accountability, titled *Biotechnology Clusters Developing Slowly; Startup Assistance May Encourage Growth*, the $1.5 billion in state and local taxpayer funds to turn the state into a biotech hub had so far only generated some 1,100 jobs. Lacking proper private-sector venture capital funds, the Legislature in 2007 set up the Florida Opportunity Fund to direct public money to biotech startups. But the massive investment of cash, according to the report, "has not yet resulted in the growth of tech-

nology clusters in the counties where program grantees have established facilities."

Some deals in Ohio haven't worked out as well as others, Third Frontier officials say, but the overall default rate is only one-tenth of 1 percent. The new voter-approved extension of the program shows the public's support for the job-creating potential of the program, says Norm Chagnon, executive director of the Third Frontier Commission. "Most people say they want to stay in Ohio and want to raise families, but they can't find the jobs," he says. "This signals our commitment."

Between 2004 and 2008, total venture capital investment in Ohio grew by 13.2 percent per year, from $243 million to $445.6 million, according to a 2008 report published by Michael Camp, academic director of the Center for Entrepreneurship at the Ohio State University's Fisher College of Business. That's more than double the annual growth rate of total U.S. venture capital investment during the same period. And the state continues to invest in startups through the Third Frontier, as well as its Technology Investment Tax Credit Program and the Ohio Venture Capital Authority. Gov. John Kasich, who took office in January, brought in longtime friend Mark Kvamme to run the Ohio Department of Development and analyze the state's capital investment programs. Kvamme, a Silicon Valley venture capitalist, took the interim development director job for $1, and by midyear he plans to complete the transition of the state agency into a new public-private partnership, JobsOhio. "We're evaluating programs to figure out where we want to double down," Kvamme says. "We want to fund entrepreneurs who have intestinal fortitude."

Back in Youngstown, Cossler says he truly believes technology has the power to change the local landscape. "We're not Palo Alto," he says. "We don't have indigenous tech companies here. But no one wants to know the origin of software."

In other words, unlike the massive steel factories of the past, a Web-based company can deliver products from anywhere with a computer and an Internet connection. Now Cossler's on a mission to bring home "the Youngstown diaspora" and grow the tech campus to support 5,000 jobs. The incubator currently occupies three buildings in downtown Youngstown, a mix of renovated historic structures and a modern glass addition. Cossler plans to expand into a fourth building soon, putting to use a long-dormant brick warehouse next door, where a weathered sign still reads, "Furnitureland of Youngstown."

"This is a city that essentially was dying," says the SSTI's Berglund. "And they've taken a really innovative approach with their incubator program."

While some may consider it a waste of taxpayer money to heap funds on luring high-tech firms to the Rust Belt, Cossler says Ohio's venture capital investment is critical. And, he says, it's not even all that different from the industry that built Youngstown in the first place. "If you reduce software to a common denominator, it's a steel company," he says. "You're taking raw materials and blending them together to create a value-added product. It's all manufacturing."

27. Thinking Differently About Development*

JOE MINICOZZI

Communities often experience some level of disconnect between economic development policy and ensuring sufficient tax revenue to cover the cost of the services the government provides. Suburban projects tend to be favored over denser downtown development, but data from more than 30 jurisdictions across 10 states show that a municipality receives a greater level of revenue from its denser and more walkable urban patterns than its suburban pattern of development. Considering this information provides local government officials with an opportunity to consider development from a different angle.

The studies this article is based on cover municipal revenues per acre across states from California to Maine and Montana to Florida, including wealthy cities such as Mountain View, California, and less affluent towns such as Driggs (pop. 1,600), Idaho, and Dunn (pop. 9,700), North Carolina. The data consistently confirm that mixed-use, dense development produces greater revenues per acre than low-density patterns. In most cases, the proportion of revenue growth is exponential, not proportional, based on density increases. The "per acre" measurement is important; it is simi-lar to judging the efficiency of a car in a "per gallon" basis. Both land and gasoline are finite resources, and comparing the consumption of the resource can be the easiest way to understand the efficiency of the product. This is especially true when annexation is difficult or impossible, limiting the amount of land available.

Case Study: Sarasota County

Consider the example of Sarasota County, Florida, which asked the following question: Can properties and cashflow be isolated, geospatially, as revenue model? The state of Florida hired a consultant to assess the cost of public facilities for residential properties to help demonstrate the costs associated with spreading out land development patterns (Duncan and Associates, 1989). Using this report, an apples-to-apples comparison was made between a suburban multi-family unit and a multifamily unit located downtown.

Assuming a finite limit to the downtown example—if tax value and density were cut in half—the suburban ROI would still be much smaller. Projecting this kind of cash flow out 20 years puts the county in the red

---

*Originally published as Joe Minicozzi, "Thinking Differently About Development," *Government Finance Review*, August 2013. Reprinted with permission of the publisher.

by $5 million, using the suburban model, while the urban model shows a profit of more than $20 million. (These numbers did not account for the revenues that go to the city or the additional services the city must provide.)

Decades of research indicates that municipalities do need to account for costs and revenues within a geographic location. In addition to accounting for administrative costs, jurisdictions also need to account for the cost of government "on the ground." A municipality can be looked at as a very large real estate development corporation; in that light, city administrators would be fund managers for (in some cases) multibillion-dollar portfolios. Although we don't think of running a municipality this way, there's something to the idea.

Following this logic, a "value per acre" analytic was applied to the entire city of Mountain View. This is the hometown of Google, and as an homage, the data were exported into Google Earth, allowing users to experience the value difference in three dimensions. The results were interesting, and logical. The downtown area was expected to show a great deal of value, but the difference between that core area and immediately adjacent neighborhoods is dramatic. It should also be noted that the majority of downtown buildings have fewer than three stories.

Additionally, the data show that "downtown scaled values" were popping up in other areas of the community. This analytic helps community leaders identify the high-performance parts of the community and, perhaps, identify new policies to make the best use of those areas. High-scaled value is not limitless, but even adding more of the development patterns that are happening at the transit-oriented developments (TODs) could add significantly to public coffers.

Real estate developers are constantly looking for ways to advance their portfolios by seeking new retail tenants, looking for new properties to develop, and keeping an eye on broader capital markets and real estate trends. Savvy developers understand who is in their marketplace, who their competition is, and even what that market will look like 20 to 30 years into the future. They are also conscious of how all the parts of their portfolios are performing—giving local government officials another way to think about their communities.

The Value of Communities

Thinking differently about how local governments might be run is an argument for how we think of the places we make, and their inherent value. Jurisdictions sometimes make policy decisions that actually undermine their ability to create value. Our taxation system is based obliquely on "value" as a non-invasive way to assess a taxation rate, which is calculated through a complicated rubric that mixes in estimates of market demand and inherent value.

But assessment methodology cannot always bring about the intended consequences. For instance, a basic standard is "the larger the parcel of land, the lower its unit value on a per unit basis." The rationale is that as the unit of land gets larger, fewer buyers can afford it. Missing from that equation, however, are the public costs tied to that parcel. Land is not like a manufactured item that gets less expensive with each additional unit produced. The larger a tract of land, the more expensive it becomes to provide services to it—especially when those large parcels sit at the periphery of the community. That's because the farther away from the center of the community a piece of land lies, the more roads, pipes, and wires must be put in place to reach that land. Sending fire, police, and medical teams is also more costly. It might make sense, then, to reconsider the common practice of discounting the tax rates for owning that land.

As an example, the community had a distinct dichotomy. On one side of the street, there was a shopping mall and a parking lot, surrounded by streets, totaling three square miles. Across the street from this parcel were smaller commercial parcels, each with about 150 feet of frontage along the road. On a per acre basis, the land under the mall (not including the buildings) was valued at about half the rate of the smaller parcels—the mall received a volume discount, compared to properties that stood literally across the street. Why wouldn't land on one side of the street have the same value as land on the other?

Architecture has similar incentives. When less expensive buildings are taxed at a lower value than more expensive buildings, developers have a direct incentive to erect low-cost buildings with limited shelf lives. Many such buildings are destined to eventually sit vacant—a typical big-box retail store, for example, is designed to last, on average, about 15 years. On a square-foot basis, its taxable assessment is also much less than that of most residential properties in the community.

Time Value and ROI

Of course, assessors do not create development policy; they just have the unenviable task of figuring out "value" in a real estate marketplace that doesn't always make rational choices. Also, even though they create the pricing structures for public revenues, they are rarely brought into the conversation about the costing variables that are literally at the front stoop of the parcels they're pricing.

The time value of money and the return on the investment also need to be accounted for. As the Sarasota case demonstrates, investments made in the urban downtown area pay for themselves in just three years, compared to 42 years for development in the surrounding suburban areas. Cities might want to require a faster return for public investments—perhaps 15 years, rather than 40.

Conclusions

Jurisdictions need to look closely at their financial models for development and be sure that they are separating out the numbers considered in development decisions. This includes analyzing all the information in a comprehensive manner. Research shows that regardless of the size of the municipality, its most potent property tax-generating areas are its downtown or Main Street. Those parts of the community should, therefore, receive reinvestment commensurate with the revenue they produce, and policy should be adjusted, where necessary, to capture the costs of development patterns within a reasonable time cycle. Doing so will help keep our communities from operating in the red.

Reference

James Duncan and Associates (1989). "The Search for Efficient Urban Growth Patterns," Florida Department of Community Affairs (Governor's Task Force on Urban Growth Patterns).

28. The Search for Infrastructure-Driven Transformation[*]

WILLIAM FULTON

Upstate New York's declining industrial landscape masks one of the greatest contributions to economic development in American history. Across it lies the old, struggling industrial cities of Buffalo, Syracuse and Utica, as well as once-proud small towns like Lockport and Palmyra. What these cities and towns have in common is a prosperous history created in large part by the Erie Canal's opening in 1825. And that prosperous history holds a lesson for economic development today.

The Erie Canal is usually characterized as America's first great infrastructure project—but it was much more than that. It was America's first great economic development effort. The canal's pace seems glacial to us today: A 5 mph speed limit meant it took the better part of a week to get from Buffalo to Albany by horse-drawn barge. In fact, the canal transformed the time and geographical restrictions on the movement of people and goods—connecting the Great Lakes and America's Midwest to the Atlantic coast and Europe for the first time.

When we think of economic development, we don't always think of the transformational infrastructure project. We think of recruiting businesses and factories. Or we imagine nurturing the ecosystem of researchers, educators, entrepreneurs and financiers. Repeatedly throughout history, however, Americans have turned to infrastructure to stimulate economic development. And at a time when voters are resistant to higher taxes and skeptical about subsidies to business, they remain enthusiastic about building big infrastructure projects.

The American Recovery and Reinvestment Act was heavily tilted toward capital projects on the theory that "shovel-ready" projects could put people back to work—mostly for private contractors rather than government agencies. The Barack Obama administration is also using federal transportation money to promote "placemaking"—the creation of parks, plazas and squares that attract people in addition to simply improving travel. In California—a state that's perpetually bankrupt—state and local voters regularly resist taxes, but constantly vote in favor of multibillion-dollar bond issues for schools, parks, roads and even affordable housing. So if we're going to make big progress on the economic development front in the near future, we're probably going to have to do it by leveraging big infrastructure.

---

[*]Originally published as William Fulton, "The Search for Infrastructure-Driven Transformation," *Governing*, November 2010. Reprinted with permission of the publisher.

However, the record on using big infrastructure for economic development is decidedly mixed. Besides the Erie Canal, there are many other transformational examples—both national (the Transcontinental Railroad and interstate highway system) and local (the Houston Ship Channel, Port of Los Angeles and Dallas/Forth Worth International Airport). But there are also many make-work examples. The New Deal spent billions on public works projects to keep people working and left us with many national treasures, but it didn't pull us out of the Depression. And of course, wherever there's big infrastructure there's also big pork. State and federal funding for infrastructure projects is rarely distributed with long-term economic transformation in mind. Short-term political benefit is usually the order of the day.

The challenge facing state and local government today is not merely to spend money on infrastructure, but to spend that money in a way that will foster economic development. Economic development leaders often approach this in a one-off way—an off-ramp, rail spur or property that benefits a business they're trying to attract. Such an approach may help a specific business, and in turn, help the community. But it's not likely to lead to transformative economic development efforts. Transformative efforts are usually system wide, and they generally do one of three things:

Make it easier to move goods and people, as the Erie Canal, Transcontinental Railroad and interstate highway system did.

Make it easier to move information vital to commerce. Think of the telegraph, telephone and Internet.

Radically reduce the cost of doing business—or alternatively, greatly increase the capacity to do business. The introduction of electricity as well as the Internet served both of these purposes.

Of the many infrastructure investments on the table today in the United States, only a few serve any of these three purposes. The creation of a high-speed rail system is one. The conversion of the electricity system to a smart grid is another. Both of these are not small projects and are likelier to be efforts led by states—using federal funding in the first case and working with private electricity providers in the second.

Where does that leave localities and metropolitan areas—today's Syracuses and Lockports? These days, any metropolitan-level effort toward big infrastructure—the Houston Ship Channel, for example—is likely to include state and federal involvement. But that doesn't mean these can't be instigated locally. With major metropolitan areas facing unprecedented congestion, perhaps the most compelling infrastructure projects—at least from an economic development perspective—are those that fill small gaps but break big logjams.

Think, for example, of L.A.'s Alameda Corridor, a $2.4 billion infrastructure project, which took 30 miles of congested rail traffic out of the L.A.–Long Beach Harbor and put it underground. Or look at Philadelphia's Center City Commuter Connection. This two-block transportation tunnel built in the 1980s, at a cost of $330 million, allowed a complete rerouting of all commuter rail traffic in Philadelphia that led to a much better use of the entire region's rail system.

High-speed rail and the smart grid may turn out to be tomorrow's Erie Canals. But in a mature society such as ours, it may be that small infrastructure connections—expensive though they may be—will be transformative in the future.

29. Revving Up the Rails*

Josh Goodman

If a train leaves Charlotte, North Carolina, heading north to New York City, when won't it arrive?

It probably won't get there in 13 hours, even though that's what's listed on the Amtrak schedule. In 2006, more than 80 percent of trains on this route arrived late. And the line's performance is not unique. One-third of Amtrak trains pulled into their destination stations behind schedule. The Coast Starlight—the train that runs between Seattle and Los Angeles—was the worst: It was on time for less than 4 percent of its trips. Shorter regional routes performed a bit better than the longer passenger-rail routes, but none scored above a 90 percent on-time record.

Making the trains run on time is a vexing problem. Rails' supporters, which include state governments that subsidize passenger trains, tout train service as a necessary transportation option with important implications for economic development. But it's an option that can live up to its potential only if the trains don't turn off ridership by being late. The problem is frustrating because the source of most of the tardiness is well known: Trains hauling freight delay their passenger-carrying counterparts. And the solution is something few want to hear: massive capital investment.

The Freight Factor

By global standards, passenger trains in the United States are painfully slow at best. While trains in Europe and Asia speed along at 150 to 200 mph, in this country, an Amtrak train can be outpaced by a lead-footed motorist. Most trains aren't authorized to go faster than 79 mph.

But if foreign passenger trains zip along like Ferraris and American ones lumber along like minivans, then freight trains putter around like golf carts. Trains carrying goods often creep along at 30 or 40 mph. After all, it doesn't matter whether a shipment of coal or grain arrives in 10 hours or 15. The extra cost of moving the goods quickly, including higher costs of maintaining the tracks, doesn't justify the expense.

In many places, the minivans are stuck behind the golf carts on the equivalent of a one-lane highway. The American railroad system is bound together in a tenuous public-private partnership. Private railroads, which are freight-oriented, own the vast majority of the track, requiring the publicly managed passenger trains to share space with slower freight trains. "On-time performance is slipping and continues to slip," says Frank Busalacchi, secretary of the Wisconsin Department of Transportation,

---

*Originally published as Josh Goodman, "Revving Up the Rails," *Governing*, March 2007. Reprinted with permission of the publisher.

"because we all have these problems with freight rail."

This problem is coming to a head now because American freight rail is booming, having just completed its ninth consecutive year with record volume. This success represents a dramatic reversal for an industry that had spent decades downsizing. In an effort to stay profitable in the lean decades, the industry had been tearing up tracks and letting others fall into disrepair. Federal deregulation of freight rail in the early 1980s accelerated this process as rail companies consolidated and looked to cut costs.

Richard L. Beadles, who serves on Virginia's Rail Advisory Board, notes that railroads today are learning a lesson that any child playing with blocks already knows: It's much easier to destroy something than it is to rebuild it. "There was an appalling lack of planning and vision," he says.

Private railroads are now spending billions of dollars on improvements, but track maintenance and construction is so capital-intensive that it's a challenge just to keep up with the growing traffic. Maintenance is also a mixed blessing. Track work is necessary but compounds delays—and that's before any benefits are realized.

Officials from the private railway sector admit that, when making upgrades, their priority is to serve their investors who don't see any profit from improved passenger service. "It takes time to build capacity, and you have to make sure you're getting an adequate return on investment," says Tom White, a spokesman for the Association of American Railroads. "We can't make investments that are primarily public service in nature."

The State Role

Had this dilemma played out 15 years ago, state transportation officials might have shrugged and said intercity passenger rail was a federal responsibility. Today, however, more than a dozen states have a financial stake in intercity passenger rail, with California, Illinois, Maine, North Carolina, Pennsylvania, Washington and Wisconsin among the most active. They see passenger rail as a solution to a host of disparate problems, from congested highways to polluted air to economic stagnation.

Part of this shift is the embrace of a concept that's a dirty word in the private sector: redundancy. Roads, airports and now rail all face challenges with overcrowding. The operating theory is that none of them alone can get a growing population where it needs to go, so all are necessary pieces of the puzzle. Rail represents a way to move people from city center to city center (unlike air travel) and allow business travelers to work while in transit (which is difficult in a car). In an era of high gas prices, traffic jams and airport security delays, trains are often a more appealing way to travel than they were in decades past.

That's certainly what California has found. In 1990, Golden State voters used the ballot-measure process to provide state funding for passenger rail. One of the uses of that money was to start up service between Oakland and Sacramento, cities that are 80 miles apart and where passenger-rail service didn't exist. In 2006, the route, known as the Capitol Corridor, expanded to 16 daily round trips, with seven of them continuing beyond Oakland to San Jose. Healthy ridership (more than 1.2 million passengers on the Capitol Corridor in 2006) has been possible only through a major investment, one that Amtrak, the federal government and freight railroads weren't and aren't willing to make. But California has pumped $1.7 billion from bonds into the Capitol Corridor and two other routes since 1990.

Regional corridors such as Oakland to Sacramento are the passenger-rail system's silver lining. They're the routes where ridership is growing, new daily trips are being added and revenue comes closest to meeting expenses. And, many of the most successful routes—Seattle to Portland, Oregon; Milwaukee to Chicago; Chicago to St. Louis; Harrisburg to Philadelphia; and California's Capitol Corridor—have been enabled by state money. These investments have been fueled by states' desire to augment service and by the need to step in where Amtrak, because of its perpetual funding crisis, will not. "Amtrak has an entire country to worry about," says Karen Rae, a deputy secretary in the Pennsylvania Department of Transportation. Noting the faster and more numerous trips on the Keystone Service, from Harrisburg to Philadelphia, she added, "If this had been left to Amtrak, you would have seen minor improvements and half the service that we're providing."

Double Tracking

These gains, however, are cause for hope rather than elation. Rail still represents only a tiny fraction of intercity trips in the United States. Many transportation officials don't think that's because Americans are inherently in love with driving but rather because trains in this country are slow and unreliable. "It's where you have an appointment and end up being an hour late," says Busalacchi, who is also chairman of States for Passenger Rail. "That's where people get disenchanted and go right back to the automobile."

While the problem is intensified on longer routes, it exists on regional ones, too. For example, Amtrak's Cascade is a mid-length route from Eugene, Oregon, to Vancouver, British Columbia, and includes the important Portland-to-Seattle corridor. Only 48 percent of Cascade trains arrived on time in 2006. Freight traffic was the biggest source of delays—even though federal law stipulates that Amtrak trains be given priority over their freight counterparts.

Faced with the freight-delay problem, states have a couple of imperfect options. One is to offer the freight railways incentives— bonuses if they clear out of the way enough to let passenger trains run on time. Wisconsin has been using such incentives to get the Hiawatha—the Milwaukee-to-Chicago route—running on time. In 2006, Hiawatha had the best on-time performance of any intercity passenger line. Maine also uses the bonus approach to help get its Downeaster, the route from Boston to Portland, to the station on time.

But the inducements don't always work. Amtrak has been offering its own incentives to the private railroad companies but the freight lines have left tens of millions of dollars on the table as the passenger trains that run on their tracks have continued to be delayed. Part of the reason that these payments don't work is that the dollars involved aren't enough to influence multibillion-dollar companies.

But there are other fundamental reasons why the bonus approach doesn't work. Incentives are based on a premise that if freight railroad operators just tried a little bit harder, the passenger trains would be able to run on time. However, with the tracks overcrowded and regular maintenance necessary, delays are inevitable. Slowly, the passenger-rail community is realizing that, despite some horror stories to the contrary, their freight counterparts might be doing the best they can. "We have come to grips with the reality that the freight railroads are not out to make life difficult for Amtrak," says Cliff Black, an Amtrak spokesman. "The tracks are congested."

This congestion can be solved with fewer trains or with more tracks. Rail officials across the country talk of turning single track into double track and double track into triple, creating more parallel lines so that the faster passenger trains can pass their freight counterparts more easily. Their wish list includes new or expanded sidings—places where slower trains can pull over to let faster ones speed by. Some sidings are too short to accommodate today's longer freight trains.

But building and expanding rail service to offset rail congestion would require much bigger investments than states are making today. For example, Busalacchi longs to start up passenger service between Milwaukee and Madison, but the cost for that 80-mile project is pegged at $400 million. That kind of price tag raises the question of whether intercity rail warrants that sort of investment. The answer may be "no," unless the trains get faster.

Speed Demons

There are two keys to getting people to ride the trains: price competitiveness and time competitiveness. With regard to the latter, it's often faster to drive regional corridors—barring traffic jams— even if the trains run on time. High-speed rail would change that and state rail officials are starting to move in that direction.

Fifteen years ago, the federal Department of Transportation designated five high-speed rail corridors around the country. "What that meant was, 'Bless you, go forward and do good things with your own money,'" says Patrick Simmons, director of the rail division of the North Carolina Department of Transportation. When North Carolina got around to studying its high-speed corridor—running from Washington, D.C., to Richmond, Raleigh and Charlotte—it discovered something unusual for a public transportation project: The projected annual revenues exceed operating expenses. North Carolina and Virginia are now moving forward on a project that would have trains moving at 110 mph; they are conducting environmental impact studies that will be required to secure federal funds.

California's high-speed-rail proposal is even more ambitious: It would run trains at twice the North Carolina corridor's speed, whisking passengers from Los Angeles to San Francisco in a little over two-and-a-half hours. Supporters hope to place a measure on the 2008 ballot to supply funding for this project.

Pennsylvania is ahead of them both, having just begun running trains at up to 110 mph on the Keystone Service last fall. The project required $145.5 million in track upgrades, with costs split between the state, Amtrak and the Federal Transit Administration. With those upgrades complete, the 100-mile trip takes just over an hour and a half, slightly faster than by car. Rae says her state had two factors working for it in starting the high-speed service: First, Amtrak owns the tracks on the Keystone Service— it doesn't on most corridors. Second, the route has very little freight traffic.

Just as the tenuous freight-passenger relationship hinders present intercity train travel, it imperils its future, too. Rae's previous job was as the top rail official in Virginia. In many ways, the Richmond-to-Washington, D.C., corridor is similar to Harrisburg-to-Philadelphia: Both connect a major metropolis to a smaller capital city that is 100 miles away. But Rae says that hooking up Richmond and Washington with high-speed rail is a much tougher task and therefore more expensive. The cost of high-speed on the Charlotte-to-Washington, D.C., line, will be billions of dollars, not the millions for the Keystone Service. Don't even ask about California's high-speed project. It comes with a $40 billion price tag, which is why Governor Arnold Schwarzenegger announced in January that he opposed the rail ballot measure and preferred to focus on roads.

With no hope for help from private freight-bound railroads and limited funding of their own, state rail officials are looking to an institution that hasn't been known for its financial largesse for passenger rail: the

U.S. Congress. What they're shooting for is legislation that, besides funding Amtrak at much more generous levels, would also provide matching funds at the same formula as highways—80 percent of the cost of capital rail projects. This legislation passed the Senate last session on a 93-to-6 vote but never went any further. The bill has been reintroduced, but until something happens in Washington, states, much like the passengers aboard the trains, are left waiting.

30. Bridge to Somewhere*

ADAM REGN ARVIDSON

There is a family-owned business in Sauk Rapids, Minnesota, called Manea's Meats. It's a prominent retailer that draws shoppers from across the St. Cloud metropolitan area to this town of 12,000 on the Mississippi River.

A couple of years ago, Manea's moved its entire operation one block east to make room for a new river bridge that now touches down in the heart of downtown. It moved into a brand-new building that fronts a brand-new streetscape and sits on a newly cleared downtown site chosen especially for the store. All of this was paid for largely through federal highway dollars.

If that sounds like a pretty sweet deal for a small butcher shop, know that Manea's isn't the only land owner in town that got such help. Its building is just one of nine constructed through the one-of-a-kind Downtown Impact Mitigation program. DIM addresses businesses whose land or buildings were taken for construction of the new bridge and associated streets. The program offers financial incentives to encourage those businesses to stay downtown.

It is a logical extension of other mandates to mitigate transportation projects' environmental or historic resource impacts. DIM is, however, far more complex. Because of that complexity, and the fact that

doing this as standard practice (especially in larger cities) would open a Pandora's box of funding problems for the Federal Highway Administration, it is unlikely to happen again.

Calling a Bluff

In Sauk Rapids, the whole process began with the need to replace the old Mississippi River bridge that linked the city to St. Cloud. The bridge was to be funded, according to standard practice for replacing obsolete infrastructure, by the Minnesota Department of Transportation, the Federal Highway Administration, and two counties (Benton and Stearns).

The project would be led by the two counties, not the cities, and the initial designs were, to say the least, unappealing to Sauk Rapids. As proposed, the bridge would fly over Benton Drive (the city's main drag), turn 2nd Street (a primary downtown cross street) into an elevated roadway, and essentially divorce the commercial district from the regional transportation system.

The city rejected the design, its engineer refusing to sign off on necessary local approvals. "It was our unwillingness to participate in a transportation project that we felt would destroy downtown," remembers

*Originally published as Adam Regn Arvidson, "Bridge to Somewhere," *Planning*, November 2009. Copyright 2009 by the American Planning Association. Reprinted by permission of *Planning* magazine.

Sauk Rapids city administrator Ross Olson, "that made Benton County say, 'If you think can do a better job, then you can have it.'" The city called the county's bluff and took over.

With a new design, the city replaced the flyover with a touchdown at Benton Avenue and 2nd Street. That intersection, however, would be raised eight feet and moved westward, away from the river. It would still require significant right-of-way acquisition, and 15 buildings housing 25 businesses would be demolished.

A study commissioned by the city found that overall downtown sales could decline by as much as 30 percent. "That just wasn't acceptable to the city," says Todd Schultz, Sauk Rapids' community development director. "The businesses we would lose had nowhere to go." A major concern was that all the buy-outs would relocate to highway commercial districts outside of town, and that Sauk Rapids' historic commercial core would simply wither and dies.

This was in 2002. Over the course of the next three years, Olson and Schultz organized a team that would ultimately create the DIM program. The landscape architecture and planning firm Dahlgren, Shardlow & Uban created the Downtown Framework Plan following extensive public involvement. Next came a set of architectural guidelines for new construction. Then architect Janis LaDouceur undertook perhaps the most contentious and difficult aspect of the process: the relocation and development plan.

LaDouceur spent weeks interviewing downtown landlords and business owners likely to be affected by the bridge project, trying to place their business needs and wants appropriately within the downtown context. Her plan is an illustrative shell game that describes where an impacted business might go in the "new" downtown, what would have to be removed to clear a site in that new location, and what would

eventually be built on the sites that would be demolished and regraded during bridge construction.

Meanwhile, Olson and Schultz were talking up Sauk Rapids with various outside allies: the St. Cloud Area Joint Planning District (which maintains a lobbyist in Washington), the Minnesota Department of Transportation, the FHWA, and the region's congressional representatives. Mn/DOT and FHWA ultimately agreed to provide $8 million for the DIM, which the city could use to acquire blighted or substandard properties in the downtown area, raze existing buildings, relocate those residents, and subsidize the construction of new buildings for DIM-participant businesses.

Remarkably, little of this was controversial in the community, since many of the buildings considered blighted were well recognized as such by the townspeople. In addition, the city staff consistently focused on the overall plans for the downtown, rather than on individual buildings.

Making It Happen

Manea's is a representative case study. It relocated from Benton and 2nd Street North to make room for the new bridge touchdown. The building would be bought by the city in a typical right-of-way acquisition process.

First, according to the DIM program, Manea's would relocate to a city-owned site at 2nd Avenue and 2md Street North, which had been identified in the Framework Plan as an area that would benefit from downtown-style retail. Manea's would buy the land from the city.

Second, Manea's would have to build at least as many square feet as were demolished. This is the critical "economic mitigation" requirement for participation in the program, and it ensures that the downtown's retail square footage remains at least the same. Construction would be subsidized by the DIM, provided that the building met the design guidelines.

Finally, Manea's would agree to own the new building for 10 years, at which time the DIM subsidy would be forgiven. The big trick was coordinating Manea's move and other business relocations with the bridge construction—while disrupting commerce as little as possible, Olson notes.

With minor variations, the process was similar throughout the downtown area. Although it is difficult to put a firm number on the number of businesses involved—because some owners relocated their buildings but have new tenants—the amount of retail square footage has actually increased, says city attorney Igor Lenzner.

Status Report

The overall plan for the community is only about half done, Schultz notes. In addition to the bridge and the business relocations, the plan includes new streetscapes on the core downtown thoroughfares (complete), a new park on the old bridge abutment (in the bidding process), infill development on other vacation lots (under study for the best uses and marketing options), and improvements to other downtown businesses (partially complete).

The total price tag was more than $60 million, with funding from Mn/DOT's bridge reconstruction program, federal transportation dollars (including the $8 million DIM program), a $1 million grant from the Minnesota Department of Natural Resources for bicycle transportation, a Small Cities Development Grant, federal earmarks (thanks to legislative support and regionwide lobbying efforts), and a regional half-cent sales tax, which generated about $3 million for streetscape improvements.

Yes, the Downtown Impact Mitigation program cost taxpayers extra money. "It really does make transportation prjects more expensive; it definitely does," says Olson. "But the benefit is saving a community, saving the economic vitality of a downtown area." Olson and Schultz feel that the DIM program saved their downtown not just from an unsympathetic transportation project, but also from years of erosion of urban form.

The seeds of that new downtown are there: Two-story commercial and mixed use buildings flank the main intersection, a fitness center moved in, and all the new buildings nestle up to the right-of-way with parking lots behind or to the side. But the urban fabric is still a little spotty, with some vacant lots and run-down buildings remaining. Even Olson and Schultz admit to a few disappointments, namely an auto parts store with its back to the bridge touchdown intersection.

Still, Sauk Rapids efforts have largely been successful. "Seven or eight years ago we started a comprehensive planning process," says Olson. "We just had an incredible opportunity via the bulldozer to make it a reality."

31. Romancing the Factory[*]

WILLIAM FULTON

Not long ago, *Area Development* magazine, one of the leading site and facilities location publications in the country, released the results of its 22nd annual survey of corporate executives. The results: Cost, speed and labor force matter. Quality-of-life issues don't. Incentive packages are important but need to be tailored to the situation.

Surprising as these results may seem, they are an accurate reflection of the views of corporate executives—at least in the manufacturing sector. Almost 90 percent of the executives who responded to the survey run manufacturing companies. And that alone reveals an often-overlooked nuance about economic development these days: It's not just about the new, knowledge-based economy.

The old economy is still really important. And while technological breakthroughs and increasing skill levels are ever more important in manufacturing, some things don't change. The key criteria for manufacturers and other old-economy sectors are not taken from the pages of a Richard Florida book. The quality of the symphony and the quantity of the gay bars doesn't compute. The cost of labor, access to the rail and highway system, and the speed with which plants can get built matters a lot.

Which is why we sometimes get conflicting messages about what it takes to create economic development success these days. Different things matter to different types of companies. And although the Richard Florida-style creative companies—the ones that come up with technological breakthroughs and set the table for economic progress—want quality of life in spades, it's still the old-economy companies that actually make what we use.

And they need different things than their creative counterparts. According to *Area Development*, the six things manufacturing executives want the most—and they want these considerably more than they want anything else—are:

1. Highway accessibility
2. Low labor cost
3. Cheap and available energy
4. Skilled labor
5. Low construction costs
6. Available land

All of these things, except possibly skilled labor, are becoming harder and harder to come by in the booming metropolitan areas in the United States. These are the regions typically viewed as the winners in the nation's competition for top-level jobs—the ones that are capturing the research institutions and growth companies. And that creates an opportunity for the rest of the country.

---

*Originally published as William Fulton. "Romancing the Factory." *Governing*, August 1, 2008. Reprinted with permission of the publisher.

To a surprising degree—headlines to the contrary—we still make a lot of stuff here in the United States. According to the National Association of Manufacturers, manufacturing still accounts for almost 12 percent of the nation's gross domestic product. This is down significantly from the 1990s, but that's mostly because other parts of the economy are growing faster, not because manufacturing is declining in absolute terms. There are still more than 300,000 manufacturing companies in the United States and they employ more than 13 million people.

The future of American manufacturing will probably be a story of increased productivity, although it is not likely to be a tale of increased employment. In many ways, factories are the new farms. They require lots of capital and technology but not nearly as many people as they used to. And there will still be a considerable amount of churn—obsolete plants will continue to shut down or retool. But this means that there will be great opportunity to recruit and retain manufacturing companies. The *Area Development* survey found that 34 per-cent of manufacturing companies had expanded their operations in the past year, while 13 percent had contracted.

That's why it makes sense for cities and states to understand specifically where they should position themselves in the economic development marketplace. Sure, everybody wants to be "the next Silicon Valley," and once a decade or so somebody actually succeeds in this great quest. But not every place is a San Jose, San Diego, Austin or Research Triangle—places with great universities, a highly educated workforce, and a cachet that keeps the venture capital flowing.

Cities are likely to succeed if they're realistic about what they've got, and if they can differentiate themselves in important ways from the increasingly expensive and congested places that get all the cool "new economy" stuff.

If what you've got is highway access and land—and this is increasingly what most struggling cities have lots of—then that's what you should sell. Because, as the *Area Development* survey suggests, there are more folks out there looking for what you've got than you might think.

32. Historic Train Depot Breathing New Life into One Small Town*

JILL FITZSIMMONS

Nestled in a valley between Mount Rainier and Mount St. Helens is the small western Washington town of Morton (population 1,000). Annually, thousands of tourists speed past Morton on their way to national attractions. The town may be found at the junction of State Route 7 and the scenic byway U.S. Highway 12. The region offers fishing, hiking, and skiing at nearby White Pass. It's at this gateway to the South Cascade Mountains that Morton sits.

Still, town leaders haven't been able to find a way to pull tourists off the roads and into their timber town. Mayor Bob Worsham, who doubles as the town's historical-society president, quips that he'd like to put a gate across the highway, forcing visitors' attention to the charming town that's been his home for seven years.

Worsham just may have found his attention-getter. This past year, the Cowlitz River Valley Historical Society led an effort to move a nearly 100-year-old train depot from its original site to a more tourist-friendly location along the tracks but closer to the town's hub. The Morton Train Depot is the only remaining original structure on the former line of the Tacoma Eastern Railroad Company.

Today, some city leaders are hoping the depot will become an anchor for redevelopment in a town hit hard by the fading of the timber industry. Plans are to rehabilitate the building, not only for the purpose of developing Morton's tourism industry but also to restore the structure to a functioning train station.

The depot could indeed provide many redevelopment opportunities, says George Sharp, marketing manager for the Washington State Department of Community, Trade, and Economic Development (CTED). The key to grabbing tourists, Sharp says, is to create an experience that will make visitors want to stay in your community for more than an hour. Day visitors spend about $100 in a community, while overnight visitors spend about $200.

"All of our smaller communities are looking for a unique selling position," says Sharp, who's worked closely with Worsham on this project. The depot could be Morton's selling position and a vehicle for redevelopment, he adds: Storeowners may jump on board and clean up their buildings. New businesses may open to capitalize on tourism. What could be generated is another tourist destination for Washington, Sharp maintains.

*Originally published as Jill FitzSimmons, "Historic Train Depot Breathing New Life into One Small Town," *PM Magazine* 88, no. 5 (June 2006). Reprinted with permission of the publisher.

But pulling off such a big project in a town of little more than 1,000 people is no easy feat. Morton has no full-time economic development office. And the project has faced its share of hurdles. Originally, some community leaders opposed the project. Then, the land chosen for the relocation was found to be contaminated.

And don't forget the lack of funding for economic development in small towns like Morton. "It takes a huge amount of energy for these small communities to do something like this," says John Means, who was hired as project manager in 2004. "I can say this is really an extraordinary project for a city the size of Morton."

It was the historical society, a group primarily made up of senior citizens, that pushed this project forward, according to Means. The older generation recognizes the project's value to Morton and its future generations. "I've never seen a group that's as dedicated. They just have a long-term perspective on this," Means says. "On the one hand, they're short on resources and sophistication [about such projects]. On the other hand, they're persistent."

Railroad Tie Capital of the World

Morton, still home to many descendants of its pioneers, grew out of the logging industry. When the Tacoma Eastern Railway extended into Morton, the town was opened up to the rest of Lewis County, where the railway had prompted growth in logging companies, sawmills, and shingle mills. At one time, 100 sawmills operated in the area.

Tacoma Eastern Railroad, however, wasn't only hauling logs. In 1905, its passenger-excursion service, the Train to the Mountain, brought thousands of tourists from around the world to see the newly established Mount Rainier National Park, says Russell Holter, project compliance reviewer for the Washington Department of Archeology and Historic Preservation and coauthor of *Rails to Paradise*, a comprehensive history of the Tacoma Eastern Railroad. Passenger service from Morton continued until 1929, while the mail was delivered by train into the 1930s, Holter says.

The railroad played a big role in Morton's crowning as the railroad-tie capital of the world. Railroad ties made in Morton were shipped throughout the nation. During and after World War II, the ties were shipped overseas to Germany, Poland, China, and other countries hit hard by bombing.

Originally built just north of town in front of the Tubafor Mill, the depot remained at this location for 95 years. The balloon-framed, stick-built structure was one of about seven depots built along the Tacoma Eastern Railroad; today, it is the last on the line. The two-story building stands 32 feet high and is 52 feet long by 24 feet wide. The building looks today much as it would have looked 90 years ago.

When Tacoma Rail developed a new loading facility for the nearby mill in the 1980s, the depot found itself in the middle of the expansion plans. Weyerhaeuser sold the depot 20 years ago to the town's historical society for $10, with the stipulation that the organization move it. But that didn't happen. Over the years, the historical society secured three grants to move the building, but in 2004, the grants were in danger of expiring. Someone needed to step up and get the project moving.

A New Home for the Depot

That moving force would prove to be the Worshams. Bob Worsham, fulfilling his many roles in the community, and his wife, Eleanor, who is a historical-society member, pulled together the chamber of commerce, the historical society and the city, securing one of the early grants to get the depot moved. He says he did it because he saw an opportunity for the community to prosper. With more activity at the depot could come more jobs.

Though John Means was hired in 2004 to help the historical society move the depot, still, getting the building ready for the October 15, 2005, move was an obstacle in itself. Using the Environmental Protection Agency's brownfields model for environmental cleanup and redevelopment, Means pulled together a team of technical people with expertise in historic preservation, environmental cleanup, and community and economic development to work on the various aspects of the depot move and cleanup project.

The historical society secured more than $235,000 in state and federal grants and local contributions to relocate the historic depot. It took 14 permits—environmental, national historic preservation, and building—to negotiate the move, Means says. More than 13 government agencies are involved at some level, he adds.

Before the moving of the building, the task of lead abatement had to be done on the depot so it wouldn't be dropping lead paint chips along its route. Money was saved by contracting with the state department of corrections, which conducts a hazardous-waste training program for inmates. Inmates removed the lead paint and applied a primer to the building.

The building would be transported to the site of the former Chevron/Texaco bulk-fuel facility. Because contamination was found in the soil and groundwater, Chevron was ordered by the state's department of ecology to clean up the site. To prepare for the move, Chevron excavated what would be the depot's new foundation, pulling out 1,000 cubic feet of soil and backfilling with clean soil.

The building, of course, also had to be raised from its old foundation before it was moved. Under it were placed 70-foot-long steel beams. After being lifted onto the beams and stabilized, the depot was put on three dollies, each the size of a Mini Cooper car, Means says. The dollies could be steered individually to maneuver the depot. All was hooked onto a semitrailer and towed along the route by the moving contractor. Though the depot traveled only 1,500 feet, preparing the route took an incredible amount of planning. Trees had to be trimmed, and power, phone, cable, and fiber-optic lines lifted up and over the depot as it passed. The lines were 40 feet tall when jacked up.

The move turned into a community event. People lined the streets, cheering and applauding as the depot was moved toward its new home. The Mount Rainier Scenic Railroad joined in the celebration, offering free rides to spectators. Adding to the excitement was a film crew from the History Channel, who filmed the site preparation and the move for a new series called "Mega Movers."

Looking to the Future

The Morton Train Depot, once a forgotten icon of days gone by, could play a major role in the town's growth. Project supporters have big plans and dreams. Mayor Bob Worsham talks of a plaza being built around the depot, with gift shops, antique stores, and other tourist-friendly businesses. He'd like to see streetlights, restrooms, a loading dock, benches, and sidewalks.

Bob Worsham anticipates trains holding as many as 400 or 500 people stopping at the depot. Vehicles, maybe even carriages, will be needed to take visitors around town. Parking will be needed. He sees a modern, interactive museum at the depot that relives the history of Morton and the logging and railroad industries that played such an important role in its creation. He'd even like to see a sign out front, made from railroad ties.

While the town is a highly attractive place, it needs something to provide the motivation to pull it out of its economic downturn, Means says. Morton is on the cusp of moving forward, and the depot can provide that momentum, he believes. When community members see that an initiative of this scope can be accomplished in Morton, they'll be ready to tackle the next program: "I think so many things can build off of this project and grow from this project," Means says.

At the time this article was written, the depot was elevated about five feet in the air. A foundation is to be constructed under it, and the building lowered onto it. The next phase of the project will be exterior rehabilitation. Though the building is in good shape, much work needs to be done to restore it to its glory days. The state of Washington's U.S. Congressman Brian Baird has secured $191,000 to repair windows, paint the depot, and rebuild a passenger platform.

Project officials recognize that the depot is unique, a physical record of a time gone by. Plans are to preserve the building as closely and well as possible because it is eligible for the National Register of Historic Places.

Site-wide cleanup of the contamination also must be completed. While the ground-water aspect of the cleanup work is still in the remedial phase, the soil cleanup is scheduled for this summer, says Guy Barrett, site manager for the Washington Department of Ecology.

Once the site cleanup has been done, the project will be a strong contender for a Washington State Department of Transportation Enhancement Program grant, Means says. About $287,000 would be used for sidewalks, curbing, parking, lampposts, signage, landscaping, and benches. The next phase would be interior rehabilitation. The depot needs new electrical heating and ventilation, as well as refurnishing. The historical society petitioned the state legislature for $200,000 in supplemental budget funding. "I would say that by the end of 2007 we should have this project wrapped up," Means estimates.

For now, the Morton Train Depot is ready to come alive again. The depot is a symbol of the town's past, as well as of its future. According to John Means, "Morton really needs to get some kind of spark going, and I think this is a core project to get that moving."

33. Creating a Land Boom*

WILLIAM FULTON

Brownfields. Infill. Redevelopment. Land recycling. One of the biggest trends in economic development isn't about jobs or taxes—it's about land. Specifically, it's about reusing land that's already been urbanized but is "lying fallow" in the form of vacant buildings, parking lots and so forth. The public policy efforts in this arena are intense these days—cleaning up contaminated land, winning political support for increased densities, cataloging vacant and underutilized land in a more sophisticated way than ever before.

But there's one factor that's hard for public policy to change, and that's the recalcitrant attitude of a lot of the property owners themselves. In city after city, especially in depressed areas, property owners sit on their land—usually if they've owned the property for a long time and taxes are low. Landowners often view their property as their retirement investment or a nest egg for their grandchildren. If carrying costs are low, there's little motivation to compromise their financial dreams for short-term gain.

Now some older cities are playing with a new idea that might change the thinking of urban property owners. Actually, it's an old idea, going all the way back to Henry George, the 19th-century social reformer: the "two-rate" property tax, which imposes a much higher tax rate on the value of the land itself than on the buildings. George's idea, of course, was that land should be taxed extensively to recapture the windfall profits of speculation, which rarely came about as the result of the landowners' own actions. Today, the two-rate tax idea is being put forward with a different idea in mind: to get urban landowners off their backsides.

The idea of a two-rate system is simple. If you make it more expensive to own land and less expensive to own buildings, landowners are more likely to be aggressive about building on their land. This system has not been widely used in the United States. But many cities in Pennsylvania use it, and other depressed cities in the Northeast and Midwest are talking about it.

In many of the 20 Pennsylvania cities that use the two-rate system (Altoona, pop. 45,000, recently became the latest), the tax rate on land is four times higher than the tax rate on buildings. There is considerable evidence that the system helps. One widely cited example is Harrisburg (pop. 49,000), the state capital, which was once one of the most distressed cities in the nation. Since the early 1980s, when the two-rate system was put into place, the number of vacant structures in Harrisburg has dropped from

*Originally published as William Fulton, "Creating a Land Boom," *Governing*, August 2003. Reprinted with permission of the publisher.

4,000 to 500. Another widely cited example is Pittsburgh, where the value of building permits grew by 70 percent after the city increased its land-to-building tax ratio from 2:1 to 5:1 in 1979. Of course, lots of other things changed during that period—an urban renaissance occurred practically everywhere—but the two-rate system clearly played a role.

Not surprisingly, the idea has been examined by a number of localities in depressed Upstate New York. But in Amsterdam, the only city where it was actually implemented, it was repealed after getting caught up in confusion about a reassessment that happened to move forward at about the same time.

Then there's the question of what to do about the political clout of low-tax landowners who want a system that rewards them for sitting on their land. That's the dilemma in California, which just celebrated the 25th anniversary of Proposition 13, the tax-cutting initiative. Proposition 13 caps the property-tax rate at 1 percent, which does little to motivate landowners. But it also permits reassessment only on sale, which discourages property owners who are "sitting" on property from selling it to someone who might be more construction-oriented.

Understandably, Proposition 13 has the steadfast support of the state's millions of homeowners. But it may be also part of the reason why—in spite of astronomical land prices and bottomless demand for practically everything—older parts of Los Angeles remain a sea of parking lots, mini-malls and swap meets.

Building economic development off of a property-tax system can be tricky. To overcome the Proposition 13 problem, a two-rate system can be constructed so that homeowners' property taxes go down while non-residential taxes go up. But that brings with it a whole separate set of political problems. (The similar "split roll" idea, in which commercial property is simply taxed at a higher rate, has been a non-starter in California because of opposition from business leaders.)

Also, the need to motivate landowners is not the same everywhere; it's more urgent in depressed cities and depressed neighborhoods. And what about all those property-tax abatements? Isn't that using exactly the opposite tool to try to stimulate growth?

Property taxes can be political minefields. But a two-rate tax may be part of the solution to the economic development puzzle—especially in older cities and older neighborhoods, where landowners don't always act in the rational way that economists would expect them to.

34. A Brownfields Bonanza[*]

HOWARD LALLI

Coralville, Iowa, a heartland community of 18,500 people adjacent to Iowa City, successfully used $1.9 million Brownfields grant funding from the U.S. Environmental Protection Agency (EPA) to catalyze redevelopment of an industrial park located at the gateway to the city. The cleanup that ensued became the largest in Iowa's history, including removal of 72,000 gallons of diesel fuel, a significant coal pile, and thorough groundwater remediation. Although Coralville is still in the process of executing its redevelopment plan, the community is already realizing benefits.

In the late 1980s, the city targeted Iowa River Landing as a distressed location with great potential due to its location next to the Iowa River and Interstate 80, which is passed by more than 58,000 cars per day. Many of the vehicles are on their way to the University of Iowa and its basketball arena and football stadium, as well as the VA Hospital and the University of Iowa Hospital and Clinics, which is the largest teaching hospital west of the Mississippi River. The identified site, however, was home to waste-transfer stations, dumpsters, abandoned warehouses, adult entertainment establishments, trucking firms, and recycling yards.

Setting Priorities

Once the site was identified, the city council set priorities and work began with a volunteer committee inviting public input on an ambitious master revitalization plan for the Iowa River Landing development. The plan resulted in a design of a mixed-use district with a multimillion dollar hotel and conference center that would create an inviting gateway to the city.

Data resulting from EPA grant-funded phase I and II environmental site assessments was used multiple times over several decades to drive realization of the ambitious redevelopment. Multipronged public engagement ranged from involvement with the 75 owners of 110 parcels of land in the redevelopment area, to outreach at schools to promote education about contamination and what students can do to help clean up their environment for the future.

Engagement of property owners included addressing initial concerns that testing results would become public information. The process included helping them realize that these issues would surface eventually—whether during sale, redevelopment, or financing of an expansion—and that testing up-front minimizes the impact on a property's long-term value. Today, property

---

[*]Originally published as Howard Lalli, "A Brownfields Bonanza," *PM Magazine* 95, no. 3 (April 2013). Reprinted with permission of the publisher.

owners in the area readily seek the assessment.

The city continually sought the most sustainable possible redevelopment processes, which included recycling existing concrete streets, sidewalks, and building foundations for use as granular backfill under new streets. Recycled asphalt overlay material was stored for future use. Four metal buildings were disassembled, taken off-site, and reassembled for reuse on other sites so that the material did not go to the landfill.

Existing wetlands were not bulldozed over but rather enlarged and enhanced to become an integral part of the riverfront park for public use. Other sustainable practices that Coralville implemented included permeable paving, stormwater control, green roofs, LED lighting, and electric-car charging stations.

The Coralville Marriott Hotel and Conference Center was completed in 2006 with 286 rooms, and 6,000 square feet of meeting and exhibit hall space. The city-owned hotel generated more than $4.5 million in room revenue in its first five years. Artwork displayed in the hotel is created by Iowa artisans, and its library features books by writers who have attended the world renowned Iowa Writers Workshop at the nearby University of Iowa.

In front of the hotel, the privately financed River Bend was built with three floors of residential condominiums above 26,000 square feet of first-floor commercial development that catalyzed other private investment in the area.

During the redevelopment process, it was important to the community that an existing softball complex not be lost, so the city purchased property in other parts of the community to expand the facilities for adult and youth softball, baseball, soccer, and additional sports activities.

Greater community connectivity has also resulted from the redevelopment: Coralville and Iowa City created a new pedestrian-bicycle trail over a rehabilitated dam across the Iowa River.

At every step of the redevelopment, EPA funding—and when there were gaps between eligibility for such grants, funding from the city—made it possible to answer concerns about environmental risk. The assessments made it possible for the city to either demonstrate that there was no risk on a particular parcel or, when there was, to determine its extent and develop a plan to address it.

By 2006, Coralville had realized $140 million of investment: $70 million in the Marriott, $40 million in acquisitions and demolition, $18 million of public infrastructure, and $12 million of other commercial redevelopment.

In addition to the usual analysis, data from the early assessment was also used to negotiate property values with existing owners. The information depicted different scenarios ranging from unrestricted residential to heavy industrial use. It was used again to assist the city in ensuring that it maintained its due diligence and its liability protection as purchasers of contaminated property.

The data was used in infrastructure applications to help develop such sustainable infrastructure for the area as a cleanwater loan to create bioswales, infiltration practices, wetlands, and planning practices to minimize the stormwater runoff impacts from the development. Most recently, the assessment data is being used to help developers pursue state tax credits, once again leveraging the original EPA grants.

ICMA Partners with EPA on Brownfields Conference

Brownfields redevelopment projects often require the expertise of such multiple disciplines as environmental science, economic development, infrastructure engineering, civic planning, financing, and community development. In most jurisdictions, however, practitioners of each of those disciplines are housed in separate departments, making coordination a challenge to Brownfields' program managers.

"The key to successful redevelopment projects is effective interoffice coordination within a local government that can often be facilitated by the local government manager. ICMA, in partnership with the U.S. Environmental Protection Agency, organizes the National Brownfields Conference to educate local decision makers about sustainable land reuse and to share successful collaboration techniques. Since 2003, the conference has steadily grown from an event with roughly 2,500 registrants at Brownfields 2002 in Charlotte to more than 7,000 for Brownfields 2011 in Philadelphia; no conference was held in 2012. Brownfields 2013 is expected to be one of the largest conferences to date," according to Grant Sparks, Brownfields 2013 conference director, ICMA, Washington, D.C.

A Path of Redevelopment

Perhaps most importantly, all of this has led to formally establishing and defining a brownfields program, allowing a variety of properties to be assessed and started on the path of redevelopment, which would have been extremely difficult without the EPA grant funding.

A second phase of redevelopment has been underway since 2006, led by a partnership with the University of Iowa Hospital and Clinics. Its $70 million Iowa River Landing state-of-the-art facility opened in October 2012, serving 600 patients a day with a full-time staff of 300. The University is now in the early stages of planning for a second, similar facility in the Iowa River Landing.

Earlier in 2012, Backpocket Brewing, a 225,000-barrel production and bottling facility with public tap room, opened its doors. Just up the street from the brewery, a 100-room Homewood Suites extended-stay hotel with first-floor retail space opened in early 2013, and June 2013 will bring the arrival of an 80,000 square foot Von Maur department store. This phase of redevelopment will signal a total public and private investment of more than $300 million.

A small portion of the 60 acres of land that were transformed over the past 12 years of redevelopment, where Coralville sought sustainable processes, included recycling and reassembling metal buildings for reuse on other sites.

Tips for Successful Projects

Coralville City Administrator Kelly Hayworth is a loyal attendee of the National Brownfields Conference. "Attending these conferences helped me see what other communities have done," says Hayworth. "I've seen a range of types of reuse, and I've learned the practical aspects of getting residents and businesses involved." Here are his tips for successful redevelopment projects:

Engage the public. Coralville recognized the need for public involvement and therefore created a planning committee made up of city council representatives, leaders from the community and local businesses, university employees, and residents. Clear communication with the community as to what the master plan entailed and the process of getting there was key to the city's success.

Gain a Brownfields Education. Local governments play a huge role in brownfields redevelopment. Typically, it is the responsibility of local government officials to identify sites, create action plans, implement programs, apply for funding, and monitor a project to completion. Coralville, Iowa, City Administrator Kelly Hayworth continues to attend the National Brownfields Conference because he and his staff colleagues have benefitted from ideas and inspiration that have fueled the redevelopment of a 160-acre brownfields site in his community. "It isn't just for large cities. Small communities can take great advantage of the information at the event," he says. To learn more, visit www.epa.gov.

Harness funding. Coralville has received seven EPA Brownfields Assessment Grants to date, totaling more than $1.8 million. Obtaining grant funding is a competitive process but the determined city persistently applied for grants knowing the long-term benefits would pay off. Coralville also used a mixture of local and state funding in order to complete the project.

Create partnerships. Much of Iowa River Landing's success is attributed to the public and private partnerships that were vital throughout the redevelopment plan. At each step of the process, partnerships offered a range of expertise, guidance, and support. The EPA, Iowa Department of Transportation, Iowa Department of Economic Development, U.S. Army Corps of Engineers, city council, University of Iowa, and numerous private organizations were instrumental in this project.

During the redevelopment process, it was important to the community that an existing softball complex not be lost, so the city purchased property in other parts of the community to expand the facilities for adult and youth softball, baseball, soccer, and additional sports activities.

35. Attracting Development to Brownfields Sites[*]

Catherine Finneran

Development interest in brownfields sites has been growing steadily since the Environmental Protection Agency's (EPA) initiation of its national brownfields pilot program in the early 1990s. While, traditionally, environmental risk has been considered the major impediment to developing these sites, programs at the state and federal levels have gone a long way towards addressing these risks.

It is important to recognize that deterrents to the redevelopment of brownfields sites can come in other forms as well. Deteriorated infrastructure, out-of-date zoning, and overly complicated local approval processes often can severely hinder a brownfields redevelopment project in moving forward. With many key approvals for these projects needed at the local level, local governments are in a great position to "level the playing field" and better attract developers to these properties.

Local officials are finding new ways to streamline local approval processes, better market publicly owned sites, and offer incentives for redevelopment. These new approaches have been highly successful in attracting investment to high-priority properties in their communities.

Many developers agree: One of the most important things that a community can do to encourage development of brownfields sites, whether privately or locally owned, is to establish a single point of contact in the locality to deal with development issues.

A Single Point of Contact Is Important

Pete Pedersen is an investor in and developer of formerly industrial properties. In his company's efforts to buy, entitle, and master-plan contaminated properties, his firm, Renova Partners, LLC, has worked in several communities with no centralized point of contact for handling brownfields or development issues. The result has often been a prolonged and inefficient process of being bounced from one staff person to another. Navigating this maze can prove frustrating, and potentially can stall the progress of a development project.

In contrast, Pedersen's experience in working with the city of Phoenix has been extremely successful, thanks to the efforts of an established, central point of contact within Phoenix's office of environmental programs. When approached with an ap-

[*]Originally published as Catherine Finneran, "Attracting Development to Brownfields Sites: A Local Challenge," *PM Magazine* 88, no. 10 (November 2006). Reprinted with permission of the publisher.

propriate development proposal the city's brownfields program manager, Rosanne Sanchez, assumes the role of shepherding the project through local, county, and state approval processes.

Sanchez begins by bringing together all pertinent departments for a coordinated review of the development proposal. She also serves as an advocate for the project at the state and county levels, making first contact with outside agency staff to ensure that projects are prioritized for review. This high level of focused local attention has significantly expedited project approval and removed potential roadblocks for developers interested in locating in this community.

Unhappily, the reality is that many communities can't afford to employ a full-time staff person with the time and expertise to guide projects comprehensively through this process. Designating someone at the local level to direct questions is, however, important. Whether this person is a city or county manager, planning or economic development representative, or other staff member is relatively unimportant.

Have a Plan

Charlie Houder, senior vice president for acquisitions of Preferred Real Estate Investment, Inc., agrees that it is of key importance that a local government adopt a proactive, can-do attitude when approached by a new developer with a plan that fits the community's vision for the site.

As developer, owner, and operator of office, industrial, and mixed-use real estate properties throughout the country, Houder's company specializes in sites with environmental, entitlement, and other challenges. Houder has seen some cases in which a high level of animosity is built up between town officials and past property owners of brownfields sites because of past losses of local employment and subsequent losses to the property tax base. According

to Houder, a community must provide a clean slate for discussions with new developers so that these sites can get back into productivity as soon as possible.

A close partnership between the city of Chester (pop. 34,000), Pennsylvania, and Preferred Real Estate Investment, Inc., made the Phoenix Award winning PECO Energy waterfront redevelopment project a reality.

The 2005 EPA Phoenix-Award winning PECO Energy Project in Chester, Pennsylvania, is a case in which Houder's company has had great success in working with local officials through the development approval process. This 90-acre, former Philadelphia Electric Company property was home to an enormous coal-fired power plant that released hazardous material into the soil and groundwater, including the Delaware River. When the Pennsylvania Department of Environmental Protection and EPA began cleanup at this site, the property owner sold 63-acres to Houder's investment company to lease for offices, restaurants, shops, marinas, and housing along the city's waterfront.

Chester's city staff was committed from the beginning to working collaboratively toward offering a rigorous yet streamlined approval process. The concerted efforts of the community to help this project move forward resulted in a combined public and private investment of more than $300 million in the community, the creation of more than 2,000 jobs, and the donation of land to the city for greenspace and waterfront access.

When a local government issues a request for proposals (RFP) to sell a site, Houder suggests, it should avoid an overly burdensome RFP process. According to Houder, one of the most important things an RFP should contain is a clear path toward ownership that will ensure full site control by the selected developer.

RFPs in which the process for buying the property, or even whether the property is for sale, is left unclear will receive a relatively low response. Entering into a quasi-partnership with a locality on ownership is also not an attractive prospect. Knowing they can get site control expeditiously is highly important to interested developers.

Lowell Is a Case in Point

Lowell, Massachusetts—a Brownfields Showcase Community and mobile workshop location for the Brownfields 2006 Conference—has had great success in attracting developers to municipally owned brownfields sites. Currently, Lowell is marketing the 15-acre Hamilton Canal District site, a prime location in walking distance to the downtown and to the third-largest intermodal transit station in the state.

According to Brian Connors, director of economic development for the city, before marketing the site the city assembled the property through eminent domain and negotiated acquisitions, to ensure clear conveyance of title to the selected developer. To market the property, Lowell also developed a comprehensive Web site that contains key information on the project and the benefits of locating in the city.

World headquarters for the biotechnology company Genzyme is located on a large brownfields site in Cambridge, Massachusetts.

As a result of this Web site and an extensive marketing campaign undertaken by the city, Lowell has received hundreds of developer requests for the site's RFP. This number far exceeds the responses to other local disposition processes that Lowell has undertaken.

Another remarkable aspect of the Hamilton Canal District project is that the city will offer an expedited permitting process to the chosen developer. Once a team has been selected, Lowell will work with this developer to conduct a multiday planning charrette toward developing a master plan

for the project. The goals of the charrette will be to solicit input from the community on the reuse of the site, and ultimately, to write a form-based code that will replace the underlying zoning within the district boundary.

At the end of this process, the site will be fully entitled, eliminating the procedural delays and risks typically associated with such projects. For more information on the Hamilton Canal District project, visit the Web site at http://www.hamiltoncanal.com.

Make Incentives Available

Incentives are the most obvious draw for a developer considering locating in a particular community. According to Ed Daley, city manager of Winchester (pop. 27,000), Virginia, incentives like tax-increment financing or the creation of a community development corporation demonstrate to developers the local government's willingness to assist with a project. Daley believes that an infusion of local dollars, whether through direct funding or reduced taxes, is an important commitment that communities can make.

Phoenix, Arizona, has appropriated $4 million of its capital-improvement bond funds to provide grants to private developers and nonprofit corporations undertaking brownfields projects through their Brownfields Land Recycling Program. While this funding cannot be used for cleanup, it has proved invaluable to developers facing high infrastructure and development costs.

One project that benefited from this funding was the Copper Leaf subdivision, a 750-home, mixed-income community in the South Mountain area of Phoenix. At first, the developer hesitated to assume environmental cleanup costs above a certain amount. To give the developer the confidence to move forward, the city agreed to assume all costs over a negotiated dollar amount, using funding from these grants.

Communities can create further incentives for developers by using funding gained through federal programs. According to Cedric Kam, an economic development specialist at HUD, a change in community development block grant regulations made in May 2006 promotes brownfields redevelopment by formally including environmental remediation as an eligible cost.

The grant fund program the city of Phoenix, Arizona, created using capital improvement bond funds made the Copper Leaf subdivision project a success.

Local officials can use CDBG and Section 108 funding to offer grants and loans to developers for acquisition, remediation, demolition, and construction at these sites. Also, local governments can offer loans to developers for remediation under the EPA Brownfields Cleanup Revolving Loan Fund program.

And, of course, it is essential that a community be fully familiar with state incentives available to developers. Access to low-interest loans, tax credits, environmental insurance, and liability protection can often make a deal happen that otherwise would not.

In Massachusetts, a local government can request that the key state agencies administering brownfields programs—MassDEP, MassDevelopment, MassBusiness, and the Office of the Attorney General—work with local staff to navigate the brownfields redevelopment process. In some states, economic development agencies and brownfields organizations help communities market these sites, too.

36. Chelsea's Path to a Vibrant Downtown*

Brett Common

The last thirty years have been anything but easy for America's small towns. The reasons why are mostly due to macroeconomic factors beyond their control. Foreign competition and technological progress have hit the manufacturing sector especially hard, leaving factory towns reeling. The proliferation of big box retail has driven consumers out of downtowns and into malls. And the continuing trend toward urbanization is leaving the small town increasingly underrepresented in policy discussions.

Chelsea (pop. 5,100), Michigan—a small town about fifteen minutes west of Ann Arbor—felt these same effects. By the mid–1980s, the village (now a city) was losing its downtown. Small businesses were moving out, leaving storefronts vacant. To make matters worse, the businesses that were closing were retailers that offered useful staples—a drugstore, a grocer, and a department store. A new strip mall located closer to the interstate also created competition for businesses in the area, representing a new threat to downtown.

Today however, downtown Chelsea is thriving. It has evolved into a destination city with a blooming restaurant scene, independent retailers, and events that draw visitors into the city's core. Chelsea has been able to take advantage of its unique assets to promote growth while retaining the historic charm that visitors relish. Chelsea is not without challenges, but it successfully fought off the encroaching malady that was at its downtown's doorstep only a short time ago.

This case study focuses on key elements contributing to Chelsea's success through its downtown development story. It closes with some lessons for cities that find themselves in similar circumstances.

Realizing the Need to Change

There are almost always proactive leaders behind any positive change, and Chelsea is no different. In the early to mid–'80s, a select few citizens, city leaders, and business owners became concerned about what was happening to their downtown. Two of these leaders included Ann Feeney, a former Chelsea mayor and current councilmember; and Mark Heydlauff, owner of a downtown appliance store and current member of Chelsea's Downtown Development Au-

*Originally published as Brett Common, "Downtown USA: Chelsea's Path to a Vibrant Downtown," NLC Case Study (Washington, D.C.: National League of Cities, April 2013). Excerpt reprinted with permission of the publisher.

thority (DDA). They were seeing a downtown that was slowly dying, so with the help of other interested stakeholders, they formed a vision group and decided to do something about it.

The group got together in 1985 and outlined a vision ("Vision 1995") for the downtown, which was formulated around a very basic question: "What should the town look like?" They focused first on incremental changes intended to make Chelsea's downtown a more inviting destination—removing the electrical wiring from Main Street, improving the sidewalks, planting trees, and improving the lighting. To help fund these aesthetic improvements, Chelsea took advantage of a relatively new state law at the time that allowed for cities to designate downtown districts that could use tax increment financing (using additional revenue generated by a completed project to pay for development costs) to "correct and prevent deterioration in business districts." As a result, Chelsea's DDA was formally established in 1985 with the following goals:

- To maintain the strength of the city center as an active market—the community and the retail center of Chelsea. It is important to capitalize on the historic character of the downtown.
- To continue to enhance the historic character of the downtown through restoration and renovation, while allowing the opportunities for healthy growth that complements the existing retail mix.
- Focus on the importance of off-street parking to gain a quality pedestrian shopping environment.
- Maintain the distinction of the different character and function of the highway commercial district (I-94 and M52) and downtown Chelsea.

Chelsea took cues from the city of Northville, a suburb west of Detroit, which had successfully built a vibrant downtown using its own DDA. Like Northville, Chelsea's DDA used a combination of tax increment financing and a tax of up to 2 mills on all property within the downtown district. Northville had more land to work with and its downtown was larger, but the idea was the same: implement an effective strategy to make the downtown the centerpiece of the destination.

Making It Happen Through Collaboration

The glue that held the process together was the uncanny collaboration between all of the stakeholders involved. The DDA, elected officials, community banks, Chamber of Commerce, small business owners, and regulatory departments worked together, and were—and still are—fully invested in making Chelsea a better place. Chelsea's downtown development was truly a group effort. In order for everything to fall into place, all stakeholders had to be on the same page and committed to the plan.

Each institution in town worked together, but they also didn't step outside the bounds of what their core functions were. The DDA resisted the temptation to become a bank; it left that function to the community banks, which were committed to help fund new local businesses. The council was slow to get on board, but after it did, it became a reliable partner, consistently making it easy to operate downtown businesses by waiving fees if necessary and fast-tracking permit processes, among other actions. And the Chamber of Commerce heavily supported the development plan; after all, it would be good for business. The Chamber also helped by steering clear of political positions, focusing on serving as an intermediary between its members and the council instead, and seeking out strategic partnerships.

Chelsea's citizens had to be on board too, and they ended up providing a big boost. When the vision group was raising funds to implement the beautification plan, it came up a little short. The fully funded plan would cost about $1.6 million, but they were only able to raise $1 million through a traditional bond issuance. To fill the gap, the group ended up raising the extra funds through pledges by the citizens themselves, which, under the tax code were defined as tax deductible gifts. Councilmember Ann Feeney notes that business owner Mark Heydlauff literally "begged" for money from the community because he believed in the cause so strongly. Because Chelsea was able to raise funds directly from the citizenry, this demonstrated the significant community buy-in of the plan.

Finding a Catalyst (or Two)

A cleaned up downtown is all well and good, but if there aren't open storefronts lining the streets, there's little point in spending money on aesthetic improvements. Chelsea needed a catalyst, and it got two. One was in the form of the Purple Rose Theatre Company, a nonprofit theatre founded by actor/musician Jeff Daniels, a Chelsea native and longtime resident.

For the second catalyst, the group wanted a downtown restaurant to complement the theatre. Bob Daniels—Jeff Daniels' father and president of the Chelsea Lumber Co.—was appointed spokesperson and lead recruiter in the effort to bring a fine-dining restaurant to Chelsea. He approached Craig Common, a metro Detroit chef looking for a building to open his first restaurant (disclosure: Craig Common is my father). Common recalls Daniels being "very positive" about the prospects of Chelsea's downtown and portrayed a clear vision as to what the town needed (and wanted) to be suc-

cessful. Common took the plunge and eventually opened The Common Grill in an old vacant department store in the middle of the downtown. Both the theatre and restaurant, now Chelsea institutions, opened in 1991.

Heydlauff claims that they didn't quite know what to expect when the Purple Rose and Common Grill opened downtown. Fine dining and fine arts aren't traditional small town staples. But it turned out that they were both instrumental in providing momentum to the town's development efforts. The theatre, combined with the restaurant, brought patrons into Chelsea's downtown from close by and from out of town and kept them there, allowing for pedestrian traffic in the shops on the main drag.

Does a Friendly Business Environment Create Vibrancy, or Does Vibrancy Create a Healthy Business Environment?

Chelsea's development strategy was about creating a vibrant downtown that was friendly to business, but would also provide a desirable quality of life. Bob Pierce, executive director of the Chelsea Area Chamber of Commerce, alluded to the element of vibrancy and the importance of creating a sense of place when discussing the role of the Chamber in downtown development. The Chelsea Chamber, while focused on business, puts a lot more weight in community responsibility and a belief that if a community is desirable, vibrant, and offers a superb quality of life, business will follow.

In recent years, business has followed, particularly in the restaurant sector, bringing to Chelsea dining options not always associated with small Midwestern towns. Adding to the trend of the flourishing microbrew scene in Michigan, Chelsea Alehouse Brewery opened its doors in January. Back to the Roots, a fair trade clothing store/knick-knack shop/tea and coffee house/ sushi bar that gives at least 25 percent of revenues to charity opened in the summer of 2011. It's a creation that seemingly opened in the wrong location, opting for small town Chelsea instead of hippified Ann Arbor, only a few miles away. But one of the owners of the business finally moved to Chelsea after "hearing about Chelsea as a destination" from his business partner. And Chelsea just welcomed a barbecue restaurant, Smokehouse 52, a homage to M-52, the road that cuts through downtown.

Phillip Tolliver, the man behind Smokehouse 52, is a Chelsea native and wouldn't think of opening his flagship restaurant anywhere else. He can testify to the incredible support he received from the city, as well as community residents, when preparing to open. In Tolliver's words, he "couldn't have asked for any more," from the city council and DDA. Anything he needed was done "instantly" and they were extremely helpful in guiding him through the paperwork process. Tolliver's commercial kitchen hood cleaner even remarked that the building department inspector must be his uncle, since they worked so well together.

The restaurants and independent retailers that line Main Street draw visitors into Chelsea's downtown, but the city has also focused on holding festivals and events that attract visitors from outside the area. One such example is Sounds and Sights, an event held every Thursday throughout the summer in which impromptu stages are set up throughout the downtown for musicians, artists, and performers to entertain pedestrians that are shopping, eating, or just wandering. Also, an annual Sounds and Sights Festival draws a large number of guests into town each summer. These events are funded and operated mostly by Chelsea's private businesses in conjunction with the DDA and other public stakeholders.

Measurable Progress

In small towns, it is often relatively easy to see if the town is doing well just by strolling through its center. If there is a healthy amount of pedestrian traffic and minimal vacant properties, it is safe to say that the town is probably on firm economic footing. There have been some recent closings in Chelsea's downtown district, but for the most part, it is a bustling environment and most storefronts are filled. The Chamber of Commerce also captures tourist inquiries, queries for events, membership information, etc., and in Chelsea, these metrics have all steadily increased over time.

Raw data from Chelsea's downtown bears out the success of its development strategy. In 1985, the State Equalized Value (50 percent of market value) of the property in Chelsea's designated downtown district was approximately $4 million, which is almost $9 million in 2012 dollars. In 2012, the SEV of Chelsea's DDA property was approximately $26 million—an increase of around 196 percent.

Today, Chelsea's downtown makes up 9.5 percent of the city's total tax base, up from 9 percent in 1985. According to city administrator Kim Garland, the reason why this figure has not increased dramatically is that the city outside the downtown has grown significantly in that time. So while the downtown district's slice of the economic pie has grown exponentially, the city's overall pie has expanded as well. This growth included an expansion of the local hospital (one of the city's biggest employers), a residential boom, and a new business plaza located outside of the downtown, among other developments.

There Will Always Be Skeptics

Chelsea's development has not been without challenges. Whenever potential changes are introduced in any environment, there are bound to be stakeholders or residents that aren't willing to take risks or make drastic changes. In Chelsea's case, the city council, along with a smattering of local residents, were initially hesitant to disrupt the status quo.

Once again, local businessman and DDA member Mark Heydlauff proved resilient, visiting dissenting citizens individually to try to get them to understand what this whole process meant—that the downtown truly holds the town together. He understood that Chelsea was taking a big risk and making a huge investment, but the way the city was going, something had to give. And by creating a downtown worth visiting, this could potentially spur growth outside the downtown district, which would bolster the town's tax base.

The best way to change the opinions of skeptics is to produce visible successes. Once Chelsea's residents and Council started to see the positive changes that were taking place and the momentum it created, it was easy for them to be supportive.

What Does the Future Hold?

Immense challenges lie ahead for Chelsea. While the city made it through the 2008 financial crisis relatively unscathed, macroeconomic pressures continue to mount. The recent closing of a longtime hardware store and the relocation of both the post office and a small independent market out of downtown is evidence that Chelsea is not—and may never be—out of the woods.

The closure and relocations has brought to light a challenge that all of the community leaders stressed is a daunting issue, which is losing the ability to bring citizens downtown to buy essential products. Heydlauff cautions against becoming a "restaurant row," where all other retail is conducted out of the central core at big box franchises. Feeney stresses the need to maintain downtown as a destination for the local population; it needs to be a place where people buy ordinary products. She makes clear that if a city doesn't have a credible plan for supporting local retailers, big box stores can and will have a negative impact.

Lessons from Chelsea

Like a lot of small towns, Chelsea has a lot of history and great architecture within its downtown district that provides a lot of charm. Also, one of the largest state parks in Michigan's Lower Peninsula is located right on Chelsea's doorstep. It's important to identify and preserve key assets that lie in or around a city's region. Chelsea made sure that these assets would be preserved alongside economic growth. Pierce says that the city can parlay these two assets to "balance nature and commerce," further contributing to Chelsea's sense of place.

Being a small town has some disadvantages, namely a lack of resources to initiate large-scale development projects, but it also has some great advantages that fly under the radar. Small towns can be more nimble in their business development practices. This means more quality face time with current and prospective businesses and quicker and more effective responses to questions or issues that arise. Chelsea's regulatory apparatus has taken advantage of this by expediting permitting processes and committing to exemplary customer service.

In Chelsea, because of its small size, everybody knows everybody else, and this isn't necessarily a bad thing. Its sense of community contributed to the unlikely procurement of funds from the citizens themselves. It also bred a collaborative and group mentality amongst the business owners and city leaders that ultimately led to a focused strategy for economic development. Heydlauff stressed the importance of Chelsea's development being funded with private dollars, which meant that the community had a stake in seeing positive returns on their investment.

Developing a lively downtown is a formidable challenge for small towns, especially when facing so many challenges in the short- and medium-term. But with a committed and passionate group of leaders, a collaborative can-do environment, buy-in from citizens, persistence in the face of skepticism, and a few key catalysts to get the ball rolling, a seemingly nondescript town can transform from empty storefronts to a regional destination in no time.

37. Top Ten Myths of Downtown Planning*

PHILIP WALKER

The 1970s were an innovative era in design for many facets of American life, including clothing, hairstyles, architecture, and, yes, urban planning. By the early 1970s, a number of forces were already in full play, resulting in unparalleled residential and commercial growth in the suburbs and a steady spiral downward for many downtowns.

In a desperate attempt to turn that situation around, numerous downtowns across the country jumped onto the pedestrian mall bandwagon. In an effort to compete head-to-head with suburban shopping malls, these downtowns blocked off vehicular access on their primary retail streets in order to create open-air pedestrian malls.

Because the market forces that were causing the downtowns' downfall were much larger than the issue of vehicular access, these panic-stricken efforts, not surprisingly, did little to reverse the fortunes of these downtowns. In fact, in most cases, the "malling" of Main Street only exacerbated downtown's problems, resulting in a slow and painful death for many of them.

During the 1970s, Burlington, Iowa, then a town of 26,839 people, converted the block of Jefferson Street between Main and Third streets into a pedestrian mall. By the late 1990s, it was clear that the pedestrian mall was not helping businesses along that block, so the downtown organization, chamber of commerce, and business association pressured the city to reopen the block to automobiles.

Downtown Allentown, Pennsylvania, erected a canopy along Main Street on the same day that its first suburban mall opened, but it was recently dismantled and replaced with historic streetscape furnishings. Even major cities with seemingly critical masses in their downtowns, such as Louisville, Memphis, and Seattle, have undone their downtown pedestrian malls to reintroduce vehicular traffic.

These failed examples are not an indictment of all pedestrian malls. Some large downtowns, such as those in New York City and Baltimore, can support them. College towns, such as Charlottesville, Virginia, can support them. Those cities constituting both, such as Madison, Wisconsin, can clearly support a pedestrian mall, as evidenced by State Street.

However, because the "mauling" of Main Street resulted in failure for so many other communities across America, not to mention

---

*Originally published as Philip Walker, "Top Ten Myths of Downtown Planning," *Planning*, June 4, 2009. Copyright 2009 by the American Planning Association. Reprinted by permission of *Planning* magazine.

the tragedy of "urban renewal" programs that razed countless blocks of historic architecture, the 1970s are rarely recollected by most downtown advocates with any degree of nostalgia. In short, any downtown master plan proposing a pedestrian mall should be met with extreme scrutiny before receiving a stamp of approval.

The true essence of every downtown plan is a collection of ideas. The misinformed notions below are among those frequently voiced by citizens, sometimes voiced by elected officials, and occasionally voiced by professional planners and downtown "experts" who should know better. Many have some element of truth, but none is entirely accurate.

1. Our downtown just needs one "big ticket" development to turn things around. Rarely does a "quick fix" really repair a downtown over the long haul. Developments such as sports facilities and casinos can vanish as quickly as they arrived, and even if they stick around, their novelty to the public may not.

Downtowns that have reversed their downward spirals to become success stories have typically done so incrementally, through numerous small steps over time. Most struggling downtowns did not reach their current conditions overnight, so turning them around overnight is unquestionably unrealistic.

2. Replacing some existing buildings with parking lots will bring more shoppers downtown. Buildings are the most fundamental element of any downtown. Generally speaking, more buildings in a downtown—particularly occupied ones—are better than fewer buildings because the activities that occur inside them attract people and their money. People do not visit downtowns to park their cars.

Furthermore, in the case of historic or unique buildings, it is their character that helps make the downtown unique. While parking lots located interior to their blocks are necessary, those fronting directly onto streets create dead spaces along the streetscape and are visually unattractive. Parking is a challenging issue for most downtowns and one that must be addressed, but razing buildings is rarely the long-term solution.

3. Our strategy for revitalizing downtown should focus on retail. Successful downtowns enjoy a rich mixture of diverse uses, including offices, housing, institutions, entertainment, and, yes, retail. However, a singular focus on retail is usually an ill-advised strategy, despite that fixation for so many downtown revitalization programs.

In fact, given its importance to most downtowns, housing is often the best bet of any component of downtown to promote—though success with housing is frequently difficult to achieve. In addition to providing further market support to retail and other uses, residents make their downtown feel inhabited and safe, thereby attracting those living outside of downtown to visit for shopping, dining, cultural events, and other activities.

4. Attractive new brick sidewalks will bring more people downtown. New sidewalks, as with streetscape improvements in general, are certainly useful in broadcasting a message that downtown is important to the community. As part of a comprehensive urban design strategy, they will sometimes even stimulate adjacent private development, which can indirectly attract more people to the downtown. However, very few people visit downtowns simply to enjoy their high-quality sidewalks, so their value must always be kept in perspective.

5. Downtown needs a large national department store to compete with the suburban malls. Unless a downtown is large enough to enjoy the market support of thousands of people on any given day, in most cases time should not be wasted trying to recruit a national department store. National stores' numeric criteria for trade-area employees, residents, and vehicular traffic, as well as sales volume potential per square foot, are typically too high for all but the largest downtowns to meet. Instead, most downtowns are better served by focusing on niche retailing that suburban malls are not filling, in addition to other uses such as offices, housing, and institutions.

This principle does not preclude targeting smaller stores that happen to be national chains or franchises, as a limited number of such tenants are usually desirable to supplement locally owned businesses. However, unique, independently owned stores are among the strongest draws for most downtowns.

6. On-street parking should be converted to another driving lane to improve traffic flows for the benefit of downtown. The inability of vehicles to flow quickly through its streets is not the root of a downtown's problems. A lack of destinations to attract vehicles and their drivers to the downtown is more likely the challenge. On-street parking is important as a convenience to shoppers and diners, as a traffic calming device for drivers, and as a physical and psychological barrier protecting pedestrians from moving vehicles. The conversion of on-street parking to driving lanes simply results in faster moving traffic that makes downtowns less pedestrian-friendly and less business-friendly.

7. Existing one-way streets should be maintained for traffic flows that will benefit downtown. Even more alarming than simply maintaining the status quo, some communities that are still stuck in a 1960s mind-set will proactively contemplate the conversion of existing two-way streets into one-way couplets. One-way traffic is more beneficial to through traffic than it is to traffic for which downtown is the destination.

For most downtowns, one-way streets prove unnecessary and even counterproductive because they encourage speeding, limit the visibility of retailers, and are con-

fusing to new visitors to downtown. Confused visitors can easily become irritated visitors, and irritated visitors may never return.

From a traffic flow perspective, one-way streets create many of the same problems caused by the conversion of on-street parking into driving lanes, which, in turn, can generate the need for remedial traffic calming measures.

8. Downtown special events are a waste of time and money because few dollars are spent in businesses during the events and a great deal of preparation and cleanup are required. In most cases, special events are more important for their long-term benefits than for their short-term gains. Special events often attract some people who rarely or never frequent downtown, but their attendance at a downtown event makes them aware of businesses or activities that they might seek out at a later date.

Furthermore, a positive visitor experience during special events can reap tremendous future rewards, including word-of-mouth advertising. Given the relatively low costs of preparation and clean up, particularly if volunteers are mobilized, special events are a worthwhile form of promotion when strategically linked to the downtown's particular marketing strengths.

9. One of downtown's primary streets should be closed to traffic and converted into a pedestrian mall. While that concept was in vogue during the 1970s, downtown experts are now recommending that these streets be transformed back to drivable ones. Most Americans are still, and might always be, too automobile dependent to completely abandon their cars. Pedestrian malls typically work only in downtowns that have a high resident or employee density, large volumes of tourism, or some other unique circumstance, such as an adjacent university.

10. Too many regulations will kill downtown's businesses. Perhaps in theory it would be possible to regulate a downtown to death, but not in political reality. Politicians enacting a detrimental level of regulation would likely be voted out of office. Well-crafted and detailed codes, such as design standards for buildings and signs, might be considered overly stringent by some, but they can clearly elevate the quality of the built environment if used properly.

A physically and aesthetically enhanced downtown typically results in increased property values because of one simple principle: Real estate values are ultimately based upon the degree of a place's desirability. While the associated increased rents can result in some businesses having to relocate, they are usually replaced by more profitable ones.

Some of the most highly regulated downtown districts in America, such as Princeton's Palmer Square, Charleston's King Street, Cambridge's Harvard Square, and New Orleans's French Quarter, are also some of the most commercially successful. In fact, in 2005, the Old Town district in Alexandria, Virginia, added yet another regulatory layer to limit chain stores and ground-floor offices, yet its virtues as a fertile environment for prosperous businesses show no signs of abating.

38. Revitalizing America's Downtowns During This Century[*]

Roger L. Kemp

Many residents have left downtown areas for the suburbs over the years. A considerable number of businesses also have moved from downtowns to shopping malls over the years. Much of this was brought about by the development and expansion of our nation's interstate highway system, a product of the mid–1950s, which is still evolving today! Traditionally, a family wanted to raise children in a single-family house with a yard, away from the traffic and noise in the downtowns. This seemed like the American Dream for many years, but it is now changing.

A quick overview of American history would reveal that as our highway system expanded, residential subdivisions were developed in the suburbs. Families moved there for the reasons noted above. This trend went on for several decades. When I was a young child, a typical family owned one car. As mothers went to work over the years, they acquired cars, too.

Now, it seems like children older than the legal driving age in every state have cars. I recall seeing old homes with single-car garages, newer homes with two-car garages, and more recent homes with three-car garages. I was recently visiting one of our nation's growth states, and I saw some homes with four-car garages. Wow!

But things are changing! Parents of grown children would like to relocate in urban, downtown areas. Young professionals would like to focus on their jobs before starting families. They wish to locate in inner-city areas and relocate to the suburbs later in life.

There's also another group, consisting of those folks who would like to live their lives without having a vehicle, hence the new type of residential developments, called transit-oriented developments, located near public transit stations. There is also a rapidly developing market for condominiums and townhouses that are located next to public light-rail transit systems.

There is a national need—a community one, too—to make downtowns attractive, which requires a redevelopment effort to make them more livable. Such positive movements require states and their local governments, and especially those folks who are responsible for managing downtowns, to advocate for changes that will benefit downtown areas. I think history has gone, or is going, full circle in this regard.

I was recently looking at a century-old

[*]Originally published as Roger Kemp, "Revitalizing America's Downtowns During This Century," *PMPlus* 92, no. 11 (December 2010). Reprinted with permission of the publisher.

picture of a high-rise residential area in the Lower East Side of New York City. Individuals and families lived in residential structures several stories high, with an assortment of commercial businesses located on the ground floors of these buildings. All of the restaurants, markets, and other types of commercial activity took place at street level. Then, over the years, we separated our zoning areas based on different land uses. The thinking was that you would not want citizens living in commercial or industrial areas. This way of thinking is now rapidly changing.

If communities want to revitalize downtown areas, they must change the zoning laws to allow for mixed uses of commercial (on the ground floor) and residential (on the floors above that). Also, arts, entertainment, and culture are coming back downtown. Communities are using libraries and museums as tools to stimulate economic development.

Also, communities are trying to lure educational institutions and nonprofit organizations back downtown. I've also read that some states are relocating their offices from the suburbs back into downtown areas. There's a big trend to preserve what's left of nature as well as restore what's been removed over the decades and also expand various aspects of nature. These restorations include parks, wetlands, waterways, and ways to enhance pedestrian access and movement through the use of walkways, bikeways, plazas, and the widening of public areas to accommodate people instead of cars.

I've always thought that our downtowns were designed by cars. It seems like people were a secondary consideration. Times have changed! Streets are now getting narrower and are losing lanes. Sidewalks are getting wider as well as greener. This trend has facilitated the movement of people back to downtown areas! It's also great for commercial businesses established on the ground level to have their customers residing above

them. No need for those one-story commercial centers and blocks of the past. Rezoning them and placing residential units above them is the wave of the future. If you build them, people will come, especially if there's public transit in the area.

Here are some of our nation's major evolving downtown trends:

- Restore and enhance all aspects of nature.
- Build mixed-use buildings that are multistory in height.
- Make public transit available, usually light rail systems.
- Restore the public infrastructure to favor people over cars.
- Combine landscaping with the restoration of all aspects of the public infrastructure.
- Convert surface parking lots to parks, gardens, and open spaces.
- Attract culture, arts, and entertainment facilities.
- Attract educational institutions and nonprofit organizations.
- Move smaller, specialized businesses downtown.
- Encourage downtown locations for such ethnic and niche stores as markets, delicatessens, bakeries, and restaurants.
- Restore a sense of public place in the core of our new downtowns.

Above all, these trends make our downtowns more people friendly, rather than favoring the movement and parking of vehicles. Items on this list, if accomplished by a local government, would stimulate the local economy and attract the type of businesses, educational institutions, and nonprofit organizations that would benefit the rebirth and growth of a downtown area.

Additional incentives would further facilitate the attraction of desirable private, educational, and nonprofit sector additions. These incentives typically include:

- Low-interest loans.
- Façade improvement programs.
- Provision of a friendly development process.
- Property tax incentives, usually in the form of reductions or rebates.
- Zoning to accommodate mixed land-use developments.
- Public investments on downtown improvements.
- Programs to market the new image of your downtown.

As we all know, to sell economic development incentives to local public officials, they must be reasonable as well as promise a long-term benefit to taxpayers.

More important, those public officials elected by the citizens must feel comfortable with such incentives as well as feel that they will improve their downtowns. Downtowns must also benefit all of the citizens within the community. A nice downtown should serve as a great public place not only for those folks who live there but also for other residents in the community, too. They should be attracted to "their" downtown, and they should also feel comfortable within the entire inner city area, including the surrounding neighborhoods.

Both elected and appointed officials should always keep in mind that prudent economic development incentives are a wise way to increase a local government's revenues without raising its taxes. During these difficult economic times, the above practices should be embraced and facilitated by politicians, downtown professionals, and citizens alike, since they will assist in balancing their community's budget with the increased revenues that result from renewing a community's downtown.

Most communities evolved piecemeal over the years and now need to be retrofitted and redesigned for the future. Planning and zoning regulations should be in place to accommodate mixed-land-use, infill, and redevelopment projects. Call it new urbanism, sustainability, pedestrian communities, healthy communities, inner-city renewal, or the green movement, whatever you wish. We must all work together to get things moving in these evolving positive directions.

The practices facilitated by these downtown trends can be increasingly applied to projects of all sizes—from a single building, to a full block, to a neighborhood, and even to an entire community.

39. Debunking Time
12 Myths About Downtown *

MARK BRODEUR

Successful downtowns are distinctive and unique.

Still, many communities seeking to improve their downtowns hold a set of beliefs about problems and solutions which may—or may not—be consistent with the way their specific downtowns function.

One dozen myths about downtown redevelopment are so persistent that they regularly reappear. By impulsive, emotional, or copied from other successful downtowns have very limited application.

Myth #1: What We Need Is a Film Festival. Some downtown advocates take the Silver Bullet approach to revitalization. They base an entire revitalization effort on landing a department store, baseball team, examining them, it's possible to ferret out what can be truly useful in downtown development. Moreover, it's possible to discern that approaches to revitalization that are library, or major event like a film festival. This approach is a house of cards because if that one thing doesn't come downtown, the rest of the plan doesn't work.

Many communities have proven this myth by actually attracting the Film Festival or department store and then thinking that their revitalization work was done. They waited for customers and investors to return. And they waited for customers and investors to return. And they waited.

Unfortunately, these communities discovered that attracting one major user does not result in renewed downtown vitality. Instead, the lesson to be learned is that a Silver Bullet only works when it's in conjunction with economic, design, and other promotional elements to support revitalization.

Myth #2: Zone for Vertical Mixed Use. Think of this as Silver Bullet, Part Deux. It's a revitalization strategy based on the notion that one type of land use solves everything.

Due in part to California's housing shortage, new urbanists think that mixed use is the new panacea. Mixed use can be good for a downtown if it isn't forced into areas where it may have never been historically.

A downtown without mixed use is not predetermined to die. There are several successful downtowns without mixed use zoning in place. This occurs primarily where there is single-story retail on Main Street, and housing is in close proximity. Typically, if residential uses are allowed close to Main Street, then introducing vertical mixed use for the sake of nostalgia can be a controversial forced effort. What's critical is to

*Originally published as Mark Brodeur, "Debunking Time: 12 Myths About Downtown," *California Planner*, January-February 2006. Reprinted with permission of the publisher.

have a local residential populace within walking distance, say within four or five blocks.

Myth #3: Get a Theme. The Disneyfication approach to downtown revitalization is rarely successful. Downtowns are a reflection of a community's past, and the past can be translated into a variety of architectural building styles. People consistently return to what's real, to areas with a sense of place and scale, not thematic shopping centers with franchises and plastic signs erected and finished in an eight-month construction span.

Of course, downtown merchants sometimes equate the economic success of suburban malls and lifestyle centers with thematic architecture and consistent sign programs. They believe that if a place has order and control, then all they need do to sit back and reap the benefits.

Two notable downtowns have used the theme approach successfully, and both are principally tourist stops. One is Solvang, California, and the other is Leavenworth, Washington.

One is Bavarian, and the other is Danish. It has to be the pastry!

Myth #4: Parking Is the Problem. Every downtown likes to blame its woes on parking. Frequently, people perceive that there is a parking problem if they cannot park directly in front or behind the actual business that they are visiting. Often, the supply of parking in downtown is adequate; yet, the directional signage to the parking is nonexistent. In those instances, it is only the savviest of residents who know where the best parking spots are.

This circumstance surely makes the case for better downtown parking management, consistent clear signage, and enforcement of parking regulations. It's almost never about more spaces.

Myth #5: McDonald's Will Ruin Our Quaintness. This attitude is another version of David v. Goliath: if we keep Goliath out, we'll be fine! Turns out that quite the contrary is true.

Franchise businesses weigh their location selections very carefully before committing to an area. The fact that a reputable franchise wants to make its home in your downtown should be viewed as a very positive economic indicator. What your downtown has to do is make sure that the franchise storefront fits with the architectural character of its location. You certainly don't want your downtown transformed into a row of gaudy plastic signs, false mansard roofs, and illuminated blue awnings. You have the right to control it.

So how does a downtown stay true to its unique character, retain local business, and be successful?

Downtown Coronado (pop. 23,500), California is a National Main Street "Best Downtown." It has adopted zoning regulations limiting the number of franchise establishments allowed in its downtown. Coronado's approach was to allow enough franchises to show a healthy economic picture, but not so many as to homogenize the flavor of local entrepreneurial establishments. Coronado adopted design guidelines and standards that essentially prohibit the corporate look of chain stores.

Myth #6: Everyone Should Open During the Same Hours. During the last ten years, downtowns across the country have attempted to standardize the hours of operation kept by retailers. Think about it for a minute.

Should the children's toy store stay open as late as the Starbucks? Or as late as the local tavern? This is the "Let's-Pretend-We're-a-Mall" approach.

Given the independent nature of local business owners as well as the costs involved in staying open late, this approach has failed repeatedly.

Recognizing that a single set of uniform business hours is difficult to achieve, and possibly not advantageous to the district's retailers as a whole, the most successful efforts are promoting "customer-driven" business hours. With this approach, retail businesses stay open late one evening per week. Once customers get comfortable with those hours, expand the hours later on other nights. Uniform retail hours are impossible to achieve in a downtown setting. Instead, customer-driven hours, kept and coordinated by businesses that can share customers, are the secret to success.

Myth #7: Competition Is Bad for Business. This is the "Head-In-The-Sand" plan for revitalization; a better approach would be "Head-to-Head."

The most successful commercial districts have compatible businesses located side by side in convenient clusters, proving that groupings of compatible merchants are actually good for business.

Rather than providing dangerous competition, retail clustering expands and magnifies the focused audience that retailers want to draw. This occurs because convenience and variety attract customers.

Prime examples of successful downtown retail clusters include the art galleries clustered in Laguna Beach or Palm Springs, offbeat clothing boutiques on Melrose in Los Angeles, and antique shops in Pomona, California.

Myth #8: Brighter Is Better. While an unsafe downtown is bad for business, making streets as bright as a prison yard is certainly not the answer either. There is a fine line between providing an adequate amount of light and giving the appearance of solving a crime problem.

The approach to lighting public spaces has to consider two elements.

First, lighting sources must be varied. Simply providing streetlights is not enough, and streetlights alone are often not attractive to pedestrians. The warmest type of light is reflected off building surfaces. This light is more sensual and avoids overly bright hot spots. Look for alternative light sources such as storefronts, bollards, and architectural wall wash lighting.

Second, the brightness and color of the light must be correctly matched to the public space. Super bright streetlights with a yellow tinge make pedestrians cringe and give off the wrong message about a place.

Myth #9: Downtown Will Re-emerge as the Community's Retail Heart. It is time we all start admitting that for most downtowns, reestablishing or becoming the retail heart of the community is unattainable. Once the malls opened and then the big box Costcos and Walmarts moved in, the game was pretty much over for most small independent retailers who sold similar goods and didn't offer extraordinary service.

Some downtown organizations are just too stubborn; they refuse to see the writing on the wall. The fact is that unless the small, independent downtown retailer offers unique product lines or superior customer service, the big retailers maintain a huge price point advantage. While we all like to think we "buy downtown," we still go to K-Mart to buy anti-freeze for our car.

Americans love our big boxes. They give us discounted prices, easy parking, and endless retail choices. Making matters worse is that many of us are now shopping online.

Turning our downtowns into cultural/entertainment or specialty retail areas will dominate the restructuring of our inner cities, and create a truly thriving destination for communities. Also, housing in and around an urban center has suddenly become vogue. Empty nesters, young urban professionals, and two-income couples will stabilize the market for downtowns. Inner cities that cater to this market segment can provide entertainment, government, specialty retail, culture and restaurants that are interesting and upbeat.

Myth #10: Design Controls Scare Developers Off. Pure nonsense. In fact, quality developers prefer to do business in communities that demand quality projects. By using design guidelines, they know their investment will be protected. Developers do not want to create a beautiful building design if they suspect that the vacant lot next door is going to be an architectural atrocity.

The most successful revitalizations are the result of partnerships between the community, city government, and local developers. These partnerships can be highly successful in providing a quality project for the community and an economically successful project for the developer. The essential ingredient for making the partnership work is attitude. All parties in the partnership must agree to cooperate, so that a mutually beneficial project derives from all the hard work.

Myth #11: Don't Do Anything Until We Have a Market Study. While this myth presumes "A Technical Study Will Protect Us," it's more like a CYA approach. Instead of first performing a market study, downtown stakeholders should envision what types of uses they want. This serves two purposes. First, it shortens the list of potential targets the economist will study, and it also avoids having the economist report to the downtown association that a Costco, Home Depot, or auto dealership shows real promise in downtown. Yikes!

Keep in mind that it is the mix of retail uses that is most important in making a downtown successful. An economist can rarely pinpoint the actual uses that are specifically needed for a successful downtown district. What an economist does is report the market segments that could be fulfilled within the city limits. The economist can suggest business sectors that are saturated, neutral, or needed. So, figure out what mix of uses you want in your downtown, and then hire an economist to ascertain if the market will support that mix.

Myth #12: Downtown Needs Drive-By Traffic. This is the largest myth out there! It presumes that the more cars that drive by a business, the better retail sales are. This is the highway strip approach to downtown revitalization. This premise is partially true but for only a few select market sectors, such as convenience stores or gas stations.

What is important is to have cars that have downtown as their destination, not a place they drive through to get to another place. Pedestrian-friendly downtowns need walkable, human-scale streets, with easy parking, not two-lane mini highways.

Countless cities across the United States have state highways running through the heart of their downtowns. In most places, the highway commercial uses that originally located along the state highway have relocated outside of downtown.

And in Conclusion… Myths are exactly that—myths—and are not real solutions. A collaborative solution between planners, designers, the community, and public agency decision-makers is the answer to a community's needs. Communication throughout the process is the key to a successful downtown revitalization effort.

Though solutions to any downtown revitalization are as varied as the downtowns that implement them, it is critical for each downtown to start with an open and honest dialogue about its strengths and weaknesses. Adopting solutions that may have been right in Timbuktu are foreign to your community's environment.

Remember, by engaging downtown stakeholders to find local answers, the community is less likely to fall prey to the most common pitfalls.

40. Main Street Facelift*

Tracy Brown *and* Scott Lazenby

Local governments often use matching grants to encourage renovation of the facades of older downtown buildings. These programs are often passive, with the results driven by the owner of the private property. Although the city or county exercises some control over the improvements—often by paying an architect directly—the building owner must still come up with matching funds and deal with the red tape the locality imposes.

In many cases, the results are spotty at best. Even with a low private match requirement of 50 percent or less, the building owner may be reluctant to put money into aesthetic improvements. This is especially true for absentee building owners who are satisfied with the rents they earn from their business tenants.

Even when property owners take advantage of the incentive, the improvements may be scattered throughout a downtown area, with attractive, renovated buildings surrounded by less attractive ones. The challenge a local government faces is to get a bigger bang for the public buck.

Case Study: Master-Plan Approach in the City of Sandy

Sandy, Oregon, is a city of 9,655 on the western foothills of Mt. Hood. The City is celebrating the Centennial of its incorporation, and its historic downtown is on the route of the Oregon Trail. U.S. Highway 26 is the downtown's main street, and businesses benefit from the 30,000 to 60,000 cars per day that pass through.

Downtown buildings are a mix of historic wood and concrete structures; other historic buildings marred by 1960s and 1970s "improvements" using stucco, out-of-date mansard roofs, and cheap siding; unremarkable buildings built new in the 1960s and 1970s; and more modem buildings done in a variety of architectural styles.

In recent years, the City has adopted design standards for new commercial buildings in an attempt to tame the architectural chaos that was taking place. Rather than create an artificial theme, the design standards simply call for elements that are compatible with the "Cascadian" style that characterizes Mt. Hood's Timberline Lodge, built by Portland-area craftsmen employed by the Works Progress Administration during the Great Depression. Exceptions to the standards in the downtown core preserve

---

*Originally published as Tracy Brown and Scott Lazenby, "Main Street Facelift," *PM Magazine*, October 2011. Reprinted with permission of the publisher.

the historic character of existing clusters of buildings by encouraging infill development to complement the appearance of those buildings.

These standards have helped with new development, but the planning commission and city council wanted a mechanism to spruce up the existing, older downtown buildings. The City operates an urban renewal agency using tax increment financing, and it participates in the Main Street Program developed by the National Trust for Historic Preservation.

During the past decade, $5 million has been invested in downtown public infrastructure including parking, sidewalks, streetlights, and burying utility wires. The time seemed right to direct some of the urban renewal funds to improving the storefronts of private buildings. City staff explored the matching grant programs offered by other communities and worked with the Main Street committee to tailor a program to meet local needs.

In the middle of this process, this article's coauthor, Tracy Brown, attended a national Main Street conference in Chicago. The recession had caused a sharp decrease in subdivision activity, so he had time to serve as Sandy's Main Street coordinator in addition to planning director. At the conference, Randy Wilson of Community Design Solutions described a program he had used in South Carolina to spruce up entire blocks of downtown buildings at the same time.

The innovation in this approach was to buy the cooperation of the building owners by paying 100 percent of the cost. At the same time, money was saved by having a single contractor do all the work, which reduced the overhead and mobilization cost of multiple individual contracts.

How the Program Works

This idea was shared with the city council and other main street leaders in Sandy. The

consensus was: "Let's give this a try." Here are the elements of Sandy's Master Plan Facade Program:

A total of $1.8 million in urban renewal funds was budgeted for the project over 6 years. This is a large investment in private buildings. But with only ⅓ of the funds spent so far, the impact on the appearance of the City has been more dramatic than the result of the $5 million spent to date on sidewalks, street lamps, and other public improvements.

City staff worked closely with an architect in designing the program. The architect, Ralph Tahran, had also helped establish the design standards for new construction. He was masterful in evaluating buildings, sketching improvements, and working with building owners and the contractor.

The architect and Sandy staff members first "triaged" all existing buildings, with a goal of maximizing the visual impact of the city's investment.

The team then met with the owners of the targeted buildings. The final design was arrived at by mutual consent, but because the City was picking up the full cost consensus was easily reached in most cases. A picture is worth a thousand words, and the architect was skilled at sketching concepts on tracing paper and using a digital display board to dress up the digital images of the buildings.

The out-of-town owner of a typical, boxlike 7-Eleven store, when seeing the Cascadian embellishment proposed for his building, said, "Tell me again: you're paying for all this?"

In the end, the City did require a 1 percent match, but even for the most expensive project-a $50,000 makeover of a concrete building at the gateway to the downtown-the owner quickly agreed to his $500 contribution.

Each property owner signed an easement allowing the City to perform the work on the building and agreeing to maintain the improvements for at least seven years.

A single contract was bid for the first batch of building improvements. The resulting economy of scale, in combination with the depressed construction prices caused by the recession, allowed the City to stretch its dollars. In the first phase, 11 buildings were improved for a total cost of about $310,000, not including architectural fees.

The program did not cover such major structural changes as new roofs or additional space, but it did cover-depending on the condition of the building-new windows, doors, awnings, siding, paint, stonework, and the heavy timbers characteristic of Cascadian architecture.

Results

The contractor worked from one end of the downtown to the other during the summer of 2010, and the results of this first phase of the project were dramatic. With the proximity of the Mt. Hood and central Oregon recreation areas, traffic through town peaks in the summer, and many visitors stopped to comment on how good the place was looking.

Other property owners then wanted to jump on the bandwagon. The owners of two buildings-a historic log structure and a former grocery store-decided to make major structural improvements, including new pitched roofs and expanded space. The city provided matching funds on a sliding scale (80 percent up to $5,000, 50 percent for the next $45,000, and 30 percent for more than $50,000), but the owners made investments in their buildings that exceeded the city's requirements.

One concern expressed by business members of the Main Street committee was that the building owners would have relatively little skin in the game. As it turned out, though, many of the owners or their tenants made concurrent investments in sprucing up the interiors of the building or redoing the outside landscaping.

Even in the midst of the recession, new businesses began opening in the downtown. One older building with several tenant spaces went from 100 percent vacancy to 100 percent occupancy, and the owner of the building, who was still on the waiting list for the facade program, immediately invested in upgrading the lighting and HVAC systems.

With the excitement generated by the program, the Main Street committee launched an event series, First Fridays, that included wine tasting, music, art displays, and sidewalk sales throughout the downtown. In spite of rainy spring weather—not a big surprise in Oregon—the series of Fridays was a huge success, and the participation rate by businesses has skyrocketed. Other activities and evets have followed.

Lessons Learned

The city approached this as a pilot program and an experiment and kept careful note of what was working and what wasn't. A few of the lessons learned so far:

As a practical matter, it might be necessary to place a cap on the owner's cost. Given the reality of older buildings, the city's contractor sometimes uncovered such structural problems as dry rot. Ideally, this would remain the building owner's financial responsibility. Without a cap, owners of old buildings might be reluctant to participate if they are afraid of what they'll find when the building skin is removed.

In one case, the building owner, who was the landlord, enthusiastically supported the proposed improvements but didn't communicate with the owner of the tenant business (a restaurant) who had other ideas about such improvements as paint color and deck material. Legally, the city could have proceeded without the business owner's buy-in, but in the interest of peace and harmony the project was put on hold for a year until a compromise could be reached.

Different circumstances may require different approaches. Working with a single contractor made it easier for the staff to manage the project. But, especially because many small, local contractors are out of work, we are considering a general contractor-construction manager approach for the next phase, when small local firms can bid for parts of the subcontract work.

The program needs to have built-in flexibility to deal with the unknowns inherent in working with old buildings. A new awning was a key component for one of the building makeovers, but the contractor soon discovered that the 80-year-old building couldn't hold the awning as originally designed. The project was set aside for the next phase to give the architect a chance to rethink the design.

Be prepared for problem negotiation along the way. The contractor wasn't given detailed engineering and architectural designs for each building but was instead given drawings and descriptions of the expected outcomes. The architect worked closely with the contractor when problems came up, and the city had to negotiate when the contractor asked for more money to address the unexpected problems. This is simply the reality of remodel work.

Community Support

A 99 percent grant program for private storefront improvements with no fixed limits is certainly more expensive than, say, 50 percent grants limited to $5,000 each. But Sandy's concept of much larger grants was the key to moving the city from its role as a passive spectator to an active participant in upgrading the appearance of an older downtown.

The city was in the driver's seat as it selected which buildings would be treated, and how. And sprucing up many buildings in a brief period of time suddenly created a critical mass that spurred other investments and downtown activities.

The business owners were enthusiastic about the project in spite of the temporary mess during construction, and the community has supported the program strongly. Even though public, tax increment funds were used, residents are proud of the way their city is looking.

41. Main Street Pursuits[*]

PATRICIA MITCHELL *and* CHARLES ABERNATHY

In our opinion, a downtown area is one of the most important impressions for a visitor evaluating a tourism experience or a location decision. A main street and surrounding downtown area can convey the character, economic vibrancy, and the "mood" of a community. The development and implementation of programs to enhance the attractiveness and vitality of a community's downtown is the responsibility of elected officials and administrators and should receive considerable attention.

The Main Street Program (Main Street), established in the early 1980s by the National Trust for Historic Preservation and now a subsidiary of that organization, is economic and community development in its best form. It is a place-based program where a community's assets are analyzed and an economic development program built from those assets. It is more importantly a place-making form of economic development.

The physical environment is created through attention to visual appeal and historic preservation, and with them, a community is created where people want to live in or near. The conception of place-making can create viable economic development with a hometown feel that community members enjoy, and which visitors find appealing as a destination place for shopping and vacations.

The purpose of this article is to suggest a broader context to downtown development through place-making economic development and specifically through the Main Street Program, a program now found in 46 states. Downtown business districts and downtown development authorities certainly have their place in enhancing commerce or improving the ability of merchants to increase sales.

The Main Street Program broadens the opportunity to create place, to enhance the visual appeal of communities, and to engage in various forms of preservation. We will demonstrate this approach through photos of Main Street communities, specifically looking at street and sidewalk enhancements (streetscaping), facade treatments, transportation improvements, and historic preservation.

It is our intent that local government managers will be enticed to further explore the potential of a Main Street or Small Town Main Street Program and begin to think conceptually about place-making as an important component of an economic development plan.

Main Street is three things: (1) a proven approach for the revitalization of down-

*Originally published as Patricia Mitchell and Charles Abernathy, "Main Street Pursuits," http://icma.org. Reprinted with permission of the publisher.

towns, (2) a network of interrelated communities, and (3) a well-respected national program with support services to membership communities. The program advocates an all-inclusive method of downtown revitalization focusing on organization, design, economic restructuring, and promotion.

Transportation Enhancements and Streetscaping

Streetscaping is an important factor in revitalization. Through visual appeal, outdoor benches, widened sidewalks, and walkable community improvements, visitors and residents are encouraged to walk the downtown area enjoying a community's amenities and providing merchants with ready-made customers.

Such transportation enhancements as removing stoplights and creating attractive crossings and bump-outs for the planting of flowers and trees can create a slower pace and calmer feel to the main street area and encourage spending time in the comfortable environment.

Departments of transportation (DOTs) and district health departments are often key partners in revitalization. For example, the North Carolina DOT agreed to the removal of traffic lights in downtown West Jefferson, and the Appalachian District Health Department helped fund such improvements as removing overhead utilities to make the area a more attractive walkable community, thus creating health benefits.

Local Programs

It's good to be able to report that local programs designed to enhance the appearance and vibrancy of downtown areas are plentiful. Examples include establishing events and festivals to bring people and tourists to the downtown area. Marketing, branding, and promotions to encourage business activity are also typical. Resident advisory committees are critical components of each of these initiatives.

Local governments have established business associations with an economic development office focused solely on promoting the downtown business district. Some places are taking the aggressive and perhaps controversial step of providing incentives for the location of businesses into the downtown area (e.g., rental assistance or utility reduction programs).

Facade renovation programs are often the centerpiece of a downtown renovation program. These programs typically provide matching funds, oftentimes with a community-sponsored program or a Main Street grant program.

Such improvements as painting, facade replacement, awnings, and window replacement can be eligible for these matching grant funds. Marion (pop. 8,000), North Carolina, which began implementing a facade program in 2011, has participated in 14 funded projects, where projects received 50 percent of project cost up to $5,000. Here are some details about Marion's program:

- Matching funds are specifically tied to building improvements involving such structural improvements as windows, facade restoration, painting, and awnings.
- Marion agreed to use its own public works crews to provide limited assistance with debris removal, historical research, and paint-scheme suggestions.
- An application process and review committee were established with the review committee making recommendations regarding color schemes, creating historical accuracy, and maintaining consistency.

Broad participation in the process has occurred in Marion with county and city government, the economic development association, and the Downtown Business

Association involved in funding and decision making.

Historic Preservation: Important Component of Main Street

The preservation of a community's past is often an emotional commitment for a community. Well-preserved historic buildings are increasingly used as the anchor of local government activities.

As evidence, the Burke County, North Carolina, courthouse in Morganton (pop. 16,800) and an old textile mill are anchors in historic preservation and activity. The courthouse houses a museum for Senator Sam Ervin of Watergate fame, who began his law career in the building.

Place-Making as a Development Strategy

Using a community's assets for developing an economic strategy provides a logical approach to revitalization activity. Taking the asset-based strategy one step further and thinking about place-making provides a concept to create an environment where we want to work and play, as well as attract others to our community. Today's busy society is often looking for an attractive and calming atmosphere in which to spend some leisure time.

The revitalization of small towns also makes economic sense. PlaceEconomics, a Washington-based consulting firm analyzing the economic impact of the North Carolina Main Street Program, determined that from its inception in 1980, $2 billion has been invested by businesses and local communities and 4,700 new businesses created. It is estimated that "each year $1.6 million in sales taxes are generated just from the net new businesses in Main Street districts."

The North Carolina program operates a Main Street Solutions Fund, which is a legislatively appropriated grant program established in 2009, with $1 million being appropriated for FY2015.

Main Street is a proven strategy of place-making for economic development and quality-of-life activity.

REFERENCE

Ledbetter, D. (July 8, 2014). Discussion of West Jefferson Streetscape Project.
North Carolina Main Street Program. www.nccommerce.com/rd.
PlaceEconomics (2014). *Decades of Success: The Economic Impact of Main Street in North Carolina.* Executive Summary. North Carolina Department of Commerce and the North Carolina Main Street Communities, Washington, D.C., February 2014.

• H. Retail •

42. City-Developer Relations*

Christiana McFarland

Challenge

Many city officials express frustration when working with developers toward redevelopment. Some claim that developers are not mindful of community vision or that they have unrealistic incentive expectations. Developers, on the other hand, note that local government administrative processes can be obscure and that the needs of the community are generally not communicated in a timely fashion. Many times these issues become insurmountable challenges to otherwise potentially successful redevelopment projects.

In the hopes of overcoming some of these obstacles, National League of Cities' First Tier Suburbs Council began a partnership with the International Council of Shopping Centers (ICSC) in 2007. The focus of the partnership is on city-developer relations for retail redevelopment with the goal of helping city officials and developers better understand each other's perspectives and work together more effectively. As part of this partnership, the First Tier Suburbs Council steering committee held a roundtable dialogue with developers from across the country in a pre-event during the 2008 ICSC Global Retail Real Estate Convention in Las Vegas, Nevada.

This Municipal Action Guide presents parts of the conversation between the city officials and developers on four key themes: public benefits; the local development review process; project selection; and community visioning. Specifically, it provides a rare glimpse into the views of developers and is intended to facilitate a redevelopment process that is receptive to developers while meeting the needs and goals of local communities. The guide also offers suggested strategies and examples of cities that have used these strategies to more effectively engage with developers.

Public Benefits

Public benefits are additional amenities that developers contribute to the community in which they are building, generally in exchange for some allowances by the city such as density bonuses, quicker approvals, or fee waivers. Public benefits can include using green building practices, building affordable housing, providing cultural centers or parks, or employing local contractors. In addition to the philanthropic aspect of public benefits, developers also have an economic objective. They are more likely to sustain or increase the long-term value of

*Originally published as Christiana McFarland, "City-Developer Relations: Working Together Toward Successful Redevelopment," *National League of Cities Municipal Action Guide*, November 2008. Reprinted with permission of the publisher.

their property by assisting the city with its efforts to enhance quality of life and economic competitiveness.

Q. City official: What type of public benefits can a city realistically expect a developer to provide?

A. Developer: Responsible Property Investing is an emerging movement in the development community. It is meant to increase the social well-being of a community by engaging in sound investment practices such as smart growth, energy conservation and worker health. In addition, more and more developers are negotiating public benefits as part of their commitment to the community. Although developers are starting to move in the direction of social responsibility, it should be noted that developing a property is still an investment and the bottom line will always be a primary concern. If the community has a project that will attract developers, then the public benefits associated with the project will be a matter of negotiation and part of the overall economic equation. Additionally, developers are mindful of community responsibility, but cities should carefully assess the extent to which one development project can effectively solve broader community issues.

Possible local strategy: Many developers are open to providing public benefits if it is economically feasible. One local strategy is to incentivize the provision of public benefits by developers to create a win-win situation.

City example: Austin, Texas (pop. 717,100). Instead of establishing strict public benefits guidelines, the City of Austin has developed a program that rewards developers who choose to provide benefits to the community. The program is based on density bonuses; developers are permitted upzoning to build denser and taller in the urban core in exchange for the provision of public benefits such as affordable housing

and green building practices. Sometimes impact fees are also waived. For example, in the Baron Place condominium project, developers provided $1 million for affordable housing in the neighborhood surrounding the project; preserved mature, native trees; and spent over $250,000 to transplant trees to neighboring city parkland. In return, the city waived $300,000 in fees, provided in-kind city services, and expedited the reviewing and permitting processes for the project. Additionally, the city and developer worked together to provide a dedicated public access trail through the property to offer improved neighborhood access to the Town Lake Trail.

Local Development Review Process

A local development review process provides a means for the city and developer to negotiate the details of a proposed project. It usually includes an assessment of site constraints, the need for special approvals, and compliance with building and land development codes. A high-quality development review process is an indicator to businesses and developers that your community will be a strong partner.

Q. City official: At what point in the negotiation process will developers tell cities what the cost will be? It seems as if they tend to hold back. More generally, what do public-private partnerships mean to developers and what role does the local development review process play?

A. Developer: Developers tend to hold back on stating a final cost of the project because it's often difficult to know exactly what new costs may arise. When we provide the city with a figure, the city tends to hold us to it even if the costs change. Projects change over time and an integral part of a public-private partnership is staying committed for the duration of a project. A public-private partnership is just that—a partnership, and partners don't walk away. Cities and developers need to stay the course, share in the risk and gain, and be reasonably flexible if new needs arise.

Many times, having a reliable review and decision-making process helps alleviate much of the uncertainty involved with a project and helps get all parties on the same page early on. Even if there is no public investment, there is a lot to be said for certainty in the decision making process. Does the developer have comfort that he can get from point A to point B with the help of the city? Has the city gotten its residents on board with the project? Are zoning and other requirements flexible and communicated in a timely manner?

Possible local strategy: A development review process that is transparent and streamlined enables both the city and developer to be clear about expectations, regulations, and costs. The Michigan Suburbs Alliance recommends the following strategies:

- Examine the reviewing agencies and procedures for rezoning or conditional zoning, special land use, planned unit development, site plan review, variances and related activities and implement changes that increase efficiency and simplify processes.
- Applications for rezoning, special land uses, site plan review, and variances should be made easily accessible and include fee schedules, plans required (number and content), meeting schedules (regular and special), review process and timeline.
- Identify any special permits or approvals required (e.g., wetlands, brownfield, tree removal) and at what point in the process they need to be obtained.
- Designate a qualified staff member as the "intake professional" who is

responsible for receiving and processing the application and plans, maintaining contact with the applicant, facilitating meetings, and processing the applications after approval.
- Require a pre-application meeting with the reviewing agencies.
- Allow for special meetings to expedite the review process and establish a fee structure.
- Allow for and encourage community meetings at the outset of the application process in which a development proposal can be discussed with residents and businesses of the affected area.

City example: Napa Valley, California (pop. 77,011). In an effort to keep both developers and the city engaged and updated throughout the development process, the City of Napa has introduced a new "check-in" system. The check-in system encourages frequent interaction between the developer and the city, primarily during the initial planning stages. Once a developer submits an application for a project to the city, he is invited to present his project to a special committee representing city departments impacted by the project. Developers and city staff discuss the project to identify any major issues. The developer has the opportunity to adjust the plans and then meet with the city staff again for a full evaluation of the project.

The check-ins benefit both the city and developer. The developers are made aware of any problems that the city has with the project from the outset. Identifying challenges sooner helps developers get from the initial planning stages to groundbreaking more quickly; there is an explicit acknowledgment from the city that for developers, time is money. Additionally, the check-ins help to keep developers informed of all of the city policies that need to be satisfied in order to progress with the project. From the city's perspective, although there is an understanding that new challenges and costs may arise as the project develops, having discussions with developers early on enables the city to more accurately anticipate how much it will need to invest in the project. Check-ins also allow the city to better prepare for new development and evaluate how a specific project will contribute to municipal planning goals.

Project Selection

Often a city has in mind a particular project that it would like to see at a site, but this isn't always what the developer or the market considers to be the appropriate use.

Q. City official: When a city has an idea of what they want to do with a property, can they pitch it to the developer, or does the developer ultimately decide what to do?

A. Developer: The market ultimately decides what type of project will be best suited for a property. If the city wants what the market will give it, then it is likely that the city will get that project. Therefore, it is important for a city to have reasonable expectations about its market conditions. For example, not every city that is looking to add retail development will be able to support a large department store. "Not everyone gets a Nordstrom!"

Also, in terms of selecting projects, developers tend to follow the lead of anchor tenants. A reliable anchor that knows what it wants is going to reassure a developer that a retail center will be successful. Large retail stores and anchors generally rely on their own market and economic research, so investing large sums of money in consultants to do this for you may not be the best use of your funds. Rather, invest in your staff. Developers will look at how knowledgeable a city's staff is regarding economic redevel-

opment, whether it is the elected officials or department staff.

Possible local strategy: If it seems clear that your city's ideas about the development or redevelopment of a site are not sustainable in the current market, you may consider the suggestions of a developer while also carefully assessing how the proposal supports your community's longer-term goals for growth and development. As noted by one developer, leaving a site vacant or blighted until the perfect developer or project is presented can pose some risks to the economic viability of community. If a city holds out too long and the property remains undeveloped, especially in the case of properties needing substantial redevelopment, it's possible that blight associated with one site may negatively impact surrounding businesses and neighborhoods.

City example: Bartlett, Tennessee (pop. 47,603). After learning the hard way that you can't market an area based solely on what you want, the City of Bartlett has shifted its collective marketing perspective and joined with local landowners to better understand the suitable uses of a particular plot of land ripe for redevelopment.

"We've had to take a step back and focus on the forest instead of the trees. Although the City originally wanted to market a commercially zoned tract into a lifestyle center offering upscale retail shops, one conversation with a developer changed our direction completely. The tract we'd centered the plan around was directly across the street from the County's hottest retail area. We hadn't considered that the area simply didn't need any more retail," said Mayor McDonald.

The City's marketing plan has since shifted focus to what the broader area is lacking—a Class A office campus, a full-service hotel and pedestrian-accessible restaurants.

Mayor McDonald added, "Although we haven't had a developer commit to the project, we've had increased interest, and more importantly, from a long-term perspective, we've learned a valuable lesson. While we know the City of Bartlett has plenty of quality sites, we now understand the importance of recognizing the area's needs in creating an attractive marketing strategy."

Additionally, the City has partnered with the local chamber of commerce in hiring a director of economic development whose main purpose is to assess and market viable projects to developers.

Community Visioning

Community visioning entails developing a vision for the community with broad-based input, translating the vision into long-term plans and regulations, and encouraging development which builds from this vision. Community visioning has long been touted as a good planning practice, but some cities are concerned that having a strong community vision will deter developers.

Q. City official: How do developers feels about communities with a vision and development goals?

A. Developer: Cities that have a plan for development are more likely to attract a developer. "We prefer to develop in communities with a well-developed vision and comprehensive plan—it's easier to know what the community expects." Developers who are just offered money with no plan are suspicious about the intentions of a municipality. Developers prefer that cities have a plan supported by residents, but that they can also be flexible when new needs arise.

Community vision is important both in the planning phase and longer-term code enforcement. Cities should know that good, reliable developers are not afraid of code enforcement. It won't scare us away. "We actually prefer to develop in communities with strong, equitable code enforcement. It's one of the few ways we know that our investment in your community will be protected."

Possible local strategy: Using a community vision to guide development decisions and then implementing code enforcement to maintain the vision enhances quality of life and demonstrates to developers that they are making a sound choice by investing in your community. It is important to be flexible as new needs arise, but the guiding principles of the development should come from the community vision.

City example: Mission (pop. 9,526), Kansas. Mission, Kansas, a community less than three square miles in area, was at a crossroads when many large parcels of land became available for redevelopment. Mission began a planning process that involved all facets of the community, including residents, businesses and shoppers, to create a vision that would serve as the framework for future development. The community vision, which ultimately called for more compact, walkable, and sustainable development, was challenged when faced with a lucrative offer by a big-box developer. With a strong commitment to the vision, Mission denied the big-box store and has accepted an offer for a new mall from a developer who has embraced the city's vision for a vibrant, pedestrian-friendly, mixed-use destination. Although the developer typically only works on retail projects, his collaboration with the city and understanding of the community vision has led him to include residential, hotel, office and entertainment as potential project components. The city's resolve to stick with its vision also resulted in overwhelming community support for the project. In Planning and Zoning hearings, instead of busloads of Not in My Back Yard (NIMBY) opposition, city officials received acclamation from those in attendance and questions like "When will the project be complete?"

RESOURCES

America Downtown: New Thinking. New Life. www.
   nlc.org/resources_for_cities/programsservices/Am
   ericaDowntown.aspx.
"Collaborating With Developers to Make Strip Redevelopment a Reality." *Nation's Cities Weekly*, www.
   nlc.org. Oct. 29, 2007.
Good Jobs First. www.goodjobsfirst.org/
International Council of Shopping Centers. www.icsc.
   org
NLC's First Tier Suburbs Council website. www.nlc.
   org/inside_nlc/committees councils/465.aspx.
"Obstacles to Redeveloping Obsolete Suburban Strip
   Centers." *Nation's Cities Weekly*, www.nlc.org. Oct.
   29, 2007
Redevelopment Ready Communities, Michigan Sub-
   urbs Alliance. www.michigansuburbsalliance.org/

redevelopment/redevelopment_ready_communi
   ties/.
Renaissance Programs for Cities and Towns: City
   Practice Brief. www.nlc.org/ASSETS/8EC82A838
   BF5410B9204C7EA10B B9704/City%20Practices%
   20-%20Renaissance%20Zones%200708.pdf.
Responsible Property Investing Center. www.respon
   sibleproperty.net/.
Retail Redevelopment: City Practice Brief. www.nlc.
   org/ASSETS/287C47186D754ECABF9EA0F61B231
   88C/City%20Practices%20%20Retail%20Redevel
   opment%200508.pdf.
"Revitalizing Strip Centers Vital for Cities Economy."
   Nation's Cities Weekly, www.nlc.org. Oct. 8, 2007.
"Strip Redevelopment in First Tier Suburbs: A Success
   Story." *Nation's Cities Weekly*, www.nlc.org. Nov. 5,
   2007.

43. The Retail Chase*

CHRISTOPHER SWOPE

When legions of retailers, developers, bankers and brokers descend on Las Vegas it will be for one of the biggest schmooze fests in the world. It's the International Council of Shopping Centers' spring convention, and to anyone who hasn't been there, the scene—literally a city under a roof—can be a bit overwhelming. Exhibitors set up booths as wide as office buildings, and the aisles are platted into a sprawling street grid. At the corner of "38th Avenue & Q Street," mobs swarm the Cold Stone Creamery booth for free ice cream; a "block" away, they get free pretzels from Auntie Anne's. But the real business happens behind closed doors, where the bigwigs of chain retail shake hands on hundreds of deals that decide where America will shop and eat for years to come.

Because the commercial stakes are so high, the ICSC conference isn't just an affair for the industry anymore. It's a big event for local government as well. Mayors, city council members, city managers and economic development officials have become regulars at this annual carnival of dealmaking. Some 4,000 public-sector people are now members of ICSC, and they are one of the fastest-growing segments of the association.

It's easy to see why they feel the need to come. One out of every three retail real estate deals are either conceived at this meeting or completed there. "If you're a retailer looking for 25 sites to expand to, the only place to do it under one roof is Las Vegas," says Catherine Timko, a Washington, D.C.-based retail consultant who has accompanied a few big-city mayors to ICSC.

Many of the public officials who go are people like Wayne Seybold, the mayor of Marion, Indiana, who first went in 2004 and, despite his initial shock at the scale of the event, has been back every year since. "We're a town of 33,000," Seybold says. "There were 40,000 people at this convention. So our first year we were like deer in the headlights. OK, we're here—what do we do now?"

Like everyone at ICSC's convention, Seybold was looking for deals. He wanted to attract more retailers to Marion so that his constituents could enjoy a wider variety of places to shop without having to drive an hour to Indianapolis or Fort Wayne. That first year in Vegas, Seybold went home empty-handed. But he learned a few things about the retail business and how to go about romancing the chains. For example, he figured out that big retail companies usually prefer working with favorite developers. That meant he was better off talking

*Originally published as Christopher Swope, "The Retail Chase," *Governing*, March 31, 2007. Reprinted with permission of the publisher.

to the developers rather than simply chasing around after familiar brand-names. Seybold also learned how crucial data is to retailers—not the Census Bureau stats that every mayor knows by heart but detailed spending patterns of Marion residents mined from their credit card accounts.

Seybold's more recent outings to Las Vegas have been more productive. Now he goes with a group of local builders and a list of specific development sites he wants to discuss. Seybold also carries data compiled by a retail consultant showing that his small city actually anchors a respectable trade area of 250,000 people. "That really enabled us to change our marketing and our message," Seybold says. "We can take that information and say to retailers that this is the reality of what's going on in the city now. People are starved for certain types of retail."

It's taken a while, but Seybold's Vegas trips seem close to paying off. Two large mixed-use retail projects are in the works in Marion, one near a local university and another near Interstate 69.

What's more, the town has its first Starbucks. That may not be a big deal in Seattle, but in Marion, 200 people showed up for the groundbreaking. "For a lot of people, going shopping or eating out has become their entertainment," Seybold says. "I keep hearing people say there's not a lot to do in this city. What they mean is that we don't have enough retail. If you don't have retail and restaurant choices, people look at that as the city not having such a great quality of life."

Faddish Business

Not every community sends its mayor to ICSC or goes about recruiting retailers in quite the way Marion does. Yet more and more cities are chasing after chain stores and restaurants these days as an explicit economic development strategy. Some do it solely to boost sales-tax revenue. Increasingly, however, they talk the way Seybold does—about the less tangible "quality-of-life" issue.

For cities, suburbs and small towns alike, retail presence has become closely intertwined with self-image. As the sociologist Sharon Zukin once wrote, we are where we shop. That's more true than ever in a mobile country whose retail landscape is increasingly dominated by national brands. Mom-and-pop stores may provide local flavor, but chain stores are societal benchmarks. Mayors hear it from their constituents all the time: Why don't we have a Trader Joe's? Why don't we have a Bass Pro Shops? What are we, some kind of backwater?

When local officials get into the retail chase, however, what they quickly find is a curious business that doesn't follow the same rules that govern site selection in other industries. Most big corporations that governments recruit are interested in the quality of the local workforce. Chain retailers don't worry much about that. They don't need many highly educated employees. What they want to know is how many of their customers live nearby and how long it will take them to get to the store. Chains also want to locate near other stores that serve a similar clientele. Chico's, the women's clothing store, likes to be near Pottery Barn or Crate & Barrel. As Tim Angell, the head of economic development for Des Plaines, Illinois, says, if municipalities want to attract retailers, then "they have to think like a shopping center developer."

Retail is also a notoriously faddish business. Strangely, that's another reason why some older localities have become more visible players in recent years. Enclosed regional malls built in the suburbs are no longer much of a growth industry. In fact, many of them are dying—wounded fatally by consolidation of department store chains.

What's hot now is the "lifestyle center"—

an open-air mall, essentially, in which street-level shopping is mixed with housing, restaurants and public gathering spaces. And developers typically can't pull off these complex, mixed-use projects without some help from city hall on zoning, land assembly and parking. So there's more reason than ever for local governments to gravitate toward ICSC and the deals that emerge from the massive annual meeting.

Meanwhile, the attitude of retailers toward central cities has changed. Now that they've tapped out all the easy development sites in the suburbs, many of the big companies desperately want to penetrate urban markets. Even the big boxes have shown a willingness to tinker with their cookie-cutter store designs, to fit tight urban sites in ways that would have been unthinkable five years ago.

Home Depot recently opened a store in the middle of Manhattan. It's pedestrian oriented—there's no parking—and located in a historic building. Target is experimenting with two-story formats in Southern California. According to Robert Gibbs, a retail consultant based in Birmingham, Michigan, only two things are holding back urban retail now: the cumbersome permit process in many cities and a bias against chain stores that a growing number of cities are writing into law in the form of anti-big-box ordinances. "Cities have a supply problem, not a demand problem," Gibbs says. "There's a new willingness among retailers to flex their models, but cities for the most part aren't doing their part."

Much of the change in the retail market is happening not just within cities but in the middle of downtown. All over the country, young professionals and empty nesters—people with disposable income to spare—are moving into new lofts and high-rise condos. Those new residents have to shop somewhere. In downtown Minneapolis, now home to 30,000 people, three grocery stores are coming, and not one of them

requested government subsidies. "For years, all the cities in the Midwest wanted to have a Michigan Avenue," says Minneapolis Mayor R.T. Rybak, referring to Chicago's famous high-end shopping street. "Michigan Avenue is spectacular, but we're not all going to have a Michigan Avenue." What's evolving downtown now, in Rybak's view, is a hybrid retail model where destination shoppers can still buy $200 shoes, but where the people living upstairs can find a dry cleaner. "Focus on the housing first," Rybak says, "and the retail will follow."

Webcast Warnings

At the end of February 2007, nearly 100 local government officials from around the country participated in an online webcast, called "Winning at ICSC," advising them on how to get the most out of their visit to the conference. Some of what they heard wasn't especially reassuring. Valerie Richardson, vice president of real estate for the Container Store, warned the group that if they hadn't already made their appointments with the top retailers, it might be too late—three months before the conference even started. "We have folks calling now," Richardson said. "Our schedules do book up very quickly." What's more, the officials were told, it might be a waste of time to show up unless they could bring with them a roster of developable sites on which they were ready to make deals. In the absence of such a list, developers often refuse even to talk.

The webcast had a cautionary tone all the way through. David Miller, the city manager of Forest Hill (pop. 12,700), Texas, told first-timers that it could take three years at ICSC just to make sense out of the chaos of the convention hall. "You'll spend a lot of time learning the layout and how it works," he said. "The second year you'll be more productive because you'll know how to deal with the intensity of the conference itself. By the third year, you're a seasoned pro."

"Winning at ICSC" was presented by The Buxton Co., a retail site selection consultant. There is, in fact, a whole cottage industry of consultants whose main line of work is helping retailers vet expansion sites but who have recently found a lucrative public-sector business on the other side of that equation. Companies such as Buxton, Claritas, ESRI and MapInfo use sophisticated data mining and mapping tools to help cities pinpoint customers and hone their pitch to retailers.

Buxton, for example, goes beyond demographics by drilling down into consumers' credit card accounts and magazine subscriptions. In the industry, this kind of data is called "psychographics." As Buxton vice president Joseph Fackel explains, "you and I could be the same age, both white males, educated and making the same amount of money. But you may be into traveling, collecting wine and subscribe to Gourmet magazine. Well, maybe I like to hunt and fish, I drive a pickup, I wear boots and I subscribe to Guns & Ammo. Bass Pro doesn't need you, but they need me." By running this kind of analysis, Fackel believes he can help cities determine what sorts of retailers their markets can support—and tell them which companies they shouldn't even bother chasing.

According to Seybold, this kind of data has helped Marion make sense of its retail market. "They're pinpointing customers as opposed to drawing circles," the mayor says. "We were traditional: Here's a point, and here's a 15-mile circle around it, a 20-mile circle, and a 30-mile circle. They came in and said the way we do it today is with drive times—10 minutes, 15 minutes, half an hour. Where we are in rural Indiana, there's not a lot of stoplights, so our market became a lot bigger."

Not everyone thinks the consultants are worth the money—Buxton's services cost $70,000, and some of the psychographic data is available more cheaply from other sources. Likewise, not everyone is con-

vinced that jetting off to Vegas is what every mayor or economic development director needs to do. "Vegas has taken on a life of its own," says James Kaplan, a suburban Chicago shopping center developer. "But the developer that's going to work in your small town is the guy who's already within 25 miles of you. You're not going to go to Vegas and find someone from New York to go to your town of 15,000 people."

"I roll my eyes when I hear about another city running a team out to ICSC," says Brad Segal, a Denver consultant who helps cities plan for revitalizing their downtowns. Segal believes that the best retail strategy is not, per se, a retail strategy. He says smart businesses these days are looking for urban amenities that draw people for reasons other than shopping. "To me, a successful downtown is a multidimensional environment that includes housing, office workers, arts, culture and entertainment. And it includes retail. Retail is a means, not an end. Still, some old ways of thinking on retail leads us to the ICSC convention and trying to recruit the trophy."

Corridor Strategy

Whether or not cities send delegations to Las Vegas for three days in May, recruiting retail is becoming a more time-consuming job. In Louisville, it consumes eight full-time jobs. A few years ago, Mayor Jerry Abramson began noticing how shabby some of Louisville's retail corridors were looking, especially where stores such as K-Mart had pulled out and left behind empty big-box buildings. So the mayor set up an economic development program focused entirely on retail attraction and growth. A few cities, such as Chicago and Philadelphia, have similar offices, but Louisville's effort is notably aggressive.

The "Corridors of Opportunity in Louisville" office is headed by John Fischer and consists of four economic development officers working for him. Each has responsibility for one quadrant of the city, and all share responsibility for promoting retail and restaurants downtown. Two staffers help with administration and one, a geographic information systems expert, runs psychographic analyses that Fischer's team can take to retailers and show where pockets of underserved customers are. At the end of February, Fischer was busy trying to convince Kohl's that the discount department store would do well in a location recently vacated by Dillard's.

Fischer's office leans on city departments and utility companies to expedite permits and hookups, and brokers relationships between retailers, developers and landlords. The office has worked on over 200 deals. An early one involved the Bashford Manor Mall, an enclosed shopping center that was losing tenants, looking ragged and attracting criminals. The local neighborhood association wanted something done about those problems. So Fischer contacted the mall's owners in Illinois and talked about finding a new direction for the site. The city offered a low-interest loan to help demolish the old mall and helped recruit a Walmart SuperCenter and a Lowe's.

Home Grown

Louisville's model also pays attention to local mom-and-pop retailers. The thinking is that most successful chains started out as a single successful store—the first Starbucks in Seattle, for example. Abramson routinely approaches local businesses that are doing well in one location and asks the owners if they might be willing to open a second, third or fourth. That's how Wick's Pizza, a well-known establishment on Louisville's east side, expanded into a strip center on the other side of town. "Those are easy," Abramson says. "We go to the local businessmen and women who already have the cleaners or the shoe-repair shop, and we

show them a strip center where they can get low rent and we help them out with a low-interest loan. We're not asking for gifts or charity. We're telling them we've run the numbers, and the neighborhood is willing to support the cleaners or the shoe-repair shop or the bookstore or the coffee shop. And we've done every one of those."

Abramson and Fischer take pride in Louisville's effort to generate a home-grown retail expansion. On the other hand, they see a combination of mom-and-pops and big national chains as the healthiest retail mix. Fischer, an ICSC veteran who knows the convention's quirky rules, is headed to Las Vegas—he's been lining up his appointments with developers and retailers for weeks. And for the first time, Abramson expects to join him. There may be hot deals available; there might not. Either way, they figure the mere possibility of rubbing shoulders with the right developer or retailer is too much to miss. As Fischer says, "The basis of everything we do is relationships."

Romancing the Store

Going shopping for retailers? Here are 10 things to know:

1. Get your hands on the same detailed consumer data the retailers are using. Fill holes in that data with on-the-ground intelligence. If your community wants a hardware store, find out the number of home renovations and building permits that have been issued. "It's important to know what metrics these folks are using," says Alyssa Stewart Lee, head of the Urban Markets Initiative at the Brookings Institution. "What your ground truth says about a place can inform their decision matrix."

2. Time is money. Chains face tremendous pressure to expand locations quickly. They'll skip your town if the permitting process is too long and complicated. "Stores have to open to keep their stock prices

rising," says retail consultant Robert Gibbs. "A development director for a chain is told to open five stores in a region by a certain date, and if they don't open he gets fired."

3. Be realistic. Retailers simply won't go where they can't find a critical mass of customers. It doesn't matter how much a few vocal people in the community may want them. "At the end of the day for retailers, locations are data-driven decisions," says Joseph Fackel, vice president of the Buxton Co. "If the data doesn't line up, they don't do the deal."

4. Make a retail master plan. Know what types of businesses your community can support (see No. 1), and have viable development sites ready to go. "Cities should have a written policy saying they want to be competitive and gain market share," says Gibbs. "And they have to have a public parking strategy."

5. Don't fight the chains. Instead, work with locally owned stores to help them survive. If mom-and-pop can't afford high rents in a newly revitalized area, help them relocate to another part of town. Or, offer low-interest loans to help successful local retailers expand into chains themselves. Don't forget: Starbucks was once just a small Seattle coffee shop and Wal-Mart a single store in Rogers, Arkansas.

6. Mix uses. Retail often follows other functions and activities. So the best retail strategy sometimes has nothing to do with retail. It has to do with housing, entertainment and culture. "Stop thinking so much about sales tax dollars," says retail developer

James Kaplan. "And think about ways and reasons to get people into town."

7. Invest in the public realm. Retailers may be leaving shopping malls for more urban settings, but they still want a predictably clean environment where their customers feel safe. Lighting is especially important: 70 percent of all sales occur after 5:30 p.m. "Cities need to have high design standards for signage, lighting and building design and be willing to enforce those standards," says Gibbs.

8. Consider incentives. Retailers won't go where their customers aren't—see No. 3. But many chains are risk-averse and are unwilling to locate in unproven markets without a little help. Plus, anchor stores are accustomed to cutting deals on rent at shopping malls. "Bigger-format retailers come with an expectation of lower rents," says Paul Levy, president of the Center City business improvement district in Philadelphia. "In most cities, they've been able to get their way. That's the reality of the marketplace."

9. Be patient. Although retailers are often looking for fast returns, many also plan for expansion several years out. Retail recruitment efforts may not pay immediate dividends, but relationships formed now may pay off five years from now.

10. Keep up with the times. Retail trends come and go like women's fashions. But you can't hide a dead Marshall Fields or Tower Records in the back of the closet. Enclosed malls are out. Lifestyle centers are in. What retail concept will be hot next?

44. Tourism Impacts Economic Development*

DAVID ROBINSON

Tourism, as an economic development tool, at times gets a bad rap. Opponents focus too much on the low wage service jobs generated by the hospitality industry and fail to see the larger value of tourism to many successful regional economies. Tourism is a critical element to the quality of life a region offers its residents.

No one questions that a region or state's quality of life is a major factor in its economic success. First, natural amenities affect population growth and natural amenities are often central to tourism. Regions with warmer climates, mountains and beaches have been the growing areas in the United States for well over 50 years. The widespread use of air conditioning solved the challenge of warm summers and large concentrations of customers have been following the sun for decades.

Tourism also benefits urban and rural markets. Big cities are not the only location where tourism impacts the economy. New York City, Chicago and San Francisco certainly have a substantial economy, built in part on a billion dollar convention and visitors program. However, rural economies with mountains, rivers and beaches also have a larger number of jobs and wealth created based upon visitors spending freely on vacation and second homes. These amenities act as "export" opportunities for land in rural communities. For example, state parks in rural Georgia produced nearly $65 million in gross economic output. They are an important economic development tool for a region with few customers and little wealth otherwise.

Tourism also provides economic opportunity for workers with less than a college degree. Eighty percent of the American economy is in the service industry. It now takes 140 workers to manufacture what it used to take 1000 workers in 1950. The challenges of low wageworkers in global locations, a 21st century economic reality, are that jobs are needed for workers starting on the economic ladder from an academic standpoint. Jobs in the hospitality industry, tied to the tourism trade, create that first step in the economic ladder for many workers. Wages in this industry are not high like in the advanced service industry. But with only 30 percent of Americans with a college degree and fewer manufacturing jobs available, the tourism industry is an economic outpost for many Americans searching for work.

---

*Originally published as David Robinson, "Tourism Impacts Economic Development," *PA TIMES*, 2014, http://patimes.org. Reprinted with permission of the publisher.

Natural amenities of a region also influence the larger economic development pitch made by regions and states to every company considering staying or locating in a region. The workers for regional companies also enjoy the same natural amenities developed for the tourist market. Surveys of corporate site selectors consistently show that the quality of life of a region affects the company location decision. Now all communities claim to have a great quality of life but regions developing their natural amenities can illustrate how their region provides access to them.

More importantly, quality of life as a factor in economic development decisions varies in relevancy among industries, but is important to workers in the high-wage, high-tech sector dominated by highly educated and mobile workers. America is a mobile society with transportation and telecommunications networks connecting everyone. Consumers and companies maximize the utility of goods and services through their decisions as to where to locate. This mobility illustrates the relevancy of tourism for successful regional economies.

Finally, tourism can be a dominant feature in a region's economic success. The prime policy argument in favor of recreational amenities as an economic development tool is its ability to shift population. Look at Utah. Utah's investment in winning the Winter Olympics continues to pay big economic dividends.

The 2002 Winter Olympics at Park City (pop. 7,800) turned into a global tourism model for regional economic development on the backs of impressive mountains and skiing. Park City also offers a downtown hospitality experience that made the region a destination point. Utah's skiing industry has an economic impact of $1.6 billion.

The 2002 Winter Olympics and the global media coverage turned this sleepy village just outside of Salt Lake City into a global tourism powerhouse. The economic impact of the 2002 Winter Olympics included $4.8 billion in sales during the Olympics, but there was more than a 25 percent hotel room increase from 2002 to 2009. The statewide hotel occupancy increased from 58.8 percent in 2003 to 59.7 percent in 2010 based in large part on tourism tied to skiing. Direct expenditures from skiers and snowboarders increased 67 percent from 2002–2003 through 2010–2011. The Park City/Salt Lake City region is proof that tourism can create wealth and major events, such as the Olympics, can be used to launch such an initiative to new heights.

Tourism is rarely the total economic answer for a region or state. However, one industry is rarely the total economic panacea for any region or state. Tourism impacts the economic growth of a region by creating a better quality of life, offers jobs to those starting on the economic ladder and can create billion dollar industries often tied to major regional investments.

45. Tourism in the City of Pigeon Forge, Tennessee[*]

Madlyn M. Bonimy

Nestled in the foothills of the Great Smoky Mountains, the city of Pigeon Forge, Tennessee, is a thriving tourism destination. However, until 1940, the city of Pigeon Forge, located in eastern Tennessee, was primarily known just as a two-stoplight, sleepy farming community. The city gained in popularity with the dedication of the Great Smoky Mountains National Park. It is the most visited park in the United States with more than 10 million people passing through each year. Pigeon Forge, adjacent to the park, is just minutes away.

The impetus for tourism in eastern Tennessee was the 1982 World's Fair held May 1, 1982, through October 1982. Thus, the tourism boom hit the city in 1982 and since then growth has been rapid.

Today, with a permanent population of just 5,988, the city of Pigeon Forge receives more than 9 million tourists annually. To accommodate this growing influx of tourists, hotel rooms in the city increased from 2,000 in the 1980s to more than 14,000 in 2013. Accommodations include more than 85 properties, 15 campgrounds and a number of fully equipped rental cottages, villas, bed-and-breakfast inns and condominium units.

Tourists are lured to the city of Pigeon Forge as they are attracted by the Great Smoky Mountains. Snuggled in the foothills of these mountains, the city is also home to Tennessee's largest single attraction, Dollywood. A 140-acre theme park owned by eastern Tennessee native Dolly Parton, Dollywood is the state's only theme park and it welcomes more than 2 million tourists each year from April through December.

In addition, the city offers a multifaceted tourism product with activities such as visiting historic and cultural sites. It also offers shopping (over 300 factory outlets), mountain visits, country music reviews and festivals. One such festival, Winterfest, a four-month long festival (held November to February), was created to help businesses increase revenue in the city's offseason months. Winterfest provides tourists with musical entertainment, games, family fun, a light display of 5 million lights, smoky mountain storytelling and a Wilderness Wildlife week, where guest speakers give presentations about the flora and fauna found in the Great Smoky Mountains National Park through workshops, lectures and guided hikes.

Tourism generates economic development in the city of Pigeon Forge. With

[*]Originally published as Madlyn M. Bonimy, "Tourism in the City of Pigeon Forge, Tennessee," *PA TIMES*, http://patimes.org. Reprinted with permission of the publisher.

tourism as its main industry, it is estimated that most people in Pigeon Forge (approximately 85 percent) are employed in tourism-related jobs. In fact, the tourism industry in Pigeon Forge, Tennessee, creates both direct and indirect employment.

Direct employment is necessary to serve the tourism industry. It is evident in jobs created at hotels, restaurants, shops and so forth, to serve the tourist. Indirect jobs are produced through the creation of the components of the infrastructure with skilled and unskilled jobs, such as mechanics maintaining rental cars, artisans creating items sold in shops, farmworkers, telecommunications employees, police and all manner of other jobs generated to serve the needs of the tourism industry in the city of Pigeon Forge, Tennessee.

Thus, the economy of Pigeon Forge depends heavily on the tourism industry—for employment and the generation of revenues brought into the city by business receipts and state tax revenues. In 2004, visitor spending totaled more than $713 million, reflecting a 7 percent increase over 2003 when visitor spending totaled more than $669 million. This is a 98 percent increase from 1990. Visitor spending has continued its upward trend. For example, from 2011–2013 visitor spending increased from more than $830 million to $937 million, representing a 13 percent increase.

The city of Pigeon Forge sends 6 percent of its gross revenue to the state of Tennessee. In 2013, Pigeon Forge provided $56.2 million in tax revenues to the state of Tennessee. In 2005, gross business receipts generated more than $777 million, an increase of 9 percent from 2004. From 2011–2013, gross business receipts saw a 12 percent increase totaling more than $937 million.

In conclusion, governments exist for specific purposes and they intervene in every facet of life. Governments exist to provide people valuable services that businesses or individuals are unwilling or unable to provide independently, such as natural defense, pollution control, disease control, police and fire protection and primary education. However, governments have economic functions as well. John Mikesell argues in his book *Fiscal Administration: Analysis and Application for the Public Sector* how "governments have economic functions: [...] stabilization, and growth, the combat against unemployment and inflation and provision for increases in the standard of living for the citizenry [...]." In line with Mikesell's argument, tourism is the principal economic development generator in the city of Pigeon Forge, Tennessee.

Tourism in the city of Pigeon Forge involves providing recreational facilities and services, such as lodging, transportation, attractions, entertainment and food for people traveling for rest, relaxation, sport and access to culture and nature. Thus, by its very nature, tourism is characterized by urbanization and commercialization; and its obvious economic manifestations are job creation, tax revenues and income.

Governments, such as in the City of Pigeon Forge, Tennessee, use tourism as an important economic development activity to combat unemployment, increase tax revenues and income and provide for the increase in the standard of living for citizens.

46. Want Tourists in Your Town?
*Brand It, and They Will Come**

J. Michael Lillich

While the advertising concept of branding generally applies to products, a Purdue University professor thinks regional branding is what rural communities need to succeed in making tourism a viable part of their local economies.

Liping A. Cai, a Purdue assistant professor of hospitality and tourism management, defines tourism branding as "a process of building a unique destination image that evokes a specific set of the travelers' thoughts, feelings and associations, which in turn add value to their visiting experience."

He says rural communities that decide to market themselves for tourism often think too small. "Sometimes even a county is too small. Visitors don't think about county boundaries. Regional branding of four to five counties is more effective if they have the same attractions."

Rural towns, according to Cai, need to evaluate the nature of their regions' attractions in terms of "destination mix," which has five components:

- Attractions, both natural and cultural.
- Infrastructure: highways, utilities, sewer.
- Facilities: hotels, motels, bed-and-breakfast establishments.
- Transportation, including taxis and buses.
- Hospitality training, which involves the whole community in knowing what the area's attractions are and how to present them in a positive manner.

"Hospitality training is very important but often ignored," Cai says. "Tourism marketing is a community effort, and having friendly, personable, knowledgeable people is very important. For example, a gas station attendant on the interstate who is trained and part of the system may recommend a restaurant or a local attraction to travelers. This can make all the difference."

Cai says states with agricultural traditions have rural tourism to offer. "Rural tourism in America goes back to the early 1980s when agriculture, mining, timber, energy and agriculture-based manufacturing communities experienced an economic decline," Cai says. Rural tourism is much more advanced in Europe, he says, where it is common for farms to open up to visitors on "rural trips."

*Originally published as J. Michael Lillich, "Want Tourists in Your Town? Brand It, and They Will Come," *Purdue News*, February 2001. http://www.purdue.edu. Reprinted with permission of the publisher.

Regional tourism planning should also select target markets, according to Cai. What attracts families may be very different from what attracts newlyweds, which, in turn, may be different from what retirees are looking for.

Then, there is globalization to consider. "The United States is the third most-visited country in the world, after Spain and France," Cai says. "Many times, repeat visitors to the United States, having seen New York, Chicago and San Francisco, want to see the 'real' America. When I first introduced the idea of Indiana tourism to my students, they laughed, but we often ignore what is in our back yards."

Cai has done research on rural tourism in New Mexico, which employs regional cooperative branding in the seven-county Old West Country in the southwest part of the state. The paper he wrote on the research won the best paper award at the Council on Hotel, Restaurant and Institutional Education's national conference in New Orleans in July. Cai's New Mexico branding research focuses on the area's cowboys-and-Indians heritage.

"What this shows is that if a prevailing image of a region already exists, communities should align their images with the regional one," Cai says. "If there is not yet a regional brand image, communities should work together to build one based on their common strengths."

His research also shows that using cooperative branding causes advertising costs to decrease markedly and return on advertising investment to increase significantly. This research is part of a larger effort by Cai and his colleagues at the Purdue Tourism and Hospitality Research Center to measure the economic impact of tourism "as communities become more sophisticated about tourism and recognize the need for good, accurate, credible information," says Alastair M. Morrison, the center's director and professor of marketing and tourism.

"All of this is not to say that an individual community should not promote its own uniqueness," Cai says. "But unless there exists an overpowering organic image of the town in the public consciousness, the community should consider creating a subbrand based on its uniqueness under an umbrella regional brand."

But Cai cautions that tourism is not an economic quick fix for every town seeking an alternative to agriculture and Old Economy manufacturing businesses.

"Business people like tourists. Residents may not," Cai says. "Tourism is sometimes called a factory without chimneys, but that's not true. There are too many social and environmental issues inherent in a community's developing tourism. The question is how to make tourism sustainable over the long term."

Cai says the answer is to "regionalize, plan and brand."

47. Work of Arts[*]

ZACH PATTON

The house Mark Palmer lives in is a brick beauty. Built in the 1850s in the Lower Town section of Paducah, Kentucky, it also houses Palmer's gallery of paintings and the studio where he puts watercolor to paper.

Palmer, who moved to Lower Town in 2002, had been a Washington, D.C.–based artist until he got wind of Paducah's Artist Relocation Program: a variety of financial incentives aimed at luring artists to live and work in Lower Town. The neighborhood had its drawbacks: It was a crime-ridden slum. But it just happened to be full of century-old Victorian, Romanesque and Italianate homes and once-charming bungalows that time and neglect had diminished. Palmer's house, in fact, had been so structurally decayed that it had been condemned.

But Paducah was offering Palmer a good deal to move there. And it was doing so on a bet that if it could attract artists to the area—own homes and become full-time residents—it could transform the derelict part of town back into a vibrant, viable and productive neighborhood.

The program was launched six years ago, and today, Lower Town is on its way to becoming a national destination for artists. The 30-block neighborhood is full of studios and restored older homes, with newly constructed buildings mixed in. During the week, artists work in their studios, mow their lawns and shop at the supermarket. Toward the weekend, visitors fill the sidewalks, wander in and out of the galleries, eat at newly opened restaurants and stay at local hotels.

The concept behind the relocation program isn't revolutionary. Economic development officials in cities and states all over the country have already keyed in on the start-up value of artists.

Through the use of subsidized rents or sales tax breaks, painters, sculptors, glass blowers, weavers and the like can be enticed to open studios and set a tone and stage for turning around a set of city streets. The programs in use are wide ranging. Maryland and Rhode Island, for example, exempt artists from paying sales and income taxes on their work—provided the works are produced and sold in specially designated arts districts.

A handful of states—Connecticut, Kentucky, Maine, Montana, New Mexico and North Carolina—allow an artist's estate tax to be paid in artwork he or she produced. Cities from Fort Lauderdale to Grand Rapids have developed "live-work" spaces for artists in an effort to revitalize an ailing neighborhood. These localities typically

---

[*]Originally published as Zach Patton, "Work of Arts," *Governing*, July 2007. Reprinted with permission of the publisher.

partner with a developer to rehab an old warehouse or cluster of buildings into residential lofts and studios, which are available to artists at a reduced rent.

Paducah's program goes way beyond these approaches. By focusing on home ownership and personal loans directly to artists themselves, the Artist Relocation Program is creating a stable, permanent arts community in Lower Town—one house at a time. And the program has achieved a success its original planners never could have envisioned. "We thought it would be great if we could get 10 artists," says Tom Barnett, Paducah's planning director. "With 15, we thought we could change the neighborhood forever." Today, more than 70 artists have moved to Lower Town from across the country, and they are defining the city in the process.

Cleaning Up

Paducah lies in Western Kentucky, at the point where the Tennessee River joins the Ohio. An industrial rail and steamboat center, the city of 26,000 sits halfway between Nashville and St. Louis, on the way from Chicago to Memphis. While its own population is relatively small, Paducah is a draw for 70,000 county residents and an outlying population of many more. The relatively dense downtown of tall buildings and the city's close-knit inner neighborhoods speak of a history as a center of trade.

Lower Town was Paducah's first real residential neighborhood, located just a few blocks from downtown and the riverfront. Its first houses were built before the Civil War, and by the 1920s, it had grown into a leafy, compact grid of some 300 structures. Gingerbread Victorians and stately Queen Annes mingled with brick stores and warehouses, along with smaller houses and bungalows. During the second half of the 20th century, however, as residents moved out to the suburbs, Lower Town began to deteri-

orate. Slumlords bought up the houses and sliced them into apartments; by the 1990s, Lower Town was 70 percent rental property. As the buildings decayed, so did the quality of life in the neighborhood. Crime shot up, and Lower Town became known as the place to find drugs and prostitutes. "This was a neighborhood that had been abandoned not only by the government, but by the citizens, by everybody," says Barnett. "In Lower Town, you were either passing through or looking for trouble."

In the early 1980s, Paducah made a half-hearted attempt to preserve the neighborhood's buildings by designating the area a historic district. That helped stabilize the conditions of some of the homes and enhanced the city's regulatory powers in the neighborhood, but it didn't do anything to improve the homes. There was no proactive initiative, and there certainly was no grand vision of how to improve Lower Town.

That all began to change in 1999, when Mark Barone stepped out onto his front porch. Barone is a painter and printmaker who had moved to Lower Town 10 years earlier. When he walked out his front door and witnessed a drug deal across the street, he was both angered and energized. He began to envision a plan to revitalize Lower Town—a plan he could take to city hall. "We needed to save the neighborhood," Barone says. "Either the city was getting on board or I was getting the hell out."

Barone started by working with Barnett in the planning office to get Paducah to adopt a tougher rental license ordinance— a means of getting rid of the slumlords in Lower Town. The city increased the number of inspections it conducted in the area and strongly enforced new codes to gain control of the neighborhood.

But Barone and Barnett were thinking on a much bigger scale. With the Paducah city manager and a city commissioner, they traveled to Rising Sun, Indiana, a small town that had initiated a modest program to attract artists to its Main Street. They began to see how a similar program could be tailored to fit Paducah. Within months, they were able to persuade the city to let a Barone-Barnett team develop the Artist Relocation Program. The city even gave them a first-year operating budget: $43,000. The planning duo also was able to put together an additional $100,000 in seed money, which they used to purchase Lower Town homes. "Then we just sat around a little table in my office and started making up the program," Barnett says. "We sat around telling lies to each other—or, as Mark would say, a vision— and that became the program."

A Defining Moment

What they created differed from other cities' efforts in a few very important ways. First and foremost, the Artist Relocation Program is based on homeownership. The city partnered with Paducah Bank, a locally owned financial institution, to give loans to program participants. The bank, which is itself located in Lower Town, offered 100 percent financing to artists to purchase and rehabilitate the homes. Even more important, Paducah Bank agreed to offer loans at values well beyond the actual appraisal of a house—sometimes as high as 400 percent over the appraised value. That was crucial because property values in Lower Town were so depressed.

As an example, Palmer's house had, in its condemned state, only dirt for its floors and no glass in the windows. The city bought the 3,500-square-foot house for $1,200 and spent $37,000 to stabilize it before giving it to Palmer at no cost. Palmer then spent $250,000 to restore the home. But at the end of the day, the house was only appraised at $100,000 because the neighborhood was still so undesirable. That's why it was so critical that Paducah Bank extended loans that were in excess of the appraised value

of a house. "Eventually we made the decision to just stop having appraisals done at all," says Larry Rudolph, senior vice president of the bank. "That will give a lot of bankers some real heartburn. But the first thing you have to do is take your loan policy and disregard it."

The bank evaluates each artist who wants to participate in the program on an individual basis. And it has turned down what Rudolph calls "a fairly good number" of applicants who didn't make the cut financially.

The loans underscore the idea that the program is designed for artists to own their homes. In most other cities' programs, an initial developer rehabs the space and then rents to artists. When the neighborhood starts to take off, property values go up and the artists are forced out. "They treat the artists like urban manure," says Barnett.

In addition to the easier loan terms from Paducah Bank, artists participating in the relocation program have access to a number of other incentives. The city pays a $2,500 bonus for artists to help cover professional rehab fees such as architecture consultations or landscaping plans. None of the materials purchased for construction and rehabilitation are taxed. In addition, the city works to keep the artists' professional life stable: It pays for the artists' Web sites and markets their work nationally.

The city also has taken steps to keep the new homesteaders and their neighborhood safe. It has opened a police substation in Lower Town, lowered speed limits and installed more stop signs. And to make Lower Town visitor- and resident-friendly, the city has invested in additional sidewalks and streetlamps.

For Charlotte Erwin, a painter and printmaker who specializes in marbled watermarks, the change in Lower Town in the five years since she first moved in "is incredible." She and her husband, Ike, a bookbinder, were the first couple to take part in the Artist Relocation Program. Their 1898

Queen Anne home was in desperate condition when they bought it in 2001. The roof had leaked for decades, trees were growing through the foundation and the house's delicate gingerbread detailing was lying in pieces in the overgrown flower garden. Today, their rehabbed house, which includes their studios and a gallery, sits on a sunny corner popping with hibiscus, iris and daylilies. "This has been an amazing thing for us," says Erwin, a native Kentuckian who had moved to Illinois before coming back to her home state.

While the Erwins' home typifies the renaissance of this neighborhood, the city has also made efforts to retain the low-income residents who lived in Lower Town for decades. The city housing authority has replaced some dilapidated low-income housing with new single-family homes. And the revitalized area has attracted other businesses to Lower Town, including restaurants, attorneys' offices and small architecture firms. "We wanted this to be about keeping the neighborhood," says Barnett. "We don't want this to be a neighborhood of just artists. You need a lot more than that to make a real neighborhood."

Performance Measures

The success of the Artist Relocation Program has surpassed anything Barnett or Barone imagined. Artists have moved to Lower Town from as far away as Los Angeles, San Francisco, Tucson and New York. Nearly 35 structures have been renovated. Another 25 are in the works, and more are in the planning stages. There's new construction in Lower Town—overseen by a historic and architectural preservation board—for the first time in half a century.

Barnett and Barone have met with dozens of officials in other cities across the country who are interested in the program. "There's a number of cities working on programs like this, but the one example almost everybody points to is Paducah," says Bruce Knight, the planning director of Champaign, Illinois, and the chair of the American Planning Association committee that selected Paducah for a national award in 2004. "They developed a creative solution that can be transferred to other places."

In the end, the Artist Relocation Program has been a powerful economic tool for the city. Officials estimate the program has attracted $20 million in direct, private investment and brings in hundreds of thousands of dollars per year in sales taxes and other tourism-related revenue. And, of course, property values in Lower Town have skyrocketed. "We didn't set out to make this a national model for economic development," Barone says. "We just wanted to make the neighborhood better."

Picking Picasso

When a city decides to spur economic development by attracting artists, it faces esoteric questions: How do you define art? Who is an artist? What kinds of works are art?

In some places, the answers have led to lists of pre-approved art forms and styles. In Maryland and Rhode Island, for example, where artists who work in specially certified districts are exempt from sales and income taxes, artworks must fit into one of several predetermined categories approved by the state.

But planners in Paducah wanted something different in Lower Town. When they developed the Artist Relocation Program, they decided to open it to artists of all kinds, says Mark Barone, the artist who originally envisioned the plan. "We didn't care whether they were amateur, mid-career or professional—writers, musicians, painters or sculptors."

The program has attracted textile weavers, songwriters, photographers, bookbinders, fabric makers, illustrators and jewelers. "We just want to see that they're producing shows, have a portfolio, have an arts education," says Paducah city planner Tom Barnett.

Because the program hinges on home-ownership and personal loans from the locally owned Paducah Bank, artists who want to participate in the program have to meet certain financial standards.

Aside from ensuring an artist's ability to pay back the loan, though, no one vets an applicant's artwork to see whether it conforms to some predetermined definition of art. "We're not going to judge the quality of the work or the content of it," Barnett says. "We just want to know that an artist is serious."

48. Assets Building in a Small Appalachian City[*]

WILLIAM HATCHER *and* MATT OYER

Communities should focus on their assets rather than their needs when developing economic strategies. Needs-based development often causes communities to offer unwise tax incentives in hopes of luring job growth. Often the money lost due to these tax breaks would be better spent on education, infrastructure, and public safety. A simple refocusing of the development discussion away from needs and toward assets can help a community develop a meaningful vision. Beyond this advice, there is no universal model of development that works for all communities, but there are best practices found in many cities that can provide a guide for community development. On the edge of the Appalachian Mountains, Berea (pop. 14,000), Kentucky, is implementing a number of these best practices.

A Tolerant City

Berea has a history of being a tolerate college town. When founded in 1855, Berea College was the first integrated institution of higher learning in the nation. Today, the college has a well-known arts program. Students accumulate little to no debt because they work at the school or local arts-related shops to help pay their tuition. The school is known for this student support and a superb liberal arts education. The city of close to 14,000 people has a diverse economy.

Berea's robust community of artisans has developed innovative means to make a living off of their art. The city's motto is the "Folks Arts and Crafts Capital of Kentucky—Where Art's Alive." Many of community's artists sell their art in the Kentucky Artist Center located closely to an I-75 exit. These artisans represent an important cluster for the community's economy, but the local economy is not limited to the arts. The college provides a large number of middle class jobs, and there are around 3,500 manufacturing jobs in the city—a significant percentage of the overall employment base. The overall economy is fairly productive. The city's unemployment rate is slightly less than 7 percent.

The city does face the challenge of retaining manufacturing jobs in a state that has been shedding these types of jobs in recent years. Since 2005, Kentucky has lost around 11 percent of its manufacturing jobs. The

[*]Originally published as William Hatcher and Matt Oyer, "Assets Building in a Small, Appalachian City," *PA TIMES*, http://patimes.org/assets-building-small-appalachian-city/. Reprinted with permission of the publisher.

city came to appreciate this challenge when an industrial company left a few years ago. In hopes of avoiding such an economic shock in the future, the community has developed a vision around its assets and not its needs. This vision seeks to strengthen the city's local businesses and cultivate its cluster of artisans.

Leakage Analysis and Localism

To help implement this vision, the community hired the consultant, Michael Shuman, who is known for his promotion of local businesses. Schumann is a strong proponent of communities using leakage analysis to identify areas where a community's assets are "leaking" out of the local economy. To perform this analysis for Berea, Shuman used data from the Business Alliance of Local Living Economies (BALLE). The organization seeks to formulate strategies for communities to retain and foster their local businesses for meaningful development. Community development is not only about economic growth but also the improvement of local institutions. Local businesses are a key component of this betterment. Local jobs keep more money in a community than big box jobs. In fact, a number of studies have shown how big box stores can also contribute less in city taxes than local businesses. By keeping more money in the community, local businesses lead to job growth in other sectors. Localism activist refer to this as the local multiplier effect. Shuman's analysis for Berea claims that by strengthening local businesses, the community could add approximately 5,700 jobs to its labor force—a significant number for a small community. A great deal of this local growth is depended on Berea's creativity cluster.

A Cluster of Artisans

The creative class theory of development is one of the best well-known academic theories in the social sciences. In *The Rise of the Creative Class*, Richard Florida argues that communities with large percentages of workers involved in the arts and other creative progressions are more likely to prosper than localities with traditional labor forces. The arts-based professions produce creativity externalities that improve the overall community. This theory is often criticized as being urban-centered and offering little help for rural and small communities. However, creative clusters can grow in these environments. Stuart Rosenfield describes how a combination of talent and innovation has produced a cluster of glassmakers in the rural mountains of North Carolina. Berea's artisan-based development is another example of a cluster of artisans found in a small community.

Lessons Learned

The creative types certainly add to Berea's economic and comprise a large part of the community's vision to cultivate local economic opportunities. Nevertheless, the community's officials and residents have been savvy enough to develop other assets as well—in particular a fairly robust manufacturing sector. Still, the city's vision of developing local creative business offers future betterment for the community and a buffer in case there are decreases in manufacturing jobs.

From Berea, a few lessons for other communities can be learned. First, the college has help create the community's creativity cluster. Residents are trying to further develop this cluster by growing local businesses. Also, the proximity to I-75 ensures a volume of potential customers for these local businesses and helps maintain a health manufacturing section.

Lastly, in Berea, local residents and officials work together to develop meaningful development strategies driven by assets-based vision. The city's public engagement campaign stands out as one of the top development lessons to be learned. Berea shows us the role of vision, creative local businesses, and economic diversity in assets-based development. Next month, we will discuss another important component of the assets model of development—communication between public officials and citizens.

49. Can Green Technology Propel Economic Development?[*]

Chad Vander Veen

Traveling east along U.S. Highway 12 from Helena, Montana, it's entirely possible to drive for an hour or more without seeing another human. Windswept plains dotted by curiously named hamlets wait for signs of life to come careening down the mostly empty road.

Past Townsend, a small burg on the southern tip of Canyon Ferry Lake, the deer on the highway far outnumber vehicles; and when dusk settles in, they prove much more dangerous. But the farther east you travel, the more you notice one particular man-made structure—electric transmission towers. Specifically cross-like high-voltage direct current towers, which stand in stark contrast to the empty land that spreads in every direction.

The towers eventually terminate in an area known as Judith Gap (pop. 216), notable for its name and not much else. That is, until recently, when from the waving grasses and grazing cattle rose 90 masts looming hundreds of feet in the air. But here there are no sails whipping, no ropes cracking; rather atop these mammoth masts sit wind turbines, each with three enormous blades that turn gently in Big Sky country.

The wind farm at Judith Gap is one of many that have taken root in the vast expanse of central-eastern Montana. And the seeds are being sown for many more. Montana is part of a "wind belt" that envelopes Wyoming, Colorado, New Mexico and northern Texas. These states are in the midst of a wind rush that has driven Montana Gov. Brian Schweitzer and other governors to open their arms and offer incentives to businesses looking to harness the wind, in turn creating jobs and delivering a new kind of green to feed the economy.

In Montana, the abundance of both wind and state incentives have drawn investment from renewable energy companies like Chicago-based Invenergy and Spanish firm NaturEner. These and other companies say they find the state an ideal place to do business.

"What we find in Montana is a very open environment for development, both socially and politically," says Bill Alexander, chief development officer for NaturEner. "That's typical of a new market, an emerging market. But we found the legislative body in Montana has been very interested in helping to continue the incentives for development."

In 2007, Montana passed HB 3, "Clean

---

[*]Originally published as Chad Vander Veen, "Can Green Technology Propel Economic Development?," *Governing*, March 1, 2010. Reprinted with permission of the publisher.

and Green" legislation aimed at attracting renewable energy businesses to the state. The bill created new tax classifications and new, lower property tax rates for renewable energy firms operating in Montana. There are also grants available for renewable energy research, and loan and bond programs. In all, companies will find more than 30 additional state programs for renewable energy. For example, companies generating wind power would likely qualify for at least seven state tax incentives—not to mention a host of federal renewable energy programs.

"Montana has, according to recent studies, the second-best wind energy resources in the country, some of the best on the planet," says Schweitzer. "We have many energy resources that can be cleaner and greener. We're excited about developing our wind."

Schweitzer is among an emerging group of state leaders who are staking at least a piece of their futures on green technology. With states across the nation looking to kick-start their economic engines, green technology increasingly is viewed as, if not the engine, at least a piston helping drive it.

That's the case in Colorado, where Gov. Bill Ritter ordered his Energy Office, Economic Development Office and state CIO to collaborate on ways to nurture green technology start-ups and create demand among consumers for emerging—and typically more expensive—green products.

Colorado is testing a new Discovery Grant Program designed to help early stage companies, which are often simply groups of researchers attempting to take an idea out of the lab and into the commercial market.

"At that point, there's not a lot of available seed capital. So to give them some small grants at the very beginning really shows great support from the state," says Matt Cheroutes, director of communications and external affairs for the Colorado Governor's Office of Economic Development and International Trade.

Cheroutes, a founding member of the Colorado Cleantech Industry Association, says strong executive support for green technology in Colorado will lead to job growth and economic prosperity. But that won't happen, he says, unless companies can deliver their products to a public that can afford them—a tall order in green tech markets that are often too immature to deliver at affordable economies of scale.

Cheroutes says the state works closely with renewable energy firms to develop incentives for consumers. Take solar power, for example, where the cost of installing solar panels typically doesn't pencil out for the average homeowner.

"We've had a lot of people in our state say they want solar on their homes," Cheroutes says. "But they simply can't afford the initial investment to do it. We've seen estimates anywhere from $8,000 for a very small home to $15,000 for a medium-sized home. These days, not a lot of people have the ability to pay that."

The state worked with two Colorado solar firms—SolarCity and SunRun—to develop a financing model that makes solar installations more affordable. Instead of paying the full installation fee upfront, consumers instead put up a down payment that is a fraction of the total cost. Over the next three or four years, the energy savings the consumer realizes goes back to the solar company to pay the remaining balance. After the company is paid in full, the consumer's energy bill decreases significantly.

The Obama administration expects green technology companies to become important players in the nation's economy. The U.S. Department of Energy (DOE) estimates that the wind industry alone will support a half million jobs in the nation by 2030. In the western United States, this activity also would boost annual property tax revenues by more than $1.5 billion and increase payments to rural landowners to more than $600 million over the same time period, according to the DOE's *20% Wind by 2030* report.

The report explores the challenges and implications of generating one-fifth of the nation's electricity needs through wind power. Under that scenario, Montana stands to benefit handsomely from embracing wind power. Given the current and planned wind power capacity for the state, if 20 percent of the nation is in fact using wind power by 2030, Montana could expect 2,875 long-term new jobs, 16,888 short-term jobs, a $78.2 million increase in property tax revenue, and a $230 million annual economic boost over the long term. In addition, data indicates a two-year wind farm construction phase could generate a $900 million short-term economic boost.

But not everyone buys into the rosy predictions. Numerous industry analysts, economists and academics say the green technology sector is too small to drive economic recovery, or that the amount of government subsidies needed to make it successful would effectively cancel out any benefits. Observers also claim wind-power numbers, such as those in the DOE report, are wildly optimistic or simply made up.

"Green jobs estimates include huge numbers of clerical, bureaucratic and administrative positions that do not produce goods and services for consumption," according to the authors of *Green Jobs Myths*, a March 2009 University of Illinois Law and Economics research paper. Written by a group of business and economics professors, the paper also contends that, "Government interference—such as restricting successful technologies in favor of speculative technologies favored by special interests—will generate stagnation."

One of the authors, Roger Meiners, a professor of economics at the University of Texas at Arlington, went into further detail on the VoiceAmerica Talk Radio Network's Free Market program. "The numbers thrown around about the number of jobs that will be created by these alternative energy programs, primarily wind turbines and solar sources of energy, just range all over the place," he says. "One group will say a million jobs, another will say 3 million, and I think they're really just pulling them out of the air, because when you look for where they come up with these numbers, there's nothing there; they just simply make the assertion that this many jobs will be created."

Green technology may indeed create jobs, but it's worth questioning how much money will be spent upfront to create them, Meiners adds.

"If the administration pours tens of billions of dollars into this program as is built into the budget, then obviously there are going to be a lot of people put to work helping to build wind farms, a smart energy grid, expanded solar grids and so on. It could well be in the hundreds of thousands [of jobs created]. The question is, what's the cost, what's the benefit?"

Still, one California group says its research shows that green jobs are growing while the state's economy suffers. Next 10, a nonprofit focused on building the green economy, found significant expansion of California's green economy in a report released in December 2009. From 1995 to 2008, the Sacramento area saw green tech jobs grow by 87 percent, followed by the San Diego region (57 percent), the Bay Area (51 percent), and Orange County and Inland Empire (50 percent).

"Data shows that green-sector businesses are taking root across every region of California, generating jobs across a wide spectrum of skill levels and earnings potential," says F. Noel Perry, founder of Next 10, following the release of the data. "While green jobs clearly cannot solve the state's current unemployment challenges, over time these jobs could become a growing portion of total jobs in California."

Others add that government agencies can nurture green job growth by being early customers for green technology products.

"Government is a big buyer of products and services," says Gary Simon, co-chair of the Sacramento Area Regional Technology Alliance's CleanTech program. "If one pays attention to buying the cleaner, greener products over the standard, that's what we're trying to show is available. Really you're not paying that much more to be clean, green and sustainable. And if you look at the economics over time, it's actually cheaper to be green and sustainable."

But with the green technology industry still largely in its infancy, it can be difficult to know where to look for, say, a thin-film solar vendor. It wouldn't be surprising to find the staff of a green startup focused on simply trying to keep the lights on, to say nothing of navigating the treacherous waters of government procurement. But Simon says the companies are out there and that it may be on government to find them.

"[State and local governments] simply have to look a little bit harder. For everything they buy and use now, there's going to be a clean, green, sustainable alternative," he says. "Finding where those companies are now is a bit of a hunt because it's a small part of the overall economy in the U.S. But they are there."

In Montana, Schweitzer follows what could be described as a "Field of Dreams" approach to developing the state's green economy. In other words, build wind farms and companies that provide supporting technologies-and jobs-will come.

So far, Montana's clean energy incentives appear to be working. NaturEner is spending billions to construct wind farms in the state. Last October, the company opened the state's largest wind farm, a 210-megawatt facility in Glacier County. It's also in planning stages to open a second, even larger 309-megawatt facility a few miles north of the Glacier farm. These wind farms have al-ready created hundreds of temporary and full-time jobs.

NaturEner's wind farms dwarf even the massive Judith Gap wind farm built by Invenergy. That 135-megawatt facility began operation in 2005 and features more than 90 wind turbines. It also generated hundreds of construction jobs and about a dozen full-time jobs, filled primarily by residents of the nearby and remote town of Harlowton.

"We took advantage of [an incentive] for new and emerging businesses for our first two wind projects there in Toole County," says NaturEner's Alexander, adding that the incentive is why the company is pursuing development of a third wind farm in the state. "The Rim Rock project is a 309-megawatt project that should go to construction sometime this winter. It will have 206 turbines. The one we just finished was 140 turbines, so this one will be 50 percent larger than that."

Schweitzer hopes this activity will spur technical breakthroughs that make clean power generation more practical. For instance, better storage technology would reduce the need for expensive transmission lines, a key concern for wind power and other renewable energy sources that generate electricity far from population centers.

"We actually have an unlimited supply of energy, whether it be tidal or wind or solar," Schweitzer says. "The most important technology of our time, and for the next decade, will be storage technology. If we could build a transmission system that had storage on the other end, so the consumer who had that battery in their car could be buying electricity or selling it back into the grid, we would need less transmission."

These obstacles are exactly what Schweitzer is counting on to drive economic progress in Montana, as innovative companies spring up in the state to tackle such issues. If these plans seem overly optimistic, consider the fact that San Diego Gas &

Electric, a Southern California utility serving more than 1 million people, is currently a customer of the Glacier Wind Farm. California has also set a goal for 33 percent of the state's energy to come from renewable sources by 2020. That's an enormous business opportunity for Montana, even using traditional transmission lines. If investment in transmission technology results in significantly improved capacity and efficiency, or if a next-generation storage technology is developed, the level of economic opportunity in Montana becomes so sizable as to be difficult to fathom.

To be effective, however, green incentives must be carefully designed to avoid unintended roadblocks. Many businesses, having been promised grants or other financial perks, have opened shop only to discover the crippling disincentives of bureaucracy.

"If I were governor, I would have a full analysis done of the state's incentive programs, as well as certification programs, and look for those things which do serve to support investment in infrastructure, but also identify those things that work against it, like zoning laws," says K.C. Healy, director of Deloitte's Energy & Resources practice. "There are various sorts of structural things governments can do to where they incent one side but then they make it extremely difficult to carry it out on the ground."

NaturEner's Alexander said Montana takes a less "regulatory" approach than other states his company deals with. "The primary approach we get from Montana is how can they help us? How can the local community help us? How can the government help us expedite the permitting process, what do we need to help promote the projects?" he says. "In other areas, the first approach is sometimes for us to disclose everything we want to do, and let them vet that internally so they can decide if we're doing to right thing for the environment, if we're doing the right thing for the cultural and historical sites within the area."

Besides executive leadership, grants, financing packages and tax incentives, green technology's success as an economic engine may hinge on simple evolution. Despite the best efforts of government, it may come down to whether society has reached the point where the traditional economy, driven by fossil fuels, is no longer acceptable.

"The culture has changed in Colorado," says Cheroutes. "It's something that everyone in Colorado has sort of agreed to and bought in to. And whether that's out of a desire to protect our mountains or to keep our kids from being sent halfway around the world to fight, or if it's to keep kids who are home employed and working, it's a cultural mind change, and sometimes those are the hardest things to deal with in the beginning. So if you have the will of the people, of industry and of political leaders, you can make anything happen."

Of course, it doesn't hurt to have government leadership shepherding that evolution.

50. Metro Wi-Fi Networks[*]

Bert Williams

Walk into virtually any Starbucks and, in addition to lattes and espressos, you'll see people working on laptop computers. A computer networking technology known as Wi-Fi enables users to access the Internet as well as send and receive e-mail globally at more than 100,000 locations called "hot spots." With Wi-Fi, people are no longer shackled to their home or office Internet connections. Internet access is available in many locations throughout their communities.

But hot spots are the Internet equivalent of pay phones-you have to travel to a location where service is available. In the past few years, an emerging technology known by a variety of names, including "metro-scale Wi-Fi," "municipal Wi-Fi," and "mesh networking," has taken the hot-spot concept to the next level, providing community-wide Wi-Fi access and doing for high-speed Internet access what cellular telephones did for voice services. A metro-scale Wi-Fi network can connect all sorts of Wi-Fi devices, including laptops, personal digital assistants (PDAs), and Voice over Internet Protocol (VoIP) phones.

How Does Metro Wi-Fi Work?

Mesh technology makes practical the distribution of Wi-Fi throughout a community by eliminating a significant logistical and economic hurdle—the need to connect each Wi-Fi access point to a wired network. Instead of using conventional access points, Wi-Fi mesh networks provide user connections with mesh routers.

Approximately 10 percent to 20 percent of these routers connect to the Internet via a wire. The rest are completely wireless. Information is transmitted from Wi-Fi router to Wi-Fi router, hopping across the wireless network until it reaches a wired connection to the Internet. Each Wi-Fi router in the mesh network is the size of a breadbox and is attached to a lamppost, telephone pole, or other fixture with a power source. Because there are no large towers, no zoning ordinances or variance approvals are required. No specialized skills are needed; installation averages 15 minutes per pole. The equipment is designed and built for environmental extremes.

If the network expands or is altered, there is no need to return to adjust the routers already in place. Expeditious and straightfor-

*Originally published as Bert Williams, "Metro Wi-Fi Networks: What Are They and How Can They Benefit Your Community?," *PM Magazine* 89, no. 2 (March 2007). Reprinted with permission of the publisher.

ward construction (combined with the lack of wireline connection to each router) delivers enormous cost savings and short deployment time frames. Tropos Networks has provided the wireless routers used in more than 500 metro-scale Wi-Fi networks around the world, including networks in Philadelphia, Anaheim, Corpus Christi, Oklahoma City, Pittsburgh, Houston, and a number of smaller cities.

Metro Wi-Fi Applications

Local governments and service providers are deploying these networks for a wide variety of applications, including public safety, public access, and economic redevelopment:

Locally owned and operated networks in Chaska (pop. 24,400) and Moorhead (pop. 39,300), Minnesota, among others, offer residents broadband (more than one megabit per second [Mbps]) Internet access at dial-up prices ($17 to $20 per month). In a typical city of 10 to 15 square miles with this service, we see that about 20 to 25 percent of households use the service (similar to rates of use of digital subscriber line [DSL] service over telephone lines plus cable broadband penetration), 1,550 are steady daily users, and an average of 2,640 use the service each week. These users generally download, in aggregate, more than 100 gigabytes (one gigabyte equals one billion bytes) per day (that's the equivalent of 1 million typical Web pages, or 25,000 typical MP3 [digital audio] files per day).

New Orleans, Louisiana, installed a public safety video surveillance network using a metro-scale Wi-Fi mesh network. The innovative combination of Internet-based high-end camera technology, Wi-Fi mesh, motion detection, and other elements reduced the murder rate by 57 percent in six months and auto theft by 25 percent in the covered areas. After Hurricane Katrina, this network was converted to a public access

network and remained, for nearly a year, the only source of broadband Internet access in parts of the city.

First responders in Milpitas, California, shave precious seconds off of response times using a metro-scale Wi-Fi network coupled with an automated vehicle location system.

In Corpus Christi, Texas, a metro-scale Wi-Fi network is automating utility meter reading to cut costs and improve service. Using the system, the city is now reading 73 water meters per second compared with minutes per meter with the old manual process. This network is also used by municipal field workers, including public safety officers and building inspectors.

In St. Cloud (pop. 40,900), Florida, a metro-scale Wi-Fi network, built with public economic development funds, provides low-cost broadband access and thus cuts costs for downtown businesses. This leaves the businesses with more money to invest in the local community, creating more jobs and more growth.

In Philadelphia, Pennsylvania, more than 30 citizens per day log-on and use the network installed around Love Park in the city's downtown. Many of these users are from low-income families in Philadelphia, and they use the network to do homework and other research. This is only one small example of how metro-scale Wi-Fi networks foster digital inclusion.

Metro Wi-Fi Business Models

A number of different ownership and operational models, shown in Figure 1, have emerged from early metro-scale Wi-Fi deployments. These ownership models are being used today by localities and across multiple carrier segments to promote broad adoption of metro-scale Wi-Fi for many different users and applications.

Even if the metro-scale Wi-Fi network is privately owned, local government cooperation is usually required to enable the service. This is no different from other forms of broadband: DSL is delivered over wiring installed using rights-of-way often acquired by eminent domain. Cable modem services run over systems installed under local government franchise. Even when built by private service providers, wireless services often require similar city cooperation so that devices can be mounted on city assets such as streetlights.

No matter what the ownership model, most metro-scale Wi-Fi networks are mixed-use networks that provide services simultaneously to multiple sectors (business, government, and consumer). Further analysis shows that these networks leverage up to five "revenue engines" as part of a successful business operation.

Access and Revenue Engines

Consumer and small-medium business (SMB) access. Market analysts estimate that by 2008 there will be more than 500 million Wi-Fi-enabled devices worldwide. Both fixed and mobile users are currently taking advantage of metro Wi-Fi availability. At the start of the metro-scale Wi-Fi deployments in the cities of Chaska and Moorhead, Minnesota, 20 to 25 percent of potential customers signed on within 90 days of service introduction.

In addition, more than 70 percent of subscribers in Chaska and Moorhead reported being extremely satisfied with the speed and the reliability of their service, and 69 percent of subscribers recommended the service to others.

Fee-based consumer and SMB metro-scale Wi-Fi access networks are in place today at Moorhead and Chaska, Minnesota. EarthLink, which will own and operate the networks in Philadelphia, Anaheim, New Orleans, and other cities, offers wireless broadband services with monthly charges ranging from $17 to $25.

Local government and enterprise access. Applications that provide increased productivity and pervasive services work well in this market. Whether improving the productivity of public safety officers, providing increased security through video surveillance cameras, or reducing losses through Wi-Fi-enabled parking and water meters, always-on connectivity helps reduce costs and increase revenues. Some localities are signing on as anchor tenants, thus helping to assure a steady revenue stream as other users and applications come online.

Other communities choose to own the metro-scale Wi-Fi networks, so local access becomes a cost avoidance (in other words, the community provides the service to itself rather than paying access fees to a commercial provider). An excellent example of local access is Corpus Christi, Texas, which uses network access for automated meter reading, public safety, and a number of other operations.

Mobile device-driven applications. Wi-Fi isn't just for laptops anymore. A new wave of mobile devices, such as gaming, mobile TV, Voice over Wi-Fi (VoWiFi), music, photo sharing, and personal communicators offer revenue opportunities. These devices help drive multiple accounts per subscriber, much as cellular accounts have reached 1.9 devices per subscriber.

Advertising and content distribution. Advertising revenues are shifting from traditional printed media to online channels. Online advertising revenues are growing dramatically. Service providers are generating incremental subscriber revenues through revenue-sharing arrangements that monetize the white-space areas on the log-on page, landing page, service provider portal, and so on, in addition to deriving revenue from partnerships with global search firms.

Key to maximizing revenue is the ability to target the advertising based on knowledge about the subscriber-for example, location and behavior. Location-specific cost per click for advertising is 4 to 10 times greater than global or national advertising. Approximately 25 to 30 percent of all search requests are for local information; the combination of mobility and location-specific advertising can drive two to three times more advertising revenue and increase ARPU. Google, for example, will be providing a low-speed, advertising-supported service on the San Francisco metro-scale Wi-Fi network.

Other benefits. St. Cloud (pop. 40,918), Florida, has chosen to forgo revenue altogether. It offers free Wi-Fi to all residents and visitors. St. Cloud calculated that, on average, residents could keep the money they spent on their Internet connections supplied by private telephone and cable companies headquartered out of the local area and instead spend that money in St. Cloud. The average citizen in St. Cloud was paying more for Internet access to out-of-area companies than that citizen was paying in local taxes to support all local services. The city chose to offer free coverage to all citizens, businesses, and government entities in order to keep the money within the city and broaden service to all citizens.

Economics of Metro Scale Wi-Fi

Metro-scale Wi-Fi offers compelling economic advantages over other wide-area wireless and broadband solutions. The technology provides higher throughput; enables richer, more compelling data services; and provides a substantial competitive advantage in the wireless data market. Consider the following:

- Capital expenditures are typically 15 to 50 percent of the cost per megabit per second (Mbps) of subscriber capacity when compared with competing mobile technologies. Use of low-cost Wi-Fi technology and limiting backhaul to a few points per square mile contribute to the superior economics. Metro Wi-Fi network infrastructures are being deployed for $100,000 to $150,000 per square mile or geographically expanded at $90,000 to $130,000 per square mile.

- Operating expenses are similarly 15 to 50 percent of the cost of competing technologies. Truck rolls for customer installations are all but eliminated. Metro-scale Wi-Fi mesh technology dramatically reduces backhaul costs. User-device investment (Wi-Fi phones, gaming devices, or music players, for example) is minimized because devices incorporate Wi-Fi technology as standard equipment or a low-cost option. Virtually all maintenance and optimization of the network is handled remotely via smart mesh analysis and control software.

These tested revenue engines have emerged from the early efforts to deploy metro-scale Wi-Fi networks. Whether the network is locally owned or service provider-owned, using multiple revenue engines delivers profitable services to consumer, business, and government users. Choosing the right technology, products, and integration partners can reduce capital expenditure, operating expense, and time to service.

51. Mississippi Hotspot*

Justin Fritscher

Police in Pelahatchie, a small, central Mississippi town, recently responded to an evening call from a resident concerned about a man sitting in a vehicle in front of her business after hours. Police arrived and discovered the man was using his laptop—an out-of-towner tapping into the town's free Wi-Fi.

"He said, 'I'm just a businessman coming through,'" Pelahatchie police chief Glenda Shoemaker says. "He needed a place so he could send some information on the Internet."

As it turns out, he could have gotten online from almost anywhere in the tiny town (pop. 1,500). Leaders of this community began installing wireless Internet infrastructure in 2009, and Pelahatchie Mayor Knox Ross says the Wi-Fi was worth its $7,000 price tag. "It's one more extra thing we can do to differentiate ourselves from everybody else. I suspect in a few years other places will have it, but right now, very few do," he says.

Town leaders say the new Wi-Fi—as well as other projects to enhance quality of life—is key to drawing more businesses to Pelahatchie and making life better for residents. The town lies just 30 miles east of Jackson and has an average household income of about $31,600, lower than the state average of $36,400.

Small-Town Hustle

Because of its location on the edge of the metropolitan area, Ross notes that the town has to be highly competitive to draw businesses. "We don't have the same resources that larger cities have, and we have to hustle," he says. None of the other municipalities in the area offer free Wi-Fi. Neighboring cities—larger in population and closer to Jackson—are big competition, offering more housing and retail options for companies wanting to locate.

The move also helps the town's image. "Perception, in our business, is as important as actual reality," says Tom Troxler, director of the Rankin First Economic Development Authority. "Sometimes in Mississippi, we have to overcome negative perceptions."

The mayor says he got the free Wi-Fi idea from Troxler, whose job is to bring businesses to Rankin County, where Pelahatchie is located. Troxler says he read about a town in Iowa going fully wireless and thought it could help Pelahatchie grow.

While it's hard to establish a cause-and-effect relationship, Pelahatchie's economy has managed to remain stable lately, and the Wi-Fi perk certainly hasn't hurt. Since its installation in January, a woodworking studio, an insulation installation company, and a county service building have made concrete plans to open shop—and to employ at least 30 people.

Sales tax revenues have stayed steady while other local municipalities are seeing a decline. Part of what keeps Pelahatchie afloat is its variety of industry. With 216 employees, Mississippi Baking is the biggest employer in town. "While one business might not be doing so well, others might be picking up the slack," Ross says.

Ross also notes that he has talked to a handful of businesses considering relocating to town since the Wi-Fi launch, and the service makes a good selling point. "When I talk to a company about coming here, when they see tangible evidence that we are putting our money where our mouth is, it gets their attention," notes the mayor of 12 years.

Starting Small

The downtown—a four-block area—was the first area covered by the Wi-Fi cloud. Now, schools and commercial areas on the outskirts of town can access the free wireless Internet, and the town plan to extend it further as more money comes available in its general fund.

The town has installed 10 transmitters on buildings and light poles—each able to transmit a signal from 400 to 600 feet, notes James Murphy, the owner of WebWerks, the company that installed the system. The monthly bill to the Internet service provider is about $200.

When Ross first started researching options, a larger Wi-Fi company quoted a price of about $50,000 for the whole project, way too much for the town's annual $1 million budget to absorb. Ross, an avid camper, noticed that many campgrounds offer free Wi-Fi, and he knew they wouldn't have paid that much for Internet service.

Ross called the Jellystone campground just outside of Pelahatchie, and learned that WebWerks installed its system.

Pelahatchie's Wi-Fi is for the casual user, for someone checking e-mail or just wanting to surf the web from a park bench. It was not made to replace existing businesses' Internet connections, but some use it that way, Murphy notes. The town can see how many users are on at one time, and Ross says eight to 10 users are there on average. He expects the number to keep increasing. People are using it across town, inside homes, and at businesses, the park, and playgrounds.

Downtown plays host to a cluster of businesses, including a pharmacy, salon, insurance and accounting offices, grocery store, and woodworking shop. Ross says he would like to see a coffee shop or more restaurants, and he's hoping the Wi-Fi and the improving face of downtown will be the lures.

"At first I thought it was a weird idea," say town clerk Bettye Massey, who has worked in town hall for 20 years. "It's pretty unique for a small town like us." Although larger cities like San Francisco, Atlanta, Austin, Texas, and Portland, Oregon, pioneered large-scale Wi-Fi, Pelahatchie's decision is having a ripple effect among small towns in Mississippi. One town considering a Wi-Fi push is Quitman (Pop. 2,500), located about 90 miles southeast of Pelahatchie.

Wi-Fi isn't the town's only tech-savvy push: Four webcams that were installed downtown will allow people to watch what's happening there via the town's website, www.pelahatchie.org. Also available on the town's site is the mayor's blog, which Ross updates a couple times each week.

The town has $2.7 million in projects now under construction, including renovations of town hall and a former hardware store that is being converted into a community center.

Plans are also under way to redo Second Street, the main drag through town. Included in the Second Street streetscape plans are landscaping and crosswalks with scored concrete. These projects should be completed by summer 2010. "It will be something that people can be proud of,"

Ross says. Another project in the works is a two-mile bike path linking downtown to the nearby Jellystone campground. A town museum and a new library opened.

"A lot of this stuff is what people dreamed about" for Pelahatchie, Ross says.

52. The Supermarket as a Neighborhood Building Block*

Mark Hinshaw *and* Brian Vanneman

For at least 50 years, Americans have held fast to the ideal of a neighborhood that essentially derives from the one described by Clarence Perry in 1929: a geographic area bounded by arterial streets, with a school in the center and shops and apartments along the edges. Although this classic map is now considered quaint because of its unworkable intersections, random street pattern, and odd scraps of public space, it has endured and informed countless subdivisions. Popular literature and even blogs refer to some variant of this neighborhood unit as if it were sacrosanct.

What the nostalgia buffs don't take into account is that the classic pattern was meant to accommodate families with four or five children. With families like that, communities might logically locate an elementary school, playgrounds, and a community center within walking distance of homes.

Unfortunately, this construct all but mandated automobile use for shopping and other tasks, offered no recognition of transit, relegated people living in high-density housing to noisy streets, and created isolated enclaves separated by wide arterials. Nonetheless, the idea was so compelling that many neighborhoods in the U.S. today have those precise traits. However, both the nation and family composition have changed tremendously in the past several decades.

What Demographics Tells Us

Today, while the number of households in the U.S. has vastly increased, household size has declined dramatically—to around two people per unit. Our population is aging rapidly, with as many people older than 65 as under 18. And that shift will become even more pronounced in the next several decades as millions of older citizens live longer lives than ever before. Extensive research by Arthur C. Nelson, FAICP, at the University of Utah, among others, has called attention to these transformations in our culture.

At the same time, we are seeing tremendous shifts in attitudes and behavior. High levels of consumption are winding down because of the recession, but even before that many people were looking for other ways to live.

Now many people are looking for the small and beautiful. According to the U.S.

Census Bureau, the average size of new homes has decreased for the first time in decades. Richard Florida has noted, too, that the "creative class" is eschewing the scattered suburban pattern in favor of denser urban living.

This past year, the first wave of the baby boom reached retirement age—a major milestone. Think what will happen when boomers begin to lose their driver's licenses. Many of them will simply have to find new places to live where walking is possible and transit is available.

Environment and Human Health

President Barack Obama recently announced a national goal of a 17 percent reduction in greenhouse gases by 2020. To get there, we will have to make major changes in living patterns over time. But even without that goal, people have been seeking ways to reduce their own carbon footprint, often by walking, bicycling, or taking transit.

Researchers at the University of British Columbia have found that residents who live in denser, mixed use neighborhoods drive up to 30 percent less than people living in outlying areas. The Oregon-based Climate Trust suggests that households can cut their carbon footprint in half by sticking with a single car and living in denser housing. They can halve their footprint again by having no car. A recent study published by CEOs for Cities found that homes within denser, mixed use, and more walkable neighborhoods have generally maintained significantly higher values compared with outlying locations—despite the recession.

Combine all that with the slow food movement, restaurants featuring local products, farmers markets, and rooftop and community gardens. Community plans are beginning to recognize the interdependence of land use, energy use, affordable housing, public health, social equity, and the supply of food. Some cities are working to get grocery stores into lower income neighborhoods that have little access to fresh food at reasonable prices.

With all these new trends, perhaps it's time to look at a new neighborhood model, one that allows people to live complete lives without depending on cars. Such a neighborhood might not be carbon neutral, but at least it would be carbon-reduced.

A New Neighborhood Building Block

One idea is for the grocery store and its siblings to reemerge as cornerstones of great places to live. Americans already are seeking grocery stores for wholesome food and personal connections.

One of the nation's most successful greenfield new urbanist developments, Orenco Station outside of Portland, Oregon, was based on this principle: "the ability to walk to get a quart of milk," as developer Rudy Kadlub put it. The neighborhood features a grocery store close to housing, offices, and other retailers.

A study completed there in 2009 found that half of the Orenco residents surveyed "report walking to a local store to shop five or more times a week, compared to only five percent of respondents in the typical suburb who report that level of walking."

In downtown Houston, a 2004 survey found that "residents and workers consider a grocery store to be the missing element of downtown," and that for Houston residents over 40, grocery shopping was ranked as the second most popular leisure activity. Last December, following years of planning and sweat equity, the long-anticipated Byrd's Market & Cafe opened in downtown Houston. "Nothing says downtown like a neighborhood grocer," says Angie Bertinot, director of marketing for the Houston Downtown Management District.

Houston and Portland are not unique:

One of the amenities urban residents most desire is a grocery store.

Hanging Out

Supermarkets have become social spaces. Some include espresso bars and seating so shoppers can eat a meal on the spot. People hang out, read, and meet friends—even when buying groceries isn't part of the trip. The New Seasons markets in Portland, Oregon, host special nights for wellness classes, Scrabble, yoga, and crafts. Clearly, they're not your mother's supermarkets.

Meanwhile, many grocery corporations are rethinking their business model, giving up the longstanding template of a single-story box surrounded by acres of asphalt. Increasingly, these markets are going into mixed use developments with little or no parking.

The December 2009 issue of *New Urban News* reported on a couple of supermarkets being built as part of mixed use developments in Washington, D.C., as if that were a major innovation. But in some cities, such as Portland, Chicago, Seattle, and Vancouver, where public investments and growth policies have emphasized urban infill for some time, this trend has been prevalent for years—in the latter two cities for more than a decade. The Seattle area alone has more than a dozen mixed use developments that incorporate full-service supermarkets.

In the past, the lack of parking was often cited as a factor that kept markets out of urban neighborhoods. This is because for decades markets assumed that every customer would arrive by car. But this view seems to be changing rapidly as well. Some recent markets have provided only a few dozen stalls, far fewer than the standard rule of thumb. Some provide no parking at all. And these stores are doing quite well. The recently opened IGA market in downtown Seattle has not a single parking stall; customers tote their purchases home in cloth sacks.

It's one of a growing number of urban markets that cater to shoppers who carry two bags of groceries out by hand every few days, rather than transporting 10 bags by car twice a month. Buying fresh also means buying more frequently. Some chains now deliver right to your door, with purchases made on the Internet. In San Francisco, Mollie Stone's Market provides a free shuttle bus to the store on demand—a service that is especially popular with seniors.

Carbon-Reduced, Market-Centric

Let's conceive of a neighborhood with enough customers to support a contemporary supermarket with a relatively typical 45,000 square feet of floor space. Shoppers get there by foot.

While we're at it, let's reconsider a quarter-mile as the ideal walking distance between home and the store. Recent studies by the University of California, Berkeley, have shown that many people will walk much farther for daily needs. Many years ago, researcher William H. Whyte concluded that people will walk farther if the walk is interesting. So let's make the walk more interesting, even if somewhat longer. No parking lots, no blank walls; parks, gardens, and public spaces instead. And let's provide a true Main Street.

The neighborhood would also have convenient schools, but they would not be central. There might be a compact branch of a community college catering to adults—a format we are beginning to see in many places. And there would be a range of other civic buildings and spaces, such as a library, community center, a village green or square, and perhaps a community health clinic.

A supermarket would be at or near the center of the neighborhood. Interestingly, achieving enough density to support a full-service market, with most of its customers arriving on foot, is also enough to support other services. A contemporary market requires the support of 8,000 to 10,000 people (or around 4,000 households). According to economic rules of thumb, that number of people is sufficient to support at least another 50,000 to 80,000 square feet of shops and services.

This would translate into a two-sided street three or four blocks long—a quite walkable "main street" (equivalent to the principal streets in both classic small towns and mature neighborhoods.) In this model, the neighborhood is contained within a radius of four or five blocks (1,500 to 1,700 feet) from the main street. Each end of the main street would be anchored by community uses.

This is our catchment area. It resembles one suggested by Christopher Alexander and his coauthors in the seminal 1977 book about architecture, A Pattern Language. But in contrast to old neighborhood models, the main street is at the center, rather than a school. Further, traffic is brought right into the center, rather than kept to the edges, to provide access and activity. And while the model does not depend on transit, accommodation could be made for buses, commuter rail, streetcars, light rail, or a combination.

This model is distinct from the new urbanist "transect" in that a wide range of medium- and high density urban housing, as well as low-, mid-, and high-rise development, could coexist within one relatively small geographic area. This pattern reflects the messy vitality of many different types of uses, building types and sizes, and human activities within a condensed area.

Visualizing the Model

The model we are describing allows residents to use automobiles very little or not at all, and it offers a range of housing choices—the two critical factors in reducing household carbon emissions. Housing would range from town houses around the edge to high-rise apartments near the center. Some buildings would have live/work units on the ground floor. Office buildings would provide incubator space for both mature and start-up businesses.

We imagine all residents living within walking distance of the main street, which is anchored by a supermarket. Various types of public space—parks, public squares, greens, and community gardens—would be located throughout the neighborhood. Public uses are clustered at one end of the main street: schools for both children and adults, a community center, and a park shared by all these institutions. Office buildings, a library, a civic square large enough for a regular public market, and health services are located at the other end of the main street. Dedicated bicycle lanes or shared lanes are found on many streets. Transit could offer access to jobs elsewhere in the region.

For those who need to drive, one parking stall would be provided for each dwelling and some on-street parking stalls would be set aside for shared electric vehicles and charging posts. Rooftops would house photovoltaic arrays and wind turbines, green roof systems for water absorption, and space to cultivate crops and raise chickens.

Although the neighborhood recognizes the needs of various household types, there is a particular accommodation for an aging population. Finally, below-market-rate housing units, many built by nonprofit organizations, would be distributed throughout the 100-block area.

Clearly, a new model for neighborhoods is in order. And it shouldn't hark back to nostalgic notions of life in the 19th century but instead should address, head-on, the challenges of this century. The neighborhood suggested here attempts to combine principles of environmental, social, and economic sustainability with concepts of density, diversity, and demographic change.

Alternatives

Several other urban food-selling formats are emerging besides the full-service grocery, each suited to different aims and local contexts: farmers markets, food co-ops, healthy corner stores, and a new crop of small urban grocers, with about half the size of the traditional footprints.

Fresh and Easy markets, introduced in the U.S. in 2007 by British retail giant Tesco, has made an impression in some cities. The stores are much smaller (10,000 to 13,000 square feet), and emphasize high-quality prepared foods, quick in-and-out trips, and daily purchases such as produce, flowers, cheese, and wine. Many shoppers find the size—with 5,000 different products rather than 40,000—more manageable. Safeway, Whole Foods, Giant Eagle, and even Wal-Mart are looking to imitate the Fresh and Easy model, which now operates about 100 stores in California, Arizona, and Nevada.

Food co-ops and healthy corner stores are proliferating as well. While these local business and nonprofits may be desirable neighborhood anchors, they also require an entrepreneurial spirit, time, and determined community organizing. As a rule, larger stores tend to be owned and operated by national or regional chains, while smaller stores are locally owned. And, just as store sizes differ, so do the metrics related to them, such as the supporting population, the number of parking spaces, and the area of the required site.

REFERENCES

Climate Trust. www.climatetrust.org .
Healthy corner stores. www.healthycornerstores.org.
Nelson, Arthur C., FAICP, and Robert Lang "The Next 100 Million." *Planning*, January 2007.
Walk Score. www.walkscore.com.

53. Fresh Fight*

ZACH PATTON

Woodbury County (pop. 102,000), Iowa, isn't the first place you'd expect people to worry about where their food comes from. The county, which includes Sioux City (pop. 82,000) and its surroundings, boasts some of the most fertile farmland in the United States. And Iowa as a whole leads the nation in the production of pork, corn and eggs, and ranks second in soybeans and beef. Yet two years ago, Woodbury became the first county to mandate that food purchased by the county—for consumption in its jail, juvenile detention centers and other cafeterias—be grown and processed within a 100-mile radius.

Why would such an agriculturally productive place feel the need to promote local food? The truth is, in Woodbury County, as in much of the country, large corporations are increasingly farming the land. Unable to compete, family farms are folding and rural communities are declining. As it turns out, what's grown in Iowa doesn't generally get eaten in Iowa. And a lot of what's eaten in Iowa comes from all over the globe.

The Local Food Purchase Policy was the brainchild of Rob Marqusee, who was hired by the county in 2005 to help rejuvenate the rural economy. Marqusee believes that the county already is sitting on its best revitalization strategy—or more precisely, it's already eating it. Woodbury County residents spend about $250 million a year on groceries, and only 1 percent of that spending goes to local food. Using the county's purchasing power to buy local food has the potential to shift nearly $300,000 a year to local farmers. More importantly, it may help create a network of area growers and, in turn, encourage more consumers to buy from them.

Woodbury County is joining the fast-growing movement to "eat local." Supporters say the benefits include everything from a stronger sense of community to a healthier planet. Local governments see advantages, too, and a growing number of them are trying to encourage purchases of local, seasonal produce. But those efforts often are stymied by state and federal farm policies, which for decades have favored larger farms. As governments are realizing, it can be tough to eat locally when your policies act globally.

Love for Locavores

The local-food movement, of course, is something of a throwback. Eighty years ago, most people had no choice but to eat crops grown close to market—and if it wasn't strawberry season, there were no strawberries. That began to change after World War II, as improvements in transportation and

*Originally published as Zach Patton, "Fresh Fight," *Governing*, March 31, 2008. Reprinted with permission of the publisher.

refrigeration made it possible to ship fresh food long distances. People started eating pineapples in Boston and shrimp in Kansas City.

Since the mid-1990s, however, local food has grown popular at the grassroots. One manifestation of that is in the number of farmers markets, which has grown from about 1,750 in 1994 to nearly 4,400 today. Another trend is the growth in community-supported agriculture groups, in which customers buy "shares" in a farm and each receives a portion of its produce. These were virtually nonexistent in the United States two decades ago; today, there are more than 1,200 of them. Thousands of people have participated in the "100-mile diet," an online challenge to eat only locally grown food for a month. "Locavore," a noun meaning someone who eats only what's grown nearby, was recently added to the New Oxford American Dictionary.

Proponents of eating locally say it's fresher, healthier and tastier. Supporting farmers close to home, they say, can help stop suburban sprawl by keeping farmland economically viable. The newly popular reason for going local, though, is the sense that it's better for the Earth. By choosing local vegetables over supermarket fare— which has traveled, on average, 1,300 miles to get to your produce aisle—you're reducing your carbon footprint.

At least that's the idea. In truth, reducing "food miles" may not always translate into greener groceries. Is it really better for the environment to have 30 farmers driving gas-guzzling pickup trucks to greenmarkets three times a week, instead of one refrigerated truck delivering produce to grocery stores along its route? It's hard to know.

Legal Obstacles

Nevertheless, many state and local governments want to capture and encourage consumer demand for local foods. They have a few options. The first, says Marion Nestle, an author of several books on food policy, is to just get out of the way. "What states and cities have to do is make room for farmers markets. That means closing streets and all that. But it also means removing other barriers."

Nestle advocates less restrictive policies regarding cleanliness and processing for foods sold at farmers markets. Strict regulations—such as requiring livestock to be slaughtered in a federally inspected facility, or mandating costly permits and site visits from supervisors to certify produce as organic—make it hard for small farmers to compete. In one month last fall, officials in Virginia, Michigan and Pennsylvania arrested farmers for failing to comply with food laws. But changing those kinds of policies could be difficult. For starters, many of them are mandated at the federal level. And since they protect consumers from eating unsafe foods, easing restrictions like that could be a tough sell.

For its part, the city of Chicago kicked off the "Eat Local Live Healthy" program. The city hopes to boost local produce by creating more farmers markets, and by raising public awareness about the benefits of healthful eating. Many cities are directly supporting area growers through farm-to-school programs, which provide school cafeterias with local produce. There are currently more than 1,100 such programs in the country, involving nearly 11,000 schools in 38 states. Another tack, taken by some 30 localities and 11 states, is to promote local eating through a "food policy council." Such entities bring together farmers, distributors, restaurateurs and consumers, in hopes of fortifying the supply chains that deliver food from farms to nearby dining rooms.

Government-sponsored promotional programs, particularly at the state level, do highlight one problem: How do you define "local"? A locavore in Cincinnati, for example, would rather eat lettuce from northern Kentucky and carrots from eastern Indiana than pumpkins from Cleveland. Just because produce comes from your own state doesn't necessarily mean it's local. "There is a little bit of a disconnect there," says Rich Pirog, associate director of the Leopold Center for Sustainable Agriculture at Iowa State University. When it comes to local food, he says, state boundaries aren't that important. "You can see the drawbacks from having state-based programs, because they'll dilute the benefits of local food."

For that reason, Pirog says, initiatives at the city and county level may be more effective. But that doesn't mean they're easy. In Woodbury County, where the buy-local campaign also came with property tax rebates for farmers who use organic practices, it's been slow going. County departments are ready to buy their food locally, but the suppliers just aren't there yet. Local products—mostly melons and apple cider—still account for only about 5 percent of the county's food purchases.

But there are signs that the effort has been worthwhile. A few farmers have moved into Woodbury County. The county's progressive food policies have attracted new businesses, including a $40 million organic soybean processing plant that's currently being built. Marqusee is working on a major financing program that would provide low-interest loans for new farms smaller than 40 acres. And, all the eggs bought by the county will come from a local provider. It's a start, Marqusee says. "Creating a local food system is very difficult. It's a massive, 180-degree turnaround for anybody in this area. But we're really just doing the only practical thing we can do to support our rural communities."

54. Creating Jobs Over Coffee[*]

Kristen Carney

Amid the grassy plains of Greensburg (pop. 785), Kansas, Scott and Susan Reinecke recently opened Studio 54 Glass, a glass art studio. Some 650 miles south, in Austin, Texas, Tina Cannon and Christy Scovel are bringing their Internet start-up, PetsMD.com, to life. These two businesses provide vastly different products, but they are alike in that business incubator programs have helped them grow.

The Greensburg Business Incubator, which leases space to Studio 54 Glass, is a traditional incubator—leasing space and providing business services for start-up firms—but the Capital Factory incubator, which is helping PetsMD, is something else entirely.

Two Business Incubator Models

A tornado destroyed downtown Greensburg in May 2007. After surveys and public meetings identified the area's needs, the city secured $3 million from the U.S. Department of Agriculture and Frito-Lay to build a facility that would encourage downtown growth. To accomplish this goal, the city built a 10,000-square-foot, LEED platinum business incubator with enough office space for 10 businesses. Studio 54 Glass was the first tenant there.

The Reineckes' retirement dream was to open a glass art studio, and the new incubator was just the opportunity that they needed. Studio 54 Glass pays about $365 per month for its 800-square-foot retail space. "We wouldn't be able to do this without the business incubator," Scott Reinecke says, "because it's the only place in town for this business to have a go at it."

Businesses in the Greensburg Business Incubator have access to courses from the Kansas Small Business Development Center. The incubator is now completely full less than a year after it opened and is close to accomplishing its mission of serving as an anchor building and assisting in a revival of the downtown area.

Location, Location, Location? Not Always

Unlike Studio 54 Glass, online businesses like PetsMD don't require the perfect location in a downtown anchor building. PetsMD.com is an online encyclopedia of veterinarian-approved pet health information, where people can find vets and book appointments. Businesses like PetsMD can be run from coffee shops or spare bedrooms. Inexpensive space and business classes weren't what Tina Cannon, cofounder

---

[*]Originally published as Kristen Carney, "Creating Jobs Over Coffee," *Planning*, December 2009. Copyright 2009 by the American Planning Association. Reprinted by permission of *Planning* magazine.

of PetsMD, needed to help her business grow. She needed mentors.

"For us, Capital Factory was a perfect fit." Cannon says. "We gained a tremendous amount of knowledge and rapid growth from the advice of our mentors. We were able to grow our company in 10 weeks, where in the regular business cycle it would have taken us up to a year to get here."

Capital Factory is a 10-week program that provides five start-ups with weekly mentoring sessions from a group of 20 experienced mentors who have founded successful companies. The incubator also provides a small amount of start-up capital along with the services of an attorney, a publicist, an accountant, and others. The five companies in the Capital Factory program currently employ 20 people, seven of whom work for PetsMD.

Another central difference between the mentor-model incubator and the traditional model is that the city of Austin paid nothing for Capital Factory. The program is privately funded by the mentors in exchange for a small ownership stake. Participating companies sell five percent of their businesses to Capital Factory in exchange for mentorship, start-up cash, and services. And all of the Capital Factory businesses are required to be located in Austin, because the mentors are located there.

Of all of the mentor-model incubator programs, the most famous is the Y Combinator seed-funding program started by Paul Graham. Graham started Viaweb in 1995 and sold it to Yahoo three years later for an estimated $49 million, according to articles published at the time. While speaking to a group of college students interested in entrepreneurship, Graham advised them to raise money from investor-mentors with experience starting companies. After reflecting on his own advice, Graham started Y Combinator as an experiment in the summer of 2005.

Y Combinator paid each start-up founder $6,000 in exchange for about six percent of the company. The founders were required to move to Cambridge, Massachusetts, where they would work out of their apartments, meet with Graham during office hours, and attend weekly seminars. More than 200 companies applied in the first year, and Graham funded eight of them. By the end of the first three-month program, he knew that his mentor-model program had merit. Y Combinator has funded 145 companies in both Cambridge and Mountain View, California, since 2005. The Y Combinator companies have created about 500 jobs—a number that will undoubtedly grow along with their companies.

Remarkably, the $6,000 per start-up provided by Y Combinator doesn't add up to a lot of money. In fact, it typically won't even cover the start-up attorney's fees. However, $6,000 will cover the living expenses of the founders, who share an apartment and dine on Ramen noodles for three months as they build their companies. Graham's business philosophy of building lean companies focused on solving problems, plus the rise of computers and the Internet, has made the mentor-model incubator possible.

Paul Graham is not the only businessman who has run a successful mentor-model incubator. Marc Nathan, a Capital Factory mentor and the director of entrepreneur development for the Houston Technology Center, estimates that 34 mentor-model incubators have been implemented worldwide in cities as diverse as Lexington, Kentucky; Athens, Greece; and Vancouver, Canada.

Despite the economic downturn, mentor-model incubators are seeing an increase in their number of applicants. Graham is expecting more than 1,000 companies to apply to Y Combinator's next session, five times the number of companies that applied in 2005. Capital Factory had over 250 companies apply for its first summer 2009 program, well above the 100 applicants that it expected.

Get Rich Quick or Over the Long Haul?

Mentor-model incubators typically do not target a specific number of businesses or jobs. Rather, their goal is long-term profit.

Therefore, the only apparent shortcoming of this kind of incubator is that it seems like a get-rich scheme for wealthy investors—not a tool for planners to create jobs. Undoubtedly, these incubators are an investment opportunity, but there are many other motives for the investor-mentors.

Each of the 20 Capital Factory mentors owns 0.25 percent of each company. If one of the companies beats the lottery-sized odds and sells for $10 million, each mentor would make $25,000—not exactly a big windfall for people who have already bought and sold successful businesses.

By owning a tiny slice of each company, the mentors are further motivated to help those companies succeed. Leveraging private dollars for public gain is not unheard of in the planning field. Public-private partnerships have long been helpful tools in the planner's tool belt. Private funding is a vital part of the mentor model, and innovative planners with a touch of their own entrepreneurial spirit could take steps to encourage mentor model incubators in their backyards.

Which Model Is Best for Your City?

Gary Smith, who works in the Kansas office of the USDA, helped plan the Greensburg Business Incubator. Smith says the first step for planners is to ask, "What does the community have that they want to build upon?" In the case of Greensburg, it was the community's shared vision of rebuilding after its disastrous tornado. A traditional business incubator serving as a downtown anchor fit that vision. Additionally, the city was eligible for disaster funding to finance the incubator.

Consider your city's primary economic base and how you can build upon that base. If your current base includes location-needy sectors like retail and manufacturing, a traditional business incubator might be a better fit. But if your current base includes businesses that don't require a physical space, like technology and services, the mentor model might be preferable.

On the other hand, local economies can change. If your region's largest economic sector is agriculture, a mentor-model incubator might focus on teaching smaller farms how to make money from selling organic produce at local farmers markets. If your region is industrial, you might learn from the experience in Youngstown, Ohio—a classic Rust Belt city—where the Youngstown Business Incubator has received nationwide media attention for generating 300 technology jobs. But in the end, the type of incubator model for your city might come down to funding.

What to Look For

With the mentor-model incubator, there are no funding forms to fill out or any grant paperwork to complete. Instead, you need to recruit a group of business-savvy men and women to serve as mentors. Recruiting the right people is undoubtedly the most important step. The mentors you recruit will be directly responsible for the success or failure of the business incubator. Here are three absolute rules to follow when selecting your mentors.

- Mentors must actively be running a business or actively investing in businesses. Retired executives are not a good fit for this program.
- Professors make good mentors only if they have run successful businesses themselves. Their focus must be on business practice, not theory.

• You, the planner, are not a mentor. Unless you have run multiple successful companies, you are not a good fit.

Ideally, mentors will be mid- or late-career. Concentrate on finding people who run firms with 10 to 20 employees. These people will have more lessons to share with start-up companies than a CEO with a staff of 200 (unless that CEO grew the 200-person company from a start-up). How do you find these people? If your area has venture capital firms or investment banks, ask people there. Members of these two groups might make good mentors, or they'll know other people who might be interested. Plus, these groups are inherently interested in new start-up opportunities in town. Other good sources of information are other business incubators, the chamber of commerce, business reporters, and university professors.

Business Incubators:

Traditional Model Incubator

Focus: Subsidized Rent + Business Services
Cost to City: $100,000–$3 million
Typically Publicly Funded
Location Specific

Mentor-Model Incubator

Focus: Mentorship + Business Infrastructure
Cost to City: $0
Typically Privately Funded
Physical Space not Required

Recruiting Steps

To get started, commit to finding and meeting with one potential mentor a week either over coffee or during lunch.

At the meeting, explain the highlights of the mentor-model incubator: A group of successful business professionals will select, fund, and advise start-up companies. They will commit to at least two hours of mentorship a week for 10 weeks in exchange for a small ownership percentage.

Do a bit of homework on potential mentors. Then you can honestly tell them how you think their past success makes them a good fit for a mentor. Ask for their thoughts.

Be prepared for "I'm too busy," and follow up with "then that makes you the right person to teach young entrepreneurs how to manage their time." That said, graciously accept a "No." Your mentors must be committed and excited about the opportunity.

If you get "I'll think about it," give them some background information—a copy of this article or a printout of Paul Graham's thoughts about Y Combinator or the program description from the Capital Factory website. You'll have to take printouts, because busy people will forget to follow up when they get back to the office.

No matter what they say, ask them to recommend two other local business professionals that they admire. As soon as the first mentor agrees to participate, ask that person to help you recruit other mentors from their network of contacts.

The number of mentors you'll need depends on the size of the business incubator, the number and types of businesses you want to help, and incubator goals. Some mentor-model incubators have four mentors; some have 20. Get more mentors than you think you will need, because inevitably one or two of them will drop out due to business emergencies.

Once you build your mentorship team, put all of your training as a planner and community organizer to work. Help the team set goals, create a plan, and determine a timeline. Identify potential problems: How will the team find companies, how long will the program be, how often will they meet with start-ups, and who will help the companies with the everyday challenges of running a small business (like when their Internet connection fails at 2 a.m.)?

Organizing business professionals will be somewhat like herding cats. Consider using surveys and conference calls to capture people's ideas. Give firm deadlines for responding and then move on if they don't meet a deadline. Also, consider asking the mentors to nominate one to three people as managing directors who will handle the logistics of the incubator program.

Here comes the hard part: Once your mentor team has a plan in place, gracefully bow out. But keep your eyes open as you are reading the morning paper or local blogs. Don't be surprised if you hear news that companies in the incubator program are hiring employees, launching new products, or going public. That's what happened after Paul Graham started Y Combinator, and it's what is happening today with Pets MD and Capital Factory. Over a few cups of coffee, you could help it happen in your city, too.

RESOURCES

Economic Development Administration. www.eda. gov.

National Business Incubator Association's Recession Resources. www.nbia.org/resource_library/reces sion_resources/funding.php.

United States Department of Agriculture (use the link for the Rural and Community Development Department). www.usda.gov.

www.paulgraham.com (for information about how to manage mentors).

55. Reimagining a Mill Community*

DAVID E. VERSEL

This August, nearly 200 years of industrial history in Biddeford and Saco, Maine, ended quietly when the WestPoint Home blanket factory, the last textile manufacture in the cities' shared Mill District, closed its doors. Although the heyday of Biddeford-Saco textile manufacturing is long over, a new era is taking shape. Both cities are actively working to reuse their massive, red-brick mill buildings as the center of a creative economy.

"The revitalization of our Mill District is very important to our economic development," says Biddeford Mayor Joanne Twomey. "The closing of WestPoint now makes it more important than ever to ensure we provide jobs for the future." The plan recently put in place address jobs as well as infrastructure development, the design of public spaces improving riverfront access, arts and cultural programming, and most of all, public financing.

Biddeford (pop. 21,000) and Saco (pop. 18,000), twin cities on either side of the Saco River, enjoy a prime location along the Atlantic coast 20 minutes south of Portland. However, the two towns have struggled to move beyond their historic mill town identity. After peaking at 10,000 employees around 1900, textile industry employment declined to about 1,000 jobs by the 1980s, leaving the Mill District's two million square feet mostly empty.

The area's overall economy survived the textile industry's decline because of manufacturing activities in industrial parks, tourism activity at nearby beaches, growth at the University of New England, and big box retail development near the Maine Turnpike. But all these activities occurred outside of the core, leaving the cities' historic downtowns and the mill district struggling. Eager for any investment in the central area, both cities approved a controversial 1985 proposal by Maine Energy Recovery Company to build a commercial waste-to-energy incinerator on the site of a vacant mill building along the riverfront.

Also in 1985 a local developer acquired Saco Island, a six-building mill complex located between the cities' downtowns, with the thought of building a $40 million mixed use project. Those plans collapsed when only 20 of 90 condominium units sold in the first three years. Saco Island's failure was blamed on several factors: overly ambitious plans, the late 1980s recession, the incinerator right across the river, and especially,

*Originally published as David E. Versel, "Reimagining a Mill Community" *Planning*, November 2009. Copyright 2009 by the American Planning Association. Reprinted by permission of *Planning* magazine.

upscale buyer reluctance to move from Portland to a mill town.

On the Mend

Over the next 15 years, the area quietly rebounded, thanks in part to three local investors who offered multitenant spaces in the mill buildings at bargain-basement rents to small manufacturers and artisans priced out of Portland and other locations. The public took little notice until Biddeford published a 2004 study that documented 65 businesses operating within the mills—two-thirds of them newcomers within the preceding five years. More importantly, 40 of the 65 were woodworkers, artists, or other craftspeople.

According to Chris Betjemann of Odyssey Properties, which owns Biddeford's Lincoln Mil, "We've been able to attract tenants who can't find affordable space elsewhere in southern Maine. As the other mills redevelop our mill is becoming more and more valuable."

Another positive change came in 2001, when Amtrak inaugurated its Downeaster passenger service connecting Portland with Boston. Saco successfully opposed the state's plan to locate the train station in a suburban area, and the station was ultimately sited on Saco Island.

Annual ridership has doubled since 2001, fueling interest in Biddeford-Saco as a market for transit-oriented development. Last February, the city replaced the outdoor train platform with a new train station built from recycled materials and powered by a 100-foot-tall wind turbine. "A train station that is both green and in the heart of our city greatly reinforces our redevelopment vision," says Peter Morelli, AICP, Saco's development director.

Main Street Rebound

To build on this momentum, each city launched a successful Main Street program.

In 2006, a consortium of leaders in both cities joined forces to develop a cultural plan that offered a variety of short- and long-term investment, programming, and partnership strategies aimed at raising interest in the arts and creative development on both sides of the river. This planning process brought the area's arts, cultural, business, and government interests together for the first time and led directly to several initiatives, most notably Biddeford's monthly ArtWalk.

Both cities have worked proactively with mill owners in a number of ways. In Biddeford, the owners of two mill properties have obtained federal brownfield funding for abatement of lead paint, asbestos, and other hazardous materials. Saco and the new owner of Saco Island (now Island Point) enacted a long-term TIF agreement that helped the developer obtain private financing while dedicating land for public open space and a river walk.

Biddeford relaxed applicable zoning and parking regulations and amended its existing TIF district so it could fund public improvements in the Mill District. In 2008, the two cities worked together to obtain national historic district status for the Mill District, enabling property owners to apply state and federal historic preservation tax credits to redevelopment projects.

Biddeford completed a Mill District Master Plan that, according to city planner Greg Tansley, ACIP, "defines a clear vision and strategy for new private and public investment in the Mill District, which will continue the momentum for downtown revitalization in the city."

Finally, Biddeford is one of four pilot communities partnering with the Orton Family Foundation on a "Heart & Soul Community Planning" project, using storytelling and other nontraditional citizen engagement approaches to identify a vision for downtown revitalization.

Proceed with Caution

These initiatives prompted large-scale plans for mill properties in both cities, but change has come slowly. Two decades on, the Mill District boasts the new train station, 140 housing units, and 100,000 square feet of renovated retail and commercial space, but it still contains about 1.5 million square feet of vacant or underused space, including the 600,000 square-foot West-Point Home complex.

Positive change is occurring: Four mill properties have come under new ownership since the beginning of 2008. One of these, Biddeford's Lincoln Mill, embodies the over-all struggle. Its "beheaded" tower (removed and stripped for parts by a previous owner), sits on the ground while its new owners are formulating a redevelopment plan to turn the building into a mixed use complex.

After 25 years of planning, private investment, and public incentives, reimaging Biddeford-Saco's mills remains a work in progress, especially during these uncertain times. But leaders are confident it will happen. "The key to successful mill redevelopment is a shared long-term commitment by the city and developers," says Saco Mayor Roland Michaud, a 20-year veteran of city government.

56. Bike Share Isn't Just for Big Cities*

DANIEL C. VOCK

When College Park, Maryland set out to build a bike-sharing network, officials envisioned a kiosk-based system with super-durable bikes and high-tech stations—much like nearby Washington, D.C.'s popular program. In fact, College Park, home to the University of Maryland, had planned to join the district's bike share, but the deal fell through.

Luckily the city of 30,000 was able to salvage a state grant and put that money toward a different vendor. That's when city officials stumbled onto Zagster, a venture-funded startup that designs, builds and operates bike-sharing programs for smaller markets. The company created an affordable, flexible bike share for College Park that launched in May.

For small communities like College Park, it can be hard to implement a bike-share program. The upfront investment often proves too much. But that's changing. As bike shares grow in popularity, cities are discovering alternative ways to deploy and run them. Those programs are a little different than the marquee ones of cities like New York and Washington.

"We learned that there are different approaches to bike share, and that different communities can use bike share in different ways," said College Park Mayor Patrick Wojahn. "It's important for cities to think of their individual needs."

That's where companies like Zagster and Social Bikes come in. They cater to smaller towns, universities and corporate clients. Zagster operates 100 programs in 35 states, and its CEO Timothy Ericson says it's seen growth in small cities take off in the last 18 months. One benefit his company offers smaller communities is that it sells bike share as a service. Bike-share agreements vary significantly from city to city. Usually, the government owns or operates part of the service, while private vendors take up the rest. But Zagster owns the bikes, fixes them, moves them when needed and replaces them every three years. It also takes care of the stations and develops the software.

Albuquerque, N.M., a city of more than 550,000, wouldn't have had a bike-sharing system at all without a low-cost model. The system there was initially funded by donations from local businesses.

"That type of [big-city] model just wasn't going to be feasible for our community, because we didn't have millions of dollars to

---

*Originally published as Daniel C. Vock, "Bike Share Isn't Just for Big Cities," *Governing*, June 28, 2016. Reprinted with permission of the publisher.

spend on this. We only had thousands," said Valerie Hermanson, a transportation planner from the Mid-Region Council of Governments who helped launch the city's program.

To a less discerning eye, College Park's bike-share network might not look much different than the ones in D.C. and other big cities, which use specially designed bikes that can withstand frequent use on crowded streets and exposure to the weather 365 days of the year. The extra-durable bikes are parked at stations that need electricity and an Internet connection. But College Park's system is different in a couple ways: It has less conspicuous bike racks that are cheaper to build and easier to move. What's more, the most gadgetry thing about its Plain Jane bikes is that they are outfitted with GPS, which makes it easier to keep track of them and allows for analysis.

In Albuquerque, for example, administrators assumed that riders would likely stay within a 10-minute ride of the downtown stations, said Hermanson. Thanks to the GPS data, it turned out that cyclists were using the bicycles to travel across the sprawling city. That information helped justify a planned expansion of the system, she said.

Motivate, the company that operates bike-share systems in the Bay Area, Chicago, New York and Washington, acknowledges that its model is designed for high-ridership areas.

"Our sweet spot is a little higher," said spokeswoman Dani Simons. "Just like Aurora, Ill., isn't going to build a New York–style subway system, it's probably not going to have a New York City–style bike-share system either."

Before Zagster or another company will come into a city, though, applicants need to be able to show a clear reason why people would want to use bicycles in their city.

"Bike sharing is working in places people might not consider a good place," he said. "It's really about thinking through that use case: What is the gateway drug to get people onto bike share?"

57. Some in D.C. Think Livability Is Not a Small Town Value*

STEVE DAVIS

From the president down to the secretary of transportation, administration officials spent time vocally supporting a focus on livability from the federal government—doing what's in their power to encourage smarter, people-centric planning to create more great places to live where residents have numerous options for getting around and a high quality of life. Perhaps unsurprisingly in this polarized white-hot political era, there's been a backlash in Congress from some rural legislators.

But isn't livability really a quintessential small-town value? Shouldn't these legislators be the foremost advocates for the federal government encouraging states to repair their roads and bridges before building new ones, making walking and biking safer to boost mobility in places where transit isn't quite feasible and encouraging growth in historic small town Main Streets across America?

Bear with me for a personal story as I try to get to the bottom of that question.

Before coming to Washington, D.C., to work for Smart Growth America, I was a journalist for two years in Bentonville (pop. 40,000), Arkansas, a small yet booming town in the northwest corner of the state, most notorious as the birthplace of Walmart and the base of worldwide operations to this day. When my wife and I arrived in 2004, the city of somewhere around 30,000 was struggling to keep up with a frenetic pace of growth, largely fueled by Walmart's expansion and the influx of Walmart vendors that gained momentum in the decade after Sam Walton's death in 1992.

Planning commissioners and the city planning staff were treading water in an endless struggle to stay ahead of the pace of growth and demand for new housing. There were some terrific farsighted people in the city planning department, but there was little city-wide vision or consensus for what anyone wanted the city to look like in 30 years, and little time to think about it in the rush to grow. Though there was ample available land to build on in the old core of the city close to schools and jobs, it was generally easier (and more lucrative) for developers to go to the edge of town on one of three state highways, subdivide farmland or open space and throw down a subdivision of new houses with cul-de-sacs.

When moving to town, we deliberately chose to live as close as possible to the old town square, the focal point of the city since

---

*Originally published as Steve Davis, "Why Do Some in D.C. Think Livability Is Not a Small Town Value?," March 25, 2010, www.smartgrowthamerica.org. Reprinted with permission of the publisher.

it was platted in the 1830s. We wanted to be close to our office just off the square and though we liked the idea of walking to the downtown grocery store or the park around the corner, rents and home prices were also generally lower in the historic core of the city, with the influx of new residents with higher incomes fueling the construction on the edge of town, at least in part. (Speculation played quite a role as well, as evidenced by the unfinished subdivisions today.)

Though the old part of the city was dominated by single-family homes as well, the new growth took on an entirely different form from the older portion of the city.

At the core of Bentonville, there is a Walmart, at least one major employment nexus for the region (Walmart HQ), office space, a grocery store, an elementary school, a historic middle school, the city library, a nursing home, a dozen restaurants, dry cleaners, a coffee shop, several parks, a bike trail, at least four churches, and thousands of homes ranging from small garden apartment buildings to townhouses, modest single-family homes, and expensive preserved or restored historic homes costing hundreds of thousands of dollars.

Like most small towns and cities across America, the older part of the city was laid out on a street grid, uses were often mixed and most people living in the houses can get to a meaningful destination on foot, and nearly all can get to at least a few basic necessities with a short drive.

Contrast that with the form of growth that represents much of the last 10–15 years in Bentonville as their city limits expanded southwest along a state highway to the new regional airport. There's a Walmart distribution center, houses of varying sizes and price points all separated from one another, farmland and former farmland, a couple of office buildings and absolutely zero mix of uses.

Most neighborhoods have sidewalks due to a city ordinance, but none of them go anywhere outside of the subdivisions. There are restaurants, stores and other amenities somewhat close to this side of town, but every single one of them requires a drive, unless you're willing to brave a walk in the shoulder of a highway—which some have no choice about.

Growth was happening so fast that there was little very long-range planning possible to ensure that the new parts of the city would be as enjoyable and as livable as the older parts. The city did have a comprehensive plan, but the planning commission didn't always follow the plan or recommendations from the planning staff.

Unsurprisingly, with growth focused along just a few highway corridors and little option (like the street grid provides) for secondary routes, traffic along these state highways west and southwest of town soon turned into gridlock. Land use decisions seemed to be completely disconnected from transportation planning. (Also complicating matters was the fact that the city couldn't improve many of the main corridors as they were state roads under the purview of the Arkansas Highway and Transportation Department.)

So when gas prices made their historic march up to the 3 and 4 dollar territory in 2005, how would the effects be felt in these two very different parts of Bentonville? And what in the world does livability have to do with any of it?

When gas prices shot to historic levels in the summer of 2005 and following Hurricane Katrina later that year, many residents, especially in the fast-growing new parts of Bentonville, Arkansas, were stuck with few options other than to bear the pain at the pump, stay at home, work from home, or take as few trips as possible.

But for me and my wife and many others living in the older part of the city in those weeks with astronomical gas prices, a pretty normal life was still possible, even while trying to cut back driving significantly to save money. Several weekends in a row, we parked our cars entirely, and managed to do our grocery shopping, go to church, visit friends, or listen to bluegrass in the square on a Friday night without having to get in either of our two cars. We walked 5 minutes to the grocery store. We biked to Walmart a handful of times—receiving many strange looks in the process. We went to eat at a new restaurant on the square. We went hiking on a short trail in the woods right on the edge of downtown. We went to the library.

Sounds pretty "livable," right?

These sorts of fond memories about life in Bentonville are the ones rattling around in my brain when legislators from largely rural states question whether or not "livability" is a value that translates to our small towns, cities and rural areas.

Where are values like livability and quality of life more resonant if not in small towns like Bentonville? Other small towns and cities aren't that different. Even in largely rural states like Wyoming or Montana, the majority of residents are still generally concentrated around urbanized areas, the old town square, or the former railroad depot in a pattern similar to Bentonville.

When Transportation Secretary Ray Lahood talks about livability as the desire people have for a range of transportation options, the freedom to own less than 2 or 3 cars, a high quality of life with ample green space, biking or walking paths, and shopping, restaurants or health care located nearby, he's describing the very lifestyle of many residents of rural areas or small towns have, or the lifestyle many of them would like to have.

Former Meridian, Mississippi Mayor John Robert Smith of Transportation for America and Reconnecting America testified last week in Washington on the transportation challenges facing our small towns and rural areas. While the issues facing these areas may be different than large urban areas, res-

idents in these places want many of the same things—good transit networks, options for getting around, safe streets, bridges that don't fall down and highways that aren't cracked and potholed.

Transportation challenges facing small town America are not of congestion but of access—long commutes, volatile energy prices, and shifting demographics all impact the prosperity of these communities. Many small towns and rural areas lack the financial resources, planning capacity, or authority to implement solutions to their transportation needs. A bold new policy is needed at the federal level to meet those needs.

Current federal transportation policy for a place like Bentonville doesn't really work. They can try and get the state DOT on board with what they want to do, with varying levels of success. For example, the City had an ordinance to build usable sidewalks on all new and reconstructed roads, making the streets safe as possible to encourage safe walking and biking. The Arkansas DOT at the time did sidewalks as a total afterthought—sticking a sidewalk right smack next to 5 lanes of traffic on a 45 or 55 mph highway.

Federal transportation policy is clearly in need of an overhaul when cities get money from Congress they didn't ask for, to do something they don't necessarily want to do.

Will the future 8th street have sidewalks, or be another five-lane speedway?

When the last six-year transportation bill (SAFETEA-LU) passed in 2005, the City found out along with everyone else that Rep. John Boozman had secured a $37 million earmark for the widening of a city street and connection to the interstate. Walmart had gone straight to Rep. Boozman to lobby for the money, and the City found out when our newspaper did. The two-lane road runs through the very heart of town, connecting the Walmart HQ to their IT department next to the interstate, but it also runs straight through the street grid of local walkable streets. It clearly needs sidewalks, but the City is now on the hook for the contract and the project, and with money coming through the state DOT, will the City be able to build the walkable, safe, complete street they envision?

As Streetsblog noted in Mayor Smith's testimony, small towns and cities could really benefit from the kinds of innovative federal grants that would allow them to make long range plans to improve livability and steer transportation and land use investments into those parts of town that have the infrastructure now to support the growth. Growth slowed in Bentonville over the last few years, and now they're left with subdivisions southwest of town that are scattered about, have no grocery store nearby, and are generally disconnected from the city.

People who live in classic American small towns like Bentonville know a thing or two about livability. There's nothing "livable" about being stuck in your subdivision that got built too far from town, work or school when gas prices get too high. Nor is it "livable" to have the federal government incentivizing (through money to the State DOT) the widening of highways into the county to encourage more sprawl outside of town even as the city is clamoring for more investment inside of it.

Some in Congress seem to think that "livability" is some sort of urban hoodwinking of rural America. They need look no further than the sidewalks and town squares of their state's small towns to see the truth.

Call it what you want, but it looks like livability to me.

58. Can Millennials Revive the American City?*

MINCH LEWIS

The American city has been on the receiving end of devastating trends: disinvestment, disintegration of infrastructure, depopulation, deterioration of law and order and destruction of public education. Now, emerging trends might provide a counterbalance. The millennial generation and the New Urbanism movement, which both grew from the same roots in the 1980s, are providing the American city with powerful policy opportunities. Millennials, attracted to New Urbanism neighborhoods created by community development, might power the revival of the American city.

Emerging trends and merging opportunities:

- The millennial generation has an interest in urban living and the resources to support it.
- New Urbanism creates a change in traditional community redevelopment goals.
- Urban resource disinvestment has created opportunities for turning liabilities into assets.

Who are the millennials that could help revive the American city?

"Millennial" is the generational tag that classifies everyone born from about 1980 to 2000 as "Gen Y." Born into the Internet age, they have unlimited access to information. They seem to be reversing the preferences of their parents. One of those break-away choices brings them back to urban living preferences—sidewalks, front porches and neighbors they can talk to. In fact, according to a RCLCO report, "millennials want urban, walkable and high-amenity places."

What is a New Urbanism neighborhood?

The RCLCO report describes the features of a New Urbanism neighborhood. New Urbanism neighborhoods have characteristics based on standards codified by the Congress for the New Urbanism (CNU):

- Walkable access: mixed use neighborhoods with pedestrian connections within a five-minute walk.
- Higher density development: smaller lot size and multistory mixed-use structures.
- Urban scale: buildings and roads facilitating connections between people.
- Local parks: enhanced for accessible recreational activities and community meetings.

---

*Originally published as Minch Lewis, "Can Millennials Revive the American City?" *PA TIMES*. Reprinted with permission of the publisher.

- Traffic-calming transit designs: traffic circles for arterial intersections and dedicated bike paths.
- Auto-free zones: public spaces offering relief from carbon-monoxide pollution.
- People-oriented public spaces: open areas, sidewalks, cafes and front porches to host public life.

How does a community create a New Urbanism neighborhood?

As Adesanya Adekoya pointed out in an earlier *PA Times Online* article, "Millennials have changed the face of community development." Municipal governments can build on those changes. Instead of conventional activities, community development agencies can promote positive New Urbanism characteristics with public tools recommended by CNU:

Planning: establishing geographical units that relate to demographic characteristics.

Zoning: modifying traditional regulations to incorporate "New Urbanism" standards.

Building codes: revising limitations and establishing requirements for urban features.

Public investment: relocating governmental offices to neighborhood sites.

Infrastructure improvements: enhancing neighborhood amenities like parks and transit ways.

Neighborhood organizations: providing professional staff for volunteer groups.

Social service support: moving services to the neighborhood from central offices.

Social media: developing content to create neighborhood identity and cohesion.

What financial resources are available?

Resources can be redirected to finance a New Urbanism strategy:

- Existing expenditures can be refocused. Community policing offices can be opened in vacant store fronts.

Fire stations can be opened up to the neighborhood.
- Capital improvement districts can be created to finance public improvements.
- Federal CDBG funding can be allocated based on New Urbanism impacts.
- Philanthropic investment can be promoted, including funding for neighborhood community development organizations.
- Property tax policy can be changed to provide incentives for commercial development and for residential "curb appeal."
- Resources that millennials have, or will have as baby boomers pass on $30 trillion in the intergenerational transfer of wealth, can be tapped.
- School systems can adopt neighborhood schools to coincide with New Urbanism boundaries.

Implementing New Urban Neighborhoods

Creating New Urbanism neighborhoods requires a community commitment. Robert Steuteville, senior communications advisor for the CNU, lays out the process. "A community has to show millennials that it is committed to creating places where people want to live." Political, social and economic institutions must come together to adopt New Urbanism as a strategy for sustaining the urban core.

The good news: it's been done before.

The success stories are supported with formal research and with anecdotal testimony. According to a report from Smart Growth America, "Walkable urban places are now gaining market share over drivable locations for the first time in at least half a century in hotel, office and rental apartment development."

The CNU provides resources to assist

with public policy, community decision-making, marketing and financing based on the growing demand.

Steuteville recommends that the process should begin with a planning exercise called a "charrette."

A charrette is an intensive planning session where citizens, designers and others collaborate on a vision for development. It provides a forum for ideas and offers the unique advantage of giving immediate feedback to the designers. More importantly, it allows everyone who participates to be a mutual author of the plan.

CNU will provide a welcome reception and support for communities that adopt a "New Urbanism" strategy for attracting millennials. The opportunity is real. Millennials, working in partnership with community development, can play a powerful role in reviving the American city, neighborhood by neighborhood.

59. Young Professionals Return Home, and Stay[*]

WILLIAM FULTON

I grew up in the kind of place people tend to leave. Almost from the time I was born back in the '50s, the factories were closing, the population was stagnant and the kids who went away to college never came back. Much as I love my little upstate New York hometown, I couldn't help but think that the best days were in the past.

The last few times I've been home, however, I've noticed more and more people coming back. And oddly enough, the ones who come back most often tend to be people who, like me, moved across the country to Los Angeles in search of wider opportunities. One couple bailed from the entertainment industry, moved back home and started a live theater downtown. Another couple left behind a small chain of high-end restaurants catering to the film industry—and their parents, who retired in Southern California.

The boomerang effect is small but noticeable, and it's helping Auburn (pop. 27,000), N.Y., at least a little, as it tries to pull out of a half century of stagnation. Countrywide, economically depressed regions are targeting the boomerang kids—the locals who went away to college and

may be interested in coming back if they can find the right job.

Perhaps the most aggressive boomerang campaign has been set up in Fresno, Calif., a city that's growing fast in population but not in upward economic mobility. With a half-million people, Fresno is the fifth largest city in California and 36th largest in the nation (right behind Albuquerque, N.M., and Kansas City, Mo.). However, it's stuck in the impoverished San Joaquin Valley—180 miles from San Francisco and 220 miles from L.A. It's not only the center of an agricultural empire, but also the center of a low-end economy. Indeed, Fresno's continued population growth is an eternal mystery to California demographers, given the general lack of upward opportunity.

That's why Fresno's leaders have been pushing the "Fresno boomerang" idea—finding young professionals who have moved away but might want to come home. There's even a website, fresnoboomerang.com, that tries to connect native Fresnans living elsewhere with high-end job opportunities back home.

Mike Dozier, director of the Office of Community and Economic Development at

[*]Originally published as William Fulton. "Young Professionals Return Home, and Stay," *Governing*, January 2011. Reprinted with permission of the publisher.

California State University, Fresno, says his region's residents can be divided into three categories: pioneers, who moved there from somewhere else; legacies, who grew up and stayed; and boomerangers, who grew up, left and came back. Part of the problem, Dozier says, is that legacies often have what might be called a bad self-image—they compare Fresno to the places they vacation (such as coastal California) and create a negative vibe for their kids who go away to college.

On the other hand, Dozier says, "Boomerangers have left, they know what it's like outside of the valley, and they come back because they want to come back. And they tend to not be as negative about living in the valley as the legacies would have been."

It can be tough sometimes to persuade those who have left to return. The Fresno Bee recently reported about a legacy Fresnan who's working with the boomerang experts to try to get her 30-year-old son to move back from Chicago. The experts are working on finding him a job; she's working on finding him a date. So far, no luck.

By contrast, Dozier points to a co-worker, Ismael Herrera from nearby Mendota, California, (population 9,700), who received degrees from the University of California, Irvine, and Harvard University, and then served in Sacramento, Calif., as a Polanco Fellow—a program for emerging Latino public policy leaders—before returning to Fresno.

Fresno is hardly the only city focusing on the boomerangers. Youngstown, Ohio—as struggling a place as you're likely to find anywhere—has created the Greater Youngstown 2.0 website, aimed at what local leaders call the Greater Youngstown Diaspora Neighborhood. And every struggling city is on the hunt for its own Doug Burgum—the Fargo, North Dakota, native who returned from Silicon Valley to start Great Plains Software, which he sold to Microsoft for $1 billion.

It's not easy to bridge the divide between the have and have-not regions in America today. But maybe if a few more boomerang efforts succeed, the economic connections between the two will be stronger.

60. Building Intergenerational Communities*

SUE KELLEY *and* CHRIS SWARTZ

The move toward building intergenerational communities is being driven by a number of factors, including longer life expectancy, desire of older adults to age in place, changing family patterns that result in generations living apart, and growing awareness of the importance of age-friendly communities. Intergenerational communities are those that value young people and older people alike; they provide opportunities for the generations to interact and to get to know one another.

Intergenerational activities have been a part of the village of Shorewood, Wisconsin's culture since it was incorporated in 1900. As a tight-knit community where neighbors live in close proximity to one another, it is common for generations to be working alongside each other simply because it is the way things have been done.

At the same time, Shorewood has undertaken intentional efforts to ensure there are opportunities for people of all ages to feel valued and to contribute to the life of the community. As a result of Shorewood's efforts, it has been recognized as one of four "Best Intergenerational Communities 2014" in a nationwide competition sponsored by

Generations United, with funding from the MetLife Foundation. (For information on the competition and results, visit http://www.gu.org/OURWORK/Programs/BestIntergenerationalCommunities.aspx.)

About Shorewood

Located along the shore of Lake Michigan just to the north of the city of Milwaukee, Shorewood is home to 13,192 residents in an area of 1.5 square miles.

It's known as a highly walkable community, with 64 miles of sidewalks throughout the village linking residents with four schools; bus stops; an incorporated business improvement district that includes grocery stores, pharmacies, health care providers, shops, and restaurants; and three parks. Shorewood is said to be "just two feet from everything," and it is minutes away from cultural and recreational icons in Milwaukee where Shorewood residents visit and volunteer.

Lake Michigan and the Milwaukee River are located at Shorewood's eastern and western borders. On the north, it is bordered by the village of Whitefish Bay and on the south by the city of Milwaukee. The

*Originally published as Sue Kelley and Chris Swartz, "Building Intergenerational Communities," *PM Magazine*, December 2014. Reprinted with permission of the publisher.

233

University of Wisconsin–Milwaukee shares this southern border.

Shorewood is home to a diverse population and is the most densely populated local government in the state of Wisconsin. It is a community filled with people who desire to be connected—to each other and to the institutions in the community. Promoting quality of life is at the top of Shorewood's priorities list.

Knowing the Important Issues

While pride in the school system has always been at the heart of the community, Shorewood has worked hard to ensure that it is a vibrant community for people of all ages to live.

The Milwaukee County Department on Aging conducted a survey of older residents in 2008. In answering questions about the senior-friendliness of the village, respondents expressed a desire to remain in Shorewood as they age, along with a desire to become more involved in volunteer efforts.

Following the survey, the Shorewood Connects partnership was launched as a community organizing effort to bring together public and private stakeholders dedicated to increasing the age-friendliness of the community. As one of four original Shorewood Connects work groups, the Intergenerational Work Group serves as the intergenerational glue that brings together the village government, school district, and business improvement district, along with youth and seniors.

The initiatives of Shorewood Connects, including the fall and spring yard cleanup days, the Neighborhood of the Year competition, and more recently, the Senior-Friendly Business Certification Program, all serve to build and strengthen connections among residents.

Recognizing the value of the Shorewood Connects initiative to the village's quality of life in alignment with Shorewood's Vision

Plan, the village board provides funding for a paid facilitator to coordinate activities and to purchase a small amount of promotional materials. The 2014 village budget includes $7,715 for the project.

The work group decided at the start to seek a balance in intergenerational activities so as not to cast older adults as helpless and youth as helpers. Creating an inventory of intergenerational programs was one of the first activities of the work group. Here is a sample of the findings:

- Shorewood's school district benefits from having older volunteers help in the schools and at school events.
- In 2013, one of the elementary schools collaborated with older adults at the Senior Resource Center on an art project, creating an opportunity for conversation while students and seniors worked together.
- The Shorewood Men's Club and Shorewood Women's Club both fund scholarships for high school students, and they welcome youth volunteers at their fundraising events.
- Shorewood Intermediate Middle School hosts a recognition event for veterans on Veterans' Day.
- The Shorewood Senior Resource Center holds an annual essay contest for sixth graders on the topic of important older people in their lives.
- Student volunteers from nearby University of Wisconsin–Milwaukee share their expertise in technology by offering assistance to seniors in the use of cellphones, computers, and other electronic devices.

Some intergenerational activities have a service component, including yard cleanup days, while others are more social in nature. Social activities include:

- The Shorewood Public Library, in choosing its "Shorewood Reads" book, purposely picked a book read by students in English classes at the high school. The resulting book discussions included both high school students and older residents.

- The Annual Shorewood Men's Club Chicken Barbecue features an array of bands that cover the musical interests of the young and the old.
- The Shorewood Community Fitness Center offers a Silver Sneakers program as well as youth programming. On any given day, older people and teens are working out at the fitness center, side by side.
- The Shorewood Recreation and Community Service Department programs include the intergenerational community choral arts program and the Senior Citizen Pass, which allows older adults free admission to high school sporting events and performances.

The Annual Shorewood Public Library Summer Celebration is run by two groups primarily composed of seniors (Friends of the Library and the Shorewood Women's Club), along with the Library's Teen Advisory Board.

Plans are already under way to connect a new senior housing development, Harbor Chase (groundbreaking was held in July 2014), to Shorewood schools and to the Shorewood Senior Resource Center.

As a community known for a high level of civic engagement, intentional efforts have been made to include youth representatives on these village committees:

- Conservation Committee.
- Library Board.
- Pedestrian and Bicycle Safety Committee.
- Recreation and Community Services Advisory Committee.
- Shorewood Community Fitness Center Advisory Committee.

In addition to developing a host of new activities referenced earlier (Neighborhood of the Year competition, fall and spring yard cleanup, and Senior Friendly Business Certification), Shorewood Connects has also raised awareness about integrating intergenerational practices into other programs and activities.

This is best illustrated when a member of a group asks the question, "How can we do this intergenerationally?" As an example, the Elder Services Advisory Board recently discussed purchasing artwork for a meeting room used by the Senior Resource Center.

After discussion, the board decided to approach the Shorewood High School Art Department regarding a student competition, with a scholarship from the Senior Center going to the winning student who will be selected by a panel of Senior Center members.

Lessons for Other Communities

Calling attention to what is already happening in a community is a good place to start. Looking for ways to expand intergenerational opportunities will follow if there is sufficient community interest and an entity that assumes responsibility for this task, along with funding support to ensure that communication flows and the project keeps moving.

Most communities already have intergenerational programming with such traditional partners as schools, senior centers, daycare centers, and senior residential facilities. There are also potential nontraditional partners that should be considered too, both public and private, including libraries, businesses, community foundations, community organizations, recreational organizations, and others.

The extent to which there is interaction and respect between the generations can lead to mutual support on such voter issues as school referenda and the allocation of re-sources for senior programs and activities. An investment in quality-of-life efforts can also yield results in terms of attracting new residents and businesses that are seeking a place with a strong sense of community and community pride.

In short, intentional planning to cultivate a culture where intergenerational interactions become the norm will result in an engaged, caring community.

RESOURCES

AARP. http://www.aarpinternational.org/events/age friendly2012.

Generations United. http://www.gu.org.

Under One Roof: A Guide to Starting and Strengthening Intergenerational Shared Site Programs. Generations United, 2005.

World Health Organization. http://www. who.int/age ing/age_friendly_ cities_network/en.

61. Retirees

A New Economic Development Strategy*

CHRISTEN SMITH

A promising future clean-growth industry is advancing economic development in communities across the country. All forecasts indicate that the industry will offer significant short- and long-term growth. The industry: retirees.

Communities that provide a high quality of life, including broad-based, innovative park and recreation opportunities for their residents age 50-plus, are attracting seniors to relocate to their communities for retirement, and these migrating seniors are providing a significant stimulus to their local economies.

How much value do retirees add to a local economy? A quick glance at the numbers demonstrates the revenue potential. If 25 retiree households with an average annual household spending of $40,000 per household move into a community next year, the resulting economic impact of those households on the community would be an estimated $1,000,000 per year.

From the perspective of economic development investments, targeting recruitment efforts on retirees rather than corporations has a number of major advantages. Retirees do not require economic incentive packages to attract them to relocate. Capital improve-

ments, such as remodeling to enhance accessibility of public buildings that take place as a part of a retiree recruitment effort are likely to focus on community support services that also benefit existing residents.

Retirees' incomes from Social Security and pensions are stable and are not subject to the fluctuations that are experienced in the business cycles. A recent survey found that more than half of 60-year-olds are revamping their retirement plans due to the recent downturn in the economy. While these pre-retirees may be delaying their retirement dates, people continue to anticipate that they will retire.

Although the retirees' income sources are outside the community, a significant portion of their expenditures are local and directly benefit the local economy. Further, retirees are likely to transfer significant assets into local investment and banking institutions.

Retirees increase the local tax base, and they tend to be contributing taxpayers. Their taxes can be expected to support services they will not use. Seniors, for example, are not likely to enroll children in the school system or strain the local criminal justice system.

*Originally published as Christen Smith, "Retirees: A New Economic Development Strategy," *PM Magazine* 91, no. 4 (May 2009). Reprinted with permission of the publisher.

Retirees often become a rich pool of volunteers in the community. The average value of an active adult volunteer is nearly $20 per hour. More than half (51 percent) of baby boomers say they expect to devote more time to community service or volunteering after retirement.

When boomers were asked to identify the community services and programs that they currently use and that they will want to use more in their future retirement years, they identified four categories of services: social, cultural, and leisure activities; parks and recreational services and facilities; senior-designed community and social services; and education and library services.

The population projections for 2010 to 2030 indicate that younger seniors, those ages 50 to 75, will migrate to Las Vegas, Denver, Dallas, and Atlanta—communities that have traditionally been recognized for their youthful profiles. Smaller, non-metropolitan areas are also experiencing rapid senior growth, including Santa Fe (pop. 69,000), New Mexico; Bend (pop. 81,000), Oregon; Coeur d'Alene (pop. 46,000), Idaho; St. George (pop. 76,000), Utah; Olympia (pop. 48,000), Washington; and Loveland (pop. 71,334), Colorado. These choices indicate that factors other than climate are involved in decisions about retirement destinations.

Younger, more affluent retirees are migrating to areas that are rich in amenities, and community services are prominent among the amenities that are attracting them. The availability of these opportunities in the community is second only to family location as factors influencing retirees' decisions about where to live during their retirement years.

Enhancing local social, cultural, and leisure activities, parks and recreational services and facilities, and education and library services for adults over age 50 is an economic development strategy that will result in a high rate of return on the community's investments.

Resources

"Baby Boomers Envision Retirement II: Key Findings." Washington, D.C.: RoperASW for AARP, May 2004.

Crompton, John L. (2007). *Community Benefits and Repositioning: The Keys to Parks and Recreation's Future Visibility*. Ashburn, Va.: National Recreation and Park Association, 2007.

Frey, William H. (2007). *Mapping the Growth of Older America: Seniors and Boomers in the Early 21st Century* (Living Cities Census Series). Washington, D.C.: Brookings Institution.

How Well Do You Know Boomers? Counting Down the Top 10 Boomer Myths." Washington, D.C.: Focalyst Insight Report for AARP, 2008.

62. Do Cities Really Want Economic Development?*

AARON M. RENN

So many cities and regions continue to struggle economically. Even within nominally well-performing places there are pockets that have been left behind. Most of the have-nots in the current economy have been struggling for an extended period of time, often in spite of enormous efforts to bring positive change.

Why is this? Perhaps we need to consider the possibility that these places are getting exactly the results they want: Maybe they actually don't want economic development.

Economist David Friedman once told this joke: "Two economists walk past a Porsche showroom. One of them points at a shiny car in the window and says, 'I want that.' 'Obviously not,' the other replies."

That is, if the first economist had really wanted the Porsche, he would have bought it. Our choices tell us more than our words about what it is we really want.

The civic world is obviously more complex than this simple joke. But given the persistent failure to change the trajectory of so many places despite the enormous time and energy—not to mention vast sums of taxpayer money—spent on it, it's worth pondering the possibilities.

Problems are problems, but they are also sometimes solutions to certain sets of questions. One of these is how to mobilize, allocate, and deploy community resources and power. Fighting decline has become the central organizing principle in many places.

As a friend of mine from the IT industry once put it regarding what he termed "rackets": "A racket is when folks have something they complain about and commiserate about but don't fix. Upon delving into the roots of a racket one finds that the folks don't really want it fixed—the subject of the racket is a unifying force that if corrected will remove the common complaint and thus the unifying force. The cultural changes that would ensue from the change in practices that 'no one wants' are not acceptable to [the complainers]. In corporate organizational behavior, it is important to break the rackets. It is also difficult. But, I imagine, far easier in a company with some semblance of common objectives than it would be in an each-man-for-himself city."

In short, economic struggle can be a cultural unifier in a community that people tacitly want to hold onto in order to preserve civic cohesion.

Jane Jacobs took it even further. As she noted in *The Economy of Cities*, "Economic

---

*Originally published as Aaron M. Renn. "Do Cities Really Want Economic Development?" *Governing*, July 2014. Reprinted with permission of the publisher.

development, whenever and wherever it occurs, is profoundly subversive of the status quo." And it isn't hard to figure out that even in cities and states with serious problems, many people inside the system are benefiting from the status quo.

They have political power, an inside track on government contracts, a nice gig at a civic organization or nonprofit, and so on. All of these people, who are disproportionately in the power broker class of most places, potentially stand to lose if economic decline is reversed. That's not to say they are evil, but they all have an interest to protect.

Consider one simple thought experiment: If a struggling community starts booming, that would eliminate a big part of the rationale for subsidized real estate development, which constitutes the principal form of economic development in all too many places, and which benefits a clear interest group. It might also attract highly motivated, aggressive people from out of town, folks who are highly likely to agitate for better than the current inbred ways of doing business. This would inherently dilute the positions of the current powers that be.

In our own communities, where everyone seems sincere and dedicated to improvement, this can be hard to see. But when we look at other places where we have more critical detachment, it becomes obvious. For example, those of us not from Michigan can look at Detroit and see the failure of that community's leadership across the board—white and black, suburb and city, Republican and Democrat. But for all too many of them, Detroit's decline was a personally profitable affair, politically, financially, or both.

It's tempting for us to shake our heads at Detroit, wag a finger and lecture them on what they should have done better. But if we were honest and introspective, we'd realize many of the same forces are at work in our own community. There are a lot of people who are personally doing quite well even in the midst of decay. In fact, the cold reality is that they are directly benefiting from that decay.

In places long in decline, it's likely to take some outside shock to the system to break the rackets that are producing civic stasis and dysfunction. Detroit is in bankruptcy, and we'll see if that finally forces it to change its way of doing business. In the meantime, let's hope other communities find a more positive way to break free and embrace a path that leads to actual economic success.

63. The Panacea Patrol*

William Fulton

When I was attending junior college in my hometown, I was a devotee of our drama instructor. This fellow was, in a way, our town artist. He lived a bohemian lifestyle. He had a French last name. And two or three times a year, he would mount a theatrical production that everybody in town would come to see.

The problem was that his taste wasn't the same as everybody else's. In this little factory town, the shop-floor managers, the doctors and the teachers came expecting to see "Carousel." What the drama teacher kept delivering was "Waiting for Godot."

In those days, my teacher was regarded as, well, annoying. But one generation's pain in the neck is the next generation's economic development asset. Today, the drama teacher would be regarded as a critical part of our town's "creative class," in Richard Florida's phrase. In other words, he would be part of the infrastructure that would attract and keep the cool, creative people who will form the basis of the 21st century American economy.

In the past two years, every economic development manager in America has heard about Florida's "creative class" idea. The theory is simple. America's metropolitan economies of the 21st century will be driven by emerging high-tech industries (such as

biotechnology). This economic growth is driven largely by hip, almost bohemian, creative types. And this creative class prefers interesting and diverse urban places to the suburbs.

Since Florida's book, *The Rise of the Creative Class*, was published two years ago, he and his colleagues at Catalytix, his consulting firm, have roamed the country spreading this gospel and advising various cities and metro areas how to cash in on the creative class.

Now, predictably, the creative class backlash has started. In particular, Joel Kotkin, the iconoclastic urban pundit from Los Angeles, has taken the side of grunt cities. Kotkin claims that creativity is not a big job generator nationwide, and most cities are simply setting themselves up for failure and disappointment if they pin their hopes on the creative class.

Furthermore, Kotkin claims, even the creative types who drive the high-tech economy do not necessarily want to live a hip urban lifestyle. It was Kotkin, after all, who coined the memorable term "Nerdistan" to describe the supposedly boring but economically powerful suburbs—the Irvines and Sunnyvales—where high-tech engineers transform the world.

What we have here is a "panacea" battle—

*Originally published as William Fulton. "The Panacea Patrol," *Governing*, October 2004. Reprinted with permission of the publisher.

a new idea about how public policy can stimulate the economy, and a debate about whether or not this new idea can solve all problems.

This is familiar territory. Years ago, when I first started writing for this magazine, I was informally known around the office as the "panacea editor." It was my job to go check out the latest economic development fad—automobile assembly plants, convention centers, festival marketplaces, cineplexes—and write a story about whether it was a panacea.

In all cases, of course, the current fad was not a panacea. Neither, however, was the fad worthless. Most of these ideas work for some cities. And so it is with the creative class theory. The trick, as always, is to figure out where and how to use the idea so that it will work.

While every city in America has some kind of creative class, it's equally true—as Kotkin points out—that not every city can be a magnet for creative workers and creative work. But how deep is the market for the creative class? What kinds of cities will succeed in implementing the Florida theory, and what kinds will fail?

The depth of this market depends on what kind of economy America has over the next decade or two. If the U.S. can retain production jobs, then grunt cities will thrive with or without a creative class. But the long-term flow of production jobs to lower-cost countries seems like an irreversible trend. To thrive, most American cities will have to be centers of thinking rather than making.

The need for a more idea-based economy doesn't necessarily mean that Youngstown's future rests on the creative class, or that all denizens of Nerdistan will want their neighborhoods to be like Greenwich Village. And it most definitely doesn't make Florida's idea a panacea.

But it's likely that all American cities will rely on knowledge workers for most of their economic growth. And that means nurturing at least some of the urban assets that knowledge workers need. In some cities, this may mean downtown loft condominiums with coffee bars on the ground floor. But it also means the laborious day-to-day task of organizing the city's knowledge-based assets (universities, highly skilled workers and research labs) to take advantage of opportunities in the world economy. Even in a creative city, there is no substitute for hard work.

64. Bordeaux vs. Budweiser*

ROB GURWITT

There are people in Johnsburg (pop. 2,395), New York, who still won't set foot in the Tannery Pond Community Center, even though it was built in part for them. The local theater production of a play about Picasso and Einstein didn't seduce them. The monthly gallery shows hold no interest. Nor do the movies, chorale concerts or dance performances—not for the working-class people in this small town in New York's North Country, nestled in the Adirondacks, four hours north of Manhattan.

These are people who celebrate weddings and family reunions at more familiar venues in the various tiny hamlets that make up the town of Johnsburg. They gather at the small, cinder-block community center up the road in the village of Sodom, or the old Odd-Fellows Hall, now the Wevertown community center. "Tannery Pond is not a place that many locals would look to hold a family gathering; it's not a community center in that sense," says Brother James Posluszny, a Catholic priest who runs North Country Ministry, a social-service agency in the region. "The Wevertown center is theirs. The Sodom center is theirs. Tannery Pond is not."

What locals frequently choose to mention about Tannery Pond, in fact, is that it carries a $55,000-a-year price tag for the town to operate—"It was a nice gesture, but it's going to cost us money the rest of our lives," says Richard Stewart, who was born nearby in the house he still lives in.

This wasn't what Woody and Elise Widlund had in mind when they presented Johnsburg with its spacious, tea-colored community building in 2002. The Widlunds retired there from New Jersey, where they had owned a fragrance and flavor manufacturer, and they wanted the Adirondack town with its far-flung hamlets to have a central space for locals to gather and for artists to find a home. "In our travels across the country," explains Elise Widlund, "we find consistently that towns with an art component, whether theater or music or the visual arts, those are the towns that look healthy."

The Tannery Pond center certainly looks healthy. It sits in the hamlet of North Creek, right across from Johnsburg Town Hall, on the spot where a 19th-century tannery once stood. It's a welcoming space that towns four or five times Johnsburg's size—which is 2,500 year-round residents—would envy. And there are certainly those who are glad it's there. "It has helped to awaken the town," says Lyle Dye, a retired theater director and drama professor who moved to North Creek 13 years ago. The center has

*Originally published as Rob Gurwitt, "Bordeaux vs. Budweiser," *Governing*, April 30, 2009. Reprinted with permission of the publisher.

become a focal point for a large and growing slice of Johnsburg: people who moved there for its mountains, forests and proximity to the Hudson River, and are delighted to have some cultural life in what has always been a remote, hard-knock kind of place.

To say that Johnsburg is split down the middle between gentrifiers and rustics would be an exaggeration. But there's certainly no shortage of "us and them" to go around. There are the skiers and there are the snowmobilers. There are those who are drawn to North Creek's new wine bar and tapas restaurant, BarVino, and those who like the cheeseburgers and subs at Smith's on Main Street. And these days, more than anything else, there are the people pressing for North Creek to grow—to become "the next Stowe, Vermont," as one of them puts it—and the people who worry that if it does, there'll be no place left for them. Finding the right balance between growth and tradition is the number one issue for local government right now in much of the Adirondack region—and especially in Johnsburg.

That is because Johnsburg, and North Creek in particular, seem poised to attract a lot more people from outside, along with their money and their refined tastes. Just across the state highway from North Creek's business district sits the hamlet's old Ski Bowl, a tame set of descents by today's standards. But the Ski Bowl is backed up by ridgelines that lead to the far more popular Gore Mountain ski area, which drew about 250,000 skiers this past season. Gore is owned and run by New York State's Olympic Regional Development Authority, and if current plans hold, next year a ski lift and new trails will allow skiers to start from the top at Gore and ski down to North Creek.

In anticipation, new housing developments are in various stages of planning, including one right by the North Creek Ski Bowl that would replace a large patch of forest with a hotel, townhouses, restaurants, a members-only lodge, an equestrian center and a golf course. Entrepreneurs have opened up or taken over and renovated businesses on Main Street, aiming them at visitors and more cosmopolitan residents. The prospect of all this has locals talking about "workforce housing" and questioning how long it will still be available. "This is an embryonic Aspen," says Frank Boos, the housing coordinator for North Country Ministry. "If things go on as they are, they're going to have to bus workers in."

Johnsburg is hardly emblematic of all of rural America—there are immense swaths of the countryside that are not becoming playgrounds for urbanites or retirement havens for baby boomers cashing out on metropolitan life. Census numbers don't show anything like a massive migration of rich people into old blue-collar mountain villages.

But specific slices of rural America are another story. The upscale remodeling of towns in the Colorado Rockies, or parts of western Montana, are by now old stories. And similar transformations have been taking place in every corner of the country— from coastal Maine retirement meccas to Washington State's secluded Methow Valley, which has emerged as a magnet for cross-country skiers.

The trend has been driven by a confluence of factors. One is a bulge of retirees and pre-retirees, from both the baby-boom generation and its predecessor, possessed— at least, until these hard times—of wealth generated in the stock market and real estate in the 1980s and 1990s. Nina Glasgow and David Brown, development sociologists at Cornell University, found that between 1995 and 2000, 274 non-metropolitan counties saw net in-migration rates of 15 percent or higher among people age 60 or older. Since then, says Brown, there appears to have been "weak" migration overall from cities to the countryside—and recent Census numbers suggest it pretty much came to a halt in 2007 and 2008. Still, says Peter Nelson, a geographer at Middlebury College who studies rural migration, "right now the oldest boomers are in their early 60s, and that's a time period when the probability of moving from the city to the countryside increases. So even though the total percentage of people making the move might decrease, there's a larger denominator of people who could potentially make the move." That is why, even though the current recession has slowed the purchase of rural vacation and retirement homes, few experts doubt that it will pick up once the economy recovers.

Along with the retirees and vacationers, these rural enclaves have been attracting members of what author Richard Florida calls "the creative class." David McGranahan and Tim Wojan, of the Economic Research Service (ERS) at the U.S. Department of Agriculture, have studied so-called "rural artistic havens," places that appeal to artists and generate arts-related employment. In the 1990 census, they found 93 "established" havens of this kind. In 2000, they identified another 111 "emerging" havens, including relatively little-known areas such as Oktibbeha County (pop. 49,284), Mississippi, the home of Mississippi State University; and Ravalli County (pop. 40,824), Montana, near the university town of Missoula. To some extent, the arts trend and the retirement trend are related. "There is a mutually reinforcing arrangement," says Wojan, "between having a thriving arts community and being a place that is likely to attract retirees who are in-migrants—that artists are a 'consumption amenity' that people are looking for in a retirement destination."

An equally potent piece of the "creative class" migration has been "footloose" businesses. "Their owners and managers don't have to be on the factory floor or in the city," says Ray Rasker, of Headwaters Economics in Bozeman, Montana, "but can relocate for quality of life. As Rasker says, "you can go

hang out in Bozeman coffee shops and hear people say, 'Oh, I work for Microsoft' or 'Oh, we just got a billion-dollar investment from a Spanish firm and are investing in wind farms.'"

Rural growth, of course, is not the same as rural gentrification, which tends to be defined as the displacement of a community's lower-income residents by newcomers with money. Yet the two can go hand in hand, as has happened in a dramatic way in resort communities such as Aspen, and in some retirement havens—Michigan's Leelanau County, for instance. It is a rapidly increasing worry in the Adirondacks.

Ron Vanselow, who serves on the Johnsburg town council, has a vision of what a gentrified future in his area might look like. A few miles outside North Creek is a trailer park, a set of blocky single-wides, most of them with pickups parked nearby. Gesturing toward it, Vanselow recalls a vacation to Cape Cod, where, because the issue was on his mind, he made a game of trying to find the kind of housing that downscale Cape Codders might still be able to afford. Finally, spying a trailer park, he figured he'd found the spot—until his wife pointed out the Lexuses and Cadillac Escalades parked next to the trailers. "They'd even bought the trailer park!" he says. "That's what I don't want to see happen here."

One of the small ironies of the Adirondacks is that, despite their long history of settlement, scenic beauty and relative proximity to the great population centers of the Northeast, they were discovered late. "Even 10 years ago, people were still talking about the Adirondacks as forgotten land, though the needle was quivering at that point," says Brian Mann, a reporter for North Country Public Radio who has been chronicling the impact of growth on the region. "The gentrification that happened out west really bypassed the Adirondacks."

Not too long ago, blue-collar locals could afford a house on a lake in the Adirondacks.

That idea seems outlandish now, as lake-front real estate has shifted dramatically to second-home owners. In the late 1990s, the trend moved to village cores, a development that accelerated after September 11, 2001, when suddenly it seemed as if everyone in the New York metropolitan area wanted a piece of the Adirondacks to escape to. "The checks they were writing," says Alan Hipps, director of the Essex County Housing Department, "were more than the mortgages local people could afford."

A second-home boom can be unsettling to locals in more than one way. Parts of many Adirondack villages are empty now except during the summer; churches and schools have closed, and stores that once remained open all year have become seasonal. "A lot of people from Downstate and New Jersey and Connecticut started buying houses along Main Street that had been occupied by a schoolteacher or someone working at the highway department," says Tom Both, the former town supervisor of Keene, an Adirondack town about a half-hour east of Lake Placid. "I remember sitting in town hall one night looking out the window, and there were seven houses in a row with the lights out. Our K-12 school population went from 215 kids in 2000 down to 165."

Unlike most of the Adirondacks, which get very quiet from late fall until spring, Johnsburg has a year-round economy. The town sits near the Hudson River Gorge, a popular rafting and kayaking spot, and there is a knot of rafting outfitters in its northernmost hamlet, North River. A young person interested in stitching together a living can work the river in the summer, then move to one of the ski areas in the winter. A local garnet mine—which produces stones used in industrial abrasives—remains one of the largest employers in the area. And old-time families have long known how to get by on the margins. As Brother Posluszny, of the North Country

Ministry, describes it, "Many local people have had subsistence incomes for generations: They say 'I do some plowing, some hunting, a job in the summer. Or I work for this company and get a 13-hour week in winter and four hours in summer, and I get by cutting wood on the side.' They're very good at making do."

But it's far from clear how long they can continue to make do, given the rising cost of living in the area. Bouncing along the thaw-rutted mud of Back to Sodom Road, councilman Ron Vanselow gestures through the trees at a magnificent new log home—three generous stories, a porch columned with prodigious trunks, the whole thing stained an aggressively shiny reddish-brown. "This road used to look like the opening credits for the Andy Griffith Show, with kids walking down it carrying their fishing poles," he says. "But does that look like the kind of place a ski-lift operator can live?" His concern is echoed by Marco Schmale, who moved to North River in 1987 as a rafting guide and now runs one of the river outfitters. "When I came up here and started, I could buy a house, and I see people now and they can't do it," he says. "They're 25, they're a full-time river guide, in the winter they're on the ski patrol, they're making a good amount of money, but it's still not enough to get married and buy a house."

Which is why there is both trepidation and excitement about the coming expansion of Gore and the revitalization of North Creek's Main Street. The past year has seen two defunct Main Street hotels renovated and new restaurants open, including Bar-Vino, which has succeeded far beyond many locals' expectations by drawing from the ski crowd, retirees and even the river guides and ski-lift operators. There are Saturday nights in winter, now, when it's hard to find a parking spot along Main Street. The wine bar's owner, Mike Bowers, moved up from Delaware two years ago, and he sees great opportunity in the area. "North Creek has a river, a beautiful mountain, beautiful lakes, it's four hours from New York City and a couple from Montréal," he says. "The basic bones are good."

The question for town officials, of course, is whether they can keep the new development from forcing out current residents. Sterling Goodspeed, who as Johnsburg's town supervisor essentially serves as mayor, is confident they can. "We have the opportunity," he says, "to have sustained economic growth that is consistent with our environmental interests and in keeping with our history." To that end, the town government is looking into an inclusionary zoning ordinance, trying to shore up its fire and water districts, and placing great hope in the Adirondack Community Housing Trust, which aims to secure and protect affordable housing.

In this regard, it's possible that the recession will work to Johnsburg's advantage.

"Unemployment and the food pantry are not solutions to gentrification," says Ron Vanselow, "but I think we've dodged a bullet. We have some breathing room because of the economy."

Still, once development and gentrification take on their own dynamic, it is very difficult to hold on to what existed before, as plenty of gentrified towns from Mendocino to Vail have discovered. Small-town governments in particular are easily overwhelmed by the pressures that come with growth and gentrification. As optimistic as Johnsburg's leaders are that they can avoid an unpleasant fate, the record isn't especially promising.

"For the most part, I don't think the communities in our part of the world were prepared for the growth that's occurred over the last couple of decades," says Dennis Glick, who runs the Bozeman, Montana, office of a nonprofit aimed at helping communities in the West manage growth pressure. "Land use planning was not something that governments took seriously or had the resources to do effectively. As one person I know said, 'We went fishing for a little growth and ended up catching a great white shark.'"

65. As Suburbs Shift, Funding Fights Loom[*]

JENNI BERGAL

Louis Carbone, Rudy Magnan and Rocco Miano stand in front of their adults-only community in Newtown (pop. 27,000), Connecticut. Their Newtown League of Senior Voters protested tax hikes and pushed for more money for senior services instead of schools.

Rudy Magnan was shocked when he learned, a few years ago, that he'd have to pay $2,000 more in property taxes for his two-bedroom condo in an adults-only community in Newtown, Connecticut.

So Magnan and other retirees got together to protest the tax hike—and what they argued was too much spending on schools and not enough for senior services.

"It was a senior revolt. People were really pissed," said Magnan, the 74-year-old co-founder of the Newtown League of Senior Voters. "Ten years ago, we had over 5,000 students. Now we have 4,000-something and the school budget has gone up by $10 million. When it comes to supporting seniors, we get nothing. Our senior center is a dump."

This type of intergenerational political warfare could erupt more frequently in coming decades, as vast numbers of baby boomers grow old in their suburban homes, changing the demographics of their communities. Their decision to stay put may result in fewer suburban homes occupied by young families. That, in turn, could mean schools will be less full. And it could pit families with children against retired boomers in a fight for limited tax dollars.

"Their kids are graduated. Their interests are not taking care of the next generation of kids," said John McIlwain, author of Housing in America and a former senior fellow at the Urban Land Institute, a research center that focuses on real estate and land use. "The people who show up at local government meetings are going to be the boomers. The pressure will come from the boomers and, as one mayor told me, they push for what they want."

Between now and 2035, the U.S. Census Bureau projects the number of people 65 and over will explode from 48 million to 77 million, and the vast majority will be boomers, born between 1946 and 1964. More than half of boomers live in the suburbs.

Boomers are expected to work longer than their parents did. They'll pay taxes and

*Originally published as Jenni Bergal, "As Suburbs Shift, Funding Fights Loom," *Stateline*, June 22, 2016. Stateline is a project of the Pew Charitable Trusts. http://www.pewtrusts.org. Reprinted with permission of the publisher.

spend money on goods and services. And they'll donate to charities and do volunteer work.

But they will need a lot, too, because many of the features that made the suburbs desirable for young families—such as cul-de-sacs and multilevel houses—will be problematic for aging adults whose kids have grown up and moved away.

Boomers are likely to push many local governments to widen sidewalks and install benches, beef up public transit and help pay for home maintenance and repair, among many other things.

"The pressures on local government are going to be enormous," said John Feather, a gerontologist and the CEO of Grantmakers in Aging, a national association of foundations for seniors. "We spent billions of dollars building cul-de-sac suburbs, which are the worst possible design for people who lose the ability to drive."

Six years ago, a group of organizations including the International City/County Management Association (ICMA) asked more than 1,400 local governments how prepared they were to handle an aging population. The top three challenges cited were funding shortages, transportation and housing. The survey revealed only "limited progress" in preparing for the boomers compared to an earlier survey.

"It's an issue every community is going to face," said Abigail Rybnicek, deputy director of the ICMA's Center for Sustainable Communities. "We're trying to educate people on why this is important and why investment and planning now can have a big impact in the future."

Suburban boomers who are well-off will be able to downsize to expensive condos, apartments or townhomes, if they choose. Those who grow old in their homes can pick up the tab for home modifications, personal care and private transportation or ride-hailing services such as Uber or Lyft.

But many working- and middle-class boomers with fewer resources won't be as fortunate. Among Americans 50 to 65, more than four in 10 don't have enough income to support them in retirement. Many have more debt than their parents did. They may end up needing everything from affordable housing to subsidized transportation to financial assistance with retrofitting their homes.

"The question is whether the government is going to respond to people without the means who are aging in the suburbs," said Marjorie Ledell, a member of the Clark County Commission on Aging in Washington state. "It comes down to money."

That's a tough proposition for a lot of suburban communities.

In the far Chicago suburbs of McHenry County, Peter Austin, the county administrator, doesn't think there is a local government solution.

"There can be some coordination. We can help put groups together, build some networks, have some safety-net discussions," he said. "But I'm reluctant to say we're going to grow government to meet those challenges. We are finding it increasingly difficult to meet needs we already have."

Schools or Senior Services?

In some communities, particularly in Sun Belt states, seniors have been flexing their political muscle over taxes and spending for many years. Often, the fight has been over schools.

Back in the early 1980s, most of Sun City West, an enormous age-restricted retirement community outside Phoenix, was separated from the surrounding school district after a lengthy fight about paying for schools.

In 2005, voters in Dade County, Georgia, approved a school tax exemption for seniors.

A 2012 study examined intergenerational conflict over decades in American suburban school districts. It found that the greater the number of seniors who lived in a suburban community, the less it spent on schools.

"That's the consequences we're going to be facing as boomers age," said David Figlio, director of the Institute for Policy Research at Northwestern University, who co-authored the study.

The gap was particularly stark when the elderly residents were white and the school-children were African-American or Hispanic, Figlio said.

Not all seniors are opposed to school funding. But they are more likely to support schools when their grandchildren attend them, Figlio said. However, that's frequently not the case.

"We're a very mobile society and you may live in Evanston, Illinois, and your grand-kids live in Pasadena, California," he said.

Mowing the Lawn

The graying of suburbia also could result in the deterioration of some neighbor-hoods. Experts say older adults who stay in their homes often do less maintenance as the years go by. Aging boomers on fixed in-comes may be forced to choose between paying for prescriptions and groceries and keeping up their property.

That could lower property values in some suburban areas, said David Versel, an urban planner and senior vice president at Delta Associates, a real-estate consulting firm.

"Their homes are not going to be kept up. The roof might leak. The lawn might not look nice. It would devalue other prop-erties around it," Versel said. "I can see that happening on a large scale as boomers get older and don't have the resources to main-tain their house."

Some planners and aging experts think that one way to help meet the needs of aging boomers is to change zoning and land use rules to expand housing options.

That could include allowing high density apartments in single-family neighborhoods or "accessory dwelling units," so-called granny flats, an apartment in the basement or over a garage or a tiny house in the backyard that boomers or caregivers can live in.

But those concepts are highly controver-sial in suburbs designed for families and often don't sit well with local residents, who argue that it would change the nature of the neighborhood and lower property values.

Boomer Politics

Boomers aging in the suburbs may use their considerable political muscle—but-tressed by their numbers, relatively high education level and economic power—to transform the communities where they grew up.

Joseph Coughlin, director of the MIT AgeLab, predicts that boomers will demand everything from an Uber-like system for public transit to government subsidies for in-home technology to keep them healthy and safe.

"This generation has had everything else changed for them. We had to build new schools. We had to create new retail expe-riences," Coughlin said. "Now that they're getting older, they have new and different needs that will have to be met, not as a cour-tesy, but as a political demand, and govern-ment is going to have to step up."

But local government officials contend they simply won't have the resources to meet those demands. They say the private and nonprofit sectors also will have to step up, as will aging boomers themselves.

"I don't think government can handle this all by itself. I'm not even sure govern-ment should," said Amy St. Peter, assistant director of the Maricopa Association of Governments, the Phoenix area's regional planning agency.

"People feel better when they can help themselves and help their neighbors. If people are seeing themselves as a client, it can be dehumanizing."

St. Peter said her association is working with nine communities to improve services for the aging population. Several have focused on transportation and created volunteer driver programs.

"There's going to be a slew of approaches and solutions to try and deal with this," said Matt Thornhill, founder and president of the Boomer Project, a marketing research and consulting company. "The government's not going to have the money to do it all. We have to find ways for everyone who has a vested interest in maintaining their community to be parties at the table, including local businesses, the health care industry, neighborhood associations and individuals."

66. When Bad Things Happen to Good Plans*

JOSEPH MCELROY

There it sits, impossible to ignore, at a major entryway to downtown Petoskey: a vacant city block diverting attention from Little Traverse Bay, one of northern Michigan's jewels. Called Petoskey Pointe because of its location between two major roads, including U.S. 31, the stalled redevelopment project exemplifies the fallout when bad things happen to good plans.

With the economy in what Nobel Prize-winning economist Gary Becker has called "the most severe financial crisis since the Great Depression," city officials from coast to coast are grappling with ambitious projects that never got off the ground or—worse, perhaps—that stalled when they were partially built.

Petoskey's 6,000 citizens are not amused. One irate blogger wrote to a local newspaper, "They destroyed a bunch of nice buildings and gave us a dirt hole. Petoskey is the laughingstock of Michigan."

Petoskey Pointe is just one example of an increasingly common phenomenon: high-profile, public-private economic development partnerships gone sour, victims of the recession. "It's everywhere," says consultant John LaMotte of the Lakota Group, a planning and design firm based in Chicago. Before the recession deepened, he says, numerous projects were getting underway in both large and small cities as municipal officials became skilled at creating partnerships with private entities.

Real estate deals often go bad, especially in a slow economy. When private buyers or sellers lose their shirts, it's of little concern to anyone except their creditors and lenders. That's the free enterprise system's "creative destruction" at work. But when taxpayer money is part of a deal, everybody is an owner and potential critic. This puts more pressure on the public officials, often planners, who brokered the deals.

Politicians love ribbon-cutting ceremonies, but they detest being embarrassed, and big holes in highly visible locations can hurt reelection chances. The ground breaking for Petoskey Pointe took place in May 2006. In November 2008, the mayor and two council members were voted out of office. Soon after, the city manager retired after 25 years on the job.

What happened? City leaders had their eyes on the property for years, knowing it was underused. So when a team of developers with a good track record approached the city in early 2003 with proposal for a site occupied by a vacant movie theater, the local officials encouraged them to redevelop the entire block. The block, measuring 300 feet by 280 feet and zoned B-2 (Central Business District), consisted of seven parcels, including the theater and surface parking that was once the site of a car dealership and a garage.

The developers, Lake Street Petoskey Associates, based in the Detroit suburb of Farmington Hills, submitted an initial concept plan for a seven-story building. The proposal was reviewed by an ad hoc committee representing various downtown interests. Some objectors worried that the building would overpower its smaller, Victorian-era neighbors. After revisions and several meetings, in January 2004 the planning commission recommended rezoning the block as a planned unit development.

Almost a year later, in December 2004, with the national economy still doing well, the city council approved the rezoning needed for a PUD on the downtown site. Plans for the $50 million "downtown gateway" development called for 67 condos, 102 hotel rooms, a restaurant, an indoor pool, shops, and two levels of parking, with 193 spaces open to the public and 226 reserved for private use.

But Michigan land-use law allows voters to approve or reject rezonings via referendum. In May 2005, voters narrowly approved the rezoning, but the process delayed the project for several months.

"The delay caused a domino effect," B.J. Shawn, owner of Bearcub Outfitters in downtown Petoskey, told the *Northern Express Weekly*. "The repercussions ... pushed the project to a time when the economy plunged. The mortgage rate went up, the trade people got other jobs. To have to put it back together when it was moving along—that disruption was a big challenge."

Going Downhill

Meanwhile, the city sold its portion of the site—a parking lot with about 50 spaces then worth an estimated $970,000—to the developer. The city also established a tax increment financing district to help pay for parking for the new development, and the Emmet County Brownfield Authority created another TIF to cover the cost of an environmental cleanup on the former garage property. The site also qualified under a Michigan law that enables developers to receive $4.5 million in business tax credits from the state, according to Amy Tweeten, AICP, the Petoskey city planner. Acquiring the property from seven different owners further slowed the project.

Things finally started to happen in May 2006. The site was cleared and excavated for the two levels of underground parking. But just as the developers were trying to secure the second phase of construction financing, the real estate market was beginning to soften. Construction came to a halt in 2008 after the earth retention system was installed and the developers could not come up with the money to pay the contractors.

Earlier, the Petoskey city council ran out of patience and terminated its business relationship with the developers. The city then sued Lake Street Petoskey Associates for breach of contract. On September 21, an Emmet County judge ruled in the city's favor, saying the developer is responsible for paying Petoskey a total of $1.1 million.

Now, with the PUD agreement still in place, it's up to the property owners or their lenders to live up to the terms of the agreement. The PUD included a requirement for a performance bond of half the value of the project or at least $30 million. The developers did not have to submit the bond until foundation work began, but he project never got that far.

Now what? "The current economic circumstances will certainly make any redevelopment projects difficult for some time," says Tweeten. She noted that Petoskey Pointe presents the kind of catch-22 problem common in financing condo developments. "You need a certain amount of pre-sales to get the financing, but it's difficult to sell something without showing progress"—a cleared site, for instance.

Slow Start in North Carolina

Think of towels, and chances are you think of Cannon. In the 1960s and 1970s, the world's biggest textile manufacturer was the Cannon Mills Company in Kannapolis, North Carolina, a city of just 42,500, which produced an average of 300,000 towels per day and employed almost 25,000 people. So dominant was the local textile industry that the town took its name from the Greek word for looms—*kanna*.

James W. Cannon established Kannapolis in 1906, providing housing and retail establishments for his employees, much as railroad car tycoon George Pullman did on the far south side of Chicago. For decades, the town and its leading employer were barely distinguishable from each other.

That tie broke in July 2003 when the company, by then bought and sold several times and renamed Pillotex, finally closed. Kannopolis and the surrounding community saw 4,340 jobs suddenly disappear, the largest one-day layoff in the history of the state. City leaders had to decide what to do with more than six million square feet of abandoned industrial space in the core of its downtown.

Then a miracle happened, or so it seemed at first. In 2004, David Murdock, chairman and CEO of Dole Foods, who owned the textile factory from 1982 to 1986, reacquired the site and announced plans for the North Carolina Research Campus, a $1.8 billion redevelopment effort involving partnerships between Murdoch's companies—Dole Foods and Castle & Cook—and eight universities, including the University of North Carolina system, North Carolina State, and Duke. The center, with a focus on food science, was seen as a way to help Kannapolis make the difficult transition from textile town to scientific hub.

But even with a $150 million contribution from Murdock and approximately $25 million a year from the state, the stagnant economy has made progress difficult. In September, the state slashed the budget of the Nutrition Research Institute, a major component of the research campus, from $7.9 million to $6.8 million, and few of the laid-off factory workers are qualified for the new high-tech jobs.

The research campus's key facility, a 311,000-square-foot laboratory, is open, and a ground-breaking ceremony was held in May for a $26 million biotechnology facility for a local community college. The 62,000-square-foot building had been delayed because of the financial crisis, which slowed financing.

Also complete are the buildings housing North Carolina State's Plants for Human Health Institute and UNC–Chapel Hill's Nutrition Research Institute.

Plans for a 700-home golf course development on the site are now on hold because of the real estate market collapse. In June a major tenant, biotechnical giant PPD, pulled out of the project because of construction delays and an overall slump in business. Local officials say that the company, which has laid off hundreds of workers worldwide, hopes to come to the research campus when economic conditions improve.

The recession is also cutting into support from the state, which has an unemployment rate of 11.1 percent, fifth worst in the country. Research campus officials had been seeking $29.5 million from the state for fiscal year 2010, but probably will receive closer to $22.5 million. Also, the credit crunch and high interest rates have cut into the tax increment financing fund established to provide local infrastructure for the research campus.

In mid–July the Kannapolis City Council approved an alternative TIF strategy. The revised plan would provide $25 million to $35 million in local government investment, says Irene Sacks, the city's economic development chief. That's far less than the original $168 million, although the figure could rise as future economic conditions produce more development. The smaller TIF will probably fund a new building for Cabarrus County's public health authority as well as some infrastructure, she says.

Like their counterparts in Michigan, the North Carolina planners did their homework, but the recession has played havoc with earlier assumptions. A 2006 economic analysis estimated that the North Carolina research campus could create 37,450 jobs in the region by 2032. But the consultant warned that this estimate was based on the community meeting the goals of an earlier companion analysis, which pointed out the need for better schools, infrastructure, recreation facilities, and diversity efforts in order to attract and keep high-tech businesses and employees.

The consultant, Atlanta-based Market Street Services, warned that Kannapolis— perhaps best known as the hometown of legendary NASCAR driver Dale Earnhardt— would be competing with other cities that are "ranked very highly on quality of life, educational opportunities, and other typical municipal rankings."

Although the development is off to a slower start than expected, Market Street CEO J. Mac Holladay remains optimistic. "It's been difficult, but nobody could have predicted what would happen to the economy," he says. As if to prove his point, in June Kannapolis received an Excellence in Economic Development Award from the U.S. Department of Commerce for its response to the plant closure. And, even though construction has been slower than expected, "the job creation numbers are ahead of the schedule we put together," Holladay notes.

Now What?

For decades, economic development experts have stressed that partnerships between private developers and public agencies are the best way to stimulate economic redevelopment. But in light of problems like those discussed above, public-sector planners might be more cautious about committing to such relationships.

Still, LaMotte and Holladay say city officials shouldn't be afraid to think outside the box in looking for solutions. Helping elected officials find solutions is where planners can really shine, LaMotte says, "because we planner types are comprehensive thinkers and resourceful. We also have thick skin."

Holladay also urges planners to think big, especially when working on projects like the North Carolina research campus, which he describes as "transformational." To a large extent, local officials are creating a new city, he says. "It's about having a different level of anticipation. It's about thinking big and asking what we need to do to get there. What will the demands be?"

67. Examining Economic Development Dollars*

MIKE MACIAG

The John A. Wilson Building, which houses the offices and chambers of the mayor and council of the District of Columbia. Earlier, the D.C. council approved a measure to require its chief financial officer to review tax expenditures.

Just how effective tax breaks and other incentives are at boosting economic development is a crucial question states and localities should answer when they look to expand or renew programs.

Yet the extent to which local governments actually scrutinize economic development programs varies greatly, and many remain without basic accountability measures.

Most published research focuses on tax incentives at the state level, where the largest packages are typically awarded. A new nationwide survey by the International City/County Management Association (ICMA), though, provides a detailed portrait of how local governments use business incentives and employ accountability measures.

For the most part, the survey of about 1,200 local governments and agencies suggests they're taking measures that, if done correctly, will help to ensure better returns on investment. Three-quarters of survey respondents reported measuring the effectiveness of business incentives, while 73 percent conducted cost-benefit analyses.

A smaller share (56 percent) reported always requiring performance agreements, while 27 percent had agreements in place for some incentives and 17 percent did not use them at all. Only 36 percent linked economic development priorities to budget processes.

It's more difficult to gauge how effective and reliable localities' practices truly are, though. Cost-benefit analysis is a particularly controversial area of economic development, for example, and such reports are often characterized by unrealistic assumptions or questionable methodologies.

Daphne Kenyon, a fellow at the Lincoln Institute of Land Policy, said the survey results for both cost-benefit analysis and incentive measurement were better than she expected. One potential concern she cited was that some evaluations may be conducted by the economic development agencies rather than more objective outside groups.

Measuring the effectiveness of incentives is no simple task. Take, for example, job

---

*Originally published as Mike Maciag, "How Local Governments Are (or Aren't) Examining Economic Development Dollars," *Governing*, November 5, 2014. Reprinted with permission of the publisher.

creation—the most common measure used according to the survey. Tallying employment counts before and after an incentive is a far different matter than determining about how many jobs would actually be gained or lost absent an incentive.

"It all depends on who you ask and whether you're a tough judge of the numbers they give you," Kenyon said.

Still, going through the motions—even if reviews are limited—is better than doing nothing. "Just taking the sober view of looking at costs and benefits can be so vastly better than a naïve mentality," Kenyon said.

Kenyon recommends localities within a metro area work together and market themselves as a unit. Property tax incentives are relatively unimportant when companies first select a metro area, according to a Lincoln Institute of Land Policy report, but they weigh more prominently in choosing a site within a region.

Compared to local agencies, states generally possess more resources to study incentive programs. But even so, a 2012 Pew study found half of states lacked basic measures to inform policymakers on whether they provided an effective return on investment.

Evidence does suggest slightly more states and localities are starting to take a closer look at economic development. Compared to five years ago, responses for the ICMA survey ticked up a few percentage points for questions assessing use of cost-benefit analysis and measuring incentives' effectiveness. Several states responded to calls for greater transparency and scrutiny of incentives in recent years as well, passing legislation aimed at better evaluating programs.

"An increasing number of policymakers are recognizing the importance of measuring the results of tax incentives," said Josh Goodman, who researches state economic development incentives for Pew Charitable Trusts.

One reason Goodman said more states don't study tax incentives is that they're not part of the regular budget process. More, though, have moved to evaluate programs more regularly, he said.

Earlier, the District of Columbia Council approved a measure requiring its chief financial officer to review tax expenditures. It stipulated multiple considerations for analyses of economic development-related programs, such as taking into account whether outcomes would have been any different absent tax expenditures and how they may have been offset by economic losses elsewhere.

Pew has published a fact sheet outlining how a few states evaluate their incentive programs.

Evaluations of incentives must consider their goals; not all economic development awards are designed primarily to spur job creation. Some target economic development around economically depressed neighborhoods or in other areas, like transit hubs. Others may exist to raise revenue via property taxes.

One of the more common complaints levied against the subsidies is that only a few companies benefit. Using its subsidy tracker database, Good Jobs First estimated that at least three-quarters of total U.S. disclosed economic development dollars are awarded to only 965 larger corporations.

There's no comprehensive national tally of just how much states and localities have doled out. For this reason, it's hard to say the extent to which business incentives possibly increased in recent years. The ICMA survey, though, does suggest local incentive award packages generally aren't growing, at least on average. The majority of responding governments (61 percent) reported average business incentive packages of about the same value as five years prior; 23 percent reported increases and 15 percent reported decreases.

Much of the data around economic

development incentives tends to be frag-mented. That could soon begin to change under new rules proposed by the Govern-mental Accounting Standards Board (GASB) that require governments to report total resulting revenue loss. Some jurisdic-tions currently disclose much more than others, so the proposed requirements rep-resent a significant shift that's likely to en-counter resistance.

68. The Myths of Municipal Mergers[*]

Aaron M. Renn

Would the consolidation of St. Louis and St. Louis County solve bad and abusive governance?

In the wake of the events in Ferguson, Mo., much of the media coverage focused on the geopolitical fragmentation of the St. Louis area, and the abuses it has engendered. In some circles, it led to talk of government consolidation, or "big box" government, as a possible solution.

St. Louis County has 90 municipalities. (This doesn't include the city of St. Louis, which is technically an "independent city.") Believe it or not, with 22,000 residents, Ferguson is one of the biggest. A number of the municipalities have fewer than 1,000 people. This proliferation of small cities has created perverse incentives to bad and abusive governance. But while there may be clear benefits to consolidation, is it really the answer here?

Consolidation and absorption of territory by expansive central cities have been in vogue for some time. Former Albuquerque, N.M., Mayor David Rusk's influential 1993 book *Cities without Suburbs* noted that regions whose central cities had elastic boundaries that could expand to take in new territory outperformed those that did not.

It's said that consolidation brings more clarity to regional leadership and creates tax equity, since the tax burden is distributed over a larger entity. Cost savings from economies of scale are often touted as well. But as my colleagues Alan Ehrenhalt and Justin Marlowe have written, a look at consolidation as currently practiced reveals holes in all of these theories.

First, in many consolidations, there is really little consolidation at all. In the case of the "Unigov" system in Indianapolis, virtually none of the existing municipalities in the county were legally eliminated during consolidation. Police and fire departments were left unconsolidated, as were 11 school districts. Similarly in Louisville, Ky., where the city and county merged, neither existing municipalities nor fire departments were abolished. This hardly clarifies leadership and lines of authority.

There's also limited tax sharing, thanks to the political deals needed to get mergers approved. In Nashville/Davidson County, there are not only six "satellite" cities, but there is also a separate "urban services district" with a higher tax rate. Louisville has a similar designation for its former city territory.

---

[*]Originally published as Aaron M. Renn. "The Myths of Municipal Mergers," *Governing*, January 2015. Reprinted with permission of the publisher.

As for cost savings, evidence suggests that these are vastly exaggerated and that the cost of government can actually go up. This was the case in Indianapolis, where in 2007 the city finally consolidated police departments. The move was projected to save $8.8 million per year. A post-merger audit by the firm KSM Consulting found that actual savings were "negligible."

Corporations frequently manage to save money when merging. That's because they can pare costs by eliminating redundancy and harmonizing salaries. But in the public sector, nobody is likely to lose his job, and salaries tend to be harmonized to the high water mark.

Even the "cities without suburbs" paradigm may actually be backwards. In a paper criticizing the Louisville merger, University of Louisville professors Hank Savitch and Ronald Vogel argued that a better description is "suburbs without a city." That is, by allowing formerly suburban and unincorporated areas to vote for the government of the city, the locus of control shifts from urban to suburban residents. This disempowers the city by merging its interests with a far larger group of suburbanites who may have different interests and values. This can also have a racial dimension, as it dilutes concentrated minority voting power in the central city. The mere act of putting different groups of people inside the same box doesn't ensure that they will agree, as Congress so starkly illustrates.

Expansive or consolidated governments are often less responsive to citizen and neighborhood needs. A large city still only has one mayor who only has 24 hours in a day. His or her attention span is limited. And in a large city, the most influential interests tend to be its wealthy citizens along with corporate players. It can be hard for neighborhood-level concerns to get addressed.

Given these factors, it's hard to see how consolidation would help the St. Louis area. This is particularly true when, as Cincinnati Mayor John Cranley has noted of his city, the urban core is starting to see uplift while surrounding inner-ring suburbs face challenges from their own economic and fiscal declines.

Yet there's an argument to be made for consolidation of especially small cities. Unlike big-city governments, these often fly under the media and state radar unless a major problem erupts. This renders them vulnerable to abuses. It's no surprise that it was Bell—not small on an absolute basis, but only the 215th largest municipality in California—where the city manager was making nearly $800,000 per year. Combine small size with poverty, as in Bell, and these places are often doubly overlooked.

In these cases of documented abuse, state legislatures should not hesitate to simply abolish the small municipalities in question. This would result in de facto consolidation to the county level. No one should suggest that this in and of itself would solve the racial and other challenges facing the St. Louis region. In fact, it would likely produce many of the downsides described above, such as the dilution of minority voting power. But it would at least end the outright abuse of citizens, especially poor and minority citizens, by these tiny fiefdoms.

69. Economic Development in the 1099 Economy*

WILLIAM FULTON

My daughter's just about finished with college and has started the job search. It's both exhilarating and frightening at the same time, of course. Yet it's yielding a few surprises: First, there actually are jobs out there. Second, they're not exactly, well, jobs.

Most of the entry-level jobs she's running across in her field are "1099 jobs." In other words, you don't become a full-time employee with benefits. Rather, you simply enter into a contract with your employer to provide work. Maybe you have regular hours and maybe you don't; maybe you have a workstation and maybe you don't. In any event, you are a contractor, not an employee—so at the end of the year you get a 1099 form from the IRS, not a W-2.

Having watched both her parents work in the 1099 economy throughout most of her childhood, my daughter isn't particularly afraid of 1099 jobs. But she, like everybody else in the so-called Millennial generation, is a little uncertain about where this will lead. How stable is 1099 work? Will she ever have a full-time job? What will she do about medical insurance once she turns 26 and is no longer eligible to be on my policy?

These questions boil down to this: Is the 1099 simply a temporary situation because employers are skittish about the future? Or are we seeing a permanent change where most people freelance and only a few have full-time jobs?

This is a good question for economic development practitioners to ask because the answer will shape the future of the business. After all, economic development usually revolves around the whole idea of "jobs"— growing them, stealing them, adding them to the local economy and making sure constituents have them. Oftentimes, economic development success is measured in terms of the number of jobs created or saved, and economic development deals between government agencies and private companies are based on jobs as a metric.

What happens when there really is no such thing as a "job" anymore? How do you practice the art of economic development?

The answer is that even though there may not be jobs in the conventional sense, there is still work. That's the whole idea of the 1099 economy. It's just a different way of organizing the economy. Businesses need economically valuable work to be done, but instead of employing people full-time and permanently, they contract with individuals

*Originally published as William Fulton, "Economic Development in the 1099 Economy," *Governing*, May 2011. Reprinted with permission of the publisher.

to do the work temporarily. The work ebbs and flows, the businesses come and go, and the 1099 employees work for a while and then move on. It's a lot more fluid—and seemingly uncertain—than the traditional economy.

What this means is that economic development efforts become much less about individual businesses and much more about the underlying infrastructure—the dynamic flow of business growth (entrepreneurs, financiers, public infrastructure) as well as the labor force (skill levels and the density of the labor supply). The "ecosystem" of economic growth becomes more important because a fluid economy requires this system to be operating at all times—and most of it is in the community or the region, far beyond the factory gates.

Some of America's most prosperous economic sectors operate this way. The entertainment industry functions this way not only in Los Angeles, but in New York and other cities as well. Everybody's a "jobber," moving from project to project. Silicon Valley works in a similar manner, with highly skilled employees floating from startup to startup.

As a result, savvy economic developers who want to tap into the 1099 economy must recognize that they must focus on a different version of the basics. Visiting existing large businesses in the community remains important because your largest businesses are probably where your future entrepreneurs currently work. But you also have to know the subtle ebbs and flows of your local economy, especially where the clusters of small business activity are located. You have to stay in touch with your educational community, especially your community colleges, to understand what skills your labor force has and needs. And, of course, you have to read all those Craigslist ads that my daughter is reading.

It's a much more ear-to-the-ground approach than traditional economic development because the 1099 economy is basically an ear-to-the-ground economy. Traditional statistics may tell you that no jobs are being created and unemployment is high, but somewhere in your community, somebody's doing work.

I. Top 50 Best Small Towns, 2016[*]

LIVABILITY

Big stories can happen in small places. Our annual Top 10 Small Towns list has been a popular index, but we always wished we could highlight more than 10 communities each year. After all, the reason we produce this list is to shine a light on cities and towns that are often in the shadows of the big metropolises. So, we're pleased to present our inaugural super-sized "Top 100 Best Places to Live, Small Towns" edition [only the top 50 are included in this chapter].

To create this list, we used a modified version of the robust methodology we developed with the Martin Prosperity Institute for our annual Livability 100. We examined more than 40 data points each for more than 12,000 towns with populations between 1,000 and 20,000. These scores were weighted based on an exclusive survey conducted for Livability by the leading global market research firm, Ipsos Public Affairs. These cities and towns allow for the tight-knit communities key to small-town living coupled with the amenities you'd expect in larger cities.

#1 Lebanon, New Hampshire (Population: 13,474). Though it's the smallest city in the state, Lebanon offers residents natural amenities and fulfilling life experiences that you just won't find in big cities. Lebanon's visual appeal, strong economy and educational system, affordable housing, and civic engagement make it the top small town in the country. This is the second time in a row that Lebanon has appeared on our best small towns list. See where it ranked on the Best Small Towns 2014. Tucked into a valley along the Connecticut River, Lebanon is home to Dartmouth-Hitchcock Medical Center and several high-tech companies, including Timken Aerospace and GPS maker TomTom. Throughout the year, residents gather in Colburn Park for festivals and concerts, while the places like Salt Hill Pub offer live music. The Mascoma River flows through downtown Lebanon, creating a focal point. The many things to do in Lebanon keep residents active and entertained.

#2 Los Alamos, New Mexico (Population: 11,843). It's easy to see why Los Alamos is one of the fastest growing cities in the state. A deeper look shows why it's the second best small town in the country. Situated upon the Pajarito Plateau, between the Valles Caldera National Preserve and the Santa Fe National Forest, the city's rugged location belies its warm and vibrant appeal. Residents enjoy many things to do in Los Alamos, from cultural attractions to

---

[*]Originally published as "Top 100 Best Small Towns," www.livability.com. This is an excerpt of the top 50. Reprinted with permission of the publisher.

outdoor adventures. Home to the Los Alamos National Laboratory, the city is filled with scientists, engineers and creative types who enjoy ample sunshine, cultural activities, and unique western architecture.

#3 Durango, **Colorado (Population: 17,268).** The surrounding San Juan Mountains hold opportunities for Durango residents to mountain bike, hike, kayak and fish. While Durango is filled with Old West heritage, the city's restaurants and shops provide a hip, modern entertainment scene. Thousands of visitors come to experience the Snowdown Festival, which includes fireworks and a beard growing contest. Located near five major ski areas, Durango serves as a gateway to great downhill skiing.

#4 St. Augustine, **Florida (Population: 13,440).** Considered the nation's oldest city, St. Augustine celebrates its 450th anniversary in 2015. Residents here experience daily what millions of tourists come to see: historic Spanish architecture, beautiful beaches, lush parks, and a vibrant downtown filled with restaurants, shops and museums. The many things to do in St. Augustine give residents and visitors a steady stream of entertainment options. The opulent Ponce de León Hotel is now part of Flagler College. St. Augustine is home to the Florida School for the Deaf and Blind, the largest school of its type in the country.

#5 Bar Harbor, **Maine (Population: 2,524).** From its rocky coastline to the surrounding Acadia National Park, Bar Harbor offers an authentic New England experience and friendly community. Situated on Mount Desert Island, Bar Harbor is home to College of the Atlantic and Jackson Lab. Cruise ships, yachts and lobster boats constantly float past the harbor allowing passengers to admire stunning views of the shoreline. Things to do in Bar Harbor range from seaside adventures to cultural celebrations. Village Green, a park in the center of town, serves as a gathering point for residents throughout the year.

#6 Louisville, **Colorado (Population: 19,171).** Located southeast of Boulder, Louisville is home to several high-tech companies that specialize in space exploration. Families gather at Steinbaugh Pavilion for summer concerts and to ice skate in the winter. Galleries, studios, restaurants and music venues occupy many of the 100-year old buildings that line streets in the downtown area. The town's pubs are packed with personality, including Waterloo in Old Town, which offers live music, mixed drinks, beer and burgers.

#7 Hood River, **Oregon (Population: 7,311).** An outdoor lover's playground, Hood River provides opportunities to snow ski, windsurf and mountain bike, all in the same day. Perched on the Columbia River, offering views of Mount Hood, the city attracts adventurous types. Its economy remains rooted in agriculture with several apple and pear orchards and vineyards providing employment, but a handful of tech companies have brought in new jobs as well.

#8 Spearfish, **South Dakota (Population: 10,836).** Three mountains surround Spearfish, a city that attracts outdoor lovers who come to fish in Spearfish creek and wander through the canyon. Crows Peak, Lookout Mountain and Spearfish Mountain provide impressive views. Quaint shopping centers and a vibrant arts and entertainment district draws residents from across the region and provide many things to do in Spearfish. Parents rave about the highly regarded schools in Spearfish, including those within the Spearfish School District and Black Hills State University. Also serving residents is the 40-bed Spearfish Regional Hospital. This is the second time in a row Spearfish made our Best Small Towns list.

#9 Sebastopol, **California (Population: 7,535).** Ranking high in cultural and outdoor amenities, Sebastopol's small-town charm lures in new residents who easily find affordable housing across a range of home types, from 100-year-old bungalows to new subdivisions with modern features. Schools in Sebastopol are highly regarded by parents. The town's apple growing history is celebrated during the Apple Blossom Festival and a Gravenstein Apple Fair, but in recent years, Sebastopol has become a grape-growing region for high-quality wines.

#10 Port Angeles, Washington (Population: 19,125). Home to Peninsula College, Port Angeles also has a high-achieving local school district. The city connects to the Olympic Discovery Trail that traverses 130 miles of lowlands bordered by the Olympic Mountain Range and the Strait of Juan de Fuca. Other recreational opportunities for residents include mountains, rivers, lakes and forestland. An 80-bed Olympic Medical Center serves residents and anchors health care in Port Angeles, while city officials are redeveloping the downtown district.

#11 Traverse City, Michigan (Population: 15,006). Life is sweet in Traverse City, the largest producer of tart cherries in the nation. Thousands of tourists visit the town each year to enjoy for what residents experience year round: stunning views, freshwater beaches, vineyards and quaint shopping areas. Unique restaurants and fresh food options helped Traverse City earn a spot on our Top 10 Foodie Cities list. Events like the annual National Cherry Festival in July celebrate the city's history. Parents applaud schools in Traverse City, and the educational system in general which includes higher education choices such as Northwestern Michigan College and Western Michigan University–Traverse City.

#12 Los Alamitos, California (Population: 11,598). Spanish for "the Little Cottonwoods," Los Alamitos hosts the USA Water Polo National Aquatic Center, the U.S. Military Los Alamitos Joint Forces Training Base and Los Alamitos Race Course that stages several kinds of horse racing.

The community's strong health system includes Los Alamitos Medical Center and Alamitos West Health Care Center. The Los Alamitos Unified School District earns high praise from parents and students.

#13 Jackson, Wyoming (Population: 9,967). As a major gateway for travelers visiting Yellowstone and Grand Teton national parks, Jackson, WY's economy is anchored by tourism. Residents enjoy year-round access to world-renowned attractions including Snow King Resort and the National Elk Refuge. Jackson officials have developed a large shopping and restaurant district, giving residents a large range of things to do. St. John's Medical Center provides excellent health care in Jackson, while Central Wyoming College–Jackson offers advanced educational opportunities. Parents rave about the schools in Jackson.

#14 Arcata, California (Population: 17,679). Located near Humboldt Bay, Arcata is largely a college town with Humboldt State University's student base making up about half of the city's total population. The Plaza, considered the heart of the community, features a green lawn area surrounded by coffee shops, restaurants, stores, bars and live music clubs. Arcata residents have access to great health care at a 78-bed Mad River Community Hospital.

#15 Montpelier, Vermont (Population: 7,760). The smallest of the 50 U.S. state capitals, Montpelier is known as an artistic community providing cultural education options such as the Vermont College of Fine Arts and the renowned New England Culinary Institute. The city hosts the Green Mountain Film Festival each year and is home to a Union Institute & University campus. Restaurants, museums, bars and galleries provide many things to do in Montpelier. An abundance of local recreation options—from mountain biking and snow skiing to canoeing along the Winooski River—keep residents active.

#16 Carlisle, Pennsylvania (Population:

18,877). Nestled in the highly productive Cumberland Valley agricultural region, Carlisle provides a quaint setting for families. While school age children attend the Carlisle Area School District, higher education classes can be taken at Dickinson College, U.S. Army War College and the Penn State Dickinson School of Law. The Carlisle Regional Medical Center offers excellent care, and many residents enjoy the borough's 18 public parks. Green spaces, restaurants and cultural attractions provide many things to do in Carlisle.

#17 Falls Church, Virginia (Population: 13,074). Living in Falls Church comes with a premium, but residents here are treated to well-maintained parks, excellent schools and top health care. Known as one of the richest cities in the country, with a median annual household income of around $115,000, Falls Church has an extremely low poverty level. Parents applaud schools in Falls Church, especially those within the Falls Church City Public Schools, the city's largest employer.

#18 Onalaska, Wisconsin (Population: 18,148). Known as "The Sunfish Capital of the World," Onalaska overlooks the Black River and features a man-made reservoir known as Lake Onalaska. More than 300 acres of parks are available to residents, and the community is served by two quality school districts. Cost-of-living expenses are generally lower than you'll find in most cities. The majority of homes in Onalaska come in under the average national price. Health-care options in Onalaska include Gundersen Lutheran Medical Center and Mayo Clinic Health Systems Onalaska.

#19 Pella, Iowa (Population: 10,343). Pella's Dutch heritage is celebrated at the annual Tulip Time Festival and the Vermeer Mill, which features the largest working grain windmill in the country. Situated near Iowa's largest lake, Lake Red Rock, Pella offers scenic views of both natural attractions and historic treasures like the Pella Opera

House, which opened in 1900. Molengracht Plaza features a group of shops and restaurants with a canal winding through the complex. Pella Community Schools earn high grades from residents.

#20 Mount Kisco, New York (Population: 11,016). Located 36 miles from New York City, Mount Kisco offers a haven for middle- to upper-class professionals. Housing choices range from co-ops and condominiums to historic Victorian houses and multimillion-dollar estates. Schools in Mount Kisco provide excellent opportunities for learning beyond the classroom. Bedford Central School District is recognized for its quality education programs, and Mount Kisco residents preserve history with several buildings listed on the National Register of Historic Places.

#21 Tumwater, Washington (Population: 18,128). Finding outdoor adventure opportunities in Tumwater is easy. The city is situated where the Deschutes River enters Budd Inlet at the southernmost point of Puget Sound. Both tourists and residents visit Tumwater Falls Park, one of the city's top attractions, between late August and early October to watch salmon swim upstream. The highly regarded Tumwater School District prepares students for the workplace and parents applaud many schools in Tumwater. Housing options in Tumwater run the gamut from exclusive to affordable.

#22 Alexandria, Minnesota (Population: 11,465). Tabbed as a tourism center because of its many lakes and resorts, Alexandria is ranked as one of the fastest-growing micropolitans in Minnesota. Douglas County Hospital is the largest employer, with 865 professionals. Schools in Alexandria provide many hands-on learning sessions. Most children are enrolled at the first-rate Alexandria Public Schools-ISD 206. Alexandria Technical & Community College provides higher education options.

#23 Middlebury, Vermont (Population:

6,713). The village of Middlebury is listed on the National Register of Historic Places. Winding its way past historic homes and businesses, through the heart of the community, is Otter Creek (the longest river in Vermont). Middlebury serves as the commercial and business center for west-central Vermont and is home to Middlebury College. Residents have their health-care needs met at Porter Medical Center, and Middlebury has a thriving downtown that hosts an annual After Dark Music Series.

#24 Madison, New Jersey (Population: 16,043). Nicknamed "The Rose City," Madison offers residents excellent educational options, cultural attractions and well-preserved historic buildings. Located 15 miles west of Times Square, Madison is an affluent community whose median income for families is more than $100,000. Homes in Madison range well above the national average. Madison Public Schools provide a 13-to-1 student-teacher ratio, while higher education options include Drew University and the Madison-Florham Park Campus of Fairleigh Dickinson University.

#25 Golden, Colorado (Population: 19,759). Located at the base of the Rocky Mountains' Front Range, along Clear Creek, Golden is a growing community that still maintains a small-town historic identity. Several well-known companies call Golden home, including Coors Brewing Company and the National Renewable Energy Laboratory. Residents find plenty of things to do in Golden. Colorado School of Mines offers programs in engineering and science. Golden's burgeoning arts and cultural scene includes the Jefferson Symphony Orchestra and Foothills Art Center.

#26 Maitland, Florida (Population: 16,273). Long known as a vacation spot because of its tropical climate and proximity to Florida theme parks, Maitland's high-quality amenities draw many affluent families. The city has several parks along waterways, such as Lake Lily and Lake Sybelia, which attract boating enthusiasts. The real estate scene in Maitland includes a number of century-old homes on tree-lined streets. The prominent Orange County School District receives praise from parents and students.

#27 Breckenridge, Colorado (Population: 4,604). The historic town of Breckenridge is situated 9,603 feet above sea level in a sprawling valley along the Continental Divide. Besides its full-time citizens, Breckenridge also welcomes many part-time residents who have vacation homes in the area and come to snow ski. The town has plenty of shopping and arts options along Main Street and has a reputation for tourism, with summer attractions such as hiking, fly-fishing, mountain biking, boating and white-water rafting.

#28 Marshall, Minnesota (Population: 13,609). The notable Marshall Public Schools district and a handful of esteemed private Christian schools are among the many advantages of living in Marshall, which also houses Southwest Minnesota State University, a school with 3,500 students. The city serves as a regional shopping hub for southwest Minnesota, and Marshall also offers affordable housing options. Also, Avera Marshall Regional Medical Center provides exceptional health care in Marshall.

#29 Princeton, New Jersey (Population: 28,940). Princeton was established before the American Revolution and is best known as the home to Princeton University, which opened in 1756. Also gracing the community is Westminster Choir College, Princeton Theological Seminary, and an admired Princeton Public Schools district. The city offers amenities like diverse housing choices, a large shopping center, and several parks including Herrontown Woods, which features an arboretum, walking trails and wildlife viewing areas. Homes in Princeton sell for a hefty price when compared to the national average, but residents are buying into the community.

#30 Southern Pines, North Carolina (Population: 12,782). The large number of homes and buildings listed on the National Register of Historic Places help give Southern Pines a charming reputation. This tourism destination attracts visitors from throughout the south-central North Carolina region who shop in the town's boutiques, dine in unique restaurants, and explore outdoor activities like biking and equestrian sports. Schools in Southern Pines get high marks from parents. College students can attend Sandhills Community College as well as the Academy of Classical Design.

#31 Lindsborg, Kansas (Population: 3,473). Nicknamed "Little Sweden," hosts an annual Svensk Hyllningsfest ethnic celebration on odd-numbered years, with the next festival set for October 2015. Education choices include Bethany College and an exemplary Smoky Valley School District. Lindsborg is also home to the Anatoly Karpov International School of Chess. Residents rely on Lindsborg Community Hospital for health care and find a range of housing options.

#32 Takoma Park, Maryland (Population: 17,307). Spring in Takoma Park is marked by the blooming of thousands of azalea bushes which gave the city its nickname, "Azalea City." Located near Washington, D.C. Takoma Park features a range of houses from historic bungalows to Victorian mansions. Sligo Creek and Long Branch Creek traverse through this largely residential area. The largest commercial district is Takoma-Langley.

#33 Northfield, Minnesota (Population: 20,303). Students at Carleton and St. Olaf colleges help lower the median age in Northfield to 27, but this city attracts many families and young professionals. The Northfield Public Schools district is well respected, and residents have access to 35 parks along with a long-standing Northfield Hospital. Many downtown buildings have been preserved and are prime examples of late 19th and early 20th century architecture.

#34 Emeryville, California (Population: 10,497). Situated between the cities of Berkeley and Oakland and extending to the San Francisco Bay, Emeryville has experienced recent economic growth thanks in large part to biotech and software companies settling in. Schools in Emeryville rank well among the nation's top educational systems. Local students attend the well-regarded Emery Unified School District along with Expression College for Digital Arts, a private university whose graduates are often hired by Pixar, the city's largest employer. Emeryville has several shopping destinations and six beautiful parks.

#35 Newport, Oregon (Population: 10,045). Considered the Dungeness Crab Capital of the World, Newport, Ore., offers residents a peaceful seaside village that's full of great restaurants, shops and spectacular views. The city is home to the Oregon Coast Aquarium, Nye Beach, Hatfield Marine Science Center and Yaquina Head Lighthouse. Lincoln County School District and Oregon Coast Community College educate students, and activities like surfing, bicycling and hiking keep residents active. Among the distinct neighborhoods in Newport is the Deco District with art deco buildings in the downtown area.

#36 Decatur, Georgia (Population: 19,888). Retaining a small-town feel despite its proximity to Atlanta, Decatur features four historic districts along with a vibrant entertainment and nightlife scene thanks to popular venues like Eddie's Attic, Wahoo Grill, Brick Store Pub, Carpe Diem and The Square Pub. This progressive community includes Agnes Scott College, Columbia Theological Seminary and Georgia Perimeter College, while Decatur City School District has earned several academic accolades.

#37 Orange City, Iowa (Population: 6,130). Dutch architecture and a plethora of tulips help give Orange City, Iowa, a Netherlands vibe. Citizens have a variety of affordable housing options and good healthcare facilities, including Orange City Hospital. Students are privy to strong learning environments found in Orange City schools and programs within the MOC–Floyd Valley Community School District, and the city also houses Northwestern College.

#38 Williamsburg, Virginia (Population: 14,401). Serving as Virginia's capital from 1699 to 1780, Williamsburg today is perhaps best known for the College of William & Mary, founded in 1693. The city enjoys a tourism-based economy due in large part to Colonial Williamsburg, a restored historic area that attracts 3 million visitors a year. Also in the city are two major theme parks—Busch Gardens Williamsburg and Water Country USA.

#39 Pacific Grove, California (Population: 15,365). Known simply as "PG" to locals, Pacific Grove, Calif., is a coastal city nicknamed "Butterfly Town USA" because of an annual migration of Monarch butterflies that color the city from November to February. Beaches, Victorian homes and a nationally recognized 18-hole Pacific Grove Golf Links make the community a favorite vacation getaway. Community Hospital of the Monterey Peninsula provides health care to residents, while local students attend a top-notch Pacific Grove Unified School District.

#40 Dillon, Montana (Population: 4,181). Residents of Dillon, Mont., live in a prime area for snowmobiling, skiing, four-wheeling, hiking and fishing on Beaverhead River. The city's 31 independent restaurants provide plenty of dining options, while events like Montana's Biggest Weekend, a rodeo and parade keep folks entertained. Stores from Murdoch's Ranch Supply to a Patagonia Outlet keep residents well stocked. Dillon is home to good schools, the University of Montana Western as well as Barrett Hospital and HealthCare.

#41 Sheridan, Wyoming (Population: 17,699). Found halfway between Yellowstone Park and Mount Rushmore, Sheridan, Wyo., gives residents a picturesque community to live, work and play. Sheridan's outdoor amenities, which include nine parks and many acres of open spaces, help make the city a vacation destination for outdoor enthusiasts. A collection of bike trails make Sheridan one of the best places to ride a bike. Each July, the community hosts an annual WYO Rodeo. Ten historic sites in Sheridan are listed on the National Register of Historic Places, and the city is only a short distance from the Battle of Little Bighorn. Some of the best restaurants in Sheridan offer authentic western meals. Local education is provided by Sheridan County School District #2 along with Sheridan College.

#42 Bel Air, Maryland (Population: 10,240). Founded in 1780, Bel Air has 25 homes and buildings from the 18th and 19th centuries, including an entire Bel Air Courthouse Historic District and Harford Furnace Historic District. The town today has amenities like Harford Mall as well as five neighborhood parks, and residents are proud of a thriving arts community with theater, art galleries, concerts and festivals. A 182-bed Upper Chesapeake Medical Center tends to the area's health needs.

#43 Park City, Utah (Population: 7,845). A vacation haven, the tourist population in Park City, Utah, greatly exceeds the number of permanent residents thanks primarily to three ski resorts—Canyons, Deer Valley and Park City Mountain. Home to the annual Sundance Film Festival and more than 100 restaurants and bars, Park City keeps residents entertained. Schools in Park City give students plenty of specialized programs and sports opportunities. Outdoor fans can utilize several hiking and biking trails. The city's large collection of factory outlet stores and luxury retailers give residents lots of shopping options.

#44 Brunswick, Maine (Population: 15,275). Bordered by the Androscoggin River and Atlantic Ocean, Brunswick, Maine, is home to Bowdoin College. Residents and visitors have convenient access to I-295 and many outdoor amenities. Excellent health care is available through Mid Coast Hospital and Parkview Adventist Medical Center, and plenty of arts and entertainment opportunities dot the community. Fun fact: The novel Uncle Tom's Cabin was written by Harriet Beecher Stowe when she was a Brunswick resident.

#45 Middleton, Wisconsin (Population: 18,185). A nationally recognized community trail system along with national grand champion, Capital Brewery, are two of the many amenities that appeal to residents living in Middleton, Wisc. More than 60 independent restaurants and a large collection of downtown specialty shops provide lots of entertainment options. The city's strong education programs available to students in the Middleton-Cross Plains School District gain praise from parents. For healthcare needs in Middleton, citizens can visit the University of Wisconsin Medical Foundation.

#46 Hershey, Pennsylvania (Population: 14,172). Often referred to as "The Sweetest Place on Earth" or "Chocolatetown USA," Hershey, Pa., offers a range of cultural and recreational amenities that make life sweet for residents. Of course, it's home to the Hershey Chocolate Factory as well as roads like Cocoa Avenue and streetlights shaped like Hershey Kisses. Affordable housing options, Amtrak rail service and a Tanger Outlets shopping complex sweeten the scene. Schools in Hershey provide strong education options that include Derry Township School District and Penn State College of Medicine.

#47 Astoria, Oregon (Population: 9,503). Situated near the mouth of the Columbia River, Astoria, Ore., is a deepwater Pacific Ocean port that features very mild temperatures year round. The city serves as the western terminus of the TransAmerica Bicycle Trail, a popular cross-country route for cyclists. The community is graced with several parks and walking trails, and citizens receive top health care from an award-winning Columbia Memorial Hospital.

#48 Beaufort, South Carolina (Population: 12,702). Large moss-draped oak trees line downtown streets in Beaufort, S.C., creating an iconic Southern scene in a city filled with romantic views and historic charm. Chartered in 1711, Beaufort is the second-oldest city in South Carolina and situated along the Atlantic Ocean on Port Royal Island. Dotted with military bases, historic districts and excellent fishing opportunities, the city draws thousands of tourists each year. Residents find plenty of things to do in Beaufort. Beaufort County School District and the University of South Carolina Beaufort provide great education options.

#49 Decorah, Iowa (Population: 8,058). Living in Decorah, Iowa, opens doors to a variety of outdoor activities from hockey games and cross-country skiing to mountain biking, camping and canoeing. Decorah's history dates back to the 1850, when Norwegian natives built early settlements. The city's Norse heritage is celebrated each July with a large Nordic Fest. Contributing to the city's quality of life is a major trout hatchery along with many scenic parks, including some built on bluffs. The Decorah Community School District as well as four-year Luther College, which is known for its Nordic Choir, have earned several education accolades.

#50 Augusta, Maine (Population: 18,898). The state capital of Maine, Augusta is positioned along the Kennebec River where community leaders are overseeing an expansive riverfront and downtown redevelopment project. Residents stay active with outdoor recreation options that include fishing, hiking and skiing. Education is a top priority at five public schools in Augusta, one private school and the University of Maine at Augusta, and the city boasts an interactive Children's Discovery Museum. Hospitals in Augusta provide excellent care and the health scene here includes a highly regarded cancer care center.

Livability explores what makes small-to-medium sized cities great places to live. Through proprietary research studies, engaging articles and original photography and video, we examine topics related to community amenities, education, sustainability, transportation, housing and the economy. We then leverage that expertise to develop city rankings for a range of topics including small towns, college towns and our annual "Top 100 Best Places to Live."

II. Community-Based Economic Development Approach*

INTERNATIONAL CITY/COUNTY MANAGEMENT ASSOCIATION

Cities can be the engines that drive a country's economic growth, providing an environment in which private-sector jobs can be created and maintained, but they can also become barriers to economic growth and competitiveness if they do not understand the extraordinary tools that lie within their grasp.

ICMA has worked with local governments in the United States and internationally to develop strategies that allow them to compete for business in a local, national, regional, and global environment. In ICMA's experience, improving local economic competitiveness requires the active participation of local governments, which are critical to the expansion and creation of jobs in the private sector.

Because local governments are the intersection through which most business creation must flow, this regulatory and administrative gateway needs to be supportive and transparent, and local governments need to create an environment conducive to businesses. In addition, local governments are best positioned to create realistic economic development strategies grounded in the specific strengths of the community, and to mobilize resources for their implementation.

Working in developing countries, ICMA has designed an Economic Development Continuum wherein local governments serve as the nexus between jobs and basic services, adequate infrastructure, and financial management, and realize how these basic elements are interdependent and contribute to a local government's ability to create and implement proactive economic development strategies.

Once local authorities appreciate this, they are able to place into context the basic improvements that are needed to be competitive. To foster this understanding, ICMA has developed a Local Economic Development Score Card and worked closely with local governments worldwide to assess and improve municipal service delivery and physical infrastructure, create the political will for change, identify business opportunities, and develop public-private partnerships that foster economic and community growth and create more competitive cities.

ICMA's comprehensive Community-Based Economic Development (CBED) approach fosters an open, democratic process for public-private cooperation and mobilizes all community resources, including

*Originally published as International City/County Management Association, "Local Economic Development and Competitiveness," http://icma.org. Reprinted with permission of the publisher.

land, labor, capital, and technology, to improve the competitiveness of the community in the global market. The CBED approach recognizes that economic development programs involve many sectors—housing, education, labor force development, infrastructure, finance, law, health, civil society, and private sector development—and allows for the efficient use of resources in a way that benefits businesses and citizens alike. ICMA's programs have focused primarily on the following areas: strategic economic development planning; community involvement; marketing communities; support for local enterprises; labor force development and job creation; public-private partnerships; and skill building and certification.

Strategic Economic Development Planning

Sound planning is crucial to economic development success, and ICMA works with cities, nongovernmental organizations, the business community, and other stakeholders to help create strategic plans that are based on assessment of local assets and capabilities and identification of realistic opportunities.

- ICMA conducted economic development training for urban councils and chambers of commerce in two districts in Sri Lanka. The training was based on a gap analysis of the legal and regulatory environment of the districts, and the goal was to identify improvements that were needed in order to help stimulate economic development. After conducting a SWOT analysis (strengths, weaknesses, opportunities, threats), participants identified strategies that would improve the partnership between the local government and the business community. They then began outlining a strategic plan and concrete action steps.

- In South Africa, with ICMA assistance, the city of Johannesburg successfully developed a strategic plan and a business plan for an urban development corporation; KwaDukuza developed a "sustainable community" framework; and Pietermaritzburg-Msunduzi adopted an economic development vision statement.

- ICMA helped five major cities in Lebanon apply the community based economic development model. With this assistance the cities developed viable LED strategies by conducting SWOT (strengths-weaknesses-opportunities-threats) analyses and assessments to identify the sectors and projects that offered the greatest potential to create new jobs and attract investment.

- In Ecuador, ICMA provided technical assistance for the creation of an economic development strategy as well as training on facilitating interaction among stakeholders who would play a role in developing the strategy.

- In Bolivia, ICMA assisted the municipalities of La Paz, El Alto, and Cochabamba in the development of urban LED strategies developed with private entities. The strategies were approved by the municipal councils after an ample consultation process that involved key stakeholders.

- In Hungary, ICMA helped the cities of Szentes and Oroshaza analyze their community assets and identify paths for future development; helped the Kis Balaton Area Association complete a strategic planning process to promote interlocal cooperation for tourism development and enhance opportunities for citizen participation;

and facilitated a strategic planning process for Zalalovo that mobilized community resources. As a result, the community entered into agreements with Western European investors and capitalized on the government's decision to reopen an international rail line in the city.

Community Involvement

Local economic development initiatives enhance the well-being of the entire community—and the entire community has a stake in LED decisions. ICMA's approach to LED involves multiple players in the decision-making process.

- In Bulgaria, Lebanon, and Kazakhstan, ICMA facilitated the creation of economic development advisory boards or councils allowing multiple stakeholders in the community to have input into LED decision making; participants included representatives from the city council, business, nongovernmental organizations, and citizens, and significantly contributed in the prioritization of LED projects.
- Advisors from Kansas City, Kansas, helped the city of Karlovac, Croatia, develop an inclusive approach to growth by identifying issues that had hindered public participation in and support of development initiatives and helping the city improve channels of communication with citizens.
- In Georgia, ICMA conducted two courses on Principles and Practices of ICMA's Community-Based Economic Development (CBED), which explored how CBED can integrate the basic principles of economic development with the active involvement of citizens, nongovernmental organizations, community-based organizations, and businesses.

- Novgorod, Russia, gave neighborhood groups the opportunity to determine what improvements were needed in the economic and physical conditions of their respective city zones as a result of ICMA's work with the city to improve the administrative systems that support increased private investment.
- In Bolivia, ICMA introduced a performance measurement system that promoted discussion between the communities and municipalities in more than 15 municipalities to prioritize LED-related resources in the municipal budget and to monitor the use of those resources.

Marketing Communities

Whether the goal of local economic development is business attraction or increased tourism, marketing is a crucial part of the overall strategy. ICMA has helped cities worldwide identify their assets, implement "branding," and market themselves to potential investors.

- With ICMA assistance, partner cities in Bulgaria established a consortium of municipalities (Bulgarian Partnership for Local Economic Development, BPLED) to lead joint marketing efforts, including a Web site (www.invest.bg) that serves as a source of information and a point of contact for prospective investors.
- In addition, ICMA worked with all member cities of BPLED in Bulgaria to develop marketing materials. Haskovo's package entails a catalog of firms, a brochure, a DVD presentation, and a tourist map of the city, and Blagoevgrad developed and launched an electronic marketing profile and created a video promoting

the city's strengths and business opportunities.

- Faced with a declining fishing industry and a corresponding loss of population, the port city of Nevelsk, in the Russian Far East, identified tourism as an opportunity for development and began marketing its unique natural, historical, and recreational resources with the help of expertise shared by ICMA partners; the result was an increased number of visitors.
- ICMA designed and implemented the LED component of the Municipal Economic Growth Activity (MEGA) program in Serbia, which included identification of investment opportunities, information dissemination to potential investors, and other marketing and promotion outreach.
- In Bolivia, ICMA worked with highland municipalities (Curahuara de Carangas and Turco) to organize municipal fairs to market regional and nationwide livestock production (llamas). The fairs were organized by the municipality with participation of the communities that represent the private sector in that area of the country.

Support for Local Enterprises

Among the mechanisms for supporting local enterprises are incubators, industrial parks, business improvement districts, business visitation programs, and access to finance. ICMA has worked with cities worldwide to put these mechanisms in place to encourage business retention, expansion, and attraction.

- In Jordan, the USAID Local Enterprise Support Project is creating an enabling environment for growth and innovation among micro and small enterprises. ICMA is supporting changes in national policy and regularions that will facilitate better local economic development and building local capacity to design and implement successful local economic development strategies.
- Working with economic development specialists from Kenai, Alaska, the city of Bolshoy Kamen in the Russian Far East established a business incubator to help increase the number of small businesses in the city, create markets for their products, and expand the tax base; the incubator helped the city become self-sustaining to prepare for the day when it ceases to have the federal subsidies that come with its "closed city" status.
- Also in the Russian Far East, the city of Dolinsk formalized a concept for a business park, identified a potential site, took steps to identify potential tenants, and initiated a public relations campaign.
- As the city of Pazardjik, Bulgaria, prepared for the transition to a market-driven economy, ICMA and the city of West Bend, Wisconsin, helped Pazardjik develop a practical LED strategy and develop a 40-acre industrial park using innovative lease techniques; the program continued advising on the marketing strategy, and the park attracted more than $5 million in private investment, created 400 new jobs, and helped reduce the city's unemployment rate from 24 percent to 12 percent in four years.
- A traditional center for precision machining, Panagyurishte, Bulgaria, worked with ICMA and the city of West Carrollton, Ohio, to assess its economic opportunities and arrived at the conclusion that the best way to capitalize on its traditional strength

was to create a high-tech industrial park and market the city as a center for high-tech industry. The project built on existing relationships with local businesses to create a proactive growth strategy that serves both public- and private-sector interests.

- ICMA worked with the city of Adama, Ethiopia, to develop an industrial district that will emphasize agro-processing, providing an opportunity for local producers to process their products and market them to other regions of the country.
- In Bolivia, ICMA trained small businesses with the potential to perform municipal projects and then provided an opportunity for the businesses to participate in "reverse procurement fairs" where the municipality showcases its demand for goods, services, and small infrastructure projects, and local businesses bid on them.

Labor Force Development and Job Creation

When a private enterprise considers re-location or expansion, it needs to be assured that the new location has a reliable labor force. Local governments can effectively assist in matching the labor demand and supply in the market. Well trained, educated labor will help expand existing or attract new businesses, bringing new jobs to the community.

- A worker training program was an important component of ICMA's Afghanistan Municipal Strengthening Program. It targeted youth—a strategy that provides labor for small infrastructure projects and jobs for residents and also helps connect youth to the areas in which they live.
- In Bulgaria, ICMA facilitated the

development of the Gabrovo Youth Information Center and improved access to education and employment services for young people.

- ICMA worked with Pancevo, Serbia, to maximize the economic development potential of the Port of Pancevo, where it was estimated that 28,000 jobs could be created through build-out of the port and surrounding acreage.
- ICMA supported the efforts of Kragujevac, Serbia, to create a stable local economic base. When the main industrial company in Kragujevac was transitioning from state to private ownership, 15,000 jobs were threatened. ICMA created a business support strategy with the city to cultivate small businesses and programs to provide assistance to startup small businesses that accompanied the government loans given to workers whose jobs were eliminated.
- ICMA supported the creation of more than 3,500 jobs in Bulgaria as a result of a comprehensive LED program that helped the partner municipalities establish new economic development offices, train new LED professional staff, create business visitation and expansion programs and effective marketing strategies, develop business incubators and industrial parks, and develop an LED certification program.

Public-Private Partnerships

Local economic development initiatives can be significantly strengthened by the synergy that results when public and private organizations establish effective mechanisms to work together. ICMA has facilitated public-private partnerships worldwide.

- In Mangaung (Bloemfontein), South Africa, ICMA facilitated the development of a plan that focused public and private tools and methods on the development of an industrial corridor to create jobs, public infrastructure improvements, and new and rehabilitated housing and retail opportunities.

- Working closely with the city of Johannesburg, ICMA developed the framework for an Urban Development Corporation, called the Johannesburg Development Agency (JDA) responsible for directing the economic revitalization of the city. Specific components of the JDA design included a rationale for the establishment of the JDA, visioning documents, a three-year business plan, Johannesburg city center performance indicators, Johannesburg audit of city center cultural assets, and a financial plan.
- In Bulgaria, with ICMA assistance, Stara Zagora formulated a new downtown development plan that featured public-private partnerships to encourage and control development and concessions by private developers to benefit the community at large; Blagoevgrad developed a public-private partnership model for operating an indoor market; and Gabrovo developed contracts between the city and three private firms for the construction of cardboard items, a café, two shops, and kiosks.
- ICMA helped the government of Jamaica, the city of Kingston, the Jamaica Chamber of Commerce, and other public- and private-sector stakeholders articulate a clear vision for using World Cricket Cup 2007 to spur development and obtain a commitment of resources from the private sector, prioritize activities and projects, and create and train a com-

mitted management team that ensured implementation of the strategy.

- In Bolivia, ICMA promoted tourism development committees at the municipal level in the Chiquitania region in the state of Santa Cruz that included the participation of the private sector, municipalities, and association of municipalities (*mancomunidad de Chiquitania*). The committees played an important role in the application of national and regional policies at the local level to increase infrastructure standards to market the area's potential internationally.
- Also in Bolivia, ICMA retained private consulting firms and engaged the chamber of commerce in the development of urban LED strategic plans for three of the five biggest cities of the country (El Alto, La Paz, and Cochabamba). The private contractors were selected through open competition and developed the plans under the guidance of the municipalities.

Skill Building and Certification

Developing professional LED staff at the local level is a critical need for most municipalities. To fill this gap, ICMA has developed comprehensive training courses, a workbook on Community-Based Economic Development (CBED), and LED Certification Programs. The LED training and skill building activities help ensure the long-term impact and sustainability of the LED initiatives ICMA has supported.

- ICMA helped design and delivered a comprehensive LED training course for 10 Serbian municipalities as part of a program to streamline the environment for private investment and enterprise growth and develop LED capacity.

- In the Democratic and Effective Municipalities Initiative (DEMI) in Kosovo, ICMA engaged economic development staff from U.S. cities to share their expertise by providing evaluations, recommendations, and training for Kosovo cities. A study tour showcased successful U.S. practices, and U.S. partners worked with local officials to finalize local development plans and strengthen the role of local government in LED by building staff capacity and development methodologies.
- In the Russian Far East, ICMA trained more than 150 municipal officials in basic principles of effective municipal economic development, community action planning, business development, and creative marketing.
- ICMA developed a comprehensive LED Training Curriculum, and established and worked with the Bulgarian Partnership for Economic Development, a consortium of more than 50 Bulgarian cities, to design and implement a Certification Program for LED Professionals and a two-level "Ready for Business" Certification Program for municipalities.
- In Georgia, ICMA conducted two courses on the Principles and Practices of Community-Based Economic Development (CBED), which explored how CBED can integrate the basic principles of economic development with the active involvement of citizens, nongovernmental organizations, community-based organizations, and businesses.
- ICMA implemented the *Local Economic Development (LED) Speaker Series* in partnership with the USAID Urban Programs Office. USAID staff and implementers learned from ICMA's member-practitioners about the critical aspects of LED and its applications in developing and transition country contexts with an emphasis on the cross-cutting nature of LED and opportunities for cross-sectoral synergies and collaboration.
- USAID and ICMA co-sponsored the *Local Economic Development in Europe and Eurasia: Strategies that Work* workshop to take stock of USAID regional experience with LED and translate it into useful recommendations for future LED programming. ICMA framed, designed, and facilitated a four-day workshop for 60 regional USAID staff and implementing partners to share experience, results, and tools on LED programs and to discuss opportunities for greater synergies between USAID strategic objectives and sectors on LED related programs and projects.

III. Communicating Capital Improvement Strategies[*]

GOVERNMENT FINANCE OFFICERS ASSOCIATION

Public participation and stakeholder involvement during the planning, design, and construction of capital projects is extremely important. Both large and small projects will require and benefit from a communication strategy to inform the public and a method of soliciting and using feedback. This will allow the organization to effectively communicate capital needs and the impact to service levels or current asset condition in the event the project does not proceed. In addition, developing a process to involve the public during project planning is a key step in assessing priority and determining if the project will meet service-level goals and community expectations.

Recommendation: The Government Finance Officers Association recommends that organizations develop a communications plan for public participation focused on explaining capital needs, options, and strategies and facilitating feedback in advance of any major capital program. Capital programs gain from the support of the community both to ensure that capital projects will deliver expected and desired outcomes as well as to ensure there is adequate support for the investment. Organizations should consider and address the following in any communication plan on capital assets.

Stakeholder Engagement: Communications should be directed at appropriate stakeholder audiences including:

- Citizens
- Public officials
- Officials from other jurisdictions such as special service districts and neighboring organizations
- Businesses
- Community Groups / Neighborhood associations
- Interest groups
- Staff
- Regulatory agencies (oversight authorities)

Each stakeholder group may have different interests in the project and have different concerns or expectations. For example, citizens may be more interested in overall cost and impact on taxes, whereas a business may be most interested in possible loss of revenue from construction activity.

- Developing the Messaging: Regardless of the stakeholder audience, organizations should take care to

[*]Originally published as Government Finance Officers Association, "Communicating Capital Improvement Strategies," February 2014 http://www.gfoa.org. Reprinted with permission of the publisher.

ensure that there is a clear and consistent message that delivers accurate information both on the costs of the project, duration, impact, and benefit. Building credibility is essential in communications. Messaging should be developed with input from various groups within the organization (management, finance, engineering, operations, etc.) to ensure that information is complete and accurate. For high profile projects, it may be helpful to leverage external resources, such as financial advisors, subject matter experts, or public relations consultants to help gather and/or validate information or draft communication messages.

- Communication of Project Information: Organizations should clearly communicate project benefits, costs, impacts, and schedules clearly and at a level of detail appropriate for the audience and communication method. It is important that the finance officer present accurate information clearly and avoid using the communications to "sell" or unnecessarily advocate for the project. To maintain credibility, information should be transparent and accurate setting clear expectations. When communicating directly with citizens it is important to consider how citizens will be impacted by the project and discuss information in terms that are applicable including the expected impacts (both to costs and benefits) on existing services and infrastructure in the event the project does not proceed. For example, it is often helpful to relate costs back to increases in tax rates rather than present actual project costs to provide context. Communications should also discuss project outcomes and expectations that include performance measures.

- Communication Methods: Organizations should consider strategies that utilize multiple methods of communication to reach different audiences. Some communications could include:
  - Signage
  - Press Articles
  - Website
  - Social Media
  - Presentations to Interest Groups/Local Non-Profit Organizations/ and Community Groups
  - Regular communications at public meetings (public hearings)
  - Use of Media (Editorial Boards / Press Conferences)

- Use of Public Feedback: When using communications methods that are more interactive and provide the opportunity for stakeholders to provide feedback, it is important that the organization be receptive to ideas and address any significant issues. Staff also must be prepared and develop a process for evaluating public feedback. When evaluating feedback, staff should recognize the limitations and potential bias in the collection methods and take that into account in using that information. Staff should also consider differences in demographic, social, economic, or geographic segments of stakeholders that may not be representative of the entire community. For this to be effective, the communications plan must be implemented early enough in the project so that staff has the ability to use the information collected to modify the project. Some examples of public feedback methods include:
  - Community Meetings: Staff can attend scheduled community meetings for non-profit groups, or

schedule specific meetings in public locations throughout the community that can allow for presentation and discussion of project information.

o Use of Citizen Committees: Elected Officials or staff can appoint citizens to serve on a committee to collect citizen feedback and formulate a recommendation.

o Public Opinion Research / Surveys: Survey data on public preferences can be conducted either by staff or externally by a firm specializing in collecting public opinion data

o Comments / Complaints: Staff can learn from tracking and analyzing comments or questions that come up through already established channels (for example: comment cards, website inquiries, social media responses, crowd sourcing, and CRM/311 systems).

• Monitoring, Reporting, and Accountability: In addition to communications during initial phases of the project, organizations have a need to maintain communications through the end of the project and report on results. Monitoring of progress and accurate reporting on the project will provide accountability and give credibility to the next project.

IV. Glossary of Economic Development Practices

JOAQUIN JAY GONZALEZ III *and* JONATHAN ROSENTHAL

Artist Relocation Program: a variety of financial incentives aimed at attracting artists to live and work in their city or state, for example: exempting artists from paying sales and income taxes on their work.

Asset sale: is the transfer of ownership of public sector assets, entities, or functions to private or nonprofit sector entities.

Bid process: public solicitation for sealed bids from private or nonprofit developers, suppliers, or contractors.

Branding campaign: a vigorous initiative to promote the town or city as a brand to attract visitors, residents, businesses, and investors.

Brownfield: is a site previously used for industrial or commercial purposes. Such land may have been contaminated with hazardous waste or pollution.

Business climate: the environment of a given community relevant to the operation of a business; usually includes tax rates, attitude of government toward business, and the availability of capital.

Business creation: a local economic development strategy that focuses on encouraging the formation of new for-profit and non-profit companies that are locally based and will remain in the community and grow in the future.

Business Improvement Districts: or BID, is a private or a public sector (or in partnership together) initiative to improve the environment of a commercial district or area, including Main Streets and Downtowns.

Business incubator: an organization that helps entrepreneurs and startups plan, perform, and reach profitability.

Business retention: efforts by local economic developers to keep existing businesses in the community and to encourage them to expand their operations on their present sites.

Cluster analysis: the examination of employment in similar industries, or clusters, for the purpose of determining strengths for possible industry attraction, expansion and retention.

Community branding: multi-dimensional marketing on the positive differentiator(s) of a community, intended to help it stand out relative to the competition.

Community Development Block Grants (CDBG): are flexible funding tools that address a wide range of community and economic development needs, including decent housing, healthy living environments, and expanded economic opportunity.

Community Improvement Districts (CID) Act: legislation authorizing local governments to impose and collect a community improvement district sales tax on retail sales.

Competition: occurs when two or more parties independently attempt to secure the business of a customer by offering the most favorable terms usually through a bid process.

Consolidation: also referred to as municipal merger is the absorption of smaller municipalities by expansive central cities.

Contracting out: is the most popular privatization approach in the public sector involving the outsourcing of public services to business or nonprofits.

Cost-Benefit Analysis: is a systematic approach to estimating the strengths and weaknesses of development alternatives.

Creative class: a term coined by Richard Florida in his book, *The Rise of the Creative Class.* Economic growth will be driven largely by hipsters, techies, or new age creative types who prefer interesting and diverse urban places to the suburbs.

Developer: also referred to as the "contractor," is a for-profit or nonprofit company which has received a redevelopment or economic development contract from a city or town.

e-Commerce: the buying and selling of goods and services via the internet.

Eminent domain: the right of a government to expropriate private property, with fair compensation, for public use.

Enterprise development: the assistance provided to entrepreneurship in a local community to assist entrepreneurs by connecting them to financial, human, and physical resources that can help them to start and grow their business.

Enterprise zone: an area in which taxes and regulation could be lowered; these areas are usually set up in depressed areas, with the goal of encouraging investment and job creation.

General Obligation Bonds (GOB's): bonds issued by a government entity that are backed by the full-faith-and-credit of the government agency.

Gentrification: is an economic redevelopment and revitalization process in urban communities and neighborhoods, which results in increased property values but the displacement of elderly, disabled, lower-income families, mom and pop stores, neighborhood cafes, and small businesses.

Gentrifiers vs. rustics: pro-gentrification residents and businesses versus residents and businesses who are against (or for limited) gentrification.

GIS: short for Geographic Information System, which is a computer system for capturing, storing, checking, and displaying data related to positions on the Earth's surface.

Grants: public money given to an entity, and the recipient of these funds does not have to pay them back.

Gravity analysis: attraction to shopping opportunities in a regional area depends on the size of the shopping (product assortment), distance, and customer sensitivity to travel time. Generally, bigger and closer are more attractive.

Greenfield development: development of land that has never been used (e.g. green or new), where there was no need to demolish or rebuild any existing structures. When there exist grayfield and brownfield sites with infrastructure, redevelopment of those sites may be preferable.

Greyfield: land or property that is economically obsolescent, outdated, failing, moribund or underused.

Indian Community Development Block Grant Program: provides grants to develop decent housing, suitable living environments, and economic opportunities for low- and moderate-income persons in Indian and Alaska Native communities.

Infill development: developing vacant or under-used parcels within existing urban areas that are already largely developed.

Jobs Investment Fund (JIF): provides "mezzanine capital" to expansion projects or venture capital to new projects as either loans or direct investments. JIFs allow cities to engage in a number of business development activities, including capital raising conferences, entrepreneurship events, and business incubators.

Knowledge-based assets: universities and colleges, highly skilled workers, and research labs and technology parks.

Leasing arrangements: are a form of public-private partnership. Under a long-term lease, the government may lease a facility or enterprise to a private-sector entity

LEED: short for Leadership in Energy and Environmental Design, is a sustainable environmental certification for facilities or buildings.

Loans: monies given to recipients with an expectation of repayment. Public sector loans generally permit firms that have trouble obtaining loans through normal channels to secure financing either at or below market interest rates from a government entity.

Main Street Program: established in the early 1980s by the National Trust for Historic Preservation and now a subsidiary of that organization, is economic and community development in its best form. It is a place-based public program where a community's assets are analyzed and an economic development program built from those assets.

Master plan: a comprehensive, integrated development plan of action.

Mixed use development: any urban, suburban or village development, or even a single building, that blends a combination of residential, commercial, cultural, institutional, or industrial uses, where those functions are physically and functionally integrated, and that provides pedestrian connections.

NIMBY: short for "Not in My Back Yard," is a pejorative characterization of opposition by constituents to a proposal for a new development in their area.

Performance agreement: detailed write-up of expectations, targets, outputs for a task, program or project.

PIPs: short for public interest partnerships, which are development partnerships among government, business, and non-profits.

Placemaking: the development of quality public space that attracts pedestrian and other hands-on uses. The process suggests that communities can be built around well-designed places such as parks, downtowns, waterfronts, plazas, neighborhoods, streets, markets, campuses and public buildings.

PPP: short for Public-Private Partnership and also referred to as P3. PPP are economic development partnerships between or among government, business, and nonprofits.

Privatization: the government's use of business and corporate as well as nongovernmental organization and nonprofit practices to deliver public services.

Redevelopment: is any new construction or development on a geographic area or site that has pre-existing uses.

Revenue Bonds (RB's): bonds where the principal and interest are repaid from the revenues generated by a capital project (e.g., toll road, museum, stadium, etc.).

RFI: short for Request for Information which is a standard business process whose purpose is to collect written information about the public service capabilities of private and nonprofit contractors, vendors, or suppliers.

RFP: short for Request for Proposal which is an open solicitation to submit formal proposals, often made through a bidding process by a public agency interested in the procurement of a product, service, or asset.

RFQ: short for Request for Quotation which is a standard business process whose purpose is to invite private and nonprofit contractors, vendors, or suppliers into a bidding process to bid on specific public service products or services.

Smart growth: is a better way to build and maintain towns and cities. Smart growth means building urban, suburban and rural communities with housing and transportation choices near jobs, shops and schools. It is an approach that supports local economies and protects the environment.

Special assessment: a unique charge that government agencies can assess against real estate parcels for certain economic development projects. This charge is levied in a specific geographic area known as a special assessment district.

Streetscaping: street and sidewalk enhancements as part of urban renewal. It makes streets and sidewalks more senior, children, and disabled friendly.

Superfund: is a United States federal government program designed to fund the cleanup of sites contaminated with hazardous substances and pollutants.

SWOT analysis: an examination of Strengths, Weaknesses, Opportunities and Threats by a community or other entity. Often undertaken part of a community assessment or inventory especially where a marketing or promotional effort is being considered.

Tax abatement: Contracts between a government entity and a holder of real estate that stipulated that some share of assessed value will not be taxed for an agreed upon time period.

Tax Increment Financing (TIF): a public financing method that is used as a subsidy for redevelopment, infrastructure, and other community-improvement projects.

Tender: refers to the process whereby government agencies invite bids for large projects that must be submitted within a fixed deadline.

User fee: or user charge, require those who use a public service or facility to pay some or all of the cost of the service.

Vouchers: are government financial subsidies given to individuals for purchasing specific goods or services from the private, public, or nonprofit sector.

Workforce development: is a human resource strategy focused on enhancing a region's economic stability and prosperity.

Zoning: the establishment by municipalities of districts or special areas that are restricted to certain types of commercial, residential, or mixed use development.

About the Editors and Contributors

Charles **Abernathy** is the county manager and director, Department of Economic Development of McDowell County, North Carolina.

David **Ammons** is the Albert Coates Professor of Public Administration and Government, University of North Carolina, Chapel Hill.

Adam Regn **Arvidson** is a landscape architect and free-lance writer based in Minneapolis, Minnesota.

Camille Cates **Barnett** is a senior managing partner, Public Strategies Group, Washington, D.C.

Jenni **Bergal** is a senior staff writer with *Stateline*, a publication of The Pew Charitable Trusts.

Madlyn M. **Bonimy** is an adjunct faculty in the College of Public Service and Urban Affairs at Tennessee State University and has published in the areas of urban studies and tourism.

Mark **Brodeur** is the director of the Community and Economic Development Department, City of Pacific Grove, California.

Alison McKenney **Brown** is the city attorney of Bel Aire, Kansas.

Tracy **Brown** is the planning and development director of Sandy, Oregon.

Kristen **Carney** is a cofounder of Cubit Planning, a start-up firm that was funded by a mentor-model incubator.

Brett **Common** is a research assistant for the Finance and Economic Development Program in the Center for Research and Innovation at the National League of Cities.

Council of Economic Advisers is an agency within the executive office of the president that is charged with offering the president objective economic advice on the formulation of both domestic and international economic policy.

Steve **Davis** has been part of the communications staff of Smart Growth America since July 2006 and is the director of communications for Transportation for America.

Tommy **Engram** has done extensive research in municipal government and has managed three small cities in Georgia and Tennessee.

Catherine **Finneran** is brownfield coordinator, MassDEP in Boston.

Jill **FitzSimmons** is a free-lance journalist working with the Washington State Department of Community, Trade, and Economic Development in Olympia.

Thomas **Ford** heads up digital strategy for MarketingModo.

Justin **Fritscher** is a reporter for *The Clarion-Ledger* in Jackson, Mississippi.

William **Fulton** is a *Governing* columnist and director of the Kinder Institute for Urban Research at Rice University, as well as former mayor of Ventura, California.

John **Gann**, Jr., is president of Gann Associates in Glen Ellyn, Illinois.

Joaquin Jay **Gonzalez** III is Mayor George Christopher Professor of Public Administration at Golden Gate University. He has worked as an economic development planner and social justice advocate in the United States, Asia, and Africa. Jay is the author of more than a dozen books, including *Corruption and American Cities and Privatization in Practice*.

Josh **Goodman** is a former *Governing* staff writer.

Government Finance Officers Association, founded in 1906, represents public finance officials throughout the United States and Canada.

Rob **Gurwitt** is a *Governing* contributor.

William **Hatcher** is an associate professor and director of the Master of Public Administration Program, Department of Political Science, Augusta University, Georgia.

Mark **Hinshaw** is the director of urban design for LMN Architects in Seattle, Washington.

Ryan **Holeywell** is a *Governing* staff writer.

International City/County Management Association is the professional and educational association for appointed local government administrators throughout the world.

Sue **Kelley** is coordinator of Shorewood Connects in Shorewood, Wisconsin.

Roger L. **Kemp** is a distinguished adjunct professor at the Edward S. Ageno School of Business of Golden Gate University and a career city manager for 25 years in California, New Jersey, and Connecticut. A prolific author, he is also a Fellow at the Academy of Political Science in New York City.

Howard **Lalli** is executive director of the Georgia Brownfields Association in Atlanta.

Will **Lambe** is with the Federal Reserve Bank of Atlanta and was the associate director of the Community and Economic Development Program, School of Government, University of North Carolina at Chapel Hill.

Trevor **Langan** is a research associate for City Solutions and Applied Research at the National League of Cities.

Ty **Lasher** is the city manager of Bel Aire, Kansas.

Scott **Lazenby** is the city manager of Sandy, Oregon.

Minch **Lewis** is a certified government financial manager and an adjunct professor at Syracuse University's Maxwell School.

J. Michael **Lillich** is a contributing writer to the *Purdue News*, a publication of Purdue University.

Livability has worked with hundreds of communities developing content marketing programs showcasing why they are a great place to live with one simple goal: help cities attract and retain residents and businesses.

Mike **Maciag** is *Governing*'s data editor.

Becky **McCray** is an inspirational speaker who started Small Biz Survival in 2006 to share rural business and community building stories and ideas with other small town business people.

Joseph **McElroy** is a principal of McElroy Associates, a consulting firm based in Naperville, Illinois.

Christiana **McFarland** is the director of research at the National League of Cities.

Edward T. **McMahon** is the Charles Fraser Chair on Sustainable Development and a senior resident fellow at the Urban Land Institute in Washington, D.C.

Michelle **Meyer** is the assistant city manager and finance director of Bel Aire, Kansas.

Joe **Minicozzi** is a principal at Urban3, LLC (U3), a consulting company that specializes in land value economics, property tax analysis, and community design.

Patricia **Mitchell,** a former county manager and economic developer, is assistant secretary of the Rural Development Division, North Carolina Department of Commerce, Raleigh.

Jonathan **Morgan** is an associate professor of public administration and government at the University of North Carolina at Chapel Hill.

Erin **Mullenix** is the director of data driven science at Iowa State University and was research director at the Iowa League of Cities.

National League of Cities is dedicated to helping city leaders build better communities. Working in partnership with the 49 state municipal leagues, NLC serves as a resource to and an advocate for the more than 19,000 cities, villages and towns it represents.

Russell **Nichols** is a *Governing* staff writer.

Matt **Oyer** is a community development planner at the Heart of Georgia Regional Commission.

Zach **Patton** is *Governing*'s executive editor.

Aaron M. **Renn** is a *Governing* columnist and a Senior Fellow at the Manhattan Institute.

Christopher **Robbins** is an economic development committee member, Southborough, Massachusetts, and board member, Corridor Nine Area Chamber of Commerce, Westborough, Massachusetts.

Emily **Robbins** is a principal associate for economic development with the City Solutions and Applied Research Center at the National League of Cities.

David **Robinson** is a principal and founder of the Montrose Group as well as an adjunct professor of economic development at the Ohio State University's John Glenn School of Public Affairs.

Oscar **Rodríguez** is the director of the Center for Innovation and Reform, District of Columbia government, Washington, D.C.

Jonathan **Rosenthal** has more than 35 years of experience in economic development serving Syracuse and Onondaga County, the City of Des Moines, the City of New Haven, and the City of Bristol. He has built and filled business parks and assisted hundreds of business that have created thousands of jobs, and invested hundreds of millions of dollars.

Katie **Seeger** is a senior associate at the Finance and Economic Development Program of the National League of Cities.

Smart Growth America is a coalition of advocacy organizations that have a stake in how metropolitan expansion affects the environment, quality of life and economic sustainability.

Christen **Smith** is the president of Moro Group, LLC, in Ann Arbor, Michigan.

Joe A. **Sumners** is the executive director of the Government and Economic Development Institute at Auburn University, Alabama.

Chris **Swartz** is the village manager of Shorewood, Wisconsin.

Christopher **Swope** is the project director, information, at the Pew Center on the States and was previously *Governing*'s executive editor.

Chad **Vander Veen** is past editor of FutureStructure and the associate editor of *Government Technology* and *Public CIO* magazines.

Brian **Vanneman** is a principal at Leland Consulting Group, a market economics firm in Portland, Oregon.

David E. **Versel** is the managing director of Economic Stewardship, Inc., in Saco, Maine.

Daniel C. **Vock** is *Governing*'s transportation and infrastructure reporter.

Philip **Walker** is the principal at the Walker Collaborative in Nashville, Tennessee, and is author of *Downtown Planning for Smaller and Midsized Communities*.

Randall **Wheeler** is the city manager of Poquoson, Virginia.

Bert **Williams** is the vice president of marketing of Tropos Networks, Sunnyvale, California.

Index